A Political Biography of the Indonesian Lesbian, Bisexual and Trans Movement

A Political Biography of the Indonesian Lesbian, Bisexual and Trans Movement

Saskia E. Wieringa

BLOOMSBURY ACADEMIC
LONDON • NEW YORK • OXFORD • NEW DELHI • SYDNEY

BLOOMSBURY ACADEMIC
Bloomsbury Publishing Plc, 50 Bedford Square, London, WC1B 3DP, UK
Bloomsbury Publishing Inc, 1359 Broadway, 12th Floor, New York, NY 10018, USA
Bloomsbury Publishing Ireland, 29 Earlsfort Terrace, Dublin 2, D02 AY28, Ireland

BLOOMSBURY, BLOOMSBURY ACADEMIC and the Diana logo
are trademarks of Bloomsbury Publishing Plc

First published in Great Britain 2024
This paperback edition published 2026

Cover design by Adriana Brioso
Cover image: Embracing by Dolorosa Sinaga

A catalogue record for this book is available from the British Library.

Library of Congress Cataloging-in-Publication Data
Names: Wieringa, Saskia, 1950– author.
Title: A political biography of the Indonesian lesbian, bisexual and trans movement /
Saskia E. Wieringa. Description: New York : Bloomsbury Publishing Plc, 2024. |
Includes bibliographical references and index. | Summary: "In this book the history of the LBT
movement is charted, from invisibility, to visibility and now again to hiding. The author explores
the persistence of the butch/femme model of relationships; the proliferations of identities,
family violence and conversion therapy, and religion. The anti-LGBT campaign is also extensively
analysed. In its insistence on the local dynamics of this movement, the book aims to debunk the
idea that homosexuality is a Western import. It is also a contribution to the growing literature on
decolonization studies in pointing out that its
dynamics, its historical course and its present condition, different as they are from the
dominant Western view on a global LGBT movement, needs to be taken as valuable as accounts
of Western LGBT histories are"–Provided by publisher. Identifiers:
LCCN 2023043307 (print) | LCCN 2023043308 (ebook) |
ISBN 9781350422803 (hardback) | ISBN 9781350422841 (paperback) |
ISBN 9781350422810 (epub) | ISBN 9781350422827 (ebook)
Subjects: LCSH: Heterosexism–Indonesia. | Homophobia–Indonesia. | Lesbians–Indonesia–Social
conditions. | Bisexuals–Indonesia–Social conditions. | Transgender people–Indonesia–Social
conditions. | Gay rights–Indonesia. | Bisexuals–Civil rights–Indonesia. | Transgender
people–Civil rights–Indonesia. | Lesbian community–Indonesia.
Classification: LCC HQ76.45.I5 W547 2024 (print) | LCC HQ76.45.I5 (ebook) |
DDC 306.76/609598–dc23/eng/20231030
LC record available at https://lccn.loc.gov/2023043307
LC ebook record available at https://lccn.loc.gov/2023043308

ISBN: HB: 978-1-3504-2280-3
PB: 978-1-3504-2284-1
ePDF: 978-1-3504-2282-7
eBook: 978-1-3504-2281-0

Typeset by Newgen KnowledgeWorks Pvt. Ltd., Chennai, India

For product safety related questions contact productsafety@bloomsbury.com.

To find out more about our authors and books visit www.bloomsbury.com
and sign up for our newsletters.

Nasib Lesbian

Salam persahabatan untuk kawanku yang tercinta dan senasib
Umur kita dan waktu kita lalui sudah terlampau jauh
Masih adalah jalan untuk kita kawan?

Atau kita harus menunggu hingga akhir tua?
Dengan bertopang dagu saja tanpa ada usaha,
Kawan, jiwa dan perasaan kita bukan wanita
Walaupun tidak sama dengan jenis kelamin.

Kawan, ingatlah akan masa depan kita
Majulah kawan tanpa menyerah walaupun banyak rintangan
Di depan kita, enyahkan suara-suara nada yang tak
Berperasaan dan buatlah suata nada menjadi lagu.

Bersatu kita teguh, bercerai kita runtuh
Ingatlah kawan akan pepatah itu,
Kawan, prinsif harus ada ditangan kita dan jiwa
Majulah kawan jangan gentar menghapadi semua ini
Karna kita makhlu yang telah diciptakan.

Salam PERLESIN
Ryan Nurhadi
Jakarta 1983

Translation
The fate of lesbians

A friendly greeting to my beloved comrades who share my fate
Our age and the time we have been through for too long
Is there still a way for us, comrades?

Or should we have to wait till the end of our lives?
Sitting with our hands on our chins without exerting ourselves
Comrades, our souls and our feelings are not those of women
Although they are not the same as our gender

Comrades let us think about our future
Let us move forward without surrendering in spite of many obstacles
Before us, let us chase away the voices in such insensitive tones
And make one tone that becomes a song

United we stand firm, divided we fall down
Remember comrades this proverb,
Comrades, the principle must be in our hands and souls
Come on comrades do not tremble confronting all this
For we are created beings.

Greetings PERLESIN
Ryan Nurhadi
Jakarta, 1983

Contents

Author Biography

Saskia E. Wieringa is Honorary Emeritus Professor of Women's Same Sex Relations Cross-Culturally at the Department of Anthropology, University of Amsterdam, the Netherlands. She is the chair of the Foundation for the International People's Tribunal for Crimes against Humanity in Indonesia after October 1965 (IPT 1965). She has published widely on issues related to gender, sexuality and empowerment as well as on the Indonesian genocide.

Preface

This book on the history of the Lesbian Bisexual and Trans (LBT) movement in Indonesia covers a period of over forty years, from my first encounters with a group of lesbians as a PhD student working on the Indonesian women's movement in 1982 till the present. There were many interruptions; for instance, I could not visit the country between 1986 and 1998 under restrictions of the military New Order regime. After 1998 I carried out several formal research projects with LBT persons keeping in touch with my friends in between. It is impossible to thank everybody with whom I came in contact during those years. The many narrators who told me their life stories and allowed me to share some parts of their daily lives come first to mind. For reasons of confidentiality and security I have to keep their names secret, so in the following pages most of them appear with pseudonyms. I am deeply indebted to them, and this book is dedicated to their courage and to the wider LGBT community in Indonesia, especially to the new generations of activists who have to operate under ever greater legal limitations.

The first stage of my formal interviewing, which started in the early 2000s, was self-funded, as it was very difficult to get funds for such a subversive project at the time. A second stage consisted of a research project in Jakarta and Surabaya, which I coordinated and which was implemented by the Ardhanary Institute and Dipayoni. This was funded by the Riek Stienstra Fund. Riek Stienstra was a prominent Dutch LGBT activist, co-founder and director of the Schorer Foundation. Josée Rothuizen and Ingrid Foeken were also very supportive members of the Riek Stienstra Fund. Riek was instrumental in organizing support for the establishment of the Chair of Women's Same-Sex Relations in Cross-Cultural Perspective, at the University of Amsterdam, which I have occupied (it was an honorary position for one day a week) from 2006. After her untimely death, Riek left her estate to fund a research project on LBT organizations globally, which I coordinated, Indonesia being one of the nine participating countries. The Chair was established by the Stichting Homo-en Lesbische Studies. Directly supporting this Chair were Saskia Keuzenkamp, Rob Tielman and Ferdinand Strijthagen.

Thanks to Paul Jansen from Hivos and Esther Vonk from MamaCash who shared Riek's vision and made it possible to release the funds to the Kartini Asia Network. Mama Cash's director at the time, Nicky McIntyre also fully supported the project. The Kartini Asia Network was coordinated by Nursyahbani Katjasungkana, and managed by Chika Noya. I was co-founder and the secretary of the board, which further consisted of Abha Bhaiya, Amrita Chhachhi, Tesa de Vela, Sepali Kottogoda, Bernadette Resurrection and Chang Pilhwa. I am also indebted to the coordinators of the sexuality theme of the Kartini Asia Network, Abha Bhaiya (India), Anna Kirey (Kazakhstan), Erika Rae Rosario and Tesa de Vela (Philippines), Delene van Dyk (South

Africa), Shalini Mahajan (India), Kaushalya Perera (Sri Lanka), Subhagata Akanksha Ghosh (India), Hasna Hena (Bangladesh), Sri Agustine (Indonesia), Siti Mazdafiah, (Indonesia), Nomancotsho Pakade (South Africa) and Loraine Setuke (Botswana). Our discussions were rich and rewarding, and I thank all of our researchers for their political acumen, theoretical insights and their friendship.

In this book only the Indonesian part of this Kartini research project is discussed. The research was implemented by the following members of the Surabaya team: Siti Mazdafiah, Dian Lestaringsih, Wulan Widaningrum, NK Endah Triwijati, Ayuni and Dian Yulia Arianti. The members of the Ardhanary team in Jakarta were Sri Agustine, Evilina Sutrisno, Lily Sugianto, Ignatia Maria Rioza, Irene Augustine Sigit and Afank Mariani. Due to funding constraints this research was never published, though a final report was produced. Several national projects also brought out articles and booklets.

The research in Surabaya focused on community building, to support political activism. Ultimately a new lesbian organization Dipayoni was set up. The research was carried out under the wings of the Gender and Health Study Club (GHSC) of the University of Surabaya, members of which had earlier been working with LGBT groups such as the Us Community Surabaya. Dian Yulia Arianti became the coordinator of Dipayoni (light of the vagina), an LBT organization which was established during the research.

The next research phase was funded by the Ford Foundation. This focused on the workings of non-normative sexualities in India and Indonesia. Barbara Klugman has to be especially mentioned for her unwavering faith in the Kartini Asia Network. Abha Bhaiya coordinated the action research part in India, Nursyahbani Katjasungkana and Irwan Hidayana the Indonesian part. I was the general research coordinator. Training workshops with researchers from India and Indonesia were held in Goa and Khajurao. In 2006 an advocacy workshop was held in Jakarta in collaboration with the feminist legal aid network APIK on non-normative sexualities, comparing lesbians, widows, divorced women and sex workers. Researchers were Irwan Hidayana, Ratna Batara Munti, Sinta Situmorang and Widjayanto Santoso.

In the course of the many years I have been thinking of and working on this book, I met many inspiring people with whom I shared views and experiences. I cannot even begin to thank them all. Just mention a few of them: Shadi Amin, Peggy Antrobus, Gadis Arivia, Ayesha Banu, Violeta Barrientos, Louise Bennett, Kamla Bhasin, Evelyn Blackwood, Mark Blasius, Tom Boellstorff, Charlotte Bunch, Pavin Chachavalpongpun, Najma Chowdhury, Sonia Corrêa, Frances Gouda, Kuat Thu Hong, Adnan Hussain, Pinar Ilkkaracan, Peter A. Jackson, Sharyn Graham Davies, Eun-shil Kim, Lenore Manderson, Theo van der Meer, Amena Mohsen, Dede Oetomo, Dana Omari Berg, Helen Pausacker, Michael Peletz, Rosalind Petchesky, Annie Pohlman, Annemiek Richters, Renée Römkens, Yuli Rustinawati, Shadi Sadr, Douglas Sanders, Judith Schuyf, Horacio Sivori, Ian Southey-Swartz, Joke Swiebel, Beng Hui Tan, Giti Thadani, Gina Vargas, Kees Waaldijk, Vivienne Wee, Gloria Wekker, Ine van Wesenbeeck, Sonja van Wichelen and Janet Wong.

The curatorium of my chair also provided helpful advice and assistance. Thanks go to Martin Moerings, Jan Willen Duyvendak, Jan Rath, Frances Gouda and Walter Everaerd. The yearly dinners with the members of the Concilium Seksuologicum – Willibrord

Weijmar Schulz, Gerda van Dijk, Jacques Langveld, Erick Jansen, Ellen Laan and Peggy Cohen-Kettenis – always provided new insights. I was fortunate to find a welcome home at the University of Amsterdam. Especially helpful were Muriël Kiesel, secretary of the Anthropological Department, and Janus Oomen and Yomi van der Veen of the desk of the AISSR (Amsterdam Institute for Social Science Research). They provided some travel and conference funds in the later stages of this book project. My theoretical home became the ARC-GS, the Amsterdam Research School for Gender and Sexuality, with such fine colleagues as Rachel Spronk, Gert Hekma, Sarah Bracke and Julie McBrien. Robby Davidson provided eminent support and proved a warm colleague. Other colleagues with whom I had a close working relationship included Anita Hardon, Marie-Louise Janssen, Trudie Gerrits and Bregje de Kok.

I was privileged to work with a number of outstanding PhD students from whom I learned a lot. These included Irwan Hidayana, Imtiaz Saikh and the members of our 'little group' – Agrar Sudrajat, Fotarisman Zaluchu, Tu-Anh Hoang, Wanda Klein, Yu Qi, Yiran Wang and Jingshu Zhu.

Editing the *Sage Handbook of Global Sexualities* with Zowie Davy, Ana Cristina Santos, Chiara Bertone and Ryan Thoreson was a great pleasure. The two volumes we ultimately produced, with forty-three chapters, will be a source of inspiration for me for a long time to come. The Salzburg Global LGBT Forum, which was held for a number of years until interrupted by Covid-19, founded by Klaus Mueller in 2013, motivated me to keep in mind that LGBT studies need to keep a close link with what is happening in our communities all over the world. I thank all the fellows for their courage and perseverance, in the face of enormous challenges.

My close friends have lived with this book for a long time. For their patience with me I thank Sita Aripurnami, Anky and Muze Brouwer, Bianti Djiwandono, Ingrid Foeken, Edriana, Britt Fontaine, Vera Goedhart, Monika Jongerius-Jonas, Shura Lipovsky, Lies Marcoes, Daniel van Mourik, Gonnelieke van Oosterom, Pamela Pattynama, Paul and Lie Yung Polman, Elsje and Merel Plantema, Silke Studzinsky, Monica Tahuhandaru and Fineke van der Veen.

My deepest thanks, as always, go to Nursyahbani Katjasungkana, whose insights, courage, wisdom and great sense of humour made working on this book and all our other projects such a pleasure.

In the last stages I was fortunate to find Evelyn Blackwood, Zowie Davy and Ulrika Dahl willing to read (parts of) the manuscript. Their valuable comments enriched the text. Steve Russell made sure my language was faultless. Particularly helpful were my editors at Bloomsbury, Olivia Dellow and Sophie Rudland.

Note on Text

In 1972 the Indonesian language underwent a spelling change. I have elected to use modern spelling as much as possible, so 'u' is used instead of the older 'oe', the letter 'j' is used instead of 'dj' or 'c' is used instead of 'tj'. However, in names of people known in the old spelling, or in titles of books, articles or quotations in which old spelling is used I kept that. Indonesian name do not follow Western patterns. Some people go by only one name, others have two names, again others are known mostly by their nicknames. In the index I followed the Western pattern of putting a second name first, as a surname. Indonesian does not indicate the plural of a noun with an –s. I have followed that usage for Indonesian words.

Abbreviations

Adat	local customs
AILA	Family Love Alliance
ALN	Asian Lesbian Network
Amah	particular form of Islamic worship
APIK	Asosiasi Perempuan Indonesia untuk Keadilan (Women's Association for Justice)
APP	Anti-Pornography and Porno-Action Law (usually called Anti-Pornography Law)
APWLD	Asia-Pacific Forum on Women Law and Development
Arus Pelangi	Rainbow Stream, a national LGBTI association
Asas kekeluargaan	family principles
Aurat	part of the body that has to be covered in public according to Islam *Balian* (*bilian*) shaman of the Dayak communities
Banci, or *bencong*	transgender person
Basir	trans priest or healer among the Dayak
BIN	Badan Intelijen Negara (National Intelligence Body)
Bissu	trans priest among the Bugis
Boerake (burake)	priest/healer among the Toradja
b/f	butch/femme
CEDAW	Convention on the Elimination of All Forms of Discrimination against Women
CIL	Compilation of Islamic Law
CRC	Convention on the Rights of the Child
Dakwa(*h*)	proselytization
Dangdut	popular romantic style of music
DSM	*Diagnostic and Statistical Manual of Mental Disorders*
Dzikir	repetitive reciting of religious formulas
Fatwa	Muslim advice or decision, usually issued by the MUI
FGD	Focus Group Discussion
Fiqih	Islamic jurisprudence
FJI	Front Jihad Islam

FPI   Front Pembela Islam (Islamic
                             Defenders' Front)
FTM   Female to male
Gerwani   Gerakan Wanita Indonesia (Indonesian
                             Women's Movement)
GiGa   Penggiat Keluarga (Family Activists)
Hadith   saying and traditions of the Prophet
                             Muhammad
Halal   accepted, according to Islam (for
                             instance, food)
Haram   prohibited in Islam
Hijab   Muslim dress for women, intended to cover
                             their *aurat*
HIV/AIDS   Human Immunodeficiency Virus/Acquired
                             Immune Deficiency Syndrome
HIWAD   Himpunan Wadam Djakarta (Association of
                             Wadam in Jakarta)
HTI   Hizbut Tahrir Indonesia
HRC   Human Rights Committee
Ibadah   religious obligations, such as *sholat*
                             (prescribed prayers) and fasting
ICCPR   International Covenant on Civil and
                             Political Rights
ICESCR   International Covenant on Economic, Social
                             and Cultural Rights
ILIS   International Lesbian Information Service
ILGA   International Lesbian and Gay Association
IGLHRC   International Gay and Lesbian Human
                             Rights Commission
IPOOS   Ikatan Persaudaraan Orang-Orang Sehati
                             (Network [to establish] Friendship Among
                             People with the Same Heart)
Jati diri   inner self
Jilbab   headdress for Muslim women
Jin   (evil) spirit
Jinayah   criminal law
Kabupaten   district
Kerudung   loose scarf worn by women
Khunsa (*khuntsa, khuntsah*) Trans or intersex people in Islamic tradition
Kodrat   nature given by God
Komnas HAM   Komisi Nasional Hak Asasi Manusia
                             (National Human Rights Commission)

Komnas Perempuan	Komisi Nasional anti Kekerasan terhadap Perempuan (National Commission on Violence against Women)
KPI	Koalisi Perempuan Indonesia (Indonesian Women's Coalition)
KPI	Komisi Penyiaran Indonesia (Indonesian Broadcasting Commission)
KUHP	Kitab Undang-Undang Hukum Pidana, Penal Code
Kyai	Head of a Muslim boarding school
Mairil	young student in *pesantren*, desired by one or more of his/her teachers
Maksiat	sin (individual)
Manang bali	double-gendered healers of the Iban Dayak
Ministry of WECP	Women's Empowerment and Child Protection
MPR Majelis Permusyawaratan Rakyat	People's Consultative Council
MUI	Majelis Ulama Islam (Council of Islamic Scholars)
Musahaqah	consensual lesbian sex
NU	Nahdlatul Ulama (Islamic Scholars)
Pancasila	Five pillars, state philosophy
PBNU	Pengurus Besar Nahdlatus Ulama (Governing Board of the Nahdlatul Ulama)
Pengajian	quranic recitation
Perda	Peraturan Daerah (Regional Regulations)
Perlesin	Persatuan Lesbian Indonesia (Union of Indonesian Lesbians)
Pesantren	Islamic boarding school
PFA	Platform for Action (of the 1995 Beijing Fourth World Conference on Women)
PKB	Partai Kebangkitan Bangsa Nasional (National Awakening Party)
PKI	Partai Komunis Indonesia (Indonesian Communist Party)
PKS	Partai Keadilan Sejahtera (Prosperous Justice Party)
POA	Programme of Action (of the 1994 ICPD Conference)
Preman	thug
Priawan	from pria and wanita (FTM transgender transman)
PSK	Pekerja Seks Komersial (commercial sex worker)
Qanun	regulation

Roh	spirit, soul
Ruqyah	exorcism
Santri	(former) student of pesantren
Satpol PP	Satuan Polisi Pamong Praja (Administrative Police Units)
Sentul	butch
SGRC UI	Support Group and Resource Center on Sexuality Studies at the Universitas Indonesia in Jakarta
Shaman	traditional healer
Sharia	Islamic law
Sholat	prescribed Muslim prayers
Sihaq	rubbing (as a lesbian sexual technique)
Sirri	religious, not civilly registered marriage
SOGIE	Sexul Oriemtation, Gender Identity and Exprerssion
SRHR	(Sexual and Reproductive Health and Rights
Syirik	polythesist, sinful
Transpuan	trans woman (MTF transgender person)
Transmen	FTM transgender person
UI	Universitas Indonesia
Ulama	religious leader
UNDP	United Nations Development Programme
UNDIP	Universitas Diponegoro (in Semarang)
UNILA	University of Lampung
Ustadz	religious teacher
Waria	*wanita* (woman) and *pria* (man) (MTF transgender)
WH	Wilayatul Hisbah – Aceh Shariah Police
Zina	adultery

1

Introduction: Now we just whisper to each other

'We had better whisper', Agustine says apologetically. I have to strain my ears to hear what she is saying. We have just relocated from the Japanese restaurant where we had lunch, on the first floor of Margocity, a huge modern mall in Depok, a suburb of Jakarta, to the outside sitting area of a downstairs Starbucks.[1] Smokers are exiled to this place; it is windless and hot. They usually do not stay long, retreating to the AC cool of the main space inside as soon as their cigarette craving has been fulfilled, leaving behind a faint smell of cloves. But for another two hours we stay outside, huddled in a corner, sweat dripping from our brows. This steamy, isolated terrace suits us just fine. Still, even though there is nobody near us, Agustine keeps whispering, pointing her thumb up:

> You didn't see it, because you were sitting with your back to her, but the woman at the next table in the restaurant upstairs kept creeping to our side of the bench, stretching her neck to hear what we were talking about. You noticed she was wearing one of those huge *jilbab* that prevent the wearer from seeing anywhere but straight ahead? We have come to be afraid of them. All too often gay or lesbian people have been arrested because somebody overheard them, assumed they must be gay or lesbian and reported them. Here in Depok the Islamists are strong. A few months ago they hung up a big banner in front of the local neighbourhood office saying that in this area LGBT people are not welcome.

She shrugs her shoulders. 'So that's why we pulled you away and we left. Here we are safer. Do you know how many centres for homosexual conversion therapy there are in Depok?'

We had been talking for an hour or so already, sharing details of our lives, as we had not met for almost a year, before settling in the humid heat near the entrance of Margocity, shielded by banners, pots with tall plants and a screen, from both the customers of Starbucks inside the coffee shop and the customers streaming into the wide gates of the mall. 'Here I am', Agustine sighs, 'I am in my forties now, and what have I achieved? I have fought my whole life for LGBT rights, and now I have to run, whisper when I talk, always be on my guard, not daring to go out at night, afraid to enter my office.' She gives me a dejected half smile. We sip our drinks, silent.

Indonesian lesbians and gays are on the run, haunted, chased from their offices, evicted from their homes. Yet until recently homosexuality among consenting adults had not been illegal in the country, apart from in Aceh. The 2008 Anti-Pornography and Pornoaction (APP) Law was the first national law which has a clause stipulating that LGBT (lesbian, gay, bisexual and transgender) people are engaged in 'deviant' behaviour, and several regional regulations prohibit same-sex relations.[2] In December 2022 the new Criminal Code was adopted, which criminalizes all sexual relations outside of marriage, thus including homosexuality, as Indonesia does not recognize marriage equality.[3] Identity fraud is one of the other crimes LBT people may be accused of, for instance, if two women want to marry and one of them is carrying a document stating that he is a male. LBT (lesbian, bisexual and transgender) is the acronym I use more frequently in this book as an umbrella term for the group of female-bodied persons (or assigned female at birth) in same-sex relationships. The LBT organization Ardhanary Institute, which was co-founded and directed by Agustine, is at the time of writing dealing with several court cases in which lesbians or transgender FTM (female to male) people are facing trial. In other incidents working-class lesbians have been evicted from their houses. But these events do not end up in court, for the lesbians have not committed any crime; instead, the eviction might be considered a crime, but the women are too afraid to denounce their attackers. This happened, for example, in a village near Bandung, where twelve women, some of whom allegedly espoused 'unfeminine' behaviour, had rented adjacent rooms in a housing complex for working-class people. They had lived there for between seven and ten years.[4] Then, by the end of 2015 the hate campaign had started. High-up political figures lashed out about the threat that the LGBT community allegedly posed to the nation.

The activists of the Ardhanary Institute and many other LGBT organizations have witnessed the frequent and violent demonstrations of the hardliner militias, screaming against both LGBT people and communists, as if these people are the same.[5] The LBT community had felt relatively safe before the hate campaign started in late 2015. If the couples followed the heteronormative gender code, with the masculine partners being greeted with *Om* (uncle) by their neighbours, and their feminine partners as *mbak* (elder sister), or *ibu* (mother), depending on their own age and the age of the neighbour, they were generally left alone.

In 2015, however, the talk in the mosques became louder. The preachers were screaming hatred from the pulpit, and young fanatical men rallied behind them.[6] Were there any lesbians and gays in their neighbourhood? Yes, in our alley, the neighbours of the lesbian b/f (butch-femme)[7] couples in West Java admitted. Those neighbours were becoming uneasy, for had not the preachers said that forty houses around a house inhabited by a lesbian or gay couple would be cursed? And they had five of those houses in their street! So after leaving the Friday prayers in the mosque, the young men, dressed in their Muslim finery, went to the police. The police acted immediately, marching up to the lodgings of the unsuspecting lesbian couples. They were dragged out of their rooms and taken to the police station. There they were roughly questioned and ultimately released, for they had broken no laws, but they were told to leave their neighbourhood immediately and to never return.

So the women hastened home, picked up their belongings, or whatever they could carry, and, accompanied by the jeers of the onlookers, disappeared. 'And then we lost sight of them', Agustine sighs:

> For they were not formally charged, they had broken no law. Their families would throw them out if they had been known to have caused a scandal, they would have lost their jobs. It is better for them to hide somewhere, hoping to find a place where they will not be harassed. Maybe they can no longer live with their friends or their partners. This has happened hundreds of times, particularly in areas dominated by Islamists, such as Padang, Depok, Bandung, Bogor and Banten. In South Sulawesi, we heard these evictions are becoming more common also. Sometimes we read about it in the local newspapers, and when we hasten to the police stations, the officers just shrug. 'Yes, there were a bunch of lesbians yesterday. We released them. The neighbours threw them out. They have gone now, nobody knows where.'

Yet over the past two decades certain things have changed and cannot be rolled back easily, not even by a vitriolic campaign. When I first met Agustine in early 2001 she had just started working in the office of the first feminist mass organization established after the Reformasi (the democratic opening of the country in 1998), the KPI (Koalisi Perempuan Indonesia, Indonesian Women's Coalition), chaired by the prominent feminist lawyer Nursyahbani Katjasungkana. During the opening congress, held in December 1998, it was decided to establish a section on sexual minorities, Sektor 15. A support group for *waria* (male-to-female (MTF) transpeople) from Surabaya had put forward this proposal, arguing that LBT people also needed support.[8] The debate had been fierce, with the well-known radical feminist and criminologist Syarifah Sabaroedin (Ifa to her friends) together with the lesbian feminist activist Gayatri, who chaired the lesbian organization Chandra Kirana, arguing the case, while conservative Muslim women's organizations vehemently rejected the proposal.[9] Ifa was elected as the first chair of Sektor 15. She brought with her a group of older working-class b/f lesbians, whom I had also met in the early 1980s, and her mainly middle-class friends from Chandra Kirana.

For some years Sektor 15 was not very visible in the public sphere, focusing on internal discussions. Ifa and Gayatri brought in Agustine. She had been forced to leave her home in Bandung and was unemployed, with little education. She proved to be highly intelligent, a hard worker and honest – in short a great asset to first Chandra Kirana and later to the KPI journal *Semai* (Seedling). Agustine introduced a group of younger lesbians into Sektor 15. The discussion sessions broadened, and Ifa, Gayatri and I participated in several of these. Yet the members of Sektor 15 felt the unease with which other activists of the KPI dealt with the issue of sexual minorities, and when the term of Nursyahbani Katjasungkana, who had strongly supported Sektor 15, ended in 2004, Agustine decided to set up her own organization, the Ardhanary Institute.[10]

One of the first major activities of the KPI with which I assisted was a training session on sexuality in Ciloto, West Java, in 2002. Agustine and other members of Sektor 15 participated. All kinds of topics were brought up, from FGM (female genital mutilation) to orgasms and sexual fantasies. For many participants this was the first time they had been able to talk openly about the theories and practices of sexuality. Since then, many training sessions and discussion groups about the sexuality of heterosexual and LBT persons have been organized.

Since Agustine co-founded the Ardhanary Institute she has turned it into a very successful organization, training herself and her colleagues in feminist and sexual theories. In 2019 she finished her master's degree in law, and established her own legal practice.[11] This is the only way in which she can currently earn a living because all foreign funding of LGBT organizations is now (at the time of writing) prohibited, so that even the modest funding that the Ardhanary Institute had received has dried up.[12]

She has joined other legal professionals in various LGBT organizations. When we met in Margocity she had just come back from a meeting in Bali, with members from twenty-three LGBT organizations, many of them lawyers. They decided to fan out, join law firms, deal with ordinary cases, always on the lookout for occasions to assist LGBT people, for at the time anti-LGBT legislation was expected to be enacted soon. This ultimately happened in December 2022. Already they were dealing with court cases in various cities, such as Padang, Bandung, Garut, Purwakarta, Bogor, Depok and Banten. In several cases neighbours reported gay or lesbian people to the police, sometimes after peeping into their bedrooms. In other cases, gay men were arrested during raids on gay bars. Women have been harassed in the malls where they used to gather to chat and watch films. The lawyers have set up the Forum Bantuan Hukum untuk Kesetaraan (Legal Aid Forum for Equality). The Forum is composed of twelve lawyers, two transwomen, one lesbian, two transmen and seven gay men.

People are avoiding the offices of their own LGBT organizations. The headquarters of one of the largest groups, Arus Pelangi, has been shut. In mid-2018 a banner was hung in front of their gate, saying that an LGBT school was located there. This was an invitation to violence for any militia that felt like roughing up some people. The activists did not dare enter their workplace anymore. In the evenings they crept in one by one, taking out their materials.

The narrators

In this book I trace a group of people, most of whom identify as one of the groups with letters from the acronym LBT, from the early 1980s until now.[13] They are all female-bodied[14] (or at least assigned female at birth), and their gender identities include butch, femme, *lesbi*, trans, non-label or andro. Many other local terms are also used. My focus is on their activism and the changing political context in which they had and still have to survive. The majority of them have some connection to the Ardhanary Institute in Jakarta. Others belonged to the LBT group Dipayoni in Surabaya, which has shut down. Others are part of a wider community of LBT persons in urban settings in Java. Many of them live in what in the West is called butch-femme (b/f) relationships, in which the butch takes up some aspects of the gender role classified as masculine in a particular context, and the femme the corresponding feminine role. Though discredited in the West as copying heteropatriarchal patterns and considered outdated, pre-feminist,[15] this is an important way in which women who love women relate to each other in

Indonesia and elsewhere.[16] As Agustine explained to me, 'we have three generations of butch persons in our organization'. As will become clear in the following chapters, the b/f construction in Indonesia can only be interpreted in its specific cultural, politico-religious and historical context.

I trace their histories, from the dark days of General Suharto's military regime, called the New Order (1966–98), to the hopeful opening that the Reform period after 1998 offered, and to the stigma and hatred these LBT persons are again faced with at present. But the stigma and suppression in the early 1980s were not the same as it is now. LBT people are much stronger than they were forty years ago. They are better educated, and they have experienced the growth of an identity-based movement that greatly stimulated them. They also have access to the internet and to the wider world around them, which at times brings encouraging news, such as the legalization of same-sex marriages in Taiwan in 2019 and the initial approval by the Thai Parliament of same-sex marriages in 2022. On the shoulders of this older generation of LBT persons a brave younger generation, educated and internet-savvy, has arisen, many of whom identity as queer, some of them as non-binary, a term which was not available to the generations of activists discussed in this book.

The activists of the Ardhanary Institute defend themselves against the hatred of the heteronormative society in which they live by tactically withdrawing. They do not internalize the loathing of the homophobes around them, but they bide their time. On their visits to the small house in a lower-middle-class neighbourhood, which they have turned into an office, they tone down their clothing to conform more to the current feminine dress code. They may wear a *kerudung* (loose shawl) over their short hair or they may even don a full *jilbab*, as some of those do who still live at home in strict Muslim families. Agustine herself also wears her hair longer and dresses less obviously *lesbi*; she has given up on her chequered shirts. Her partner Dian has followed suit. The location of their workplace was carefully chosen, in a narrow alley behind the main street, so that the pickup trucks used by rowdy Islamist militia members cannot enter. Some of their activities continue. They still provide counselling to LBT people in trouble, most of that online, via a secret address. They have changed the name of their Facebook page to Perempuan Berdaya (Empowered Women).

The lesbians who used to gather in the malls have spread out. Before, they used to meet up in groups in special restaurants in specific malls, to share stories, watch films, chat, flirt, sipping one drink for hours. They no longer do that. When they meet, they gather in smaller groups, shifting restaurants and spending less time there.

Agustine last appeared on TV in 2018 and received thousands of death threats. She had to be raped, hanged from a tree. 'How did you feel?', I asked her. 'Sad,' she answered softly. 'I mean those people don't know me. I am a good person, am I not? Why do they hate me so much? What have I done? For a long time I looked around me furtively whenever I left our house. It eats into you,' she added. 'You lose your self-confidence.' Agustine, who always smiles, is always cheerful, always confident that their honesty and hard work on rights will eventually pay off, no longer smiled. She looked dejected.

Agustine knows that she and her closest colleagues are on a shortlist of the most well-known LGBT leaders established by the Badan Intelijen Negara (BIN, National Intelligence Services), together with such LGBT leaders as Hartoyo (Suara Kita), Yuli

(Arus Pelangi) and Dede Oetomo (Gaya Nusantara).[17] She has been offered asylum in several countries, but she does not want to leave: 'I am a leader, how can I leave them alone?' Dian and Wulan, who had been mostly silent in our conversation, nodded. They hardly work openly anymore, but submerge themselves in society, in friendly organizations, reaching out to schools, the courts, the public services, helping friends, becoming invisible, yet out of that invisibility spread good will and tolerance. The older activists can indeed do that, they gained so much experience in the past period of visibly organizing. But the young ones do not yet have such skills. They no longer have vibrant organizations they can go to, where they can grow. Agustine:

> They are so courageous they want to come out and fight! But we have to advise them to keep quiet. It is much too risky. The most vulnerable ones now are the *priawan* or transmen.[18] They are so visible, with their masculine clothing and hair styles. It is virtually impossible for them to find a job. They can only stay in school or university if they consent to wear women's clothing or school uniforms. Many of them drop out, as I did when I was a teenager.

The others nodded; while formerly b/f relations were relatively safe, as the couple ostensibly abided by the current gender codes, this is no longer the case. People now know the words *lesbi* and *butchi* and shout that whenever they see a gender non-conforming female-bodied person. The sense of persecution and insecurity is so great that LBT people even fear betrayal by their own friends. To preserve their own safety, some LGBT people have entered the most fanatical Islamist groups and pointed out their LGBT friends.

Before we parted in Margocity, Agustine told us she had been very depressed in 2016 and 2017. By that time her parents had finally accepted that she was a lesbian, and she had been happy to return to the family fold. But around that time the homophobic campaign had been raging and her parents were crying again. Not because they felt their daughter was deviant and sinful, but because they feared for her life.

The above account of one of the many meetings I had with Agustine and other members of the group of activists around her introduces some of the major themes of this book, as well as the political context in which LBT persons move, the creeping process of criminalization and the power of heteronormativity. There are several reasons why this book focuses on the LBT movement. First, several studies which have already appeared on the wider LGBT movement largely ignored LBT issues (apart from MTF transpeople).[19] Second, people assigned as female at birth face a number of distinct issues and generally traverse a different trajectory than people assigned as male at birth. Indonesia's heteronormative gender regime is highly patriarchal and misogynous. In male-oriented histories of LGBT organizations the specific forms of family violence and the violations of rights to education, housing and employment that LBT persons experience are not always recognised. Both in the wider society and in gay-dominated LGBT organizations LBT persons are often invisible. While organizations of gay men, *waria* and other MSM[20] gained access to HIV/AIDS-related funding, LBT organizations were largely excluded. As a 2020 report by ASTREA and Mama Cash concludes, resourcing for LBQ organizing has failed to keep pace with the needs and the capacities of such groups and movements that are operating in increasingly hostile and violent contexts.[21] From another angle, studies related to gender relations or women's movements in Indonesia pay little attention to LBT issues.[22]

This book does not build upon the popular umbrella concept queer, but rather sees the framework of heteronormativity as a more useful approach. It allows a broader discussion of homophobia in various institutions, and it enables an approach that foregrounds resilience, from symbolic subversion to rights-based activism.[23] The Indonesian case takes a route, not from oppression to visibility to equal (marriage) rights, as has been the case in several countries in the Global North. In Indonesia the careful process of gaining visibility has provoked an enormous backlash, making rights-based activism very difficult, as indicated above in the discussion with Agustine and colleagues. Also, in contrast with what happened in many countries in the West, the early b/f communities were not denounced. Instead, women in b/f relations are still an important group within the wider LBT community.

Political biography, the research process and my personal history

The title of this book includes the words 'a political biography'. Political, because it deals with LBT people's struggles for survival and their rights to celebrate their identities. And because it analyses the efforts of intolerant groups to criminalize homosexuality and investigates the sexual politics which cause certain people to be abjected and others normalized, irrespective of any positive or negative contributions they may make to society.

At the same time the book is a biography. It follows the life trajectories of people from several generations of LBT activists, and it contains autobiographical elements. I myself grew up in this movement, matured as an anthropologist and learnt how to analyse the sexual politics that determine to such a large extent the lives of numerous LBT people. The fieldwork on which this book is based took place over a period of over forty years. In that period, I was a friend, a trainer, an activist and advisor to both the Ardhanary Institute (since 2006) and Dipayoni (since 2012), as well as their ethnographer.[24] I also interacted with many LBT persons outside these two groups.

In the 1970s, anthropology did not deal with issues of sexuality.[25] In the Women's Group Anthropology Amsterdam, which we set up in 1974,[26] we read all the feminist literature that was being published at the time. Even though we studied Gayle Rubin's brilliant essay on sex/gender politics in 1975 and have applied a gender analysis to feminism ever since, sexuality was not an accepted topic in feminist anthropology. The dominant discourse on social constructivism in those years focused on the question of what exactly was being constructed: Communities? Identities? Perhaps desires even? With the rejection of the previous dominant essentialist model of sexuality studies, with its biologically determinist overtones, the physical aspects of sexuality were ignored.[27]

When, in 1983 the first national conference on feminist anthropology was held in the Netherlands, the session's chair, Joke Schrijvers, dismissed my proposal to include the study of lesbian groups in their proposed study of women's organizations. Hopelessly ethnocentric, she declared, lesbian women were only to be found in the West. I left the organization of feminist anthropology which I had co-founded and decided to follow my own research course, as I had already come across several groups of women-loving-women who identified as lesbians in several cities in what we then called 'the Third World', including Jakarta and Lima. Later I would write my fictional travelogue *Dora D* about these encounters.[28] From then onwards I collected all the older anthropological material I could find on gender diversity and same-sex relations. The 'sapphic silence'[29] of anthropology that Evie Blackwood and I noted extended even to the famous anthropologist Margaret Mead, who omitted her own love affair with Ruth Benedict in her 1972 autobiography, *Blackberry Winter*.[30]

In the 1980s and 1990s debates in feminist anthropological circles in the Netherlands were dominated by the gender and development school which relegated issues of sexuality to the background. The focus was on empowerment from a socialist feminist perspective. Studying sexuality was somehow considered not entirely legitimate, as if incited by a perverse inner drive. There was no training on the topic, and working on sexuality did not advance your career, arousing suspicion about one's own character. The rise of constructivism shifted attention away from bodies, their desires and their fluids, to social conditions.[31]

So for some twenty years I did my own research on women's same-sex relations in the margins of my work on women's empowerment. In 2001, I proposed a course on HIV/AIDS and the regulation of human sexuality at the academic institution where I worked, the Institute of Social Studies in The Hague. I thought the topic was long overdue, in view of the raging HIV/AIDS crisis across the world, but the management rejected my proposal. The South has problems of poverty, they told me, and that sexuality is only relevant for Western countries. And, added our then professor, Christine Sylvester, we have been working on gender issues, and sexuality is not relevant. I left the institute. After a stint as a consultant, I became a research associate at the University of Amsterdam and in 2006 was appointed as the first chair, worldwide, on women's same-sex relations cross-culturally. It remained an honorary position, for one day a week, which allowed me to supervise PhD students and elevated the status of the topic.

From being a stubborn, marginalized feminist anthropologist working on issues of gender diversity and same-sex relations in my free time, I had been declared an expert, albeit for one day a week (the other days I was the director of the Dutch Women's Archives). My involvement with the lesbian movement in Indonesia has been a major part of this journey, as I came to understand the importance of heteronormativity, passionate aesthetics and postcolonial amnesia.

The scapegoating of sexual dissidence in newly independent nation states is often bolstered by the 'postcolonial amnesia' of nations grappling with their colonial past.[32] This concept refers to a sometimes striking continuity between the sexual politics of postcolonial regimes and their colonial predecessors. Typically, gender diversity and women's political and sexual power are degraded by colonial regimes and then conveniently forgotten by their postcolonial successors, even though they profess to restore the country to its assumed precolonial greatness and values. Monotheistic religious leaders join in mobilizing emotions to naturalize the fiction of the 'always-already' patriarchal, heterosexual nation. I use amnesia here not just in its dictionary meaning of 'loss of memory' but extend its use to incorporate connotations of political convenience. Postcolonial amnesia in this book refers to a process of selectively memorizing certain aspects of a colonial or precolonial past, ignoring the aspects which are politically or socially inconvenient to those who control the mechanisms to create a hegemonic vision of society. Amnesia and the construction of moral, sexual panics are major means to establish hegemonic thinking in any society.

The thoughts, emotions, perceptions, desires and anxieties of our narrators are contingent on and embedded in their social, economic, cultural, religious and political locations; at the same time they are also triggered by their bodily potentialities and limitations. The body is not just a repository of social and cultural forces – a surface to be inscribed. Our narrators chart their life courses through a tangle of injunctions and many forms of violence and violations when their embodied desires clash with, or are sidetracked by, the formidable powers of those who personify social normativities or the institutions that uphold them.[33] Desires, based on bodily potentialities, are both intentional and pre-reflective and, as such, productive of power, while power simultaneously produces desire. Desire is more than erotic desire – it is also related to justice and self-accomplishment.[34] Our narrators live a liminal existence. They know the normative, live in it, negotiate with it yet are also always the unwanted 'others', with abjected desires.

Desires are expressed in culturally available tropes. In the Dutch East Indies and in its successor state Indonesia, particular bio-politics of gender and sexuality transformed certain traditional gender diverse social roles and embodied practices. This development was partly in response to colonial and postcolonial structures of governance, the increasing influence of conservative majoritarian Islam and Christianity, and a reflection of current Western and psychological models. In the process, a binary, patriarchal form of heteronormativity was strengthened, invisibilizing same-sex and transgender practices. Its passionate aesthetics have also informed attitudes towards the major exception to invisibility, the *waria*.[35] Heteronormativity is a core element of bio-power, regulating the moral codification of sexuality.[36] Heteronormativity creates a liminal area for forbidden, abject desires, which provides unity and consistency to the current heterosexual norms.

From 1981 onwards I was engaged in PhD research on the history of the Indonesian women's movement. A secret part of that work was interviewing surviving members of Gerwani,[37] some of whom had just come out of prison. They had asked me to write their history, as they were desolate about the effects of the sexual slander directed at their organization, which was still widely believed at the time.[38] Even now, former Gerwani members are stigmatized, and progressive women activists are called 'new' Gerwani. It is dangerous to get that label, as fanatical mobs still use the bogeyman of communist castrating women as an excuse to attack.[39]

Lesbian women were invisible at the time. The repression of the military dictatorship was so strong that apart from a few scandal stories in the press the existence of women living in a same-sex relationship was ignored. Only during my third research trip to Indonesia did I come into contact with a group of lesbian women in Jakarta who used to gather in one of their houses, a pavilion in the posh Jakartan area of Menteng. We hung out together, went to discos and had a good time. This group in 1983 set up the first lesbian organization in the country, Perlesin (Persatuan Lesbian Indonesia, Indonesian Lesbian Association) as I discuss in Chapter 4. Initially only the butches lined up as members, but when Syarifah Sabaroedin, a brilliant criminologist and a well-known lesbian activist, and I, asked their femme partners whether they too wanted to join, they enthusiastically enlisted. At that time, I never considered my meeting them as fieldwork. It was both for me and for them a fascinating experience to get to know each other. I only started analysing academically my encounters with this group in the late 1990s.[40]

As my research on the Indonesian women's movement included work on Gerwani, I was blacklisted for thirteen years and lost touch with the Menteng group. After the Reformasi, in 2001 I was invited to a meeting of that group, which had dispersed by that time to the outskirts of Jakarta. They asked me to document their lives, and restore their dignity, as I had done with the members of Gerwani. I was extremely busy at the time with several research and teaching projects and could not immediately start the interviews I needed to do. I also had no funds. Yet in the following years I conducted numerous interviews, both with members of this group, and other lesbian activists, mainly in Jakarta and Surabaya.[41] My intense involvement with the Indonesian 1965–7 genocide, including the organization of the International People's Tribunal on Crimes against Humanity (IPT 1965) which was held in November 2015, prevented me for a long time from writing a book on the lives of the brave LBT persons I had been meeting since the early 1980s. This book is a long-overdue tribute to their courage and perseverance in the face of societal hatred and stigma.

In 2003 and 2004 I made two research trips to Jakarta to work with the members of the b/f community, many of whom had joined Sektor 15 of the KPI (Koalisi Perempuan Indonesia, Indonesian Women's Coalition).[42] I collected the life histories of twenty women, ten of femmes, and ten of butches. I started with the femmes, as in general the butches are far more outspoken and get more attention. Since the rise of sexology in the late nineteenth century, female masculinity has been a topic that has received much more attention than the desires and lifestyles of their femme partners. Femme women in this view were seen as 'normal' women, duped by their butch inverted partners. The active desires of femme women have long been invisible in the academic world.

Most interview sessions were conducted in their own homes. This allowed me to observe the surrounding of the narrators. In some cases, they agreed to or preferred to come to the KPI office for their interviews. In the case of the femmes this was mostly caused by an unsafe family surrounding or by the anxiety of their butch partners to invite me, whom they saw as a fellow butch and possible sexual rival, into their homes. All narrators were fully informed about the purpose of the research and agreed to participate. The transcripts were read and discussed by members of Sektor 15, who assisted with the research.[43]

However intimate and personal, the interviews were also performances. Both the butches and the femmes presented their public personae to me, in some cases giving ideal-typical descriptions of themselves. Issues that did not fit their self-image would be left out. These silences were in themselves revealing. In conversations with other members of their own community or with outsiders I was able to fill in some gaps. The femmes in general were silent about the occasional violence some of them had experienced from their butch partners. They wanted to portray the relationship in a rose-tinted light. One of the butches, for instance, would gamble away all their money and, in his frustration, might hit his partner.[44] His wife never revealed that to me in any of our conversations. The butches, on the other hand, were more concerned with their image as responsible carers of their families and as autonomous sexual persons. Thus those of them who had engaged in unfair economic practices (deceiving a butch friend or embezzling money) would not reveal that.[45]

Two of the butches had male partners. For one of them, this was caused by economic desperation. The other one was urged by his femme partner to marry her younger brother, to cover up their own relationship.[46] In both cases other members of the community revealed that to me. The butches themselves never once referred to this aspect of their lives, even though I knew them both well and we had openly discussed all kinds of other aspects of their relationships and private lives.

Apart from these individual interviews I held a number of focus group discussions on topics that emerged out of the research process, such as the untouchability of the butches, ways to overcome problems in the relationship, sexuality, religion and community building. I engaged in various participatory activities. I went to parties, gave seminars which they attended, and hung out with them. I also interviewed key informants from the other lesbian groups in Jakarta I knew, such as Chandra Kirana and Swara Srikandi.

I also collected documents, and more recently text or documents on social media. First, the various bulletins produced by Chandra Kirana and Swara Srikandi, and second, printouts of the internet correspondence around two particularly acrimonious conflicts that had raged within Swara Srikandi, tearing the group apart. Third, other secondary sources were consulted and articles in the print media collected.[47]

During this first phase of the research process several issues emerged. My narrators talked rather easily about their private lives, including their sexual experiences, defying the cultural code of silence on sexual matters. Their alleged 'copying' of heterosexuality never was a replica of the construct on which it was modelled. As Butler argues, the 'ritualized repetition' of prevailing gender norms allows for its simultaneous subversion.[48] A masculinity that is worn with stigma signals the pervasiveness of the 'original'; at the same time it reveals its central weakness, it is not born by a male-bodied person. Masculinity and maleness do not have to imply each other.[49] By demonstrating their desire for a masculinity that is not heterosexual, femmes too disrupt the current sexual politics. Their often flamboyant femininity signals femme sexual power and, not directed at men, befuddles them while dazzling their butch lovers.

In multiple ways I was both an insider and an outsider. I was an insider as I was a member of KPI for many years. As a lesbian myself, I experienced similar issues. I shared with them my stories of sexual assault and discrimination. They recognized me as *senasib, seprofesi* (sharing the same fate, and the same 'profession') and as a long-term friend of many of the butches and femmes of the community. In other ways I will always remain an outsider. As a white person my position was controversial. I tried to remain neutral in the many conflicts that have characterized the lesbian movement in Indonesia. In particular the two TV presentations in 2002 and 2003 (discussed in Chapter 5) caused enormous stress within the movement. Conflicts arose about how 'out' certain women were and how to deal with the virulent homophobic reactions of society. In some cases, my efforts at mediation were appreciated. However, when some women disagreed with a proposal I made, I was accused of being a white outsider who would never understand the dynamics.

Although I tried to take a professional distance when interviewing, at times I also actively intervened. For example, I engaged in discussions with them about religion. The Muslim butches felt a great unease about how they should relate to their religion. Femmes had far fewer problems. As 'normal' women they could wear the appropriate Islamic feminine dress (*mukenah*) when praying. The butches, however, felt torn. They could make human society believe that they were men but Allah, they felt, would surely be able to look through their disguise. So they had to be 'honest' and would have to put on the *mukenah* when praying. But they were ashamed to be seen like that in public and thus could never attend prayer meetings. I suggested that Allah would surely know their deepest souls, where their manliness lay according to themselves. As religion is a spiritual affair, would not the communication from their souls be more important to Allah than the message given by wearing the *mukenah*? As I had recently converted to Islam I had some credibility, but most of them disagreed.

In my fieldnotes from those years I regularly noted femme sexual assertiveness and wondered how my asking about their love lives might be misread for interest in them personally.

For the femmes to show their sexual attractiveness, their daring, and for the butches to keep control, to meet this challenge is a game. If that is the issue then I kept the necessary *sentul* (butch) cool. But it is a dangerous game, for this play does lead at times to relations. It also confirms Indonesian gender ideas, women have the passion, *nafsu*, men the *akal*, intellect, do the talking in public, show control over their emotions. If the b/f community can be read to be organized around sexual attraction, femmes are the motor. All this makes butch jealousy a bit more comprehensible, for these femmes do flirt. Long glances, swaying hips appearing out of nowhere. Direct looks, suggestive silences, getting hold of my hand, my arm, my knee, which indeed are close to the respondents, for I hold the recorder, and they speak softly and quickly. But I take great care never to touch.[50]

Parties are a great occasion to observe b/f erotic games. On 11 May 2003, for instance, I attended a birthday party at the house of one of the more affluent narrators. I was sitting down with a glass of beer when Evi and her long-standing butch lover arrived. Evi was attractively made up, wearing a T-shirt with a very low neck, knee long tight fitting trousers, high open heels. Her butch lover wore a white polo neck and long dark men's trousers; he had a pleasant open face. Brushing past me, Evi whispered, 'Why didn't you phone me, I gave you my number!' I danced with all femmes I had interviewed so far in turn and tried not to show preferences, for talk of jealousy was all around, Agustine told me in the kitchen. After some hours I sat down again with Evi, who informed me that I looked like an *udang rebus* (boiled shrimp). But I did more than dancing. I observed the game of teasing, making passes, whispers, languishing eyes. Avoiding the butch lover, flirting. Later I reflected on the dance with Agustine and the politics of mating. No butch seemed to be jealous of me, so that was okay.[51]

Over the next years I engaged in two other formal research projects on women's same-sex relations in Indonesia and kept meeting my old friends in the LBT movement. The first project was in the framework of the Kartini Asia Network. I co-founded this all-Asian network in 2000 and it was formally established in 2003 in Manila.[52] It fosters cooperation between academics and activists. The philosophy is that the impact of women's/gender studies is increased if it is based on women's realities and that gender advocates can work more effectively if they are grounded in the relevant theoretical and methodological perspectives. When that synergy is created, the so-called Triangle of Women's Empowerment can function more effectively. The three corners of this triangle are usually feminist-oriented academics, activists and state actors. Academics and activists in constant interaction push for reform and more gender-sensitive policies to be enacted by the 'femocrats' in state functions.[53] The network held two major all-Asia conferences, in Dalian, China, in 2004 and in Bali in 2008.[54]

In 2006, within the framework of the sexuality theme of the Kartini Asia Network, an advocacy workshop was held in Jakarta in collaboration with the feminist legal aid network APIK[55] (Asosiasi Perempuan Indonesia untuk Keadilan, Indonesian Women's Association for Justice), on non-normative sexualities, comparing lesbians, widows/divorced women and sex workers.[56] This was the beginning of an analysis of heteronormativity as a regime that polices those within its boundaries and marginalizes those that fall outside its limits. An initial training course for researchers on the theme was held in April 2008 at the Jagori rural feminist training centre in Himachal Pradesh, India. Abha Bhaiya and I produced a training manual for that course which was subsequently widely used by women's organizations in India and Indonesia.[57] Another training course the researchers organized was in collaboration with the IASSCS, which held its biannual conference in Hanoi in April 2009.[58]

From 2009 to 2011, funded by The Ford Foundation and HIVOS, the coordinators of the Kartini sexuality theme, Abha Bhaiya, Nursyahbani Katjasungkana and I coordinated an action research project on the workings of heteronormativity among sex workers, widows/divorced women and lesbians in India and Indonesia. The project involved fieldwork in India and Indonesia, resulting in comprehensive profiles of thirty-three female-born persons living beyond the bounds of 'normalcy' or heteronormativity in Delhi and Jakarta. All of them were, at times, thoroughly disoriented when their desires clashed with societal norms and the people and institutions that uphold them and govern 'decent' sexual and social behaviour. This disorientation has material, embodied and discursive aspects. Kristeva defines the abject as 'the in-between, the ambiguous, the composite'.[59] Butler locates the 'abjected others' in a material reality, both corporeal and politicized, and stresses the unthinkable, unnameable characteristics of those considered to be 'abject'. Their realities are silenced and their modes of living are unintelligible within what Butler calls the 'heterosexual matrix'.[60] In the book that is the result of this project I reflected on the passionate aesthetics that are deployed to separate the 'normal' from the 'abjected'.[61] This book on the history of the LBT movement in Indonesia builds on the conceptual tools developed during the course of this Kartini project: heteronormativity and passionate aesthetics.

To promote the study of trans/sexualities a global network for the study of trans/sexualities cross-culturally, TRANS/SIGN, was set up in 2008. This was chaired by me, co-coordinators were Evelyn Blackwood (Purdue University, United States) and Nursyahbani Katjasungkana (Kartini Asia Network and APIK). TRANS/SIGN was a network of academic scholars, policy advocates and research-minded activists. Besides the Kartini Asia Network, the Riek Stienstra Foundation, located in the Netherlands, was also involved.[62] The funding came from the HIVOS Foundation and MamaCash.

The project lasted from 2009 to the end of 2010. Eleven studies were carried out in eight countries, and four hundred participants were interviewed in fourteen different languages.[63] The topics included female masculinity, the silencing and invisibility of women and the trajectories of LBT activists. Most projects used intensive oral history interviews. In Indonesia two sub-projects were implemented on female masculinity. In Jakarta a team of the Ardhanary Institute did the interviews. The research in Surabaya focused on community building, to support political activism. Ultimately a new lesbian organization was set up, Dipayoni (literally, Light of the Vagina). They used a community-based research approach, consisting of fun-edutainment and more formal focus group discussions (FGDs).[64] The research results were shared with the narrators throughout the research process and afterwards. I edited the final full report, and the quotes used in this book are based on that report. The transcripts and other research materials are kept in the offices of the organizations. Since these projects finished I have visited Indonesia regularly, keeping up to date with the narrators whose life stories I had collected or read – sometimes through formal interviews, at other times at parties or other events – and also collecting secondary data, sometimes via social media.

Political context

Indonesia proclaimed its independence in August 1945. After a bloody independence war with the former Dutch colonizers, Indonesia's first president, Sukarno, could start rebuilding the country in 1950. His regime was characterized initially by an open democracy (national elections in 1955) followed by a period of regional uprisings and political instability. In 1959 Sukarno proclaimed a policy of 'Guided Democracy', stifling the democratic process. Tensions between the armed forces – conservative Muslim groups who wanted a state based on sharia law for Muslims – and the fast-growing Communist Party (Partai Komunis Indonesia PKI) ended in bloodshed in 1965.

Following the abduction and murder of six generals and one lieutenant by the 30 September Movement[65] in the early morning of 1 October 1965, members of the progressive women's organization Gerwani were falsely accused of having castrated and tortured the generals, prior to killing them.[66] This sexual slander, the first sexual moral panic, was widely propagated and incited conservative groups to participate in the massacres in which hundreds of thousands of leftist people were murdered or incarcerated.[67] After creating the chaos in which this genocide took place, General Suharto was able to replace President Sukarno in 1966.[68] He called his military dictatorship the New Order. Since then, an emphasis on heterosexual normalcy based on women's docility as wives and mothers and control over their sexuality became the bedrock of the regime. The current, second sexual moral panic builds on the post-1965 one and is spurred by the rise of conservative Muslim groups.[69]

Since the downfall of Suharto in 1998, the so called Reformasi period, there was a short period of hope that Indonesia would become a democratic nation based on the rule of law and respect for human rights. The democratic opening gave LGBT people hope that their rights might be defended as well. But Muslim hardliner groups also came out into the open. Slowly they managed to dominate civil society, undermining the secular character of the state and dominating discourses on morality.[70] Political analysts like Aspinall, Mietzner and Hadiz have come to characterize Indonesia's democracy as 'illiberal'.[71] This situation was exacerbated when by the end of 2015 a homophobic hate campaign started, the effects of which are still felt strongly. The complex political climate of the past years has been variously characterized as becoming increasingly conservative, following the rise of majoritarian Muslim fundamentalist pressure, with increasing neglect of human, women's and sexual rights. Much of this is related to who controls the power and the discourse to define the nation.[72]

Indonesia built its post-independence state model on the heterosexual family unit. Indonesia's first president, Sukarno, posited himself as the Father of the Nation, and regularly drew upon tales about his own family in his famous speeches.[73] The nation's second president, General Suharto, styled himself the Father of Development and proposed the so-called family principles (*asas kekeluargaan*) as the proper heterosexual model of citizenship.[74] He built the nation on the flagrant lies he himself constructed about women's dangerous sexual excesses, as discussed above. To maintain order and stability, the heterosexual family model with a dominant father and a subservient wife was imposed.[75] Those abjected in this model could not lay claim to sexual citizenship. The bio-politics of the New Order centred around compulsory family planning and the subjugation of women through their own organizations.[76]

Indonesia's heteronormative regime is mediated by tensions between two opposing world orders: the global human rights movement and a conservative, Wahabist version of Islam. In this book I emphasize the relevance of the space in between, the localized aspects of a complex gender regime, focusing on the agency, creativity and courage of the gender justice warriors who try to create room for themselves and their non-mainstream desires. They dream of a society in which gender equity is seen as an issue of justice, a concept which is incorporated in both the nation's founding philosophy Pancasila and in Islamic teachings, but which is ignored by the greedy oligarchy that rules the country and the myopic religious conservative forces which fuel hatred against minorities. The LBT narrators in this research negotiate their lives in a society characterized by increasing surveillance through social media, restrictive laws, the deployment of security personnel and by the vigilantism and aggression of Islamist militias.

The LBT movement moves within this political context. During the New Order any organization not controlled by the government was seen as subversive. It thus took enormous courage to even think of setting up a lesbian organization, such as Perlesin. It lasted about a year, but many of its members went on to join other organizations. Slowly women in same-sex relationships realized that together they stood stronger. When society opened up and the independent women's organizations could operate more freely, lesbian women also came out in the open. They built identity-based organizations and hotly debated what those identities might entail. Emancipation was one of the stated goals; they aimed at becoming respected citizens. After 2010 and especially after the first politically motivated homophobic statements emerged, they have gone back into hiding again.

The secrecy LBT people must practice and experience now is different from that during the New Order. During the New Order they could exist under the radar. In Indonesia, as in many other cultures, women sharing one bed is not uncommon and the practice traditionally has not had a sexual connotation.[77] But the introduction of the acronym LGBT has, in particular, lifted same-sex relations out of their liminality. People of the same sex together now arouse distrust. It is more difficult to ignore the suspicion they might be intimate. Same-sex intimacy belonged to the realm of the unspoken – that which people did not need to know (*tahu* – conscious knowing). And as long as it was not in the public realm, no action needed to be taken. Neither approval nor disapproval was required. Family members, friends or colleagues did not have to be *malu* (ashamed), which would have propelled them to take action to root out the source of this shame. What is important is that the surface is not disturbed by knowledge of facts that might rupture the tenuous religious or social consensus. My narrators often replied '*tahu tapi tidak mau tahu*', ('they know but don't want to know') when I asked whether their b/f relationship was accepted by their neighbours or families. Several modes of 'knowing' can be distinguished in a Javanese setting. At the most open level people fully *mengerti* (know in a rational way) or *faham* (know with the heart) the issue at stake. A much vaguer level is that of *tahu*. This means that as long as the couple do not cause suspicion among neighbours or their families that the relationship might be a sexual union, and as long as the nature of their love is not brought to the level of *mengerti* or *faham*, their relationship need not be condemned.[78]

Terminology

I use the acronym LBT as an umbrella term to refer to the group of female-bodied persons (or assigned female at birth) in same-sex relationships who are the narrators in this book. But usage of this term is clearly inadequate when referring to the different practices, meanings, identities and periods discussed. I adopt this terminology because LGBT is at present the major term used in Indonesia to designate any person engaging in non-heteronormative behaviour, though among the younger and more educated generations some now identify as queer. Both persons (female- and male-bodied) and organizations are labelled LGBT, and sometimes a Q is added, as in LGBTQ Forum. As the term 'LGBT' arrived from the West it is immediately associated with foreignness, which in xenophobic Indonesia arouses suspicion. Gay men, lesbian women and transgender persons can be called 'LGBT'. This can lead to confusing statements, such as when a police general was accused of being 'engaged in LGBT behaviour'.[79] What the general was actually doing and what was his or her sexual orientation or gender expression remained unclear.

This ambiguity is only one of the problems associated with the use of terminology in this book. As much as possible I prioritize self-identification and I use the terms appropriate to the period discussed. But in practice it is difficult to apply these principles consistently.[80] One issue is that some women in a same-sex (but different gender) relationship may not identify as lesbian or bisexual (if they had been married to a man before) but as 'ordinary' women. Or male-identified people classified as 'woman' at birth may identify as 'men' and not as transmen.

In the early 1980s the Jakarta women's same-sex community did not identify as lesbian; the words most commonly used to describe themselves were *cewek/cowok* (Betawi for woman/man) or *kantil/sentul* (femme/butch). Many of them kept using that terminology for themselves, while other terms had sprung up around them, like *lesbi, andro* or no label. By the time of my research between 2004 and 2005, younger b/f lesbians would identify as femmy and butchy (or *femi* and *butchi*). During an FGD in Pondok Gede in 2003, Agus exclaimed 'I am *sentul sejati*' ('I am a true *sentul*'). Dede, our host, explained: 'we are the men, the husbands in the relationship, our wives are women. A *sentul* has to carry responsibility, for we are the heads of the household.[81] Agam added: 'Our *jiwa* (soul) is that of a true man in the body of a woman. This is why we dress and behave like men.' They were all proud of their *sentul* identity, this was the source of their self-esteem. All along, the *kantil* sat in the room close together, listening.

In Surabaya, around that time, butches told me that they had to possess *wibawa* (power, authority). The male-identified participants in this research might also refer to themselves as *laki-laki* (men), while their feminine partners all said they were 'women' and 'wives' of their partners. For the sake of convenience I refer to this group as a 'butch-femme'(b/f) community although it has to be understood that the way they perform their butchness and femmeness is specifically Indonesian and that there have been significant modifications over time. Though b/f is usually associated with a lower-class subculture, and most b/f couples in this book belong to the lower or lower-middle classes, lower-class women in same-sex relationships engage in a broader spectrum of gender roles and same-sex practices.[82] Women of other socio-economic classes also engage in b/f-styled sexual encounters. Outside of Jakarta other terms were used for women in same-sex relations. In Makassar, for instance, butch women were usually termed *hunter*. Lesbians in Surabaya feel more comfortable to call themselves *belog* (reversed); *lines* or *L. Lesbi*, they said, carries the weight of stereotype, while most people are unfamiliar with the term *belog*. Thus, though the use of b/f is problematic, I cannot find a better umbrella term.

Queer is often used as an umbrella term for those who resist heteronormativity. It is indeed easier to grasp than the ever-expanding list of non-hetero people LGBTTSIQQA.[83] However, I have some reservations with its use as an umbrella term. It tends to be femme-phobic, as femmes are seen by some to abide by heteronormative roles. Another problem is that it subsumes the trajectories of female-bodied persons, homogenizing all non-heteronormative people, disguising the patriarchal regime which always puts the experiences of men in the limelight. Lesbians are more invisible than gay men or *waria* due to the general invisibility of women's sexual agency, and their restricted presence in the public sphere. The same applies to terms like homosexual and gay, which also usually refer to male-bodied persons. Queer might therefore be a useful term within the academy, grouping together theories that aim to deconstruct heteronormativity.[84] Younger, highly educated political activists in Indonesia also use it, but only very few of the narrators who shared their stories with me used the term to identify themselves.

The B of bisexuality is ambiguous. While in the Global North this refers to people who identify as having the option of a same- or different-sex partner, in Indonesia women and men who see themselves as lesbian or gay may marry to give in to family pressure and yet seek relationships outside of that marriage with members of the same sex. They do not identify as bisexual, although their sexual practices point in that direction. In this book bisexuality refers to both categories – female-bodied persons who are married heterosexually but see themselves as lesbian, and women whose sexual object choice includes both women and men. In the first case it is an ascriptive term. However, I will more often refer to these women as lesbians, or as 'normal' women if they identify as that.

The T of trans is another equivocal term. I use it as an umbrella term for transsexual and transvestite behaviours of people identifying as such.[85] At present the terms *transpuan* (MTF transgender persons), *priawan* (FTM transgender persons) and transboy are used, as well as *tranny*, *tg* or just *trans*. Others consider themselves to belong to the other gender or sex and identify as men or women. I try to follow the ways they identify themselves, also in the use of pronouns, but cannot do so consistently, partly also because people's identities may change over the years. An added problem in English is that this language uses gendered pronouns, while in Indonesian, the pronouns are unmarked. I therefore hesitate to use they/them for transpersons as is becoming common now in English-speaking countries, as this form of self-identification is not necessary in Indonesian. The porosity of the sex-gender distinction, the fluidity of gender and sexual categories and the changing identifications which may occur in one lifetime and that exist between generations all problematize the use of umbrella terms and definite pronouns.

Other letters of the LGBT(etc.) alphabet soup do not figure much in this book. Intersex people, for instance, have their own issues, both medical and social, and hardly feature in the Indonesian LGBT community. As far as I know there is only one support group for intersex people, Forkis, associated with the foremost medical gender centre in Indonesia, in the Kariadi Hospital in Semarang (the slogan on the polo necks that they sell states 'you don't know what genes are in my jeans'). The term intersex, or DSD (differences in sex development) is hardly known in the wider society. Usually, intersex people are referred to as having *kelamin ganda*, multiple sex organs. I will however briefly touch on one well-known case, that of Alterina Hofan, as it affected the butch narrators. A distinction has emerged over the past decades, between transgender/transsexual and intersex, based on bodily appearance and validated by the establishment of a person's karyotype and psychometric tools.[86] Earlier, anthropologists were much more ambiguous. Often the word 'hermaphrodite' was used, denoting

Hermaphroditus, the Greek god usually depicted with both breasts and male genitals, an offspring of the messenger god Hermes and the goddess of love, Aphrodite.[87] In the absence of medical tests it was impossible for them to ascertain with any clarity whether they were dealing with transvestism, transgenderism or intersexuality.

Conclusion

Globalization and transnational flows have produced tangible effects on sexual relations, identities and subjectivities, but this impact has been very uneven. The term 'transnational' may gloss over national specificities.[88] Often this discourse is built on an assumed overcoming of the barriers of traditionality.[89] In Indonesia, however, 'traditional' societies sometimes offered more scope for gender diversity. In this book I pay some attention to the impact of global discourses on local gender orders, bodily practices and sexual subjectivities, but I focus on the specific Indonesian politics of nation formation and religious fundamentalism, in which binary gender boundaries were imposed or strengthened. In Indonesia predatory capitalism and democracy provide a shrinking public space in which the LGBT movement exists. By bringing to the fore these specific conditions as analysed in this book, LBT history globally will be enriched.

The backlash that had set in by the end of 2015 threatens to invisibilize the LBT community again. Yet present-day members of the LBT community are better equipped to take on this new situation, even when they have to be on the run from Muslim militias and the police. Agustine and her colleagues have acquired the arguments they need to defend themselves and they have built up a strong network of friends and allied organizations. These activists no longer feel they are 'deviant' or 'sick', as women in the 1980s described themselves to me. Most of them are confident of their identities and their sexual orientations; educated younger activists may identity as queer and seek alliances with the wider LGBTQ movement. However, the many individuals who have not yet built such self-confidence, who are still at home, at school or university, may not find it easy to meet like-minded friends, for LGBT organizations have been forced to take down most of their websites and other social media. No public LGBT events are held any more, such as the Q!film festival or the Pride marches against homophobia.[90] One can only attend meetings by invitation and sometimes at the last moment the venue has changed. GPS must be turned off and participants must promise not to post photos or messages during the event. Phones have to be turned to aeroplane mode. And we whisper to each other.

A genealogy of past practices can help recreate echoes of the past which resonate in present-day sex-gender regimes.[91] As homosexuality erroneously is often seen as a Western import into an assumedly naive and 'always already' heterosexual archipelago, I start this book with a discussion, in Chapters 2 and 3, of some indigenous forms of gender diversity that have historically been present in the archipelago, including transgender religious, healing and cultural practices and beliefs. I am not primarily looking for continuities with the past but want to find moments of inspiration in the rich cultural heritage of the archipelago. I am particularly interested in the mechanisms of their destruction, as these may illuminate the depth and the mechanics of present-day homophobia. The entrance of monotheistic religions and the moral constraints imposed by the Dutch colonial administrators deeply impacted the archipelago's different gender regimes, imposing or strengthening a patriarchal binary gender system. The colonial encounter with the morally conservative Dutch led to the first wave of persecution of gay men in the 1930s. After the independence war Indonesia's leaders did not restore traditions in which non-binary practices flourished. After the creeping coup of 1965–7 and the genocide committed against the country's progressive stream, in which General Suharto assumed state power, the full impact of the postcolonial amnesia of the ruling elite became apparent. Folk and religious traditions, including some with transgender performers or ritual specialists, were associated with the left and many lost their lives. Yet during Suharto's reign also the first stirrings of modern, identity-based organizations appeared.

The next two chapters, Chapters 4 and 5, deal with the growth of the LBT movement, from Perlesin in the early 1980s to the present period. Chapter 6 analyses the specific Indonesian nature of b/f relations over the past decades. Then follows a chapter on the second homophobic campaign which was starting by the end of 2015. This is followed in Chapter 8 by a discussion on family violence and conversion therapy. Chapter 9 outlines some of the major dilemmas which religions pose for the LBT narrators in this book. In the concluding chapter the latest political, legal and social developments are examined.

2

The twilight of the gods

The National Museum of Jakarta lies on the west side of the city's central Freedom Square. In early 2003 I took Agustine and her group there on a bus tour.[1] Impressed, they looked at the many statues of Dewi (goddess) Durga, the indomitable one. She is portrayed in several of her manifestations, from severe and strong to erotic. Then they searched for the three statues of the androgynous deity Ardhanary, which are in the museum. In the central yard there is an imposing fourteenth-century statue of the god. Its right half is adorned with the traditional ornaments of Shiva. The hair piled in matted locks. The left half shows well-dressed hair, a round full breast and hip and female garments. Agus, proudly, yet almost crying, exclaimed: 'That's me, half man half woman. So there is nothing wrong with me. I exist in history!' Next, we stopped at the beautiful statue of a reclining Shiva who is awakened by a sensual Parvati. This statue portrays how Shiva is roused by Parvati after which they make love for 10,000 years. Humans spring up wherever drops of Shiva's sperm touch the earth. Now the femmes are very pleased. They are always accused of having insatiable desires. Diana laughs, 'You see, women can be *genit* (coquettish)!' Both butches and femmes therefore found a justification for their existence in these Hindu statues. Butches for their male souls, femmes for their sexual desires.

Introduction

In this and the following chapter I give some examples of Indonesia's rich history of gender and sexual diversity, which has been documented from the far Western part of the archipelago in Aceh, to the far Eastern part of the country in Papua. This chapter focuses on three deities which have almost lost their presence and power in present-day society – Ardhanary, Durga and Kwan Im – and on transgender priests in various areas. The next chapter discusses transgender and same-sex practices at the courts and in rural communities, in dance and literature. The dividing line between these two realms is porous, as ostensibly secular transgender practices often had sacral connotations. Even though Indonesia's religious regime is presently dominated by monotheistic religions, particularly majoritarian Islam, echoes from its rich pluriform religious past provide a cultural idiom that still has meaning for many Indonesians. There is no indication in Indonesia's past that same-sex relations were ever criminalized among the various ethnic groups which the precolonial archipelago consisted of. This is not to say that precolonial societies were always tolerant of same-sex relations. But it does indicate that same-sex practices and gender diversity are not phenomena imported from the global West, as present-day homophobes maintain. The regional regulations that are being produced all over the nation, and which are built on alleged custom and religion as a justification for restrictions on women and prohibitions of homosexuality, find no validation in Indonesia's rich cultural traditions of gender pluralism.[2]

Transgendered practices, mostly related to certain ritual and shamanistic traditions, were a theme of both literary texts such as *I La Galigo*[3] and the reports of colonial administrators. The best-known remnant of such a tradition is the *bissu* – transgender or intersex ritual specialists belonging to the Bugis ethnic group in Sulawesi.[4] They have lost much of their traditional power and prestige since the beginning of the twentieth century.[5] This development refers to a process that Blackwood, following Andaya, more broadly calls the decline of 'sacred gender'.[6] Sacred gender is associated with a world view in which gender is defined as a 'direct link between sacred powers and a third sex/gender'.[7] The term refers to cosmologies that 'constitute gendered meanings and practices through sacred beliefs about the nature of the cosmos and the origins of humanity'.[8] Origin myths frequently stress an original unity (a snake or an egg) from which diverse beings originate. The Bugis creation myth, *I La Galigo*, speaks of originally 'androgynous' deities that produce various sacred beings, including *bissu*.[9]

Examples of precolonial and colonial gender and sexual plurality are often derived from the reports of missionaries, travellers, administrators or anthropologists, most of whom abhorred these practices, as was the custom in their countries of origin. By the end of the nineteenth century the discourse on gender transgression and diversity in the West had shifted from the juridical to the medical.[10] This move can also be noted in the writings of the chroniclers of these practices in colonial settings. An extra bias is formed by sentiments of racial superiority, which resulted in the presentation of these cases as justifications for imperial practices in which the 'pagan' objects had to be 'civilized'.[11] Homophobia in Indonesia was introduced by the colonial administration, resulting in the first anti-gay sexual moral panic of the late 1930s, discussed in the next chapter. The Wahabist Islamic reform movements in Malaysia and Indonesia in the eighteenth and nineteenth centuries, purporting to 'cleanse' Islam from pre-Islamic elements, also fermented intolerance of same-sex and transgendered practices.[12]

Historical examples of gender and sexual diversity can be found all over Asia. Transgender people were venerated for their ability to transcend the male–female binaries and by extension the boundaries between the world of the gods and that of humans.[13] Known to this day are the communities of *hijras* all over South Asia, *kathoey* in Thailand, *bakla* in the Philippines, *mak nyah* in Malaysia and *banci/waria* in Indonesia.[14]

Precolonial religious beliefs often centred around fertility, both in human society and in the soil. In Indonesia too there is ample evidence of precolonial fertility rites and beliefs. Candi Sukuh and Candi Ceto in Central Java are fertility shrines in which depictions of male and female genitals are prominent.[15] These are portrayed in heterosexual forms, but they are a clear indication that sexuality was expressed very visibly – and not shrouded in present-day manifestations of shame.[16]

In colonial encounters goddesses lost their authority and powerful women were recast from mighty warriors to mothers and wives.[17] In her exploration of the relation between gender, race and sexuality in the colonial context, McClintock points to the cult of domesticity that arose in nineteenth-century England.[18] In this process the domestic realm became separated from the public realm of trade, politics and the military, much as in bourgeois Dutch society of the time.[19] This is in stark contrast to the power and visibility not only of Eurasian women in early colonial society, but also of the women in the Javanese courts who, as Carey and Houben documented, held important commercial, military and political positions.[20]

Particularly during the so-called Ethical period in colonial Indonesia, around the turn of the nineteenth into the twentieth century, education into dependent wifehood became a central concern.[21] The Ethical Policy was introduced to mitigate the detrimental effects of Dutch colonial greed on the Indonesian population but strengthened Dutch bourgeois values on gender and racial superiority through the creation of subordinate, Dutch-styled housewives. Around the same time the introduction of the psychopathology of sexual behaviours by Krafft Ebbing and his successors coincided with a racialist conceptualization of indigenous Indonesians as prone to sexual perversion and in need of a Western guiding morality.

Postcolonial nationalist leaders were keen to emancipate their people from the shackles of imperialist oppression. But they reproduced the sexual morality imposed on them by the former colonial masters, at the expense of their own ethnic, cultural and religious traditions of gender diversity. Western colonial homophobic morality was attractive, as people admired the modern ways which seemed so much more successful than their own traditional ways of running society. The same-sex practices and examples of gender pluralism were perceived as perverse and decadent, contributing to the defeat of the archipelago by these modern Dutch colonial forces.

These discussions may have little direct meaning for many gay, *lesbi* and queer people in the present, in the sense that they might offer identities or role models that can be copied. Yet they serve a broader goal than simply denouncing the claim that same-sex and transgender practices are foreign imports. The realization that they have a history infuses their present-day lives with meaning; when in 2005 a small group of LBT people decided to set up their own organization, they named it after Ardhanary.

Ardhanarishvara

The full name of Ardhanary is Ardhanarishvara, which means 'the lord whose half is woman'. This androgynous deity is created by the union of the Hindu deities Shiva and his consort Shakti, the female energy, also called Parvati in a benevolent form or Durga as the warrior-like manifestation. This divine being represents totality beyond duality. Ardhanarishvara is associated with communication, mediating between women and men, between divine and mortal beings. Communication is located in the chakra of the throat which in tantric belief is related to oral intercourse, linking the god/goddess to homoeroticism.[22] In the past, Ardhanarishvara was served by transgendered, or cross-dressing priests. In tantrism, hermaphroditism, homosexuality and transvestism are considered sacred, and are seen as images of Ardhanarishvara. It is not clear, however, if this practice was also followed in the eleventh-century East Javanese realms of Kediri and Singosari, in which the cult of Ardhanarishvara flourished. That tantrism had many followers is clear.[23] Ardhanarishvara is variously associated with intersex, transgender and homosexual beings.[24] The deity is portrayed as half male and half female, split vertically down the middle. Each half is accompanied by its appropriate animal, the bull for Shiva, the tiger for Durga/Parvati. When by the end of the fifteenth century the successor state of Singosari, Majapahit, was defeated by the sultanate of Demak, Islam became the dominant religion in Java, and Hinduism was relegated to isolated pockets, like the Tengger mountains in East Java, and Bali.

Ardhanarishvara represents the unity of opposites; the deity's male half is related to Purusha (the male, passive principle of the universe), while the female half is associated with Prakriti (the female active force). These principles must be in harmony with each other. Together they create the universe and they are therefore also related to *kama* (lust and fertility). Another representation of this fertile unity is in the form of the *lingga-yoni* combination – the *lingga* of Shiva and the *yoni* of Shakti – as in Candi Sukuh.

This deity signifies non-duality, a unified God both destructive and constructive, reconciling the spiritual and material world. Its figure reveals 'a seemingly perfect, indissoluble unity, complete in himself/herself' who embraces masculinity and femininity. In pre-Islamic Javanese epic court poetry, the so-called *kakawin*, Ardhanarishwara is mentioned in a tantric form of the yoga of love in which the divine union of Shiva and Shakti creates the 'seed of the world' (*windu*). This cosmic union provides both sexual gratification and the welfare of the land; it ensures abundance of life in general. This fusion of male and female in one form referred both to spiritual prowess and the physical enjoyment of love.

In one of the most famous of these *kakawin*, the eleventh-century Ardjunawiwaha, Prince Arjuna engages in a fierce fight with Shiva, in the form of a hunter. In the end, they abandon weapons and wrestle. When the deity was about to be thrown to the ground, he disappears. Before Arjuna's surprised eyes a 'rain of flowers' poured down and he 'finally saw a gleaming light'. The poet goes on to describe Shiva as Ardhanarishwara, sitting upon a 'throne of jewels'. Arjuna recognized the deity and paid homage, hailing the god as 'the essence of the highest reality, … the origin and destination of the whole world, manifest in both the visible and the invisible'.

Durga and Ken Dedes

Durga is the invincible mother goddess, the only one deity in the Hindu pantheon able to conquer the buffalo demon Mahisha, when she has been endowed with the added powers of Vishnu and Shiva.[25] She is also often portrayed as Prajnaparamita, her manifestation as the mystical East Javanese queen of Singosari, Ken Dedes.[26] Durga in her angry manifestation is Kali, usually depicted with a string of skulls around her neck.[27]

Though the consort of Shiva, when fused with his male powers she is also seen as a virgin goddess who does not belong to any man. The process of creating this supergod is associated with enormous energies; when the combined powers of Vishnu and Shiva enter her body, flames are sent in all directions.[28]

As in India, where the goddess is still a powerful and protective deity, Durga was seen as the mother goddess in charge of agricultural and human fertility, when she first descended on the archipelago around 700 CE. Durga entered into the Malay-Indonesian archipelago from India as Durga Mahishasuramardini, the slayer of the demon Mahisha, a beautiful and sensual warrior goddess protecting her devotees.[29] Yet in spite of her enormous powers and initial popularity, over the centuries Durga has been demonized in East Java and Bali. The transformation of Durga to a terrifying demon developed during the East Javanese period (between the tenth and fifteenth centuries). In the popular story of Calon Arang, Rangda – a deceived and angry widow – enlists the help of the goddess Durga to bring pestilence and disease to the East Javanese kingdom of Airlangga to wreak revenge. The Calon Arang saga has led to the identification of the goddess Durga as the patron of black magic in which form she is worshipped in order to gain magical powers, or *kesaktian*. In her reinterpretation of this story the well-known feminist philosopher and poet Toeti Heraty points to the patriarchal underpinnings of 'Bali's Queen of Evil' who wreaked havoc on the eleventh-century East Javanese kingdom of Daha. Only through treachery was King Erlangga able to defeat her. In Bali, Calon Arang is portrayed as a fearful witch, Rangda, with 'matted hair hanging loose, tongue protruding, fangs and claws grasping pendulous breasts a-sway', to be defeated by the 'good' powers of the Barong. But, as Heraty adds, 'She is just an old woman, a crone with anger overflowing.'[30] Her anger stems from the fear nobody will marry her beautiful daughter, afraid of the mother's powers of destruction. Musing on the ways patriarchal controls keep being imposed on women, Heraty wonders what the obstacles are to women choosing a partner of the same sex, and to 'join the lesbian community'? She knows the answer: 'Men are angered at the first hint of lesbianism; they immediately curse it to the core.'[31] Ariati suggests that this is especially evident in the way that

> images of cruel and sexually free women were presented as 'proof' of the involvement of the women of the progressive women's organization Gerwani in the murder of six of Indonesia's most prominent generals on 30 September 1965. These images ... must have played upon deep-seated fears of the 'terrifying' power of women like the widow Rangda who are not kept 'safe' within the domestic sphere as wives and mothers.[32]

The patriarchal twisting of folk tales, myths, religion or history had long been ongoing before the introduction of Islam and Christianity and the imposition of Dutch bourgeois morality, as Ariati in her fascinating study of Durga details.[33] Remnants of the beneficent and powerful Durga, however, can still be found in Indonesia.[34]

In Northern India Durga is associated with the rice goddess.[35] Dewi Sri is the pre-Hindu Javanese rice goddess who fulfils similar functions, ensuring the fertility of the land and prosperity in general. In East Java, for instance, until the late 1960s, regular offerings to Dewi Sri would be held on the edges of rice fields. This practice has to a large part disappeared. It became associated with the banned Communist Party. East Java was the site of a gruesome genocide in the wake of the putsch in 1965. Banser, the youth group of the largest Muslim mass organization NU (Nahdlatul Ulama), participated in the killings. Many farmers thought it wise to show their Islamic credentials and gave up their offerings to Dewi Sri.[36]

Ken Dedes is often named the princess of the flaming womb, reminiscent of the way Shiva's powers entered Durga, namely with fire through her vagina.[37] Riding in her carriage her sarong falls open, revealing a gleam of light between her thighs. The adventurer Ken Arok, who had entered the service of the husband of Ken Dedes, is intoxicated by this sight. The flaming womb marks Ken Dedes also as Ardhanarishvara. When Ken Arok understands that the husband of Ken Dedes is destined to be king of the world, he murders his employer and assumes the throne.[38] The story of Ken Dedes, as told in the *Pararaton* (Book of Kings), portrays her as a victim of an aggressive usurper, unable to prevent the chain of father murders that follows (her son from her first husband kills Ken Arok, the murderer of his father, and is in turn killed by the son of Ken Arok).[39]

The status of Ken Dedes as Ardhanarishvara gives her enormous prestige.[40] A magnificent statue of her as Prajnaparamita, goddess of transcendental wisdom, is kept in the National Museum of Jakarta and a huge copy adorns the entryway of Malang from Surabaya. Prajnaparamita is the mystical mother of all Buddhas.[41] A Buddhist website calls her a *Strī Nareśwarī* (Lady Lord of Humanity), with the power to establish a royal dynasty. She became the matriarchal ancestor from whom several centuries of Singosari and Majapahit rulers descended.[42]

Her holy waters are found in Watugede, one of the natural springs on the plateau at the foot of the elegant Arjuna volcano. On the grounds is a statue of Durga. The springs where legend has it that Ken Arok first spotted Ken Dedes are still a source of spiritual power and eternal beauty and may confer on one the mystical power of Ken Dedes. When we visited it, the *juru kunci* (guardian) showed us the spot where Megawati, Sukarno's daughter, had meditated to gain power before her presidential campaign. She became Indonesia's fifth president.

A retelling of the Ken Dedes story even seems to legitimize Dutch colonial power. Watson Andaya mentions an early nineteenth-century tale in which

> a beautiful princess is taken by the upstart lord of Jacatra [present-day Jakarta] as his wife, but his attempt to consummate the marriage is frustrated because of the flames that appear from her genitals. Exiled, she eventually becomes the wife of a Dutch prince who is ruling in Spain. It is their son, Mur Jangkung (i.e. Jan Pietersz. Coen, founder of Batavia, 1619) who attacks Jacatra in revenge for his mother's humiliation.[43]

Another powerful deity venerated for bolstering feudal power is Kanjang Rara Kidul, or Ratu Kidul, the Javanese goddess of the South Sea. S/he is able to take on many forms: young, old, man, woman. S/he was the protector deity of the kingdom of Mataram and is still revered in the Javanese courts.[44] President Sukarno had his own green room (green, the colour of the sea, was associated with this goddess) in a hotel on the beach at Parangtritis, where he used to meditate.⁴⁵ The gender-switching of this deity is not mentioned in the many popular booklets devoted to Ratu Kidul; at present she is only portrayed in her female form.

Kwan Im or Guan Yin and Avalokiteshvara

Buddhism also has its gender-fluid deity, Kwan Im, the god/dess of compassion, to whom many Buddhist temples are dedicated in Indonesia. Guan Yin, as the deity is called in China, originates in northern India where s/he was revered in its male manifestation as Avalokiteshvara, a name that is also still used in Indonesia. This male bodhisattva was transformed into Guan Yin in China in the fifth century; in Vietnam s/he is called Quan Am, goddess of fertility, and is associated with Mary.⁴⁶ Avalokiteshvara is still widely known in Tibet, Nepal and northern India as the bodhisattva of compassion. In China, Japan and Korea (both North and South) s/he is known in a more feminine form, as Guan Yin, or as the more androgynous Kannon. This is an image found all over East Asia and Southeast Asia, particularly in Burma, Cambodia, Singapore and Indonesia. In Korea and Japan androgynous statues are found. In China the early representations of Guan Yin are masculine. Later s/he is largely portrayed as female but sometimes with a slight moustache, as in Korea. Since the eleventh century the Chinese Guan Yin is generally represented as female. Avalokiteshvara is reincarnated in each Dalai Lama.⁴⁷

I became interested in this deity when I researched the vegetarian, anti-marriage sisterhoods in pre-Second World War China. I learnt that Guan Yin was the protector deity of the anti-marriage sisterhoods in Guangdong in Southern China, often called the 'Golden Orchid Associations'. These sisterhoods mainly consisted of silk workers, who pursued economic independence so that they could afford to live outside of the strictly patriarchal heterosexual marriages of other Chinese women. They vowed never to marry, and if already married off during infancy, not to consummate the marriage (as proof, they had to return after the marriage ceremony with their clothes, into which they had been tightly sewn, still intact).⁴⁸

Life in these sisterhoods offered women not only respite from the oppression of patriarchal, heterosexual marriages, but also the possibility of a religious career or political status, not open to heterosexually married women. The Guan Yin temples were staffed by abbesses and nuns who were called vegetarian sisters, vegetarian thus meaning no meat and no men. When two vegetarian sisters became attached to each other and wanted to celebrate their bond they performed similar ceremonies (such as hairdressing) as those performed by heterosexual couples. These lay and religious sisterhoods, which have existed for over 100 years, were labelled 'feudal' by Mao's victorious Red Army and prohibited. The nuns and the lay sisters fled and dispersed across Asia, from Kuala Lumpur to Singapore, Hong Kong and Taiwan.⁴⁹ There, many of them were swallowed up by heteronormative society.

Although Kwan Im has this history of gender transformation and is one of the most important deities of Asia, s/he is not known as a gender transgressive deity, as her/his gender is seen as fixed in the contexts in which s/he is worshipped. In most versions Avalokiteshvara is the older form, residing in India. He is the bodhisattva who has postponed his own buddhahood in order to relieve the suffering of humanity. There are several sutras referring to Avalokiteshvara, of which the Lotus Sutra is best known (third century CE). In chapter 25 Avalokiteshvara is portrayed as a compassionate bodhisattva who listens attentively to the cries of the suffering. He is described in a total of thirty-three manifestations. But the bodhisattva is not only masculine; seven of his attributes are actually feminine, including the most characteristic manifestation, that of compassion.[50] So, from the outset, Avalokiteshvara is characterized by gender indeterminacy. In one of those forms the bodhisattva is portrayed as child-granting, possibly going back to earlier fertility rituals. This can be seen as the basis of the later manifestations of Guan Yin as Mother, Goddess of Compassion. As Avalokiteshvara, however, the physical portrayal almost always shows a bare chest, and sometimes a moustache. There are also other variations, for example Guan Yin is popularly shown to have a thousand arms, which she needed because she had promised to perform the heavy task of freeing all beings from reincarnation. Or she is portrayed with eleven heads, because her head split when having to think so hard to understand the needs of the suffering beings. In her female form she is the companion of the Amida Buddha; in other versions Avalokiteshvara is the son of Amida. Alternatively, s/he is seen as the earthly manifestation of the self-born eternal Amitaba.[51]

Avalokiteshvara/GuanYin/Kannon, therefore, transcends gender/sex binaries but is again and again pinned down to an established sex/gender pattern. In her most powerful feminine form she is able to protect the anti-marriage sisterhoods, but masculinized as Kannon s/he is used to shore up the claims to power of Japan's mighty patriarchal monks.[52] This merging of Guan Yin/Kannon and Avalokiteshvara (sometimes with Tara as well) in Buddhism is located in the Buddhist canon, where the work of compassion and liberating humanity from ignorance can be taken up by any gender and form of these bodhisattvas. Guan Yin/Avalokiteshvara is thus genderless, or sexually ambiguous, or transgender, and as such associated with compassion, mercy and love. S/he is always portrayed as elusively beautiful. Though these principles are venerated so widely and deeply, this is not translated into compassion with actual, sentient human beings who are transgender, or otherwise transgressing the boundaries of heteronormativity.

Transgender healers

Gender fluidity or gender variance does not only take place in the world of the gods. It has also been reported in relation to priests and healers mediating between the gods and humans. Such practices have been recorded in Asia, from Siberia in the north to Indonesia and further east in the Pacific islands. Various degrees of gender transformation and sexual practice have been described, ranging from temporary cross-dressing for particular rituals to fully fledged same-sex marriages. Sometimes gender transformation only took place in shamanistic seances; at other times it concerned priests or healers who had fully transformed.[53]

In Indonesia several cases are recorded of gender variance, variously called ritual androgyny, sacred hermaphroditism or transgenderism among other terms, for example the cross-dressing traditional healers, priests or shamans, the *tadu arboerakee* among the Toradja Pamona.[54] In an article on these Toradja '*banci* priests' the author (writing in the 1930s) stresses that they are honoured by the whole people.[55] In areas untouched by Christianity they still exist and are called *boerake tambolang*. *Boerake* is the name of a female priest and *tambolang* is the name of a long-legged bird.[56] A female-bodied *boerake* is called *boerake tattioe*, which is the name of a smaller bird.[57] Both types of *boerake* dress and adorn themselves as women so that they are hard to distinguish. Among the Toradja, women have to serve the gods and the spirits (*arwah*), while the men have to work on the land and to fight. But not all women like to be a priest, for there is always the danger of incurring the wrath of the gods if a mistake is made. So only a few women devote themselves to this task and they become specialists, who are honoured and receive a good income, especially when they are successful in healing people. So, the author maintains, men are also attracted to that position, for then they do not have to fight and work the land. But only those chosen by the gods can get that position. They are visited by a devil during religious ceremonies and get into a trance; this has to be repeated. Then a big ritual is held to exorcise that devil, and if that does not succeed, it is clearly the wish of the gods, and a *boerake* then teaches him the trade.

Sometimes these men already have a wife and children who they have to divorce, for it is impossible that a woman is married to a woman. Once she is fully a *boerake* she can marry again with a man. These marriages are celebrated in a big ceremony and nobody thinks that this is improper.[58] Ultimately people forget she was a man originally, for she sings and dances like a woman, joking pleasantly with men and smiling like women do. She serves her husband as a woman would, and when it is her time she is buried as a *boerake* and in the way of a beloved wife.[59]

Dayak transgender healers

Same-sex marriages are also recorded in several Dayak societies in Kalimantan (formerly called Borneo). Schärer uses the term 'hermaphrodite' to refer to the *basir* of the Ngayu Dayak community in Central Kalimantan. These male-bodied *basir* are powerful healers and diviners and dress like women.[60] Kroef states that the Dayak Ngayu community recognized the important sacral lore of the transgender *basir* as intermediaries between the gods and humans. He adds: 'Failure to act homosexually places the *basir* in a more or less inferior position.'[61] According to Perelaer, these *basir* were effeminate priests, some of whom were married to men.[62] Berkusky saw these marriages as a clear indication of homosexual tendencies among the tribes of Borneo.[63] Their marriages were formally recognized. These trans persons were considered ritually very powerful as they represented the fusion of the binary between male and female, the sky and the earth and other binaries such as the seas and the mountains.

The gender transgression of the *basir* is also found in the world of the gods. Perelaer argued that pederasty (a word used by several Dutch colonial observers, referring to sexual activity between a man and a boy) was deeply interwoven with Dayak-origin myths.[64] The Ngayu worship Mahatala-Jata. This deity is referred to as a 'water snake which is also a hornbill' and is manifest in two distinct yet interrelated aspects – male and female, a unity in duality.[65] The male part of this god is Mahatala, who rules the Upper World, and is depicted as a hornbill living above the clouds on a mountain top. The female part is Jata, who rules the Underworld from under the sea in the form of a water snake, and she has crocodile companions. The two aspects of the deity are linked via a jewel-encrusted bridge that is seen in the physical world as a rainbow. Mahatala-Jata is served by both *balian*, female-bodied priests, and *basir*, who combine the characteristics of water snakes and hornbills.[66] Kroef informs us that the transvestism of the *basir* and their homosexual practices are symbolic of the total Ngayu godhead.[67] This is indeed a more symbolic form of androgyny for the two parts are rarely represented in one manifestation, like the statues of Ardhanarishvara or the fusion of Shiva and Durga. Gender and sexual pluralism are not only seen as benevolent in Dayak society. *Hantuen* are feared supernatural beings, bisexual soulless creatures of an amoral disposition and are prone to promiscuous sexuality.[68]

The armchair anthropologist Karsch-Haack collected an extensive compilation of articles on gender diversity and same-sex practices among the Dayak.[69] Hupe noted that pederasty among the Dayak was common; these people 'without any shame' are respected, so that they are 'real slaves of Satan'.[70] According to this explorer, certain *basir* congregated with the *biliang*, female-bodied priestesses, dressed like them and formed a choir. He was surprised that these 'kings of hell' were honoured as holy people. Their decisions were recognized as the words of God. They also served as healers. Hupe recorded that these healers were considered to have the power to cause illness or death among their enemies. They also conducted the ceremonies to rid the houses of whatever that brings *sial* (disaster).

In 1853 Schwaner travelled along the river Barito and noted that *basir* 'who enjoy the favours of the gods in the same way as the *bilian* (priestesses)'. They were better paid than the *bilian* and 'feel no shame for their horrible occupation'. There were more of them than there were priestesses. He met them with the Ngadju of Pulopetak, and along the upper and middle parts of the mighty Kapuas River. Along the Barito river, the *basir* knew how to heal by way of singing, and they were able to communicate the wishes of people to the Gods.[71] According to Schwaner, *basir* means infertile. In Pulopetak, Schwaner documented *basir* who were dressed as women and appeared in religious festivals. He denounced these practices as 'sodomitic abhorrent acts'.[72]

Lieutenant Perelaer was repulsed by these practices, complaining that the *basir* all over the land of the Dayak engaged by way of profession in the 'abhorrent acts which have made the fire of heaven descend on Sodom'.[73] In mid Kahajan there were *basir* who were lawfully married and shared the beds of their husbands as wives. And this 'abhorrent act is in no way unnatural for the Dayak', according to Perelaer, who reported that same-sex practices were encountered in all social layers of the population and that both men and women engaged in them. This custom was so widespread that one could commonly assume that there were only few men who had not committed them. Together with headhunting, this 'abhorrent immorality' could be seen as one of the major causes of the low population density of Borneo, the lieutenant concluded.[74]

Basir and *bilian* were so honoured that an insult against them was fined double the amount of an insult against a commoner. Yet, Perelaer noted, parents did not like to see their children become *basir* or *bilian*. This added to misunderstandings between parents and their children who wished to become such priests or priestesses. Usually, beautiful girls and slender boys from ten to twelve years old were selected to become *basir* and *bilian*. As part of their training they first had to learn to sing and beat the drums. Once they had mastered those arts they accompanied the *bilian* to a party. Both the girls and the boys were allowed to engage in 'every immorality', which Perelaer did not further specify.[75]

When a child had already engaged in this 'horrible immorality',[76] however, their parents decided these children must become *bilian* or *basir*. When a child had reached the age of sixteen the parents could no longer oppose the choice of their children according to the customs of the Dayak.[77] *Basir* and *bilian* were dressed alike, but *basir* did not wear a headdress. They did, however, wear their hair parted in the middle, as women did.[78]

According to Perelaer, tribadism was common among Dayak women. In this pursuit they might use a dildo made of wood and covered by wax. This contraption was used both for onany and for mutual masturbation. Perelaer's observations are corroborated by contemporary travellers, Kleiweg de Zwaan and Hardeland.[79]

The German linguist Hardeland composed a Dayak-German dictionary. According to him *basir* in Kahaian refers to men (*basir hatua*) and women (*basir bawi, balian*) who make their living from 'sorcery and fornication'. The *basir* are dressed as women; they perform religious ceremonies and are engaged in sodomitic abominations (*sodomitischer Greueln*). Many of them are formally married to another man. Those who only work as sorcerers and not as sodomites are called *basir totok*. The *basir* are more highly respected than the *balian* and their fees are higher, as their witchcraft is considered to be more powerful. When the Dayak go headhunting they like to take a *basir* with them.[80]

Cross-dressing *manang bali* lived in the Iban Dayak in the formerly British part of Borneo. They were described as double-gendered healers.[81] The Iban Dayak were a seafaring, warring and headhunting tribe, and were feared pirates. They now live mostly in Brunei and Sarawak; some inhabit Indonesian Western Kalimantan. The transgender shamans (*manang bali*, which means literally a shaman transformed from a male into a female) form the third and highest level of shamanism after accomplishing the second level of *manang mansau* (cooked shaman) and the first level of *manang mataq* (uncooked shaman). They are considered to wield great powers over the spirits that cause illness. The initiation ceremony for becoming a *manang bali* is called *manang bangun manang enjun*, literally translated as the 'awakened shaman, shaken shaman'.[82] After this ceremony, a *manang bali* dressed and acted like a woman and had relationships with men.

Boys who were destined to become *manang bali* might dream of becoming a woman and of being summoned by the spirit ruler of the *manang*, Menjaya Raja Menang, or the goddess Ini Inee or Ini Andan, who is regarded the natural-born healer and the deity of justice.[83] Menjaya Raja Manang began existence as a male god, until the wife of his brother Sengalang Burong became extremely sick. This prompted Menjaya to become the world's first healer, allowing him to cure his sister-in-law, but this treatment also resulted in Menjaya changing into a woman or androgynous being. Menjaya was consecrated as the first *manang bali* by his own sister, Ini Inee or Ini Andan.[84]

The *manang bali* of the sea Dayak were dressed as women and were treated as such. They took the name and clothes of a woman and married a man to protect them and fight for them. Their husbands, however, might also marry a female-bodied wife. As with the *basir*, the *manang bali* were regarded with disdain by their ethnographers. Sutlive, for instance, describes the *manang bali* as a 'socially sanctioned status for the homosexual male who cannot function as a man'.[85]

The *manang* used certain secret words when they practised their healing, which they passed on to other *manang* but which other people did not understand. This language possibly dates back to that of older tribes via oral transmission.[86] The anthropologist and museum curator Henry Ling Roth noted in 1896 that one became a *manang* after the order to become a *manang* had appeared three times in a dream. If such supernatural orders were ignored death might follow.

Before the prospective *manang* was allowed to dress in women's clothes he was first made 'sexually unfit'. Then he organized a party and invited the community, to turn away any evil consequences deriving from members of the tribe on account of this 'violation of nature'.[87] He provided them with *tuak*[88] and sacrificed two pigs because of this 'violation'.[89] If he failed to perform any of these tasks or rituals, he might be blamed for any mishaps experienced by the community, such as a failed harvest, and be heavily fined. But when the ceremony was completed, she would be treated as a woman. The more she succeeded in imitating womanly gestures, the higher she was respected.[90] When she succeeded to seduce a young man, her merriment was highest. She gave her lover many gifts. When the *manang* was successful and had amassed wealth, she might take a husband to share her wealth. According to Henry Ling Roth, only because of her wealth would a man be enticed to marry a *manang bali*, and the husband subsequently hoped then that his wife would soon die. For he was the object of ridicule of both men and women in the community. This alleged ridicule is in contradiction with the report of another observer, Hugh Brooke Low, who maintained that a *manang bali* had great influence. She might even become a village head. The respect villagers bestowed on her was not only related to the cures that she administered but also to her role as a peacemaker.[91]

The decline of the *bissu*

The *bissu* are the best documented of Indonesia's transgender healers and priests. The five-gender system of the Bugis, in which the *bissu* occupy one position, is frequently cited as the best example of Indonesia's gender pluralism. Here I will give a short introduction to their history and present-day lives. There are few *bissu* left in the area and their status and income have been much reduced. As the factors that led to this decline have been and are at work in other contexts in the archipelago as well, it is interesting to analyse their waning influence and presence in more detail.

Originally, they were priests in the pre-Islamic religion of the Bugis, an ethnic group in South Sulawesi. They were also counsellors of the kings and court officials and guardians of the *arajang*, the holy ritual objects. They have their own language, the *Bahasa torilangi* or god language, to communicate with the gods, the spirits of the ancestors and with other *bissu*. They were responsible for fertility and matters of war and peace. The Bugis ancient text *I La Galigo* confirms their importance. They combine the strength of male and female, of human beings and the gods and are variously described as hermaphrodites, intersex persons, bisexuals, pederasts, androgynous beings and persons with ambiguous genitalia.[92]

Bissu occupy one gender in the five-gender system of the Bugis. Besides the two cisgender categories, women and men, there are also two recognized trans categories, the female-bodied *calalai* and the male-bodied *calabai*, often called *kawe* in Makassarese society.[93] *Calabai* are male-bodied persons who dress like women, perform women's roles and often have male partners. They are still visible in society and perform various functions in marriage ceremonies. They are at present often called *waria*, as MTF transgender persons elsewhere in Indonesia. *Calalai* are much less visible. They are female-bodied persons who may marry their women partners and fulfil male roles. At present they are reported to no longer perform in ceremonies.

Although some *calabai* and *calalai* become *bissu*, this latter category must be regarded on its own. A *bissu* had an important ritual function; they were seen to be bisexual or intersex, as the handling of the *arajang* required communion with the other sex, and the sex of the ritual object was generally not known. The *bissu* is thus regarded as the 'hermaphroditic partner of the ornament'.[94] Formerly one became a *bissu* through a supernatural calling; if at an early age a child gave indications that it had affinity with the world of the *roh* (spirits), it would be sent to the palace to undergo training and strenuous tests to be finally inaugurated as a *bissu*.[95] Their dress is a combination of female and male attributes, for instance, both weapons and flowers in their hair. In their ceremonies they can be possessed by *arwah* (spirits) and are then impenetrable. When they perform *ma'giri*, stabbing themselves with a *keris* on their throats, the *keris* will not pierce their flesh.[96] The chief *bissu* in a particular place was called *poewa-matowa* (old gentleman), their disciples were called *anagoeroe*. Male-bodied *bissu* were called *bisoe-tanre* (tall) and female-bodied ones *bissoe-pontjo* (short).[97]

The *bissu* fulfilled various ritual roles, for instance, in ceremonies related to marriage and childbirth, often entering into a trance.[98] In the spirit world, a *bissu* had two partners, a woman and a man. Kroef used the terms androgyny, bisexuality and hermaphroditism indiscriminately without referring to genitalia. According to Karsch-Haack, some *calabai* were hermaphrodites and were from an early age onwards received favourably at the courts. According to him they were all pederasts and sorcerers. They were held in high esteem for they had access to all corners of the court, even to the bedrooms of the princesses, as they were supposed to be impotent.[99] Van de Wal described that they are especially attracted to beautiful youths whom they attempt to caress in ways similar to a lover embracing his beloved.[100]

Matthes wondered whether the *bissu* were as 'disgusting' as the *basir*? He doubted that they were as engaged in the 'unnatural sin' ('the name of which one rather not mentions') as often as the *basir*. The female-bodied *bissu*, he remarked, can rarely be seen as belonging to the 'fairer sex'.[101] He described an initiation ceremony which might last between seven and nine days. All this time the candidate *bissu* lies on a bed in a comatose condition while their spirit is taught in heaven. The other *bissu* keep dancing to invite the gods to descend from heaven into the new *bissu*. To also make contact with the netherworld the *bissu* is clothed in a mat which is lowered into water for three days driving on the sea. Matthes added ironically that this way they were 'in danger of being transported to the netherworld in real by a crocodile'.[102] The *bissu* Haji Yamin explained:

> In order to become a *bissu* you have to be born like that … You see, *calabai* have a penis, their penis lives (*hidup kontolnya*, i.e. they can get an erection) … I do not have a penis because you cannot be a true bissu if you have a penis … Look! [Haji Yamin lifts up her sarong and, with legs spread, reveals that s/he has no visible penis].

Graham quotes another *bissu*, Mariani, who models their sexual ambiguity on the Ardhanary model. The right side of their face sprouts some facial hair, and in ritual clothing they stick some flowers into the left side of their hair and carry a *keris* on the right side.[103] Presently there are three levels of *calabai*. The word comes from *sala bai* (not woman). The *calabai tungkena lino* are the highest rank and can become *bissu*; they are also called *sala dewii* (not gods*)*. The *paccalabai* can have relations with both men and women; they are called AC-DC, or *piso sile* (a knife with two sharp sides).[104] The *calabai kedo-kedonami* only follow the styles of *calabai*, and they are actually ordinary men.[105] As Fitri Pabente, a prominent *bissu* from Watampone, recounts, the life of a present-day *bissu* is a compromise between the pre-Islamic tradition and Islam. As a young child she felt she was a *waria*. Her parents accepted that and gave her a good Islamic education. While attending Islamic rites she always wears masculine clothes and only applies make-up as a woman (*dandan*) for *waria* festivities. She became the chair of the Waria Communication Forum of East Indonesia and the chair of the *bissu* of South Sulawesi.[106]

The ambiguous gender and sexual status of the *bissu* was highly appreciated. They had a good income, as large plots of land for rice fields were allocated to them, which were worked by the villagers in *gotong royong* (mutual help). From that income they could build and maintain their *rumah pusaka* (house of ritual objects) in which they stored their attributes and lived. This income has been taken away from them. They have to work on their own fields to survive. The *rumah pusaka* are no longer maintained.

The Bugis belief system is called *riolong*. In the beginning there were two worlds. The Upper World is called *parahyangan*, heaven, where the gods such as Patotoe and its child Batara Guru dwelled. The world below the ground was called *paratihi*, which had its own gods. *Bissu* communicated with the gods of these two worlds. The *bissu* were counsellors to the kings in spiritual matters. The king needed the *bissu* to perform the correct rituals, otherwise he might not receive the *wibawa*, heavenly blessing.

Puang Temmi, a *calalai* from Pangkep who was inaugurated as a *bissu*, recounts that she had been able to communicate with the spirit world since she had been a child. When she learnt to recite the Qur'an, she was visited by a being from the invisible world, Petta Malampee Mesana. Puang Temmi maintains that the word *bissu* comes from *bersih*, clean – meaning not having menstruation. *Bissu* are a gift of God (*anugerah dari Tuhan*): 'You have to remember that the fact that the sex of the *bissu* is not sure, corresponds with the situation of the Creator of whom we also don't know the sex.'[107] According to Pelras, transgender female-bodied persons were less likely to become *bissu*, but some of them became rulers of small kingdoms in the area.[108]

The *I La Galigo* is the origin myth of the Bugis people. It speaks of originally 'androgynous' deities that produce various sacred beings, including *bissu*. In a later form of creation the primordial unity is split, and female and male beings are created. These became the ancestors of the Bugis dynasties.[109] Thus Bugis cosmology rests upon a primordial oneness, of which the *bissu* are a manifestation. The *I La Galigo* originates in an oral tradition and was only written down over the last centuries. It was mostly transmitted by singing and was hardly known outside of the Bugis community. Only in 1995 was part of it translated into Indonesian from old Buginese. In 2017 a larger part was published in Indonesian.[110] The Indonesian text contains numerous references to *bissu*.[111]

The high status of *bissu* has been much diminished, due to a mix of religious, colonial and postcolonial processes. The first encounter of Western travellers with *bissu* thoroughly confused these Portuguese merchants, in whose country sodomy was strictly prohibited. They could not understand how these both male-bodied and female-bodied persons had same-sex partners. The *calabai* committed sodomy and pederasty, they reported, and yet were held in high esteem. In Portugal, at the time homosexuals were burned. It was also described that some *calalai* lived as same-sex couples. They performed sex with the help of dildoes made from animal guts filled with wax.[112] At around the same time the Bugis were Islamized. Bone was the last Bugis kingdom to convert to Islam, in 1611.

The colonial South Sulawesi expeditions of 1905 against the once mighty kingdoms of Bone and Gowa, under the notorious general Van Heutsz, were undertaken with the objective to make these realms sign and abide by the standard agreement whereby a native Indonesian ruler agreed to accept Dutch sovereignty and the right to levy taxes.[113] The conquerors looted the *arajang*, including a magic sword named Sundanga. The booty ended up in museums in the Netherlands and Jakarta.[114] With most of the ritual objects gone, the employment of the *bissu* was also much reduced. Andaya reported that when the Bone kingdom was attacked, their adversaries included 'a hundred female-bodied bissu who went out to meet the Bone army. Chanting, swinging their weaving beaters, their supernatural power was supposed to make them invulnerable.'[115]

Fundamentalist Islam also eroded the power of the *bissu*. From the nineteenth century onwards a puritanical, Wahabist form of Islam had gained dominance in the region, replacing the more moderate version which had incorporated elements of the old Bugis belief system. Islamic officials, the *kadhi*, began to play more important roles at the courts.[116]

When the Indonesian Republic was proclaimed in 1945, the dozen or so royal courts in South Sulawesi were abolished. Until that time the royal families, though they had already lost real power in the colonial era, still patronized the *bissu* and each kingdom minimally had a head and deputy *bissu*, while major ceremonies required the participation of at least forty priests. After independence the *bissu* lost their entitlements (for instance, the five hectares of land from which they could live), while Islam became more dominant and the importance of the *adat* institutions decreased. The new state officials did not pay for the maintenance of the *arajang*. The *bissu* became dependent on the favours of local officials, who might influence the rituals and even used the *bissu* for their election campaigns and for tourism.[117]

The Darul Islam movement (DI/TII)[118] led by the notorious Kahar Muzakkar actively persecuted the *bissu*. They were labelled *musyrik* (polytheist, pagan).[119] The *bissu* were forced to cut their hair, if they were male-born, and do men's manual labour on the fields. Many *bissu* were murdered, *arajang* were destroyed or stolen by Muzakkar's gangs, named Gerombolan Pengacau Keamanan (GPK, Groups of Agitators for Security) in what they called Operasi Taubat (Repentance Operation).[120] In Bone an Islamic mob decapitated the *bissu* chief and paraded their head around town, swinging it by their long hair, so that no one would ever dare to be one again.[121]

Under the dominance of majoritarian Islam, the *bissu* were forced to embrace Islam as their religion, and they lost their powers as spiritual mediators between the realm of the gods and human beings. As Puang Temmi remembers, *bissu* had to run to save their lives. They could only hold their rituals in secret. Many *bissu* were killed. She was a young girl at the time and was chased by members of the gang of Kahar Muzakkar who wanted to force her to marry one of them. Groups of those hardliner figures, accompanied by police, often came to break up *bissu* rituals. 'Our rituals are not in contradiction to Islam,' she insisted. 'We also ask the Almighty God for the welfare of the community, but with our own rituals, while we also perform the Islamic prayers, fast and pay *zakat*.'[122] Orthodox Muslims and *bissu* differ in relation to *kodrat*. The Islamic position is that they violate the *kodrat* (i.e. they have to follow the sex assigned at birth) and therefore commit a sin, while *bissu* insist they follow their *kodrat* which is to become a *calalai, calabai or bissu*.[123]

In 1966, after the Suharto coup, a new wave of persecution followed; this time *calalai, calabai* and *bissu* were seen as communists, although they never had anything to do with the PKI. People deemed to be of 'deviant' sexuality were hunted down and killed. Many *bissu* again went into hiding, some living in caves in the jungle. One *bissu* from a village near Sigeri learned to dress so convincingly as a woman that to this day no one in the village knows she was born male.[124]

When in 1998 the dictatorial regime was replaced by a more democratic government, the *bissu* tradition experienced a modest revival. Regional autonomy was proclaimed to stem the centrifugal forces in the huge archipelago, and Bugis traditional culture became an asset for regional politicians, with the *bissu* symbolizing Bugis authenticity.[125] But most of them continued to live in hardship. Some *calabai* resorted to performing sex work in the markets, others managed to open hairdressing salons or handled bridal decorations, as many *waria* do throughout Indonesia. The responsibilities of the *bissu* are still great, but their income is much reduced. An official *bissu* is expected to live in the *rumah arajang* with no monthly stipend.

In the late 1990s, Lathief started a programme to bring *bissu* who had been hiding for decades out into the open again. Through his organization Latar Nusa, he began arranging meetings between *bissu* and the community in Sigeri and oversaw the construction of a *rumah arajang*. With the revitalization programme, the stringent inauguration rules were relaxed. In 2002 the first *bissu* in decades was inaugurated and since then, *bissu* rituals have again become a feature of public life. Lathief's programme ended in 2003, and the last chief *bissu* of Sigeri died in 2011.[126] In 2003 it was reported that in Bone there were only two *bissu* left. In Sigeri, where there were once forty official *bissu*, including a few female-bodied ones, at the time of writing this book there are only four. In neighbouring Gowa, there are none.[127] With so few left, the quality of their teachings has also declined. The surviving *bissu* pray in the mosques in traditional Muslim garb on Fridays (if born male).[128] During the week too they may dress in Arab garb, with white turbans. At present the major ceremonies to ensure a good harvest (which lasted for days) are no longer held. But when the harvest failed the *bissu* role was reinstituted to a limited extent.

The homophobic campaign that started in late 2015 is the most recent blow. This campaign will be discussed later. From sacral beings they are now seen as abjected, marginalized persons and as *banci biasa* (ordinary MTF transgender people). At most they are touted as tourist objects, their rituals becoming touristic festivals and they may be used by political leaders to spice up their political campaigns. In 2022 cisgendered women were asked to perform at such a ceremony.

The life of Puang Matoa Saidi illustrates some of the problems experienced by present-day *bissu*. S/he was one of the most revered *bissu*, following a calling at a very young age. Deeply concerned to revitalize the *bissu* tradition, s/he learnt the *bissu* language and the rituals. S/he became Puang Matoa, leader of the *bissu* in November 2001 and died in 2011. According to Hakim their reputation had declined by that time, following rumours of rape, neglect of ritual duties and misappropriation of funds. Saidi appeared in the documentary *The last Bissu* by Rhoda Grauer. S/he also participated as the main narrator in the world tour of the *I La Galigo* performance, directed by Robert Wilson. This performance was later considered by some to have violated the purity of the *I La Galigo*.[129]

Whether the *bissu* tradition will survive is a matter of debate. Ariyanto believes that the present generation is the last. The charismatic *bissu* who know the tradition are dying one by one.[130] They have to be wary of the Kelompok Persiapan Penegakan Syariat Islam (KPPI, Group Preparing the Upholding of Syaria (sharia)) which wants to install sharia law in the region, as has happened in Aceh. They face other obstacles as well. In January 2017 the South Sulawesi police banned a Bugis sports and cultural event involving *waria* and *bissu* that was to be held in Soppeng. About 600 *waria* and *bissu* had already gathered, complete with make-up and costumes. But following a protest from the Islam Congregation Forum the police decided to inform the participants that their request for a permit had been rejected. Yet the permit had already been granted by the Soppeng council. A new requirement had suddenly popped up – a recommendation from the Religious Affairs Ministry.[131]

The relative influence of three concerned parties will probably determine to a large extent whether the *bissu* tradition will remain, and in what form: Islam, the *adat* community and the (regional) authorities. The Muhammadyah, the Muslim mass organization which has had historically a large following in South Sulawesi, and which used to prohibit *bissu* activities, has become more tolerant, reports Hakim. The *adat* communities have been strengthened by the proclamation of regional autonomy, particularly in the areas of Pangkep, Bone, Soppeng and Luwu.[132] But in Gowa and Maros the *bissu* tradition has been destroyed, and *bissu* have been replaced by Muslim religious leaders.[133] In an online talk show on 17 June 2020, two *bissu*, Angel and Eka, deplored the fact that many *bissu* choose to remain *calabai* as they have to earn a living and there is hardly any work for *bissu*. Very few regional governments involve *bissu* in their ceremonies.[134] The government does not protect *bissu* as an integral part of Indonesian culture, and very few people still believe in the special role of *bissu* as healers and ritual specialists. The regional authorities in Makassar, the capital of the province, have adopted the same homophobic language heard all over Indonesia these days when they suddenly declared they wanted to discuss the adoption of an anti-LGBT regulation.[135]

Conclusion

The declining influence of the gender diverse deities and trans ritual specialists such as *bissu*, *basir*, *manang bali* and *boerake* is related to three major factors. First, the colonial regime, which brought a monotheistic religion, Christianity, and imposed a conservative, homophobic bourgeois morality. Then the introduction of Islam and its later Wahabist reform movements which weakened the position of the traditional shamans and replaced the Hindu gods. Third, postcolonial processes which strengthened majoritarian Islam and a binary, patriarchal gender system. In the early modern period, as Watson Andaya lucidly explains, religious and state authorities 'working in tandem, ... developed and promoted conceptions of male-female relationships that still resonate today. In particular the documentation of legal precedents codified ideals that reduced the flexibility of customary law and confirmed men's prerogatives in both the household and the community at large.'[136]

Colonialism with its strongly patriarchal gender division and monotheistic religions such as Christianity and Islam weakened the sacred origins of gender, resting upon a unity that needed to be periodically reconfirmed. Gender came to be associated with individual beings and lost its connection to the sacred world. Sexual bimorphism became fixed and bounded, and gender relations were divided in a binary and hierarchical way. These binary bodies did not allow any space for gender transgression as earlier cosmologies had. These processes have progressed unevenly and in some cases partially.

The decline of 'sacred gender' can also be noted from the discourse around Ken Dedes, the famous queen of Singosari in East Java.[137] In popular textbooks and local lore her deified and transgender status has become lost. What remains is a bowdlerized, sexualized version of a femme fatale, bereft of her sacred powers. She is no longer seen as the sacral, legitimizing power of kingship but as the victim of a contest between two violent men. As Peletz notes: 'Transgenderism has lost much of the religious and specifically sacred significance it once had and with a few notable exceptions (e.g., the Bugis) its cultural centrality in royal courts and the reproduction of local polities has been eroded and it has thus been delinked from religious orthodoxy and state power alike.'[138]

In South Sulawesi the few remaining *bissu* valiantly try to keep their tradition upright. In Indonesia, contrary to what religious and political leaders proclaim, trans practices and same-sex marriages were recorded in various locations in the archipelago. Postcolonial amnesia, waves of persecution and the increasing influence of majoritarian fundamentalist Islam have erased much of these traditions.

3

Liminal spaces: Court and village culture

Introduction

Until the Japanese invasion in 1942 the courts were the centres of cultural and spiritual life. Outside the courts cultural life also thrived, for instance, in the form of dance performances and *wayang* (shadow puppet) shows in Java and Bali. In this chapter I discuss some examples of gender diversity, cross-dressing and same-sex practices in both court and village life. Accepted forms of transvestism and gender pluralism did not mean a widespread tolerance of other forms of gender or sexual diversity, and might go hand in hand with the disapproval of same-sex practices outside of the accepted context. There is no record, however, that same-sex practices were ever criminalized.[1] Among the courtly texts, the twelve-volume *Serat Centhini* from Java, written in the nineteenth century (but based on earlier versions and describing events in the 1630s), depicts homosexual and transgender practices in detail.

Under colonial rule, transgender or same-sex practices that were part of traditional cultural or religious procedures were discouraged and considered immoral, but these practices were not persecuted by the Dutch colonial powerholders. Pederasty was considered most abject.[2] Under the Dutch civil and penal codes which came into force in the colony, the only type of same-sex act that was criminalized was sex between an adult and a minor. Colonial moral outrage about cases of pederasty became evident in 1938 and 1939, when raids targeting 'pederasts' took place across Indonesia and over two hundred men were arrested.[3] This Dutch-era law remained in force in Indonesia until December 2022, when a new penal code was adopted in which all forms of non-marital sexual relations were criminalized.

Many of the above-mentioned traditions and practices are now in decline, due to the postcolonial amnesia about such practices and the growing influence of fundamentalist Islam. Various popular art forms featuring transgender practices, such as the *reog* and *lengger* dances and the *ludruk* theatrical performances,[4] have waned because the performers were persecuted by anti-communist forces after 1965 on the basis of their alleged communist leanings.[5] Artists and other members of the People's Cultural Institute (Lembaga Kebudayaan Rakyat, Lekra) were singled out for persecution during the 1965–6 massacres because of the organization's alleged pro-communist, anti-Islamic orientation. Transgender practices became suspect, their adherents murdered or imprisoned. The space for gender pluralism became constricted, people were encouraged to give up the older rituals and beliefs and to conform to a stricter form of Islam, based on a binary sex/gender model.

Lekra was the leading cultural institution on the left during the Sukarno period. It promoted the so-called people's art, in which social and political critique was incorporated. After the New Order collapsed, *ludruk* shows became popular again on TV.[6] Since the ban on non-gender conforming people on TV, discussed in Chapter 7, *ludruk*, with its transvestite actors playing women's roles, once again suffered a serious setback.

A problem in the analysis of gender diversity is the paucity of documentary sources in colonial-era literature and particularly the invisibility of the gender diverse practices of people assigned female at birth.[7] Colonial accounts usually focus on persons assigned male at birth. An exception is Van Baal who noted that in the Marind-anim culture 'travesty is a theme more associated with females than with males', particularly evident in the spectacular dances that are ritually performed.[8]

Same-sex and trans practices in Bali

The island of Bali provides an example of the difficulties in finding and assessing sources on women's same-sex practices. The Balinese poet, dancer, film-maker and writer Cok Sawitri states that Bali has 'a long history of relative acceptance of intimate relationships between women'. One Balinese folk tale referring to lesbians is the story of the sole daughter of a king who decided not to marry. She inherited a whole palace along with its riches, and openly declared that men were 'forbidden to enter'.[9] Sawitri, hailing from an upper caste family herself, observes that 'a number of Brahman households also harbour histories of platonic love between Brahman women and their maidservants'.[10] It is difficult to find references to this history in the Hindu island. In the *Kamasutra*, Vatsyayana devotes a whole chapter to the art of same-sex love. But the *Manusmriti*, the first (second century BCE) treatise on law contains stiff penalties for sodomy and women's same-sex activities.[11]

The Dutch medical doctor Jacobs, who abhorred the 'vice' of homosexuality, mentions that in Bali a 'hermaphrodite' is called *banchi*, and that pederasty mainly occurs in the form of 'podication'.[12] He described boys aged ten to twelve years performing the *gandrung* dance, dressed up beautifully as dance girls. They were accompanied by a *gamelan* orchestra (*semar pegoelingan*[13]). Men would offer them *kepeng* (Chinese coins) to be allowed to dance with them on stage, where they caressed and kissed the boys. The man who offered most could have sex with them. Jacobs also reported that in Bali both men and women were known to have sexual relationships with members of the same sex. Tribadism is common in Bali and Lombok, he noted, though it was practised in a more covert way than pederasty. The Balinese use the term *metjengtjeng djoeoek*, literally 'clashing the pelvis', and this, he assumed, involves 'real lesbian love'. But, he added that the lovers also perform 'digital and lingual variations'. Girls are also prone to masturbate, with the help of a cucumber, a banana, or an apparatus for solace produced out of wax, called *koempentji*, replacement, or *tjelak-tjelakan malem*, a waxen penis. 'Many lonely hours are thus pleasantly spent,' he concluded.[14]

Citing Jacobs, Andaya mentions the common appearance of wax dildos, as well as yam and bananas performing similar functions among the women in the royal courts of Bali.[15] The eminent linguist Van der Tuuk, who in 1861 produced a dictionary of Kawi, Balinese and Dutch, also noted that Balinese women engage in lesbian love.[16] Furthermore, he described that girls dressed as men are engaged in temple service.

As Creese concludes in her detailed study on precolonial Balinese law codes, non-heterosexual relationships were not legally regulated in colonial Bali. The legal texts were derived from Sanskrit legal traditions, particularly the Laws of Manu. The one paragraph dealing with women's same-sex relations that Creese found is directly based on the *Manusmriti*. She notes that the fines and corporal punishments spelled out seemed more related to sexual assault than to a consensual sexual relationship. Anyway, Creese cautions, the existence of such texts does not mean that they are related to the legal or social practices of those times.[17]

Court life in Java

In the women's quarters (*keputren*) of the royal courts of Java, the wives, concubines and other female family members of the male rulers lived with their maidservants. Out of bounds to most male colonial observers, the translator Winter, who lived at the court of Pakubuwono V in Surakarta, provides a rare account of women's same-sex erotic practices.[18] In his report on the customs in the royal court of Surakarta in 1824, he described King Pakubuwono V as a shrewd man. However, Winter added, he was also greedy, severe, proud and jealous. As an example of the extreme jealousy of the man, Winter told the following story. The king was so dismayed that his concubines made love with each other, enjoying the pleasures provided by wax dildos, that he ordered them to sleep in a row in front of his open door, at a distance of six feet from each other. He was particularly apprehensive that because of this habit, his wives might no longer appreciate the love of men.[19] His son, King Pakubuwono VI, thought this was such a good idea that he copied the practice.[20]

Gayatri, who hails from an upper-class aristocratic family was introduced to the ways of the women in the *keputren* of the royal palace of Yogyakarta by her grandmother, who had lived there. No men were allowed to enter the *keputren*, not even the king himself. Intimate relations among the many women in these *keputren* were not uncommon, the grandmother reported. These 'female friendships' were not frowned upon, they were seen as common affectionate companionships. Bathing, dressing and sleeping together were not associated with sexual activities. Yet these emotional attachments might provide deep and intimate satisfaction to those who are engaged in them.[21] The priest and author Mangunwijaya depicts such a relationship in his brilliant novel *Roro Mendut*.[22]

A well-known example of gender inversion is found at the royal courts of Surakarta and Yogyakarta. Lady soldiers, 'Javanese Amazons' as Carey and Houben called them, were dressed in full male attire.[23] These female warriors, the *prajurit estri*, were known for their prowess in fighting and were also skilled in dancing, singing and music.[24] One of the most feared cavalry commanders of the Javanese prince Diponogoro, who led the Java War (1825–30), was Raden Ayu Yudakusuma who had shaved off her hair like many male commanders.[25] I found no records of intimate relations among these soldiers.

Gender inversion at the central Javanese courts, as recorded for the eighteenth and nineteenth centuries, involved both men and women. All roles in the *Langendriyan* dance drama of the late nineteenth-century Mangkunegaran court in Surakarta were played by women.[26] In the eighteenth century, young men would dance the sacred *bedhoyo* dances in female attire.[27] A century later only girls danced the *bedhoyo* dance in Surakarta, while in Yogyakarta boy-*bedhoyo* performed until 1914. Carey and Houben note that this form of gender inversion was reflected in the 'homosexual culture of the Yogyakarta court … where the courtiers seem to have preferred opium and boys'.[28] In 1893 Wilken reported that Javanese *priyayi* men kept beautiful young *bedhoyo* dancers as concubines.[29]

An example of royal transvestism can be found in the *Nâgarakertâgama*, an epic written during the heyday of the East Javanese empire of Majapahit (1293–1478). The mighty king Hayam Wuruk (reigning 1350–89) enjoyed wearing women's clothes while dancing in front of his ministers; he then assumed a female dancer's name, Pager Antimun.[30]

The most well-known courtly text referring to same-sex and transgender practices is the twelve-volume *Serat Centhini*, composed between 1814 and 1823 during the realm of the Surakarta Sunan Pakubuwono V.[31] Though written on the eve of the Java War, it is situated in seventeenth-century Java.[32] It is an encyclopaedic travelogue in verse (*tembang*), in which the protagonists travel all across Java, visiting learned men and women in their dwellings. The *Serat Centhini* combines an inventory of the knowledge available in Java at the time with mystical visions and visits to ancient ruins and other landmarks. The scholarly pursuits of the travellers are offset by many scenes of popular culture, involving dance, song, music and puppetry.

The text is steeped in Hindu notions of the major objectives of life, which are acquiring *artha* (wealth), enjoying sex (*kama*), obeying the demands of duty, religion, law and good deeds (*dharma*) and achieving union with God (*moksa*).[33] Because in this view *kama* is an important aspect of life, the *Serat Centhini* presents many diverse and graphic depictions of sexuality. Numerous are the descriptions of erotic dance forms, such as the *ronggeng* and the *tayuban*.[34] The dancers are variously praised and described as prostitutes. The transgender dance of *lengger lanang* is mentioned as are dances in which the strongmen, *warok*, and their young male-bodied feminine lovers, *jathil*, are paired.[35]

The *warok* are portrayed as rowdy characters who regularly get into fights.[36] They sometimes use their *jathil* as *ronggeng*, to earn money.[37] But *ronggeng* are not stigmatized, as they were by the colonial administrators, for even the two main male characters, Mas Cabolang and Nurwitri, dress up as *ronggeng* and dance a women's dance, the *gambyong*.[38] More complicated sex scenes include group sex[39] and a passage in which two women, one widow and the other the wife of a *jathil*, seduce two male *ronggeng* to have sex. In another scene, the *warok* asks Mas Cabolang and Nurwitri to have sex with him and play with his *jathil*, alternating active and passive roles. The two heroes think this is 'better than sexual play with women'.[40] So the sex between *jathil* and *warok* is portrayed as satisfying, more so than heterosexual sex. The *jathil* are not seen as passive victims of *warok* aggression; instead, quite a few of them left their wives in order to become *jathil*.

Powerful men can be sexually punished for their conceit. Ki Adipati, the arrogant regent of Wirosoko, falls in love with Nurwitri and makes love with him for two days and nights. Then Ki Adipati sends for Mas Cabolang as well who has so far played the female role for the *warok*. Mas Cabolang reverses roles and 'entered the regent from the rear', as the regent expressed his wish to experience the pleasures of a *jathil*. As Mas Cabolang has the erotic power of adjusting the size of his penis he enters with such force that Ki Adipati is terribly hurt and is humiliated.[41]

The book is full of wise advice on how to increase sexual pleasure; the clitoris is singled out for its important role in love making.[42] Women are portrayed as actively desiring sex, though they do not always get their way. A handsome youth like Mas Cabolang is desired by both men and women. A girl dreaming about the dashing Mas Cabolang despairs that she will not have success, for the boys are too much in love with him.[43] In one scene, an old widow, Nyi Sembodo, has a young, beautiful maid, Nyi Kacer, who has to ensure that the male partner of her mistress is aroused so he is able to have sex with her mistress. They end up having trio sex, with the two women caressing each other.[44] Later, at the famous *Malam Maksiat* (Night of Sin) Nyi Sembodo is dressed as a man. She is described as clever and very good at making money.

Other forms of sex featuring in the *Serat Centhini* include incest, bestiality (a man penetrating a horse to get rid of his syphilis) and rape (successfully resisted by the girl). There are many more scenes of gender reversals and complicated sex acts, both same-sex and heterosexual. Sexuality is seen as a major life force, and is not in its many manifestations associated with sin, crime or illness.

The Javanese Hinduized court culture inspired an ethos of romantic love. The most popular masculine models are the virile, ascetic Arjuna, his robust warrior–brother Bhima and the romantic, invincible Raden Panji. The first two are characters of the immensely popular *Mahabharata*; the exploits of Prince Panji are a genre in itself. The story of prince Panji and his two wives is one of the most popular Javanese legends. It probably originated in East Java in the twelfth century.[45] In the *Serat Centhini*, one of those wives, Dewi Sekar Taji, disguises herself as a man, namely as Panji Norowongso, with whom Prince Innu falls in love.[46]

Another version of this tale is the Hikayat Panji Semirang. The heroine, Galuh Chandra Kirana – disguised as a man, the warrior-Prince Panji Semirang – enters the *keputren*: 'One can imagine that the coy but unequivocal references to kissing, embracing, touching and flirting must have given rise to giggling and innuendo among the predominantly male court audiences.'[47] This very popular story contains many references to gender fluidity and homosexual love.

The Panji tales spread as far as Siam and Cambodia. As they belong to an oral tradition, there are many versions. Roughly, the story goes as follows. Prince Panji, the younger son of the ruler of Djenggala, was betrothed to his niece, Dewi Sekar Taji, a daughter of the ruler of Kediri. They had never met. Once, while the prince was hunting, he passed the house of the regent who invited him in for a drink. He was served by the beautiful youngest daughter of the regent, Dewi Angraini. The young prince fell hopelessly in love with her and decided to marry her. His father agreed to the marriage. When the ruler of Kediri learnt that his future son-in-law had married another wife, he became enraged and declared war on his brother, the ruler of Djenggala. However, their elder sister, a hermit, intervened and convinced the brothers not to wage war, because Raden Panji could still marry Dewi Sekar Taji as his official consort. Dewi Angraini, being of lower birth, would be the secondary wife. Prince Panji refused to marry another wife, wanting only his beloved Dewi Angraini, violating the orders of his father. Enraged, the ruler of Djenggala sent Prince Panji on an errand and ordered his eldest son to murder Dewi Angraini. The dutiful prince obeyed the order of his father and killed Dewi Angraini in the forest. Many adventures follow. Prince Panji found his murdered wife has turned into stone. Prince Panji ordered his slaves to dig a grave. When they wanted to lower the body of Dewi Angraini into the deep hole she suddenly flew up to heaven. This was surely a sign the Gods loved her, so Prince Panji took heart and started waging war and soon gained the reputation of being an invincible warrior.

Finally, a big battle between Prince Panji and the ruler of Metaoen was to begin. Dewi Sekar Taji, 'the fearless princess' because of her prowess in spear fighting, demanded that she join the struggle. She mounted her invincible white elephant. When prince Panji saw her he was delighted that Dewi Sekar Taji resembled Dewi Angraini and married the princess of Kediri. On the fortieth day the happy couple went to an island where they met a girl who so strongly resembled Dewi Angraini that the prince was shattered. At that moment a messenger from the Gods descended from heaven and informed him that the Upper God, Batara Guru, had decided that no two human beings should be the same. And as Dewi Angraini resembled so strongly Dewi Sekar Taji, as twin stars in the sky, the Gods had turned Dewi Angraini into a ray of the moon. To demonstrate the resemblance of these two women, Dewi Angraini returned momentarily to earth. The messenger told the prince: 'From now on they will be one person, called Tjandra Kirana, Ray of the Moon, and her beauty will be as radiant as her name.' And so this happened.[48]

Another version has it that Dewi Angraini was not killed but instead fell ill while Prince Panji and she were on their way to meet Dewi Sekar Taji. When everybody was finally together, Dewi Angraini died. Dewi Sekar Taji and Prince Panji then saw a light flying from the body of Dewi Angraini to the moon. As Dewi Sekar Taji's face shone like the full moon, Prince Panji loved both women as one. Dewi Sekar Taji from then on worshipped the full moon, called Chandra Kirana.[49]

These exploits of Panji and his wives illustrate some important points. The first is the strong bond, fusion even, of the co-wives. Far from being rivals they support each other, and either become one in the moon or the one worships the other. This bonding of the two women is presented as something beautiful, 'shining' and as an unfolding upon which Panji himself, though the husband of both, has little influence. This theme is paralleled in another couple of co-wives, Srikandi and Sumbadra. Srikandi is the warrior – wife of Prince Arjuna. She teaches her co-wife, the meek Sumbadra, the art of archery, in which Srikandi excels. As in the case of Prince Panji, Prince Arjuna is a valiant, virile and attractive husband, but the strong bond between his two consorts exceeds the conjugal bond.

The second theme, remarkable from a postcolonial perspective when the recorded histories of warrior women have been driven out of social consciousness, is the prowess of the two valiant princesses, Srikandi and Dewi Sekar Taji (or Chandra Kirana).[50] Contemporary middle-class lesbian women have been quick to grasp the potential of this strong female bonding and the association with bravery that the two princesses have. In the early 1990s a group called 'Chandra Kirana' existed, and a few years later another group of young lesbian women was established, 'Swara Srikandi' (the Voice of Srikandi), as will be discussed later.

Though these tales contain many instances of same-sex attraction and gender fluidity, this cannot be directly translated to daily life. Florida researched the 'sex wars' in the nineteenth-century Javanese courts, in which Javanese wives were strongly advised to be meek and obedient sexual partners to their Javanese husbands.[51] She suggests that this is related to the failed quest of the Javanese ruler Pakubuwana IX. His beloved, Princess Sekar Kedhaton, refused to surrender to him and instead rose to great spiritual and intellectual heights.

Wayang performances were and still are held both in courtly and in village settings. Courts may have several *gamelan* orchestras for various ritual or theatrical purposes. The Hindu epic *Mahabharata* is a major inspiration for Indonesian *wayang* stories.[52] The main characters are very well known, particularly on Java and Bali. The *Mahabharata* has several inspiring stories of gender inversion.

Princess Srikandi, a wife of *wayang* hero Prince Arjuna, is so famous for her archery skills that in the Bharatayudha, the great war between the clans of the Kurawa and the Pandawa (to which the invincible Arjuna, his four brothers, their wives and children belong), she is one of the major army leaders and kills the mighty Resi Bima, a sage of the Kurawa.

The version more popular in India is as follows. The invincible warrior prince Bhishma, who had vowed to remain celibate, rejected Amba for marriage, whom he had initially abducted to marry a brother. As she had been abducted by Bhishma and was no longer considered 'pure', Amba was rejected by the brother. Furious and humiliated Amba sought revenge. She obtained a boon that she could kill Bhishma in her next birth and to hasten that she committed suicide. She was reborn as Shikandhi.[53] A divine voice instructed her father to raise her as a son. So Shikandhi was taught warfare and eventually married a woman. On their wedding night Shikandhi's wife became infuriated when she found out her husband was a woman. Shikandhi fled and met a *yaksha* (forest spirit) who exchanged his sex with her. Shikandhi returned and had a happy married life with his wife. During the great war between the Pandawa and the Kurawa, Arjuna could not kill Bhishma. He then hid behind Shikandhi. Bhishma, knowing Shikandhi was a woman whom he was not allowed to fight, lowered his weapons so Arjuna could shoot him with his arrows.

In the Javanese tale Kandhihawa, Srikandi, as Kandhihawa, married Dewi Durniti, who thought she was a man. When Dewi Durniti found out that her husband had female genitals, she complained to her father. Kandhihawa then went to a priest to ask his help to gratify the sexual needs of Dewi Durniti. The priest bestowed male genitals on Kandhihawa so he could impregnate his wife. A son was born from this successful marriage, called Bambang Nirsita.[54]

The affection between the transgender warrior princess Srikandi and her co-wife Sumbadra is well known. It is not their husband Arjuna, the mighty and wily warrior king, who saves Sumbadra when she is abducted, but Srikandi.[55] A tomboy is often called little Srikandi in Java. The figure of Sumbadra is upheld as the epitome of female modesty.

Arjuna is the most elegant and slender of the five Pandawa brothers, and although not as strong as his mighty brother Bhima, he is a most feared and invincible warrior.[56] Arjuna becomes a dance teacher in female form, named Brihannala, during his exile with his brothers the Pandawa. In dances the role of Arjuna is often performed by women.

The courageous figure of Srikandi was a role model for Gerwani, until 1965. At present she is seldom portrayed in her autonomous form, but usually in association with her male consort. Sumbadra has also been domesticated – but she was more than a whimpering wife, she was also known for her great spiritual powers. These have been downplayed, as spiritual, ascetic power has come to be seen as belonging to men.[57] In her bashful form she became popular during the Suharto era, presented as the ideal wife/mother figure, the epitome of demure femininity.

An interesting example of how, in earlier times, male-bodied and female-bodied cross-dressing and transgender practices were more common is found in a painting on the roof of the Kertha Gosa (the palace court building of the Balinese kingdom of Klungkung).[58] The relief tells the story of Bhima Swarga, or Bhima in Heaven, which is part of the *Mahabharata* epic. Bhima travels to hell, to find his parents and bring them to *swarga* (heaven). Pandu and Madrim, the parents of the five Pandawa brothers, had been thrown into *hell* after violating a curse. The story can be seen as the Balinese version of Dante's Hell. While there, Bhima encounters numerous sinners who are severely punished for their misdeeds, such as violating the laws of the village, committing adultery or abortion, stealing rice or remaining childless. He also comes across a pair of cross-dressing *banci*, one male- and one female-bodied. On his request for an explanation as to who these 'enigmatic-looking' people were, and what crime they had committed, he received the answer that they had not committed 'a sin. It's a kind of imperfection. And that's why a *banci*, however good his [or her] life has been, still has to spend some time in *hell* before [s]he can be admitted to the highest spheres.'[59] It is telling that currently the guides in the Kertha Gosa hall do not admit to knowing this story, while the book that contains it is sold on the premises. I enlarged one of the pictures I took of the *banci* and Bhima and gifted it to the office of the members of Sektor 15 of the KPI.[60]

Dance performances

Historically, several dance forms in the Indonesian archipelago have known transgender or cross-dressing practices.[61] These include the Betawi *lenong* dance; the *gandrung* dance in Banyuwangi, in East Java; the *ludruk* plays with the *ngremo* dance;[62] the *lengger* dance of Banyumas; the *sandhur* in Madura; the *masri* dance in Makassar and the *reog* of Ponorogo. Certain dance performances include erotic practices, such as *tayuban* and *ronggeng* in Sunda, the *jaiphong* in Banten and West Java, and the *joged* in Jakarta. Some of these dance forms have disappeared, or are in decline, their practitioners having lost the status they held in former days. Other forms have adapted to the pressure of majoritarian Islam. The terminology used to describe these performances varies, as do the practices. Transvestism and transgenderism are often used side by side, and in some cases same-sex erotic practices are linked to these dance forms. They are not reported in all cases, which may be because of an oversight of the authors, or because, of course, they did not take place. I will discuss a few examples which are better documented than others.

Foley provides an interesting analysis of the development of these dance forms in West Java (Sunda), particularly the *ronggeng* dance (singing and dancing by women performers). She distinguishes three periods. First, the mytho-historic moment of the *wali* (saints, alleged to introduce Islam in the archipelago), who used arts, including *ronggeng* as a tool of conversion. Second, the colonial era, when the palaces became major centres that hired and influenced the art of *ronggeng* performances, particularly in the Sundanese area of West Java. A similar dance genre catered more specifically to an aristocratic audience, the *tayuban*. The third phase she discusses is the contemporary period, when these art forms have declined. She notes that the anti-pornography legislation enacted in 2008 (which will be discussed later) is in part aimed at eliminating remnants of these long-existing female-bodied and male-bodied transvestite performance practices.[63]

A well-known example of transgenderism and same-sex eroticism is the *reog* (or *reyog*) dance in Ponorogo, East Java. The dance traces its origins to the realm of Kediri (1045–1222). With their ritual dances, of old performed in a state of trance, the dancers would bring good fortune and fertility to the community.[64] The practice is linked to the Javanese religion called Kejawen and for centuries existed side by side with Islamic practices. The dancers – consisting of the male leaders of the group, the powerful *warok* and their young male-bodied feminine companions (*gemblak* or *jathil*) – were required to follow strict rules, rituals and exercises, both physical and spiritual. The *warok* carries a huge tiger mask, adorned with peacock feathers, and a *gemblak* sits on his neck. The total weight of the *gemblak* and the mask could add up to 100 kg. Prior to a performance the *warok* was prohibited to have sex with a woman, in case he would lose his mystical powers, but having sex with a boy between eight and sixteen was allowed. A *warok* had the same prestige as a *kyai* (a religious leader), or a village head. *Warok* and *kyai* were believed to have mystical powers.[65] The more *gemblak* a *warok* had, the more sacred he was considered by the community. A *warok* cared for his *gemblak*, providing security and education and looked after his family which received generous offerings of livestock and other gifts as dowry. A good *gemblak* might become a *warok*. *Warok* also had wives and children.[66]

The *reog* tradition suffered a major setback in the mid-1960s. The tradition was associated with the PKI-affiliated cultural association Lekra, and the performers were persecuted, in some cases their heads cut off and placed on spikes in public places.[67] With the spread of politico-religious homophobia since 2015, the *reog* tradition changed. Boys are now ashamed to be known as a *warok's gemblak*, and *warok* are no longer living with *gemblak*. Of old, when a group of around sixty dancers entered a village, led by the *warok* with his huge tiger mask, the procession was led by a dozen or so *gemblak*. Girl *jathil* now lead the procession.

Gunopati, a famous *warok*, is quoted as saying: 'A *gemblak* was a lover and a symbol of honour.' He himself had eight *gemblak* partners. The few *gemblak* that remain are now called 'foster sons'.[68] At present *reog* dancers still perform at religious (Islamic) festivals and national anniversaries. The mystical connotations have declined.

Reog performances were often accompanied by dancers wielding brightly coloured rattan horses, the so-called *jathilan* or *jaranan* dances. This dance form was widely popular all over Central and East Java, also without being associated with *reog*. They were also called *kuda lumping* or *kuda jepang*. Sometimes performances lasted a whole day, involving elaborate offerings, trance dances and the performance of all kinds of tricks. In trance, the transgender youths might eat hot coal, or glass.[69] This form of ritual transvestism is also on the decline, with its spiritual aspects diminished. The former members of these troupes have had to find other employment to survive. For a performance of a once popular *kuda lumping* troupe in Malang, East Java, in February 2003, which we had sponsored, dancers and musicians arrived in their own *becak* from all over the city. The group hardly performs any more, after their reputation was linked to communism in the heyday of the anti-communist genocide perpetrated by General Suharto, and some of their members were murdered or imprisoned. But in 2003 there were still some young transvestite dancers who went into a trance, displaying horse-like behaviour, eating coal straight from the ground and bolting like young horses. Their spiritual leader carefully led them into the trance and eased them out of it again.[70]

Ludruk is a form of dance-drama that attracted mainly lower-class audiences. It consists of a series of dances interspersed with comic scenes and is accompanied by a small orchestra. This folk theatre became very popular around the turn of the twentieth century in Surabaya, East Java.[71] *Ludruk* troupes were known for their comedians, who commented on the sociopolitical struggles of common people. The narratives are often based on folk tales or historical stories. The clowns offered social criticism, parodying those in power. The origin of the *ludruk* theatre probably goes back to the thirteenth century; like *reog* and other dance drama configurations, it originally had ritual aspects. The *ngremo* or opening dance was often performed by male-bodied transgender dancers,[72] but female-bodied dancers also cross-dress in *ngremo* dances.[73]

In the eighteenth century, *ludruk* troupes moved from one village to the next, performing in busy places like markets. Around the turn of the twentieth century they relocated to the major cities. Popular shows contained critiques of the colonial regime, and *ludruk* groups strongly supported Sukarno's nationalist policies. The prominent gay activist Dede Oetomo remembers that as a child he attended performances by the *ludruk Marhaen*, which his parents loved.[74] In the Sukarno period *ludruk* troupes were, politically, left of centre and shows increasingly contained critiques of the enemies of the people, like 'evil landlords' and 'capitalist bureaucrats'. As religious leaders such as the highly revered *kyai* might also be rich landlords, such *kyai* were also showered with critique, angering Muslims. A highly controversial story was named 'Matinya Gusti Allah' (Death of God).[75] Many Muslims saw this story as active propaganda for the PKI, proving how atheist they were. In reality the play contained the usual social criticism, stimulated by Lekra. After Suharto's coup, *ludruk* performers were persecuted as supporters of the PKI and *ludruk* performances were banned. In the 1980s, however, *ludruk* made a comeback, as long as such troupes agreed to become the mouthpiece of the New Order regime. They were forced to promote the government's programmes, such as family planning and national development. This pragmatic turn allowed some *ludruk* artists to survive.

From the 1990s onwards the new technologies of open-air cinema, video cassette players and TV severely affected the *ludruk* groups. They were considered traditional and backward. A few groups, mainly in Jombang and Mojokerto, managed to portray contemporary social problems in their performances.[76] After the New Order collapsed, *ludruk* shows became popular again on TV.[77] Since the ban on non-gender conforming people on TV, discussed in Chapter 7, *ludruk*, with its transvestite actors, once again suffered a serious setback.

The community of *tandhak waria* (male-bodied dancers in feminine roles) had a high, though ambiguous, social status. Anoegrajekti interviewed Elok, an elder, once successful *tandhak waria*. She was well paid but despised as a *waria* by the general public. As Elok muses, God is righteous and knows best, so there sure must have been divine wisdom at work (*hikmah*) when she was created? Because of that she does not want a sex change, as Dorce had.[78] For she was born with this particular body and therefore it should not be tampered with. But it made her life difficult. As a feminine boy she was evicted from her home. Elok managed to get herself an education and worked hard to be accepted by society. As a *tandhak* dancer she became well known. Elok got married, in an unofficial religious ceremony, *sirri*. The first wife of her husband had proposed it – she preferred that her wayward husband married a *waria* than that he kept having extramarital affairs (*jajan*).[79]

In Banyuwangi, at the most eastern point of Java, another traditional dance form had developed, called *gandrung*, in which the main dancers were transvestite young men. The *gandrung* dance connotes the entanglement of male and female energy. *Gandrung* has many variations and is popular in Bali, Lombok and East Java among the Balinese, Sasak and Javanese. The most popular variation is *gandrung* from Banyuwangi, and the city is often referred to as Kota Gandrung or 'city of *gandrung*'. Originally a ritual dance dedicated to the goddess of rice and fertility, Dewi Sri, it is currently performed as a social dance of courtship and love in communal and social events, or as a tourist attraction. The connection with Dewi Sri has been lost.

Around the end of the nineteenth century, the famous dancer Marsan was the last male-bodied *gandrung*.[80] After his death only girls could become *gandrung*. Anoegrajekti associates this change to the growing Islamization of the region. She asserts that the appearance of transvestite men, which was common both on and off the stage, was related to homosexuality which was widespread in the region and which had become increasingly suspect.[81] The *gandrung* dance form is similar to such art forms found elsewhere in the archipelago. Male members of the audience could climb up onto the stage and dance with the performers, sometimes slipping money into their upper clothes. As *gandrung* is seen as an erotic dance, conservative Muslim leaders have also come to oppose female-bodied dancers, recently, declaring the dance form as such *haram*, as the dancers' shoulders are usually bare and the movements are seen as sexually stimulating. They want the dancers' bodies to be fully clothed, including a *jilbab*, they prohibit male dancers climbing on stage, insist that the performers sing Muslim songs and they want to ban alcohol.[82]

In her memoir as a *gandrung* dancer in an East Javanese village, Larasati reflects that although in her *kampung* mostly women would perform the dance, until 1965 there were also men who danced the *gandrung*. After 1965 the dance was completely banned, and many artists disappeared, never to return, as this folk art was seen as a 'red' activity. The remaining dancers and musicians were forced to undergo a process of guidance (*pembinaan*) to conform to the style required by the New Order rulers.[83] In the East Javanese village where I reside part of the year, a similar process occurred. There used to be a rich cultural life, with various music and dance forms (*ludruk*, *jaranan*, *kethoprak*). And although the village Muslim leader (*kyai*) managed to save his villagers, the folk art disappeared, and the regular rituals to honour Dewi Sri, the rice goddess, stopped. Now there is only a group composed of men who play the *rebana* (or *terban*) to accompany prayers.[84]

In the mid-1970s the Department of Folk Art Culture published an interesting booklet on *gandrung*. The authors, Soelarto and S'Ilmi, record that there used to be two art forms in the region, *sangiyang* and *seblang*, which were related to animism and shamanism. *Sangiyang* had disappeared at the time they wrote, but some songs still existed as folk songs. The shamanist dances resembled those of the *bissu*; when the dancers were in trance they could not be penetrated by a *keris*. In Banyuwangi the *sangiyang* was danced by two young male dancers who wore the clothes and the make-up of young women.[85] The *gandrung* is as old as these two other dances and also has erotic connotations. Even the word *gandrung* in Old Javanese means 'implying the understanding of love'. It used to be danced by boys between fourteen and sixteen years old, with beautiful faces, dressed as girls and dancing like them. Soelarto and S'Ilmi compare this dance style with that of the *sedate* in Aceh, the *runding* in Madura and the *gemblak* in Ponorogo.[86] Though the dance form contained erotic elements, it was always associated with a goddess.[87]

As in South Sulawesi, the proclamation of regional autonomy led to a new surge of pride for the traditional culture of Banyuwangi. Government officials saw the great tourist potential of a major festival, eying the success of neighbouring Bali. In 2010 for the first time, they held the Gandrung Sewu Dance Festival. But by 2017 the Islamic Defenders Front (FPI) furiously opposed it.[88] The next year they linked their prohibition to the string of disasters that had hit Indonesia that year, including earthquakes and a devastating tsunami. They were caused, they complained, because sin and wickedness were flourishing in Indonesia.[89]

Lengger lanang

Heteronormatization and the growing influence of political Islam with its binary sexual morality is illustrated by the recent developments around the *lengger lanang* dance from Banyumas, Central Java. This is one of the most well-known dances in which transgender (MTF) or cross-dressing males perform. Originally a fertility dance, dedicated to the rice goddess Dewi Sri, it is mentioned in *Serat Centhini*.[90] There are few *lengger* dancers left. They are despised by puritanical Muslims. Performances are rare. Due to the controversies created by a recent film, *Memories of My Body*, around the brilliant dancer Rianto, the *lengger* dance came into the spotlight.

The male-bodied dancers use full traditional Javanese women's attire, such as a *kemben* (breast cloth), *kebaya*, (*batik* skirt) and a *konde* (hair bun). They apply heavy women's make-up. The dance used to be very popular, performed both at agrarian and other village rituals and at marriage ceremonies. The word *lengger* comes from '*leng*' meaning hole, vagina, and '*jengger*' meaning the comb of a rooster, a symbol of masculinity. Becoming a *lengger* dancer involves hard training, both for the dance movements and for the rituals associated with it.

Both the post-October 1965 massacres, and their aftermath, and present-day anti-LGBT sentiments endanger the traditional *lengger lanang* dance. After 1965 this style of dancing was associated with Lekra and the troupes were bridled, their members persecuted or killed. Dariah, a famous dancer between 1930 and the mid-1960s ended his life in 2018 in a small Central Javanese village close to Banyumas, dressed as a woman. She had provided make-up services for bridal couples. Until her death in 2018 she had a portrait of Sukarno on the wall in her living room. After 1965 she lost all her possessions. She was an inspiration to many *lengger* dancers, including Rianto.

It is no longer safe to perform *lengger* dances. Andrianto quotes Agus Widodo, whose stage name is Agnes, who tells him that s/he (Agnes) needs to make a security check first before performing in public before s/he accepts an invitation to dance. Agus wears male clothing off stage, but as a *lengger* dancer s/he is ridiculed and called *banci* and groped by drunk men.[91] A TV documentary in 2020 on *lengger* dancers portrays them as real men, cutting wood, climbing trees and working in the fields. One of them, Tora, is married and has a child. They see their lives as destined by God, who is after all responsible for *rejeki, jodoh* and *kematian*.[92] That most of them have not yet found a *jodoh* is therefore not due to them. When they are preparing for a show, dressing in women's traditional clothes, putting on their make-up, their movements become more feminine, their smiles languorous. They used to perform widely at festivals, weddings and harvest rituals, and now they are at times evicted if the host or some other prominent person finds out they are men in women's clothing.[93]

Just as the dance form of the *lengger* shares similarities with other Javanese dances such as the *ronggeng, tayub* and *gandrung*, the story line is embedded in Javanese literary culture, in this case, a version of the Panji tale. In one type of the *lengger* mask dance the story is told of Princess Dewi Sekar Taji. Two warriors, Raden Panji Asmoro Bangun and Prabu Klono fight for her hand. Dewi Sekar Taji is also proposed by Tanggaron, the warrior sister of Prabu Klono. The dance is associated with one of the *wali* who brought Islam to Java, Sunan Kalijaga.[94] This suggests that the dance precedes the coming of Islam to Java, in the thirteenth century, for the *wali* used existing art forms to make Islam intelligible to the local population. In the mask dance a vigorous male character, *warok*, dances with his feminine younger male-bodied partner.

The film *Memories of My Body* by Garin Nugroho portrays such a relationship. The film was released in April 2018, but it was immediately banned in Depok, Bekasi, Garut and Bogor (all in West Java); in Palembang, Pontianak, Kubu Raya and Balikpapan (in Kalimantan); in Padang and Bandar Lampung (in Sumatra); and various other places in the archipelago. Since then it has been shown only occasionally. In Pontianak a Malay youth paramilitary organization attacked a World Day Dance festival soon after the film's ban there claiming that the dances 'promoted LGBT lifestyles' and that the 'tight shirts' worn by male-bodied dancers 'dancing femininely' were incompatible with Indonesian culture.[95] The film presents a fictionalized biographical account of Rianto, who teaches and performs traditional Indonesian dances in many parts of the world, and who has his own film studio in Japan, where his art is more appreciated than in his home country. The documentary was Indonesia's contribution to the 2020 Oscar competition.[96]

Memories of My Body is based on Rianto's life story. The protagonist is Juno. Rianto himself plays the dancer as an adult and narrates the film. The documentary exposes the contemporary mechanisms that limit the chances of survival for a traditional dance form like *lengger*: the exploitation of communist phobia and bigoted Islamic teachings. The *dukun* (shaman) advises the *bupati* (regent) to seek the help of the youthful *lengger* dancer Juno for his re-election campaign. Juno first sings and then has to stroke the penis of the *bupati* with ground *menyan* (incense) till ejaculation, but Juno cannot do it, and runs away. The *bupati* has fallen in love with the handsome boy, and when Juno serves him tea at a rally, grabs his hand. A picture is taken of that moment and the *bupati*, now vulnerable to blackmail and fuelled by his ambitious wife, has to drive out the *lengger* group from the village where they had found refuge. He orders a group of *preman* (thugs) to perform this task. The *bupati* accuses them of being PKI *baru* (new PKI). This triggers reminiscences of how the father of Juno disappeared. His father had watched his family being killed during the anti-communist purges near the river, and he would regularly wildly splash around in it, watched by a young Juno. When Juno's father was also linked to the PKI, because he had followed a music workshop given by Lekra, he disappeared, leaving Juno behind.

In the documentary, the mood in the village itself has changed, for *lengger* used to be a normal part of their cultural scene, performed at harvests, festivals and weddings, but they were now seen to be destroying the morality of the villagers. The *lengger* group members bitterly complain that they used to play in city halls, and now they are driven out to the margins of society to far away villages. The leader of the *lengger* group is a *warok* who performs the lion dance. Due to their dwindling fortune, the *warok* has lost his magical powers and needs a new *gemblak*, as a spirit informed him. Juno becomes his new *gemblak*, and the *warok* proclaims proudly that Juno is now his lover and anyone who attempts to take Juno from him will be killed. Juno performs a graceful feminine dance, while his *warok* dances behind him with powerful masculine strides. The documentary integrates the theme of bodily memories as both memories of bodily trauma and the entanglement of femininity and masculinity, which ultimately opens the path to the lost mystical powers of the older *warok*.

Postcolonial amnesia in Aceh

Postcolonial amnesia in the form of enforcement of narrow-minded heteronormativity as 'always already there' is well illustrated by the case of Aceh, the only province in

Indonesia which is allowed to have its own sharia laws.[97] Following the devastating tsunami in 2004, peace was negotiated between Acehnese leaders and the central government in 2005, after a prolonged bloody conflict. The province received the status of special autonomy, and in 2009 the Qanun or Hukum Jinayat (Islamic Criminal Law) was approved by the provincial parliament of Aceh. It became implemented in 2015. *Liwath* and *musahaqah* are two terms that refer to same-sex sexual relationships addressed in Hukum Jinayat. *Liwath* is defined as a sexual relationship between a man and another man based on the voluntary consent of both, and *musahaqah* is a sexual relationship between a woman and another woman based on their voluntary consent.[98]

Since this law was promulgated LGBT people have been arrested, raided and humiliated, and targeted by the moral police.[99] This violence followed a hate campaign by political leaders such as Illiza Saaduddin. In 2012, when she was the deputy mayor of the province's capital, Banda Aceh, she posted a picture of herself on Instagram holding a handgun with both hands, declaring that LGBT people ruin the dignity of humankind. 'We in Aceh', she asserted, 'hate and fight against their behaviour which violates our customary norms and religion'.

Customary norms? In her own portrait Illiza Saaduddin is not dressed in traditional Aceh women's attire, but in a black, Western-style plastic raincoat, her head covered in a tight red *jilbab*, which protrudes so far from her face that she cannot look right or left without twisting her neck.[100] So dressed, she holds a very modern gun. This *jilbab* is a recent invention; Acehnese women used to wear a loose long shawl; so too is the province's homophobia.

Nineteenth- and early-twentieth century accounts of Acehnese culture by Dutch administrators and scientists are full of references to the so-called immorality of the Acehnese, both among the higher and the lower social groups. The Dutch were at war with Aceh and painted the region in unfavourable terms. Yet their observations are noteworthy. What shocked these observers most was the 'shameless openness' in which these men flaunted their 'depravities'. As Kruyt noted, boys from nine to twelve years old, probably imported [meaning forcibly taken] from the island of Nias, dressed in fine silks and adorned with golden and silver arm and leg bands, entertained men in the evenings and at night.[101] These so-called *sedate* were the private property of rich men; these men might also share their slave boys with their male employees at pepper plantations, who might engage with them in the 'most unnatural and immoral acts'.[102]

Julius Jacobs recorded in 1894 that parties in Aceh usually ended in 'offensive' orgies and bacchanals, sometimes even on the graves of their saints, where drinking parties took place and 'perverse' love games were played. He also witnessed elite men parading in public, surrounded by a group of 'catamites'. A particularly rich official (*bijo*) was accompanied on his official trips by a thousand of these youths, who were used for his 'perverse' desires.[103]

Every village had some *sedate* who performed poetry in the evening (*pantun*) and danced. They were owned by the male members of a so-called *kongsi*. When an official (*uleebalang*) visited a village, the members of that particular *kongsi* rented *sedate* of other *kongsi* to entertain the guest.

The renowned Islamologist Snouck Hurgronje, hated in Aceh because of his support for the Dutch military, also documented *uleebalang* who were known to enjoy sexual relations with young male slaves from Nias. He mentioned that these *sedate* danced on festivals accompanied by religious poetry.[104] Even religious leaders might have *sedate*, such as the Tekoe Panglima of the main mosque of *kampung* Emperoen near Belang, who was also married to two wives, as Jacobs recorded.[105] Praag wrote that boys provided sexual services to men at the courts of the sultan.[106] Apart from these cross-dressing *sedate*, Jacobs also reported that boys might engage in 'mutual masturbation', a practice they might continue to enjoy after they were married.

As most observers of Aceh's cultural and sexual norms were men, who had little interest in or access to the world of women, accounts of same-sex activities among women are rare. Yet Jacobs noted that tribadism, involving women with such 'perverse' sexual drives, was not uncommon in the sultanate.[107]

Cross-dressing and same-sex activities were openly practised in Aceh; flaunting one's beautiful boys was a source of pride for elite men. The *sedate* were held in high esteem, as performers and dancers, including at religious festivals. They were associated with the court and the mosques. The ones who despised such activities were not the Acehnese, but the foreign explorers and administrators, labelling them 'immoral' and 'perverse'. What the *sedate* themselves felt about their lives we do not know, but it is clear that their masters valued them. How the men who enjoyed them saw themselves we do not know either, although Karsch-Haack maintains that some of them were, in the terminology of those days, 'congenital pederasts'. Contrary to what Illiza Saaduddin claims, and what sharia courts uphold, same-sex practices in Aceh traditionally were not seen to be in contradiction with local customs (*adat*) and religion. They were part of a rich cultural life that seems severely constrained under recent sharia laws. It is ironic that present-day homophobic political and religious officials in Aceh voice opinions that would be more intelligible to the condescending Dutch colonizers than to Aceh's elite circles a century ago.

First criminalization

From the above accounts in this and the previous chapter some glimpses appear of the rich history of Indonesia's traditions of cross-dressing, transgender and same-sex practices, sometimes formalized in marriages according to local customs. Accounts of women's same-sex and transgendered practices are rarer than those of male-bodied persons. In twentieth-century Central Sulawesi, among the Wana, Atkinson recorded the cases of three women who became men and married women.[108] One woman preferred to be called 'uncle' and would be angry if someone called her 'aunt'. These women were called *bante*, cognately similar to *banci*. In 1939 in West Sumatra, a girl asked the village chief to marry her to a woman who had been widowed for eight years, saying that they had a relationship like a husband and wife.[109]

Apart from the cases mentioned in the previous chapter, male same-sex marriages were recorded in Makassar by Fernandez Navarrete as early as 1676.[110] A court case Karsch-Haack recorded in Madura illustrates that same-sex relations were accepted there. A man had murdered his 'male mistress', in a fit of jealousy. The homosexual nature of that relationship was never the offense; it was commonly accepted, also by the parents of the mistress-boy.[111]

In 1938 the colonial state suddenly asserted its powers and arrested some men for same-sex acts with minors. As Bloembergen upholds, pre-war concerns about a 'clean' and strong masculinity needed to be fostered in order to be able to defend the nation against possible aggression.[112] The so-called Indies morality scandal of 1938–9 began. Possibly 223 suspects were apprehended, ranging from high-level civil servants to teachers and workers, and from all ethnic communities – European, Eurasian, Chinese and Indonesian. Young male prostitutes, *katjong*, were asked to identify their male clients.[113] The two most well-known arrests were those of a resident of Batavia and the painter Walter Spies who resided in Bali.[114] They were charged under article 292 of the Indies Penal Code, which carried a maximum sentence of five years. Homosexual men were sent to jails, not only in big cities like Batavia, Surabaya, Semarang and Bandung, but also in smaller cities like Cirebon, Cianjur, Salatiga, Magelang, Pamekasan, Padang and Makassar.[115]

In the Netherlands, consensual same-sex acts between adults were not prohibited at the time, only same-sex contacts of adult men with minors, under Article 248b of the Penal Code. The Dutch imported that code into the colony in 1918, thereby introducing legal homophobia, in the form of the prohibition of paedophilia.[116] Though the Dutch rulers criminalized only paedophilia, it led to an increase in homophobia in general, particularly when Dutch media reported the situation by labelling this sexual phenomenon among homosexual men as an issue of morality. Transgender or same-sex practices that were part of traditional cultural or religious practices were not persecuted by the Dutch colonial powerholders. That would only happen after independence.

Conclusion

Transgender and same-sex practices are an integral part of Indonesia's rich cultural history. In the previous chapter cross-dressing or trans cultural practices were discussed, which invoked cosmic power to increase the fertility of the land and the prosperity of its inhabitants. Various terms were used to denote such practices.[117] A wide variety of such practices are documented, from occasional cross-dressing to fully fledged same-sex unions. Not all forms of such practices have been covered due to obvious gaps in documentation and research. Particularly, more work needs to be done on the eastern parts of the archipelago. The three major literary cycles – the *Mahabharata*, the *I La Galigo* and the *Panji cyclus* – as well as the *Serat Centhini*, discussed in this chapter, contain elements of gender and sexual diversity and same-sex erotic intimacy. From this exploration, certain conclusions on the transformation and decline of such practices, and the postcolonial amnesia relating to gender and sexual diversity in the country's great literary traditions and cultural practices, can be drawn. As some of these processes are still at work, the analysis has contemporary relevance.

A first conclusion is that both colonialism and the emergence of monotheistic religions have destroyed or eroded the importance of so-called ritual transvestism and gender diversity in general,[118] such as the declining role of the *bissu* in Bugis society. The religious, ritual context of gender switching has almost disappeared. This development refers to a process called the decline of 'sacred gender'.[119] In the process particular forms of heteronormativity based on a binary division of sex and gender have been strengthened. This entailed both the consolidation of patriarchal constructs and the codification of women's subordination. Watson Andaya maintains that after the advent of Christianity and Islam colonial rulers in the early modern period, 'working in tandem with religious authorities and state authorities developed and promoted conceptions of male-female relationships that still resonate today. In particular the documentation of legal precedents codified ideals that reduced the flexibility of customary law and confirmed men's prerogatives in both the household and the community at large.'[120]

Not only was women's subordination institutionalized and strengthened, but homophobia was also introduced into the archipelago and codified, contrary to what present-day conservative political and religious leaders claim. In England in the eighteenth century, sapphism was considered a foreign vice, like sodomy, and considered to be imported through contact with the East.[121] The reverse is true now; Indonesia considers LGBT to be a foreign imposition.

This is a clear example of postcolonial amnesia. The implicit mimicry of colonial homophobia suggested by the concept of postcolonial amnesia does not, however, refer to a sameness of postcolonial and colonial practices or sentiments. The postcolonial situation carries various forms of hybridity. In the case of gender and sexual relations in Indonesia one obvious form of modification is the growing influence of fundamentalist Islam.[122] Another intervening process is the association of LGBT issues with communist phobia.[123] In the wake of the anti-communist coup of General Suharto, popular art forms such as *ludruk* were associated with the Communist Party and many of its practitioners murdered or imprisoned. This moral battlefield continues till today. A third influence is the global LGBT discourse.

The decline of traditional cultural forms is not only due to political and religious processes. Modern media and culture also play an important role. Some traditional cultural forms have adjusted themselves to these developments. *Lengger* dancers are using an electronic keyboard at times, instead of the traditional instruments, and make use of social media.[124] The *sedate* dance has gained national interest, with cisgendered male dancers engaging in vigorous movements, but all references to its past as belonging to a tradition of transgenderism and same-sex intimacy have been erased. In Banyuwangi the *gandrung* is danced now by cisgendered female dancers, some with a *jilbab* covering their heads, and with skin-coloured clothes that cover their shoulders and arms. In this way the dance obeys Islamic strictures on the covering of women's bodies, while referring to the traditional way in which the *gandrung* was danced, with bare shoulders, heads and arms. In all cases the ritual aspects are ignored, or strongly downplayed. Yet present-day hardliner Muslim groups still accuse these traditional dances of promoting LGBT values. They refer to these practices as '*syirik*' (sinful, polytheist). The performers deny that and point out that LGBT modern terminology cannot be applied to them, as they belong to a centuries-old tradition.

Unveiling a history of gender and sexual diversity is therefore imperative, not so much out of nostalgia, for the past cannot be recreated. The goal is also not to represent some ideal type of cultural authenticity. The discussion of gender pluralism is relevant, as it provides moral and political support to the members of the embattled LGBT community in Indonesia, not because it offers identities or role models that they can immediately emulate. Nevertheless, it does help to disprove the claim that same-sex and transgender practices are a foreign import. Moreover, the realization that they have a history helps to infuse the lives of gay and *lesbi* Indonesians with meaning. In a meeting with members from the Ardhanary Institute in a mall in Jakarta, Pejaten Village, they proudly shared their new discoveries of transgender deities in Kalimantan, the Mahatala Jata, discussed in the previous chapter. It helps them to know they are not the only or first ones, and that they belong to a tradition. But they realize that this knowledge does not help them on the streets, for people do not want to know about these historical examples of gender diversity.[125]

A genealogy of past practices can help recreate echoes of the past which resonate in present-day sex-gender regimes.[126] Members of the LGBT community can find moments of inspiration in the rich cultural heritage of the archipelago and recreate that in their own organizations or in art forms. Tradition is often invoked to justify a certain normative order, but tradition is based on selective memory and subject to political and postcolonial mythmaking. Those who do not live their gender or sexuality in accordance with prescribed norms are at risk in the political order they inhabit.[127]

4

Delicious sins: Growing visibility

Introduction

The particular form of heteronormative marriage practised in Indonesia today is largely a product of the authoritarian and repressive New Order period (1966–98). Under the preceding Sukarno regime (1945–66), members of the powerful, socialist-feminist women's organization Gerwani had fought for women's rights in marriage, the economy and politics.[1] LGBT issues, as attention to gender diversity and same-sex practices are nowadays called, hardly played a role in public life. In the first decades after national independence only trans MTF persons received attention. Women in same-sex relations remained invisible until in the early 1980s lesbian relations came into the public sphere via media accounts of two marriages between women. Following these accounts Lambda Indonesia and the first lesbian organizations were established, Perlesin (Persatuan Lesbian Indonesia, Union of Indonesian Lesbians) and Sappho. They were short-lived, but the group of women who gathered in these groups kept in contact with each other. Perlesin was built around b/f couples. In the 1990s a feminist-lesbian organization was set up, Chandra Kirana.

Political developments: The politicization of sexuality

This chapter covers two major historical periods, the presidencies of Sukarno and of General Suharto. These two phases of Indonesia's postcolonial history were sociopolitically different, the pivotal moment being the night of 1 October 1965. In the early hours, soldiers abducted six top generals and one lieutenant – acting on false rumours of a coup these generals intended to implement. The plotters wanted, so they stated, to bring the generals before President Sukarno. Instead, three of the generals were killed immediately and the others were murdered by soldiers in a field belonging to the airfield near the hamlet of Lubang Buaya.[2] General Suharto, who knew of the actions of the soldiers, quickly crushed the affair.[3] A few leaders of the PKI were also involved in this '30 September Movement', but the party as a whole was oblivious to these plans. Suharto called the event a coup and proceeded to organize a genocide of still-unknown dimensions.[4] His troops imprisoned hundreds of thousands of people, and within a year the general had managed to seize power from President Sukarno. This is often called a 'creeping coup'.[5]

This violent takeover of government, resulting in the transfer of power from President Sukarno to General Suharto, was accompanied by a propaganda campaign to incite Muslim, Christian and other conservative mass organizations to participate in the mass killings. Suharto blamed the entire PKI and its supporters for the murder of the generals and alleged that they were opposed to religion and the national philosophy of Pancasila.[6] Through the media, which he controlled, he also accused young girls of around thirteen or fourteen years of age, who belonged to various PKI-affiliated organizations, of having seduced the generals by performing, unclothed, a lurid dance, the Fragrant Flower Dance, while singing the 'communist' song *Genjer-Genjer*.[7] The girls were charged for allegedly castrating the generals, gouging out their eyes and killing them.[8] This story was concocted to link PKI and progressive, politically active women with unspeakable sexual perversions and to portray the party and its mass organizations as inhuman, primitive and evil. This stigma has endured.

The phobia about communism is still so strong that today's younger feminist activists are often accused of belonging to an (imaginary) 'new Gerwani'. The autopsy, which was only made public in the late 1980s, proved that the generals were not sexually mutilated but killed by bullets.[9] This was the first time that a sexual moral panic was created in the Republic, and it brought sexuality to the centre of political life. This panic can be seen as the template of the second sexual moral panic that started towards the end of 2015, targeting the LGBT community, discussed in Chapter 7.

Over the following decades, state control over women's sexuality, and an emphasis on women's docility as wives and mothers, would become the bedrock of the regime.[10] To be a good citizen one had to be married according to the stipulations of Law 1/1974 on Marriage, which placed men as the head of the household and classified women as housewives.[11] This was formalized in an ideology based on 'family values' (*asas kekeluargaan*).[12] State-controlled women's organizations had to implement this New Order ideology.[13] In 1978 the National Guidelines (GBHN, Garis Besar Haluan Negara) formalized the gender ideology of the New Order: women should always make sure to behave in ways that were in line with their primary roles as wives and mothers. Clearly, LBT persons did not fit this state model. In 1998 the military dictatorship ended and the so-called Reformasi period started.

The homophobic campaign after 2015 links LGBT issues with communism.[14] Yet in the 1960s Gerwani supported heteronormativity as strongly as the other women's organizations at the time. Their members, as 'militant mothers'[15] were very progressive in sociopolitical issues, but monogamous heterosexual marriage and motherhood were central concerns. The only Gerwani leader about whom it was rumoured was a lesbian, Tris Metty, in Magelang, never made it to the top level, although her leadership qualities were highly praised; instead, she had to step down.[16] Gerwani's secretary general Umi Sarjono confirmed that there were a few closeted lesbian women in Gerwani. If it became known or suspected that any Gerwani member might be a lesbian, she would not have been able to occupy a strategic position.[17]

(In)visibility

During the 1950s and 1960s, only MTF transpeople were a visible part of the LGBT community, though not a respected one: *banci* (later called *waria*) were often forced to make themselves more masculine in order to conform to the dominant norms of masculinity.[18] In the early decades of the twentieth century, transwomen had also been quite common. As the anonymous author (1930s) in Hooykaas recorded, in every *kampung*, '*bantji*' could be encountered. They were dressed like women, had long hair and behaved like women, speaking in high women's voices. During the day they might work as washerwomen or as servants or cooks. They lived in harmony with each other in their own world and had their own organization (*perkoempoelan*). In these groups they created their own dance, which is well known, and they performed this *bantji* dance at every festive occasion the inhabitants of Batavia held.[19]

Female-to-male (FTM) transpeople as well as women and men with same-sex desires were mostly invisible during those years.[20] Public acceptance of MTF transpeople began to increase in the 1970s when the then Jakarta governor, Ali Sadikin, offered them protection.[21] Even then, this was only a partial acknowledgement of the existence of MTF people in certain professions, such as hairdressing and sex work. Most men and women with same-sex desires, particularly the women, lived in isolation, tucked away from society by their families because of their 'immaturity' – if that is, they managed to avoid being married off. In rural areas, cross-dressing transgender *wandu* and *banci*, both male- and female-bodied, somehow managed to make a living within their communities.[22] Another common location of male–male sexual practices was Indonesia's all-male Islamic boarding schools (*pesantren*), which will be discussed in more detail in Chapter 9.[23]

A unique insight into the loneliness and isolation of lesbian women in those years is provided by letters by Ger van Braam in *The Ladder*, the publication of the Daughters of Bilitis. Ger wanted to inform the readers of the 'homophilism' in Indonesia.[24] In her first letter in June 1964 she stated she knew only one gay woman, herself. The only gay men she met were 'male prostitutes along the streets, dressed up like women'. Ger wrote she liked to roam at the airport, 'looking wistfully … at the women'.[25] By her looks, she mused, nobody would be able to guess she was gay: 'We're too well concealed behind our masks of conventional habits.' She always went out with straight girls, and with some she became intimate, which was easy as 'they are very caressive of their own accord … but don't make the mistake to get any wrong ideas – they would run from you as if from a mortal danger … They are a nuisance for any hot-tempered lesbians and I have often longed to wring their pretty necks … But of course they *have* to marry'. Ger herself succumbed to the pressure to marry, but after three months 'revolted against my captivity and broke free'. She never loved her husband. 'It was just plain cowardice that made me surrender.' Her family disowned her.

Ger's news in the November issue of 1964 was much more positive.[26] She had found a lesbian friend, and a lover. Rora, the friend, knew some upper-class male homosexuals, who could not believe they were lesbians as they looked 'dead normal', very feminine. She became 'one of the gang but not for long … their one most cherished topic is SEX, and I am sorry, but after a while it gave me a pain in the neck. They are all polygamous – I thought they wouldn't differ from us!' When Ger met her lover, the latter was still married. She soon divorced, and had to leave her young son with her husband. Ger then felt she wanted to contact other lesbians, there must be thousands like them she thought, to share friendship, understanding and the 'enlightenment they so badly need'. She was disappointed in the high-class women's clubs:

> Where the women literally 'commit' lesbianism, just for the fun of it … They are just bored, with too much time and money … Their hobby is maintaining young girls, preferably art students, as their so-called protegees. Of course they ruin the girls and make perfect parasites – or worse – out of them. I know, they tried it with me too … (those hypocritical human vampires!).

The Ladder sent out a call to their readers for a 'Books for Ger' project. For any enlightenment that Ger envisaged for lesbians like her must begin with reading books. She herself learnt about her lesbianism from her husband's books, such as *The Well of Loneliness* and the *Price of Salt*. Those books were not available in Indonesia at the time. They sounded like 'fairy tales' to her, 'terrifying, fascinating and wonderful'.[27]

Ger's letters in *The Ladder* are fascinating. They afford us a glimpse of lesbian life in the 1960s, including the first stirrings of an activist consciousness. Ger hoped to raise the awareness of the many lesbians she knew must exist in Indonesia and 'contribute to their enlightenment', by providing books for them. It is unclear what happened to Ger's project, for shortly after these letters, Ger, her friend and lover, all left for the Netherlands.[28] Indonesia in the mid-1960s was an unsafe place, particularly for those with Dutch roots.

Two other issues come to the fore from Ger's letters. There was a wide gap between gay men 'only interested in sex' and lesbian women. This disparity would also become the reason why lesbian women in the early 1980s could not get along with gay activists. Secondly, class differences are striking. Rich effeminate men have their own networks, while poor *waria* work in the sex trade. Among women also class differences are strongly felt. The rich, bored women kept their protegees, according to Ger, who presumably aimed her book project more at working, middle-class women like herself.

Lesbian friends told me in the early 1980s that in the previous decades, lower-class lesbians sometimes found their lovers in the prostitution areas, while higher-class lesbians were isolated. The vast majority of LGBT people in those years lived a closeted life; the general public was not aware there were gays and lesbians among them. Above the age of thirty most Indonesian gays and lesbians had married. Women often tried to divorce.

Until the 1980s few women in same-sex relationships (upper-middle-class) identified as lesbians. The most visible ones were working-class b/f couples, an identity that at the same time invisibilized them, as it was an intelligible arrangement that neighbours could both understand and ignore. The words they used for themselves were *sekong* (slang for *sakit*, sick) as well as *sentul* and *kantil*, masculine and feminine. Only upper-middle-class women with access to a foreign education or foreign languages had access to information on women's relationships until well into the 1990s.[29]

In an FGD meeting I organized, the meanings of the words *sentul* and *kantil* were discussed.[30] They remembered hearing the term for the first time in the 1960s in the house of Dedi Oetomo (a well-known artist at the time) whose sister was a *sentul*. Dani said it was a slang term, so *sentul* would know one another as 'people of the same profession'. Reza and Yudi, both with a Betawi background, said that *sentul* in the Betawi language refers to a round fruit with a hard chocolate-coloured yellowish skin, and a white, sour content. In Indonesian it is called a *kecapi* fruit. You have to use a knife to peel it, you cannot do it with your bare hands. The association is that this fruit is masculine on the outside but feminine on the inside. *Kantil* is the name of a flower which (with some fantasy) can be likened to a vagina.[31] Its form is coquettish, seductive, the participants insisted.

As Gayatri maintains, in this period *banci* had an easier time than women with same-sex desires, as they were men or used to be men, and because Ali Sadikin (the mayor of Jakarta) helped them.[32] In Jakarta she knew a group called Fantastic Doll, chaired by Myra, a *waria*; they had work entertaining other men. Lesbian women had a hard time at school, finding work and living quarters. As Minister Mien Sugandhi[33] stated: '*Banci* I can understand, they were born that way, but lesbians I think are immoral – after all they can be cured.' This she uttered in a preparatory meeting for the 1995 Beijing Global Women's Conference in Kebayoran Inn. 'We all glared at her.'[34]

But people did not have a high regard for *banci* either. As Hegarty's research demonstrates, it was not so much sympathy for the *banci* who were roaming the streets of Jakarta trying to eke out a living, as a desire to clean up the city, and the imposition of middle-class values, which sparked the concern of the popular mayor.[35] Twice *banci* received a more respectable name. In 1968 the term *wadam* was coined, by joining together the words for *wanita* (woman) and Adam.[36] As the association with Hawa (Eve) and Adam was also made, religious figures complained. In 1978, the term *wadam* was replaced by the term *waria*, formed by combining the Indonesian *wanita* and *pria* (man). This term is still used.[37] Like female sex workers, *waria* were rounded up and brought to rehabilitation centres, where they could learn such skills as hairdressing and (bridal) make-up. The 1968 first Jakarta Fair provided an important venue for *waria* visibility.[38] The first *waria* organizations were supported by the municipal government such as PWI (Para Wadam Ibukota, Wadam of Jakarta) established in 1973. Another organization was Hiwad (Himpunan Wadam Jakarta, Association of Wadam in Jakarta), established in 1969.[39]

Butch women remained publicly invisible in those years; they were not provided with vocational training (e.g. as mechanics or drivers), and they did not have a patron like Ali Sadikin. Only after the beginning of the 1980s, articles of women marriages brought female masculinity and lesbian relations into the public domain.

The transsexual operation of Indonesian Vivian Rubiyanti Iskandar in Singapore in 1973 gained a lot of attention, particularly as the progressive Islamic scholar Hamka offered support. Citing Quranic verses on the existence of so-called *khunsa*, he opined that this was a case of 'mental suffering (*tekanan jiwa*)' that needed to be addressed:[40]

Basically, this is a person who doesn't know who they should be: they are not a man, and also are not a woman! People who are like this, who experience a long period of mental anguish are often teased by others, so their mind is a mess. They are a man. However, their behavior, comportment, and even their mind (*jiwa*) is that of a woman. In the modern era, there is an operation which releases them from their anguish. If *wadam* then decide to obtain gender reassignment surgery, then so be it![41]

In a similar vein Hamka would also assist Bhima, the transsexual FTM person I interviewed extensively in the late 1980s, when he sought an operation, as will be detailed in Chapter 6.[42] Sex change operations were discussed in a 1978 seminar in Jakarta, organized by the Department of Health.[43] They decided that the bodies of transgendered people should not be changed, but the minds of such persons should be aligned with their sex assigned at birth.[44] Psychotherapy rather than medical technology was considered the best treatment.

Literary imagination

In the literary world in those years lesbian relationships could rarely have a happy ending. The only respectable fate for a lesbian was to live in loneliness or die. This is a theme in the iconic 1928 Western novel *The Well of Loneliness* by Radclyffe Hall.[45] The first Indonesian literary text with a lesbian theme I found is a curious book published by Sukanjata in 1956, called the *Homosexual Complot*. Part of it explains how evil and sick homosexuality is, quoting American sources, and the rest consists of short stories with bad endings. Most are about men (rape, murder, neglected wife and the like), but one story is about two women. Warniti is attractive, but not interested in her many suitors. Finally, her parents marry her off to Darmidi, as Darmidi's parents are much richer and he helps them to pay off their debts. But Warniti is in love with Julia, who she considered to be more of a man than Darmidi. They had been living as husband and wife until Julia marries, has a child and follows her husband to another city. Warniti dies of sorrow.

A decade later an author calling her or himself Adinda wrote a novel called *Lesbian*.[46] The cover page already gives an indication of what the reader can expect: a half-nude, worried-looking woman, who has turned her back towards the reader, is approached from behind by a young man about to put his hand on her well-rounded buttocks. The content wavers between titillating sexual scenes, ostensibly for a male audience, and a critique on the moral corruption of the middle classes. The storyline moves from a group of lesbians, whose lovemaking is described in graphic detail, to a group of middle-aged women (derisively called grandmothers) who make out with a gang of gigolos. The husbands/fathers are away and/or highly corrupt, the mother does not care for her only daughter and as a wife she is sexually dissatisfied by her husband. Interestingly, the lesbians set up their own club, called Gateways, after the famous London lesbian club of that name. They are smoking cigarettes and marihuana and drink whisky, combining everything that a modest woman should avoid. The lesbian club, the only one I found in a novel on lesbian love, is dissolved after the protagonist, in a series of unlikely twists, has befriended the gigolo of her mother in order to teach her a lesson, after which both mother and corrupt (and lecherous) father die. This pulp novel (which would never be allowed to see the light of day after the promulgation of the 2008 Anti-Pornography Law) seems to cater to a male audience seeking a pornographic thrill. To what extent same-sex attracted women seeking some way to make sense of their feelings have also read the book is unclear. The positive message the book gives is that its protagonist, Tuti, is unharmed at the end of the book and is portrayed as a strong, actively desiring woman.

In 1994 Mira W. published the novel *The Dark Hollows in Sisi's Heart*. It tells the story of Ailin and Sisi who have a platonic love affair at school, which is suspected to be lesbian. They are separated and forced to marry men. Yet their story is uncovered and Sisi is blackmailed by her brother-in-law. Ultimately Sisi goes to practice as a doctor in a remote place. Exile, abjection and blackmail are directly associated with the 'sinful' practice of women's erotic intimacy.

The first novel with a trans FTM theme I found is the semi-autobiographical account of R. Prie Prawirakusumah, as written by Ramadhan K. H. (1988). Its title is Revealing My Life, the True Story of a Transsexual. Hen feels she is born in the wrong body. She feels herself a 100 per cent man and falls in and out of love with women. He tries to get an operation to become a true man, but for some reason this is physically not possible, so he has to stay a woman. Hen experiences many forms of stigma, but in the end he finds a woman who truly loves him and does not mind that he cannot undergo the sex change operation, whereas earlier lovers always demanded that he become a 'normal' man. In how far these books were widely read and played a role in the lives of individual LBT persons I do not know. The narrators in my research never mentioned them.

Lesbian marriages and their aftermath

In 1981 lesbian life suddenly went public. The first story of a non-fictional lesbian relationship appeared in *Tempo* magazine (23 May). It went viral and was discussed for months, as I noted while searching for lesbian women in Jakarta at the time. This article reported the story of Aty and Nona who had run away from home. Nona was only fifteen at the time, and her parents accused her lover Aty, who was twenty-one, of having kidnapped their daughter. As Aty was a well-known singer, their story gained a lot of attention. Aty and Nona had met in the housing complex where they both lived and had fallen in love with each other. They pledged their love on the Bible but could not find a way to live their love in their own surroundings. They fled home, first to Malang and later to Bali. Aty's mother chased them there and Aty was arrested. She was charged with having a same-sex relationship with a minor (Article 292 of the Criminal Code). This was the first time after independence that a lesbian couple had stood trial. During the court case, Judge Aminah stated she felt 'uncomfortable' with the story. The very direct explanation of their sexual satisfaction was too much for her, so the good judge ordered that they 'clean up' some of their testimony. Aty was sentenced to eight months in prison, with a probation period of twenty months, on charges of indecency. Nona was never detained. Her parents lamented she would never be able to lead a normal married life again. Aty was released after her four months' pretrial detainment was over, and she consented to seek counselling. Apparently, a doctor who had been able to count her 'male hormones' promised Aty's parents that he would be able to cure her condition through injections and if need be an operation.[47]

A week later (30 May 1981) the same periodical *Tempo* published an article entitled 'The Marriage of Jossie and Bonnie', an event which they had celebrated with a large party. Not being able to register their marriage officially, they had thrown a party at the Swinging Pub Bar in Jakarta, with some 100 guests, including their families, who blessed and congratulated them. The two pictures accompanying the Jossie–Bonnie story portray Jossie with short hair, in a man's shirt and a white wedding suit. Both are smoking a cigarette in their informal picture. In their wedding picture Bonnie, in a long dress, clings elegantly to her new husband. Jossie, with 'short hair and a masculine shirt', as the reporter noticed, said he had always felt like a boy. He often got into fights with boys who called her/him a *banci*, but because of his judo brown belt s/he usually prevailed. He had been arrested for rowdiness and in prison met Bonnie, who was there on similar (but unspecified) charges. Bonnie was seen to be a 'normal' girl, and had dated boys till she had met Jossie, the love of her life.[48]

In both stories the butch lovers (Jossie, Aty) are described as possessing male hormones. In Jossie's case, allegedly determined by a medical examination, it was 'revealed' he had 75 per cent male hormones. In Aty's case a psychologist figured out she had 'too many' male hormones, a condition that, the specialist argued, could be cured. Aty, however, did not feel she suffered from anything that needed healing. The defence counsel, Mrs Sri Kusumastuti, argued that both women suffered from a mental illness and thus could not be prosecuted, but that argument was not accepted. However, as discussed above, this was the conclusion that the participants of the 1978 seminar reached.[49]

These articles created a stir. They were the first ones to detail sexual relationships between women, in a well-respected national magazine. As far as I know, they were also the first articles in which homosexuality was acknowledged, apart from the transgender trope of the *banci/waria*. This was also noted by the young gay researcher Dede Oetomo, hailing from the conservative East Javanese heartland (Pasuruan), who wrote a positive letter about 'our lesbian sisters' which was published in July 1981.[50] He came out publicly at the same time. As I was in Indonesia, I also decided to send a letter to the editor of *Tempo*, to refute the many biases in the reporting. I wrote that far from such relationships being 'abnormal', research had indicated that between 5 and 10 per cent of women feel sexual attraction to other women. Lesbian love should thus be seen as quite 'normal'. There is nothing wrong with these women, I stressed, neither mentally nor physically. People have the right to be happy with partners they choose themselves. It is society that oppresses lesbian women and that needs to be cured. The complicity of doctors and psychologists with the stigmatization of lesbian women must be exposed.[51] This again triggered reactions, both hate mail,[52] and requests for more information.[53]

At the time, we discussed the issue with three of my friends, all three prominent feminist intellectuals – Marianne Katoppo, Julia Suryakusuma and Toeti Heraty Nurhadi – and decided that they would write another letter to the editor to deal with the negative reactions to my letter.[54] The authors denounced the emotional reaction of the male authors of the responses, who claimed to know that the character of the Indonesian people was always heterosexual. Issues like human rights are not limited to the Western world, they stressed. The intimacy among women that is common in Indonesia can be seen as an example of the 'lesbian continuum'.[55] They denounced the patriarchal character of heterosexual marriages. This was the first time such opinions had been publicly voiced in Indonesia, and they remain relevant today.

This debate triggered a warm appreciation among lesbian women. None of them reacted publicly to the trickle of articles and letters to the editor, but among themselves they discussed the publications heatedly. When, later in the year, I met lesbians in Jakarta for the first time, they proudly reminded me of the letter in which I had defended them so strongly.

Apart from the discussions in *Tempo*, the *Surabaya Post* of 11 June 1981 published a letter in which the attitude of Indonesian doctors who still considered homosexuality a sexual deviation was deplored. They should know that the American Psychiatric Association had already in 1973 deleted homosexuality from its list of mental diseases, the author advised.

Those first articles raised moral and legal issues around women's same-sex relations in a relatively open way. They can be seen as motivating forces for gay and lesbian organizing. Both Lambda Indonesia, established by Dede Oetomo, and Perlesin, trace their origins to these public conversations. In his letter to *Tempo*, Oetomo, who was studying at Cornell University in New York State at the time, called upon gays and lesbian sisters to build an LGBT movement. With two other gay men he co-founded Lambda Indonesia on 1 March 1982. Lambda Indonesia was one of the first groups in Asia to organize openly. As Oetomo later explained, the three of them felt that they needed to address the questions that came up in the 'agony aunt' columns in response to the *Tempo* articles, instead of them being responded to by outsiders. Replies in these columns tended to be along the lines of 'get pure', 'find a shrink' or 'pray more'.[56] Lambda Indonesia published a newsletter, *G: Gaya Hidup Ceria* (G: Happy Life Style), from 1982 until 1984.

In reaction to the letters by me and the three feminist intellectual women, Dede Oetomo wrote us an enthusiastic letter.[57] He had wanted to include lesbian women in Lambda Indonesia, but so far, he lamented, lesbians had not come forward. As the Lambda Indonesia organizers had felt that it would not be ethical that they as gay men fought for the emancipation of lesbian women, they had decided to become an organization for gay men only. But now with these letters from us, he hoped lesbians would come forward. He included a membership form in the letter, asking for it to be distributed among the lesbians we might know. He closed his welcoming letter with the request to send those forms to his home address in Pasuruan, as his friends in Lambda Indonesia were not very interested in issues relating to lesbian women. Dede remained an ally of lesbian groups, but he could not prevent lesbians who finally joined Lambda Indonesia, including Gayatri and Syarifah Sabaroedin, from leaving the organization within a year, as they felt their issues were neglected. Lambda Indonesia held its last congress in Surabaya, in 1986, where Gaya Nusantara was founded by Dede and colleagues, an organization that still exists.[58] Dede went on to become one of the bravest gay activists and scholars in Indonesia, even running for public office.[59] In 2007, Yulianus Rettoblaut (Mama Yuli), chair of the All-Indonesia Waria Forum, ran to become commissioner of Komnas HAM.[60] In 2012 both Mama Yuli and Dede Oetomo tried again, and failed.

The presence of lesbians in Gaya Nusantara was a brief affair, as lesbians from Bandung complained there was not a single session devoted to lesbian issues during the Second Lesbian and Gay Congress, held in Bandung in 1995. The input of Chandra Kirana was ignored, and the lesbians present withdrew their participation.

More articles were produced about lesbians in the following years, the reporting becoming more negative. In 1983, the popular periodical *Zaman* carried a story on a day in the life of the actress Joice Erna.[61] She openly lived with her butch lover and Erna's children. Joice observed that most lesbian actresses were not honest about their love lives: 'They are hypocrites, don't want to acknowledge their true selves. They are pure (*suci*). Yet they regularly meet each other in a certain restaurant in Central Jakarta.'[62]

The following week *Zaman* published an article in which several lesbian couples were portrayed. These lesbians often congregated in restaurants such as the Java Room in Hotel Indonesia, or in discotheques, where they could find 'new prey' (*mangsa baru*), in the reporter's words. The victims thus ensnared were lonely women, who had recently been hurt by their male lovers, and who were just trying to have a good time or who wanted to have a more sensational sex life, in the analysis of the author. Most of the women who were trapped, the reporter wrote, were those who resented their former lovers. As Joice Erna, who had been married twice, stated, 'Men are only out for their own sexual pleasure ... while [my lover] prioritizes my pleasure rather than hers.' The journalist wonders whether these women could be cured if men behaved more gently? 'No, it is not so easy,' one of the femme lesbians, Gadis, quipped, 'There are issues that I cannot explain to you.' Yet both Gadis and Joice were aware that their same-sex relationship was a sin and condemned by society, they stated. 'But I have already gone too far in enjoying this delicious (*lezat*) sin,' said Gadis smiling. The author concluded that their butch lovers were *lesbian kelas berat* (heavy-class lesbians) who were predestined to their fate. They behaved like boys from an early age on, or had male hormones.[63]

The articles in *Zaman* in 1983 invoked the spectre of preying butch lesbians, ensnaring innocent or naïve ostensibly 'normal' women. Interestingly, and this is a theme that will be discussed at more length in Chapter 6, femme sexual agency is evident. In contrast to the unsatisfactory sex the women had had with their male partners, with their butch partners they engaged in delicious sex.

Perlesin

By the early 1980s the lesbian community consisted of several overlapping informal networks. While middle- and upper-class lesbians could meet each other in cafes, lower-class lesbians, most of whom were in a b/f relationship, met at friends' houses. There were various forms of overlap, for instance, when young attractive butches were sought out by femme actresses or singers, or by older rich women, who were either divorced or whose husbands did not care that their wives had a woman lover.[64] The community in Jakarta I got to know in 1982 moved in strongly homophobic surroundings. They were faced with various forms of discrimination related to their families, education and work. The butches were stigmatized for their particular form of gender ambiguity. The words most commonly used to describe themselves were *cewek/cowok* (Betawi for woman/man) or *kantil/sentul*, femme/butch.

Although embattled, they had created a culture of resistance by their sheer existence as a community of butch/femme lesbians. As in other femme/butch communities, the butches defied convention by usurping male privilege in their appearance and sexuality. By association with their butch lovers, the femmes of the group defied public opinion as well, signalling they did not want heterosexual male-bodied persons for their sexual gratification.[65]

Sentul formed the core of the lesbian groups. They would bring their *kantil* with them to the house of the friends where they met up. They had fun with each other, gossiped, played cards, smoked weed sometimes.[66] The core group in Teuku Umar consisted of around ten *sentul*. This is the community I joined in the early 1980s. There were other such groups. In Kebayoran Baru another community of lesbians gathered. In Kebon Jeruk a group of women of Chinese descent convened. They knew Sem, in whose pavilion the Teuku Umar group convened. Sometimes they went to the disco Tanamur (in Tanah Abang Timur). Some formed a relationship with the hostesses there, the night butterflies (*kupu-kupu malam*). Generally, according to my friend Syarifah with whom I visited the Teuku Umar group and the discos they sometimes attended, the *sentul* found it easy to attract a *kantil* (femme). They were proud of their lovemaking skills, it was their social and sexual capital. They themselves needed company, an arm around their shoulders, emotional support, love – for they had invariably been ousted by their families. So they tried to be the best lovers as they could possibly be. If those relationships broke up, they would be devastated, some would smoke even more *ganja* (weed), or take to drinking. Some even threatened to commit suicide.

They were a close and supportive group; if one of them had money he would buy cigarettes and coffee for the whole group. Money was always a major issue – it was hard for them to get a good job. They respected each other, and their code of chivalry included never to seduce the *kantil* of one of their *sentul* friends. The *kantil* (femmes) usually had more money, they could do high-femme work and go undetected as lesbians. They might be cosmetics or perfume salesgirls. They were like a family. The place in Teuku Umar was their home, they could always come together, even sleep over. They found peace with each other. They would borrow each other's clothes, eat simple food. They told me they were happy in their subculture, but they had to follow rules they had set themselves. The *sentul* were not allowed to have two permanent lovers, polygyny was no go. The other *sentul* would not allow it. But *jajan*, a one-night stand beside a permanent lover, was allowed.[67]

While in 1982 Dede Oetomo was setting up Lambda Indonesia from the United States, this group of lesbians in Jakarta took the initiative to establish the first truly indigenous Indonesian homosexual group, Perlesin (Persatuan Lesbian Indonesia, Indonesian Lesbian Association). According to Syarifah (Ifa), who was close to them, two *kantil*, the dynamic Lusi and Neno, Sem's lover, took the initiative. They suggested that instead of everybody smoking *ganja* and playing cards, they should set up an organization. If anybody then had a problem, the organization as a whole could help. They were both in sales promotion in one of the new malls that were popping up all over Jakarta. They knew Lies, the butch driver of Abraham, a lawyer, who agreed to support them and allowed them to meet in his garage. Ifa never liked him, and others of the Teuku Umar group also distrusted him. What were his own interests? Did he want to sell their stories to the press?

In 1983 I attended a meeting with Ifa, where membership forms were handed out, which had to be filled in with a picture attached. There was fear that these forms could be used to blackmail them, so no form was filled in at the time, and Abraham became very frustrated. Another issue was that initially the butches felt that as they were the only 'true' lesbians, '100 per cent lesbians', as they said, they would not allow their femmes to join. Femmes were fickle, they could go back to leading 'ordinary' lives at any moment. Ifa and I suggested that the femmes should be asked their opinion, and giggling they all stated they wanted to join Perlesin as well. Ryan, one of the butch leaders, had composed a poem for the occasion, which is reproduced in the beginning of this book.[68]

A slightly different version of the establishment of Perlesin was provided by some former members in a focus group discussion I held with them in 2003. According to Agung the initiative to form Perlesin came from Pak Abraham in 1982, who asked Agung to become the first chair. Their first meeting was also attended by *kantil*. To raise funds they went to hotels, on the advice of Abraham, to collect empty bottles and newspapers, which could be sold. They held several meetings in 1982 and 1983 and formed a leadership with a vice-chair and a secretary. The meetings lasted until deep into the night and Agung became exhausted. He stepped down to become an ordinary member; but without a chair Perlesin collapsed. It had only lasted six months. Later in 1983 Lies tried to revive Perlesin, but her attempt failed. In 1996 a similar effort was made, which also came to nothing. After Perlesin broke up, the informal group in Teuku Umar went back to their ordinary activities, until the owner of Sem's pavilion wanted to use it for his own purposes, after which they became dispersed, and lost contact with each other.

Two other interesting issues arise from this brief history of Perlesin. First, Perlesin members had intended to visit women's prisons and old age homes and to provide the inhabitants with instant noodles, so that society would see they had good intentions.[69] They wanted to be seen as good national citizens, not as perverts.[70] Second, in this narrative, constructed by the butches from Perlesin, the role of the *kantil*, who took the initiative according to Ifa, is downplayed. Agung claimed agency for the butches, and particularly for himself.

Sappho

After Perlesin was disbanded, some members attended the lesbian meetings at Lambda. Around 1983, a butch called Angky invited them to the house of Joice Erna in Kelapa

Gading to discuss the issues about Lambda, as they did not feel there was space for them there.[71] During the first meeting, which was attended by some twenty people, a name for this group was selected, Sappho, and a board was created with Angky as chair. Each member would contribute Rs 15,000 per month. In the first year they managed to collect Rs 135,000 from their own contributions, at the time a substantial sum of money.

When in 1984 Sappho was formerly established, it consisted of former members of Lambda; some former members of Perlesin, such as Tomi, Aris and Dedi; and some women from a lesbian group in Teungku Cik Ditiro. Besides Angky as chair, Peggy was the treasurer and the secretary was the lover of Tomi. The initial meetings took place in the house of 'Lady' whose husband was Mr Bill, both Australians. They met every two weeks, until the couple went back to Australia. Sappho attracted members from all over Jabotabek[72] and was a closed organization. They received a contribution from Minister Joop Ave.[73] A beautiful logo was created, two swans with encircling necks.

Sappho once organized a meeting with a psychiatrist, to discuss the latest insights into the origins of homosexuality, in which he explained it was not a mental disease, much to their relief. Psychological support to lesbians was provided in regular face-to-face meetings. In their collective meetings they tried to increase their self-esteem. In Sappho both *kantil* and *sentul* came together and discussed the dynamics of their relationships. A major point of debate was the proposition or argument that 'we are all lesbians, so why must we divide ourselves between *sentul* and *kantil*?' They agreed that the answer was a simple one: 'Well we are like that, we cannot play two roles at the same time!' *Sentul* are *sentul* and *kantil* are *kantil*. In a later FGD when we reflected on these earlier discussions in Sappho, Tomi explained that it indeed sometimes happened that a *sentul* became *kantil* or the other way round, but that usually this change was difficult – they were born that way, it was 'a demand from one's soul', he said, pointing vaguely to some spot in the middle of his body: 'I myself could never become a *kantil*. If because of my work I am forced to wear a skirt I experience great stress. And what does lesbian mean anyway? That *cewek* and *cowok* are the same?'

Dedi joined in the focus group discussion: 'I also want to stand up peeing.' Tomi explained that one's underwear might get dirty. And then said: 'We are always thrown out of a women's toilet. So we always have to be careful when we enter a toilet.'[74]

Sappho was short-lived as well. I have heard several reasons why it ended. Agustine writes that it folded after five months as the sponsor/initiator, a high-placed civil servant, became too busy and there were too few contributions from the members themselves.[75] Aris, reflecting on the demise of Sappho, mused that it was a 'mistake that we invited *kantil* as board members, because when the *kantil* left we dissolved'.[76] *Kantil* at the time left the lesbian groups they belonged to when the relationship with their butch lover was over. Another reason mentioned is that Angky appropriated all the money and disappeared. The butch members were very disappointed. They needed that money to be invested in an income-generating enterprise, like a motorcycle workshop. Angky was supposed to arrange that money, she had told them that she had good contacts with COC Holland,[77] but whether she succeeded in getting funds from the COC or not, no money was ever turned into an income-generating activity. They therefore tried to retrieve the money they themselves had contributed, as well as whatever was left of the funds. Dede helped Dedi, Dani, Peggy and Mo to confront Angky, but to no avail.[78] Angky could not explain what had happened to the money. They scolded her: 'You only became chair to make use of us.' Angky stepped down, but it was rumoured that three years later she still received money from Holland.

The previous system of more informal networks was then revived, and Dani invited the group of b/f couples to her house in Bukit Duri.[79] Dedi himself at the time also longed to set up a foundation, but was too busy making a living to get around to it. He was in good circumstances then, had a salon and at one time threw a birthday party with around 100 people. Most participants were from the fringes of society, but there were also doctors and police officers. Yes, Dedi said proudly, 'I make friends easily. We might go to the gay night of a club. There are usually very few women there, but when I see a *sentul* I go to shake his hand and say hallo. So then we know that we are '*satu propinsi* (one province).'[80]

Though Perlesin and Sappho did not last long, former members kept meeting up with each other. They dispersed into smaller groups. One group first met in Trebor, Pasar Minggu, and later in the house of Yudi, in Srengseh Sawah. As the latter place was far away, it attracted fewer participants. They went back to their old habits, playing cards, gambling, drinking alcohol, finding lovers. But, as Jack explained, it was nice for we 'were in our own world. Outside of that we felt stressed, harassed. Among ourselves we felt free.'[81]

The bad experiences with Angky lingered a little, but the memories of organizing as lesbians lasted. Agustine and Dian, who were thirteen at the time Perlesin was established and lived in Bandung, had heard of the organization and longed to meet the members. That only happened in 1991, when Agustine met Angga, the lover of one of the former Perlesin members, and joined the meetings in Srengseh Sawah. When Agustine later became active in Sektor 15 of the KPI, as will be discussed in the next chapter, many of the former members of Perlesin and Sappho joined. A few of them attended the first training programme on sexuality that KPI organized in the Puncak, Ciloto, in 2002, in which for the first time I trained activists in issues of sexuality and sexual rights.

Chandra Kirana

From the early 1990s onwards lesbian organizing got a new impetus from mostly middle-class, educated women, with connections to the outside world. They also reached out to women beyond Jakarta.[82] In 1991 Chandra Kirana was founded by three women, Djuna (design of motto and newsletter), Rosawita (national coordinator) and Gayatri (in charge of international contacts and research). They were joined by Agustine, as the newsletter editor and also in charge of contacts with grassroots women, Dian as treasurer and Tari. From 1992 activities started.

Rosawita made contact with Dede Oetomo for collaboration with Gaya Nusantara, as they intended to produce a bulletin, *Gaya Lestari* (*GL*). During the years 1992 and 1993 they talked for months. What strategy to choose to reach out to lesbians from all social classes? How to break the isolation of lesbians? And the patriarchal violence they were confronted with? How could they help lesbians who had no one to turn to for their questions about their sexuality, their orientation? They often went to Bandung, where a group of upper-class lesbians met in hotels. In Jakarta they met lower-middle-class lesbians in malls. The poorer ones they approached on the streets. Gayatri, steeped in traditional Javanese culture, came up with the idea for the name of Chandra Kirana.

Chandra Kirana did not have a formal membership structure. The ambitions were high. Initially they wanted to form a network consisting of several Chandra Kirana working groups (Kelompok Kerja Chandra Kirana, KKCK) of lesbians in all (then) twenty-seven provinces of the archipelago, to provide information and to establish a lesbian culture.[83] As such they were the first outward-looking political lesbian organization in Indonesia.[84] As arranged with Dede, *GL* would appear as the lesbian section in the bulletin of Gaya Nusantara (*Gaya Nusantara*). The advantage was thought to be that many lesbians had gay friends and would read *Gaya Nusantara* at their friends' houses. The bulletin would also be published independently. The idea to establish an English-language Chandra Kirana Newsletter followed from a meeting with the Asian Lesbian Network (ALN). The first edition of *GL* was published in July1993.

Rosawita, who still lived at home, stepped down in 1993 after the publication of their second bulletin, due to family pressure. Also, her lover was jealous, as the meetings of the Chandra Kirana collective lasted until late at night on Fridays, usually in Gayatri's house, after which they went out. The Chandra Kirana members identified as lesbians. They held endless discussions on terminology. The terms that lower-class women used were still *sentul* and *kantil*, and also *ine-lilak* for femme-butch. The masculine partners also used the term *dinan*, slang for *banci*, for themselves. The femmes did not use the term *perempuan* woman, to refer to themselves, but *prewong*. Chandra Kirana members held long discussions on b/f issues. A major question became whether to accept femmes. The butches reminded themselves of the problems in Sappho's board and blamed the femmes for the separations and jealousies which caused lesbian groups to repeatedly break up. Their own role in those fights was downplayed.

Several women who joined the Chandra Kirana Friday night meetings had attended Perlesin or Sappho meetings. Gayatri said that they tried to empower those who came. Young Agustine was very quick in the uptake. The collaboration with Gaya Nusantara, however, did not go smoothly. Rosawita, who had initiated the contact, soon became tired as the gay men always expected them to follow their instructions. She found them patriarchal and more interested in finding lovers in the clubs where they held their meetings than in political discussions. They could not get along either with IPOOS (Ikatan Persaudaraan Orang-Orang Sehati, Network [to establish] Friendship among People with the Same Heart), to which Agustine had belonged. This gay group had a Betawi background. In 1995 Djuna also stepped down.[85]

In 1994 the last and sixth edition of *Gaya Lestari* appeared. The last meetings of the collective ended in 1996. For many the pressure under which they lived had become too much to bear. They all became scared when Budi, a well-known TV anchor, was sidelined, after an interview in which she was outed.[86] In 1994 two members planned to attend the ALN meeting in Taiwan, in preparation for the 1995 Beijing World Conference on Women. But not enough funds for their travel were found. After Chandra Kirana's demise Gayatri tried several times to regenerate the group. She gave up in 1998 when the KPI had established its Sektor 15, where Agustine soon started to play a central role.[87]

Chandra Kirana members established important international links, with ALN, ILIS (International Lesbian Information Service)[88] and ILGA (International Gay and Lesbian Association), as well as with IGLHRC (International Gay and Lesbian Human Rights Commission). The English version of the _GL_ bulletin, which carried the group's name, Chandra Kirana, did not last long. It was difficult to get contributions for the magazine, and a small core group of writers produced most articles. Most writers used a pseudonym; for instance, Maya, who would later set up Swara Srikandi, used the name Milablu. In the end six editions of _Gaya Lestari_ were produced, of which the first two were published in _Gaya Nusantara_. The four independent issues of _GL_ were a modest, stencilled bulletin of a few pages. They contained both longer essays, poetry, personal recollections and letters to the editor. In this last section issues like coming out and how to meet other lesbians were discussed.

The third edition of October–November 1993 contained an article about the loose association of Chandra Kirana with IPOOS in Jakarta, which organized monthly meetings in Jakarta. One hundred copies of this first independently produced issue of _Gaya Lestari_ were printed. It was the first independent Indonesian lesbian periodical. One (anonymous) reader was proud that the link with _Gaya Nusantara_ had been severed, for she wanted a modest, but high-quality lesbian periodical. The pages of _GL_ were 'polluted by the tacky illustrations of questionable quality (_picisan yang berkesan norak_)' in the _Gaya Nusantara_ periodical, and were rather pornographic at that, she asserted.

With Gayatri's network an international, rights-based feminist approach was introduced. Women's rights as human rights were discussed in this issue, for instance, the right of lesbians to form a family and raise children, including through artificial insemination. A call was included for lesbians to join the discussions around the preparations for the 1995 Beijing Conference.

The next edition (IV, February 1994) contained a short account of the first Gay and Lesbian Conference in Indonesia, in December 1993, which was attended by twenty-six men and two lesbians, Gayatri and Rosawita. _Gaya Lestari_ editor Kenia (pseudonym of Agustine) contributed an article on 'lesbian existence', to 'dispel the wide ranging societal views on the topic … there are those who feel that lesbians are not on the right path, violate the women's code of conduct/nature … there are people who judge that lesbians are dirty, not natural.' The consequence of these negative opinions, writes Kenia, is that lesbians feel 'cursed' (_dikutuk_), become shy and feel they are doing something wrong, and have a low self-esteem. Kenia explains that homosexuality has long been deleted from the list of mental illnesses.[89] Homosexuality, Kenia stresses, is just a variation in sexual orientation, some are hetero, others are homo. In Indonesia lesbianism is not prohibited between two consenting adults. She concludes that in some countries homosexual relations are legally accepted, but that in Indonesia marriage equality is a long way off. Many of the issues she raised are still relevant. They would have been new and exciting to many readers.

In the fifth edition, of April 1994, the writing team included an author who calls herself Melankolis Queen. There was a long article on the 25th anniversary of Stonewall (1969), explaining that on 27 June 1994, that iconic battle will be celebrated in New York. It also reported that the 16th ILGA conference will be held in New York at the same time, and two Chandra Kirana members are waiting for news on their travel allowances to attend that conference. Gayatri also wrote about the history of the ALN and mentioned that she attended the second conference, in Japan in 1992. She stressed that the ALN is important, as 'we need to search for our Asian roots to prove that lesbianism is not something Western'. In the section on human interest an author called Rion contributed a short autobiographical story about her love affair with Mira, who was married to Franz. The lesbian lovers had been very happy, but could not live together as Rion was unable to meet the material demands of Mira. Earlier Rion had already been ejected from Mira's parental home. Ultimately Mira returns to Franz who is able to meet the needs of Mira, leaving Rion devastated and ashamed. This story recounts the usual butch fear at the time – the valiantly struggling butch lover, hampered by a lack of education and work-related obstacles, unable to provide for her lover, and the fickle femme, who prefers economic security over love.

In the sixth and last edition of *Gaya Lestari*, in June 1994, there was a report on the Jakarta Ministerial Meeting in preparation of the Beijing Conference. Gayatri also explained the origin of their name. In Sanskrit the word *chandra* means eye and moon. Chandra Kirana means the full shining moon, and is the story of Dewi Sekar Taji who looks down on Dewi Anggraini to merge with her, so their feelings can be connected. This, Gayatri stressed, is a picture of the link of two lesbian beings who love each other.

Gayatri was the most outspoken leader of Chandra Kirana, but her leadership style was not always appreciated by others. They complained that she controlled all international contacts and information, and some said that Rosawita resigned after the first newsletter following a conflict with Gayatri.[90] Gayatri was much admired, she was older, a lecturer at a renowned institute. Gayatri was said to keep all incoming mails from the working groups to herself. After she returned from the ALN meeting in Japan she did not share the results. Also, the younger members felt that Gayatri dominated discussions and prevented others from speaking. Ultimately, Agustine, Dian and Tari resigned in December 1994 and only Gayatri remained. The various networks in the regions also resigned, for they were close to Agustine. In 1995 Gayatri made contact again with Agustine to rebuild Chandra Kirana. Agustine hesitated but agreed, as there was no other lesbian organization at that moment. This effort, however, did not succeed.

Despite its inglorious end, Chandra Kirana left a lasting legacy. The ambitious programme to set up a regional network, the bulletins and the lengthy discussions created a community of conscious lesbians, prepared to come out of the shadows when the opportunity arose, as it did after the 1998 opening up of society. A literary offshoot of this period was a book of lesbian stories entitled *Lines* by Chandra Kirana member Ratra M, published in 2000.

Sexual rights during the New Order

The New Order state was built on the creation of a moral panic based on sexual slander.[91] The stability of the nation was seen to depend on a particular model of heteronormativity, the *keluarga sejahtera* (prosperous family) with the wife and mother in a subordinate role.[92] The state was seen as one big family, with Suharto as the head, the Father of Development. Confronting such a powerful and aggressive state carried great risks. As long as lesbians remained invisible the state would not bother them. But their families could still torment them. Some kept up appearances by marrying a gay man. Others wriggled out of arranged marriages as soon as they could. Or they remained single, living an asexual life. The more daring ones tried to meet like-minded women, in discos, public parks or malls. One of the codes they used was the question are you *'lisa bonet'*? Only another lesbian would know the meaning.

In the preparations for the 1995 Beijing Fourth World Conference for Women (The Beijing Conference) lesbian issues were for the first time discussed in a policy setting. The Jakarta Declaration was prepared, to be brought to the NGO Forum in Huairou. For Indonesia the major women activists of those days participated; Nursyahbani Katjasungkana was the coordinator of the Indonesian NGO Forum. When the Minister of Women's Affairs, Mien Sugandhi, was asked her opinion on lesbian women, she answered that indeed it was the right of women to live their lives as lesbians, the government would not prohibit it. But lesbian women need not dream about getting rights.[93]

Three Lesbian and Gay Congresses were held during the New Order in 1993, 1995 and 1997. Important issues were HIV/AIDS, sexual health in general and well-being. Few lesbians attended. While the b/f lesbians I met in the early 1980s were surprised there were also lesbians outside Jakarta, even in Amsterdam[94] higher- and middle-class lesbians might have friends abroad. The first official link with the international gay and lesbian movement was via Gayatri, the Indonesian representative of the Asian Lesbian Network (ALN).[95] The first conference of this network, spearheaded by lesbians from Bangkok, was held in that city in December 1990. Lesbians from nine Asian countries found they had a lot in common, including their invisibility, in spite of women's relationships being represented in Asian (literary) traditions; the unwillingness of Asian feminists to consider sexual orientation an issue; their difficult economic position, particularly of butch lesbians; the difficulties in meeting other lesbians; the obstacles presented by one's family, notably the heavy pressure to get married; the absence of a supportive space, particularly for those lesbians who did not live in major cities; and the absence of representation of lesbians in the arts and literature.[96]

An important development was the growing link with the feminist movement. In the early 1980s feminist organizations were again established. The first feminist organization, Anisa Swasti, was set up in Yogyakarta in 1982. In Jakarta the feminist documentation centre Kalyanamitra was founded in 1984. Syarifah Sabaroedin was the only lesbian there; she was enthusiastic about the group, as the feminists did not 'make her feel that she was abnormal'.[97] But when Gayatri later also joined Kalyanamitra the board became uneasy. They did not want to be seen as a lesbian collective.[98] As feminists they were already under fire, they wanted to prove they were 'normal'. The network of feminist lawyers APIK was co-founded by Nursyahbani Katjasungkana in 1995, one of the first lawyers to be sensitive to the issues of LBT persons.

Class issues played an important role in the nascent sexual rights movement. During the New Order the gap between a class of educated wealthy people, connected to the political and military elite, and the struggling poor became wider. Education and the opportunities for better-paid jobs due to the country's economic development created a growing middle class. Because of erotic attachments the borders between upper-middle-class and lower-middle-class lesbians could sometimes be transgressed. But the differences between the classes remained great.

Middle-class professional lesbians had to remain closeted if they wanted to keep their jobs. It was very difficult for me to discuss their lives of ostracism. In March 1982 I spent a lovely evening with a well-known academic to whom I was introduced by Ifa.[99] Ifa had told me she was a friend and a lesbian, and told her friend in turn that I was a lesbian and a researcher and interested in understanding the lives of lesbians in Jakarta. However, it was impossible to discuss anything related to her private life. On our way back from Ancol, where we had dined, I finally blurted out that it must be difficult to live a closeted life. Ifa's friend snapped back that 'even now people gossip about me behind my back' and that she was sick and tired of that, and then dropped me off at my guest house. But before she drove away, she suggested that I should visit the popular disco Tanamur on Ladies' Night. The next day I tried to make up for my tactlessness and wrote a long letter about female friendships referring to Lilian Faderman, but she never reacted, and the contact was broken.[100] In spite of the great respect for her work as a scholar of Indonesian literature she never became a full professor.

The gossip circuit was relentless. The relationship between a progressive and dynamic minister[101] .and a respected historian was well known. They lived apart, the historian had adopted some children who helped her maintain an aura of respectability.[102] Although I often visited the international library she headed and we established a warm rapport, it was impossible to discuss her private life with her.

Even an out lesbian like Gayatri had to be careful. This is why she did not accept the coordinator position of Sektor 15, when she was invited to take up that position.[103] She had been attached to the IKJ, Institut Kesenian Jakarta, where she was accused of being a communist, and as she was also teaching about sexuality her teaching contract was terminated. At the time the feminist poet and philosopher Toeti Heraty was the rector. She had always defended Gayatri, but by the end of 1998 she had stepped down, leaving Gayatri defenceless.[104]

Around the beginning of the Reformasi period, while high-class lesbians met in private parties, middle-class lesbians met in night clubs if they could afford it or organized parties such as the Halloween party I attended on 27 October 2001. Around one hundred women attended, tickets had been sold out in advance. There was a witch, and two go-go dancers who performed on top of the bar clad in a bra and a short loin cloth, gyrating their pelvises wildly. Some guests wore stylish mannish costumes, others long dresses with low-cut backs. Many others were dressed in more androgynous styles. Dancing was along more fluid gender lines than in the strictly b/f parties I also attended in those years. As time progressed the atmosphere became more raucous, but never aggressive.[105]

The lack of solidarity between rich and poor women in same-sex relationships was keenly felt by the poorer butches. 'Why are poor and rich *sentul* so divided', sighed Dedi. 'Why don't they help us economically? We need proper jobs. We know each other by way of mouth, but there is no support.'[106]

Although all lesbians had to deal with the pervasive homophobia of their society,[107] the effects worked out differently for various groups and classes. Butches had a hard time getting or keeping a job. As they had often been evicted and ostracized by their families, they had no support system to fall back on. Femmes were at most risk to be married off forcibly, which might result in rape.[108] Professional women were afraid that their 'sin' would be revealed and they would be fired.

The media played a major role in the process of lesbians finding each other but also in the proliferation of hatred against them. If the first articles in the 1980s can be seen as disdainful, they at least raised moral and legal issues around sexual diversity in a relatively open way. The journalists were curious about what was going on. When Gayatri started monitoring Indonesian media from 1988 the atmosphere had changed. She reported that a later wave of articles between 1989 and 1991 was more hostile. Media coverage in those years presented a lesbian lifestyle as 'not normal' or as an in-between phase before the women in question had reached maturity and entered into a 'normal' marriage. The more masculine partners were portrayed as going 'against their nature', while the feminine partners were seen as pseudo-lesbians. She found the media coverage in those years sensationalist, focusing on low-life lesbians engaged in prostitution and drugs.[109] The word *lesbi* became a term to be avoided by lesbians aspiring to a middle-class lifestyle.

An influential figure in these years was Syarifah Sabaroedin, popularly called Ifa, who played a major role in lesbian and feminist circles during the 1980s and 1990s, until her early death in 2008. Her story illustrates some of the developments noted above. Trained in criminology and philosophy at the prestigious Universitas Indonesia (UI) in Jakarta, she also studied at Rutgers University of New Jersey and St Scholastica in Manila. She became an influential criminologist at the UI, known for her sharp analyses of issues like violence against women and pornography. A heavy smoker, always dressed in masculine clothing, her intelligent eyes sparkling behind thick glasses, she was a warm friend to many, including me. Prominent feminist intellectuals such as Nursyahbani Katjasungkana, Sita Aripurnami, Debra Yatim and Ratna Batata Munti acknowledge Ifa's contribution to their own thinking.

Ifa called herself a radical feminist and introduced the thinking of authors such as the radical lesbian French philosopher Monique Wittig to Indonesia.[110] Wittig argued that the concept 'woman' only has meaning in heterosexual systems of thought. In her view only lesbians as not-women and not-men are able to resist heteropatriarchy's programming. Ifa was one of the first Indonesian feminists to argue that heterosexuality does not only refer to sexuality, but to a political regime, which in the case of Indonesia is phallocentric, capitalist and patriarchal. With APIK's co-founder Nursyahbani Katjasungkana she coined the Indonesian term *pelecehan seksual* for sexual harassment, which is now embedded in the Domestic Violence Law. Her thoughts on women's bodies, sexual violence and pornography are contained in a book published in 2006.[111]

As mentioned above, she co-founded one of the first feminist organizations in Indonesia after 1965, Kalyanamitra, and was an important influence in most lesbian organizations set up during the New Order. She accepted to become the chair of Sektor 15 of the KPI in 1998, but the practical work of organizing was not her forte. Her main influence was intellectual and ideological. She was one of the first intellectuals to openly discuss lesbianism. She argued that ideologies are contested, and moralities are established on women's bodies. Even her death was an important lesson to her lesbian friends. Immediately after her demise, her family, from whom she was alienated, claimed her house and other possessions, evicting her loyal partner of over ten years, leaving her homeless and destitute. Ifa's friends stepped in to provide for her.

Conclusion

Despite state repression and a stifling social atmosphere, lesbian women have been organizing in Jakarta from the early 1980s onwards. Seduced by the pleasures of the 'delicious sins' they shared, angry by the isolation, societal contempt and the lack of free expression of their feelings, and barred from the enjoyment of other human rights, they came together and set up the three organizations discussed in this chapter. Many problems manifested themselves in this process: tensions between butches and femmes, financial irregularities, the mixing of personal feelings like jealousy with organizational matters, class differences and variations in ways to deal with family pressures and public threats.

The patriarchal heteronormative family regime with its oppressive passionate aesthetics also moulded the b/f dynamics of many lesbian couples. The urban friendship networks of these couples formed the basis of lesbian organizing. Some women who formed Perlesin remained active well into the Reformasi period. In the 1990s the transnational world of gay and lesbian liberation helped strengthen the emerging LBT movement.[112]

In this period experiments with the internet began, though mainly at an individual level and lesbians sought psychological counselling, both to dispel the stigma and to help ease the psychological burdens on them. Discussions started about the differences between butch lesbians and those who wanted to transition. They built up organizational skills and accessed foreign funding.

Though none of the organizations discussed here survived for very long, the activists derived a great sense of achievement from them. Particularly the butches took great pride in their history of community building, sometimes at the expense of the recognition of the contributions and courage of the femmes. The lessons learnt in this period were brought into the Reformasi era. Empowered by the search for an identity that could be defended – by organizational models that would help them fight stigma, harassment and discrimination, and by the struggle for human rights accessible to all Indonesian citizens – activists such as Agustine, Dian and former members of Perlesin set up their own political organizations: first, Sektor 15 of the KPI, and later the Ardhanary Institute. Swara Srikandhi, a middle-class lesbian-feminist organization established in the first Reformasi years, also grew out of the experiences of the later years of the New Order.

5

Shadows in the night: Post-Reformasi identity politics

Introduction

In 2001 the dancer, choreographer, poet and fiction author Cok Sawitri visited her native province Bali to search for a lesbian community. She intended to dispel demonizing stereotypes of lesbians as represented in the mainstream media. She easily found an openly gay community, but lesbians were invisible, like 'shadows in the night'. She was told that the community used a special language, that they could sense each other because of their style and their body language.[1] In this chapter I analyse how lesbian women moved out of the shadows, from their invisibility in New Order Indonesia, and demanded a place in public life. I discuss how the spread of the internet became an important tool, and how, spurred on by the emerging women's rights movement, the language of rights was adopted.

In early 1998, feminist women, disguised as ordinary housewives who complained about the inability of Suharto, the self-styled 'Father of Development', to provide milk for their babies, spearheaded the mass demonstrations that ultimately led to his fall later that year.[2] After a period of great bloodshed and unrest, a certain openness in society developed, including about sexual issues. In the early years of this so-called Reformasi period international human rights laws were ratified and a national human rights law was adopted. Freedom of expression and association were guaranteed as well as the freedom of the media. Based on their earlier contacts, lesbian activists established a close connection with the leading feminist organizations of the time, such as the KPI and the National Commission on Violence against Women (Komnas Perempuan).

Fundamentalist, vigilante organizations also thrived in this period. The notorious Islamic Defenders' Front (Front Pembela Islam, FPI) loudly denounced lesbian and gay activists as immoral, out to convert the nation's youth to homosexuality. Around 2010 their actions became openly hostile and the conference of ILGA Asia, held in Surabaya, was violently disrupted by FPI members.[3]

Like elsewhere in Asia the growing LBT movement navigated between the Indonesian feminist movement, the gay-dominated LGBT organizations and the Western LBT movement.[4] The Indonesian LBT movement differed in many ways from the gay and *waria* cultures,[5] particularly in its greater invisibility, its greater vulnerability in relation to the family, and its stronger links with the women's movement which gave them valuable insights into how patriarchy worked and how gender relations were power relations.[6] The Indonesian LBT movement also differs from the Western movement, with its focus on identity politics and rights, with coming out on all fronts as a critical marker of one's identity, plus its emphasis on marriage equality. In Indonesia coming out is a much more complex and layered process, and after a short period in which LBT organizations tried to gain visibility and wanted to be protected from discrimination, a sharp decline set in and instead of gaining more rights, homophobia increased.

In 2001 Ifa and I visited a community of femme/butch lesbians in Jakarta, some of whom I had met in the early 1980s. They wanted everybody to know that they too had suffered under Suharto's rule. And they wanted to take part in this new democracy that was being built. We decided I would record their life histories.[7] So I did, and I have followed the life courses of some of them until now. I documented the organizations they were involved in, particularly Sektor 15 and the Ardhanary Institute. Additionally, I studied Swara Srikandhi, set up in 2000. In this chapter I analyse the major internal problems they faced, their growing use of the internet and their linkages with other organizations, particularly the women's movement. I also indicate the growing hostility they encountered, as they became more publicly visible. The expansion of the LBT movement was accompanied by a proliferation of identities that women-loving-women assumed. Besides the b/f couple, the dominant model during the New Order, no-label lesbians, transmen, *translaki-laki, priawan* and people adopting other labels appeared. The publication of the Yogyakarta Principles in 2007 reinforced their claims to the rights that other Indonesian citizens also enjoyed.

Swara Srikandhi

In 2000 Wina set up a network to publish the lesbian bulletin *Swara Mitra* (Voice of Friends). The idea was to publish it every two months. Only one edition was initially published because of lack of funding. Wina, Agustine (Bungsu), MilaBlü and Aireen formally established Swara Srikandhi on 4 August 2000; on 30 August 2000 the website was launched.[8] Ree, Bonny and Ade also joined. In 2002 two new members joined the board, Alex and Riper. Swara Srikandhi's editorial team tried to steer lesbians away from a wild lifestyle, as lesbians were always portrayed in the mass media. They wanted to highlight the positive sides of lesbian life. They explained that the name Srikandhi was chosen because this *wayang* heroine has a different sexual orientation but the same capacities as heterosexual persons. Sexual orientation is a matter of preference, they claimed, just like some people love pop music and others classical music. Srikandhi, they stressed, is both courageous (she is an excellent archer) and friendly (*lembut*).

Items on the website included discussions about sexual orientation, religion, and the tribulations of love, such as jealousy and how to overcome a broken heart. Another topic was drugs. They knew that many young lesbians took drugs out of despair and they wanted to help them to give up that addiction. Many people followed the website.[9] The debates were open, with long discussions. Most of their visitors were not coming out as lesbians as that word was sensitive; they called themselves *belok* (the other side) or L. Or they identified as butch and femme, using those words rather than *sentul* and *kantil*. On the website there were many chats on the differences that distinguish who is a butch and who is a transperson.[10] Wina liked the metaphor of a butterfly: 'A butterfly refers to the transformation from a caterpillar to a beautiful butterfly and that is what we want to achieve with our website.'

Much discussed on the website was coming out as a lesbian – to whom, when, how. Usually this was a long, painful process, as it had been for many members of Swara Srikandhi itself. Riper said that coming out was the darkest and most lonely period in her life. She sought help in her religion, went to church, studied the Bible, but found no answers. Her search had started already in primary school. During her high school days she had several crushes on women. Only when she had almost finished her university education in 1997 did she find her first love. By 2003 she had still not come out yet to her wider circle of friends, to her colleagues or her family. Chair Wina was not yet out to colleagues and family either, an issue that contributed to the later rift in the group.

In conversations with me, Wina and Mila said they were careful not to confront directly the negative public opinion about lesbians. They felt it had to be done step by step, they were still too fragile. They wanted to work internally first, to understand better their own lesbian subculture. The website was used as a guerrilla strategy, to strengthen their sense of community and reach out from there. Others were more impatient. Ree, Bonny and Ade felt that they should be true to their mission to familiarize Indonesian society with lesbian life.

Two TV shows on lesbians were broadcast. They catapulted lesbian life into the public sphere but at great cost to the individuals portrayed. The first show was a programme on Trans TV on 10 September 2002. The promise of the crew who had approached Swara Srikandhi was to reveal (*kupas tuntas*) what lesbian life was like. Five members of Swara Srikandhi had accepted the invitation; they wanted to portray a positive message – that lesbians played pool, went to clubs and had a sex life as everyone else. They appeared as individuals, not representing Swara Srikandhi.[11] There were endless debates with the producer, who wanted to film the group in a café. The participants prepared well and they decided not to smoke in the programme though they were all smokers. A suitable house was found to convey the message that they were normal people who aspired to a family life. Dhani, from the Indonesian Knowledge Institute (Lembaga Institut Pengetahuan Indonesia, LIPI), provided supportive expert advice. Bonnie and Ade appeared prominently, surrounded by cigarette ends and tarot cards but also books and a laptop to illustrate that lesbians are studious people, who have not turned to lesbianism because of a heart broken by men.

Other members of the Swara Srikandhi board did not support this show. A difficult discussion on the website followed.[12] Wina explained there had been too little time to prepare (20 September 2002), reacting to a sharp remark by Terkupas (18 September 2002) that the one who held ultimate responsibility had been in deep slumber while they had taken great risks. A conflict arose between Wina and her supporters and Bonnie and Ade. Milablü wrote a biting letter criticizing Wina – you have not come out even to your own family, how can you lead a lesbian organization? Wina, hurt to the bone, reacted furiously and demanded people express their solidarity with her. Personal accusations were hurled both ways. Bonnie, who had taken thirteen books and CDs from the office to copy them so that Swara Srikandhi members could borrow the copies, refused to return them.[13] Vice-chair Mila, who had used the pseudonym Terkupas in this discussion, complimented Bonnie and Ade and withdrew from the organization. All this was played out on the public website, instead of in personal emails.[14] Others supported Wina, who called for a meeting (28 September 2002). Bonnie and Ade could not attend due to earlier engagements and left the organization.

The second TV interview was broadcast on 4 March 2003. This TV7 programme documented the lives of members of both KPI and Swara Srikandhi (Agustine appeared in both shows). The KPI logo was clearly visible. A lesbian couple from Yogya were shown as well, kissing and cuddling, but their faces were unrecognizable. Wina was angry, for lesbian intimacy had been shown on TV while she felt that the public was not yet ready for that. Women touching each other, stroking a naked thigh (leg clad in shorts), all this gave a bad impression, she felt.

They received many positive reactions on their website (women crying to see there were lesbians like them) but also threatening messages from Islamist extremists. These conveyed that it was allowed by religion (*halal*) to cut up lesbians and drink lesbian blood[15] and the hatemongers threatened to rape them with their 'big penises'. This led to a major panic in the group.[16] They also felt they were being watched when they were, for instance, playing billiards in a café they regularly visited. They were becoming paranoid.

A Muslim militant, Iman Prasetyo, directed particularly hateful comments at the members of Swara Srikandhi. This indicates that the homophobia from Muslim hardliners had been present long before the wave of political homophobia started. On 5 March 2003, he screeched: 'They should throw away those penises. Why do they need a cucumber, banana, eggplant or a candle to become a man? Why do they use the attributes of men which are created by Allah for the community of men?' He would come to their houses, as 'drinking their blood is halal, as it is clear they are devils'. And, he added the next day, they are no different from 'prostitutes working in Kalijodo or in luxurious hotels, or as murderers, robbers, rapists and thieves.'[17] Ree took him on in like fashion the next day and called him a 'mad man, a psychopath, and insane person hiding behind religion'. Other insults that Iman used that month included gamblers, corruptors, tax evaders, rapists and abortionists. On 3 April 2003 Iman announced that they would soon organize a raid and kill the women, with knives or guns. And, he stressed, there were many ways to die: AIDS, SARS, or they might have a car accident, or be electrocuted. He revealed he was associated with the well-known Wahabist mosque and *pesantren* Daarut Tauhid in Bandung. Ultimately, he accused them of wanting marriage equality and the right to adopt children.[18]

Wina invited him to an open dialogue.[19] Iman chose the *pesantren* as the location and wanted to exclude non-Muslims. The Swara Srikandhi board did not accept those conditions so that dialogue was never held. KPI chair Nursyahbani Katjasungkana advised that they search for progressive Muslim leaders to counter this terror. They had a discussion with an *ulama* from the IAIN Ciputat who explained to them that there are different gradations of dealing with homosexuality in Islam, and that violence was not advised. They shared that on the website. Iman continued to terrorize them, in the name of the Daarut Tauhid community.

Their personal lives became affected. Ree did not dare to bring her car to her office any more, for the number plate had been visible on the TV screen. The car of another member was involved in an accident caused by another party – who came out shouting at them that they were lesbians, demanding they give up their mobile phones. The femme partner took out her phone, removed the sim card and smashed the phone on the ground telling them to get lost otherwise their heads would be smashed like this mobile phone. There was an accident with a car owned by lesbians; the brake cable had been cut. They discussed their fears with Wina, who wanted proof and advised them to report to the police. But that would mean coming out to the police and the victims were not ready for that. Ree did not feel supported. More threats followed from the Universitas Muhammadiyah Surakarta, and the KPI office was called by the FPI.[20] The content was similar as the earlier threats: their offices would be burnt. There were sexual threats: I have a big dick, you lesbians have never had a proper fuck.

Again, emotions ran high. Wina reacted in a rather authoritarian manner and removed all articles by Ree from the discussion forum on the website. Ree stepped down as a board member. Wina also eradicated Ree's name from the list of ordinary members, accusing Ree of being provocative and spreading terror. Ree indignantly asked for clarification but got no answer.[21]

In the meantime, other tensions had arisen as well. The founders of Swara Srikandhi were committed to fight for their rights. But not all members of Swara Srikandhi shared Wina's ideals of striving to become butterflies. Others wanted fun, clubbing, parties and above all dating. Many of them smoked, and some of the younger ones might wear weird make-up. They were less interested in meetings and discussions.

In June 2003, after they had received a small grant from the Dutch feminist organization MamaCash, they published their second bulletin, *Lembar Swara*, with a coloured front page featuring two swans, necks intertwined. Butterflies were all over the pages symbolizing the transformation from the unattractive caterpillar to a glamorous, free flying being. This issue contained an explanation of terms, such as the difference between a transperson and a butch.[22] Another article reported on the coming out of the American TV hostess Ellen DeGeneres in May 1997. There was nothing like that in Indonesia, the author, Alex, mused: 'Some *bencong*, male-bodied characters, are presented as funny in *sinetron* (romcom). But when a lesbian character is shown such as in the show Setetes Embun (dewdrop, RCT1) she is portrayed as ill-fated, a drug addict and very masculine.'

Leadership problems had arisen too. Both Bonnie and Wina complained that the other wanted to act as the boss of the organization.[23] Wina felt uncomfortable that Bonnie pressured everybody to come out openly, while other members were not yet ready for that. The first step could be taken at Swara Srikandhi (often under pseudonym on the website), then with friends. The organization succumbed under all these tensions and members withdrew. By the end of 2003 Swara Srikandhi had only four members left, of the original fifty. In 2004 Swara Srikandhi was no more.[24]

Although Swara Srikandhi was short-lived, it made some big steps in the history of the LBT movement. Several international contacts were established. Wina joined ILGA-Asia and attended the October 2002 conference in Mumbai. She was elected chair. Nationally they always had a good relationship with the KPI. After all, their board member Agustine was employed there. An example is a discussion they co-organized on 19 January 2003, which I attended, in which an inventory of the stigmas about lesbians was made. They were called abnormal, sinners, not on the right path, violating their *kodrat*, a shame for their families, suffering a mental illness or a contagious disease, man-haters; the list goes on. So, they asked, who would voluntarily choose to live a life with this kind of stigma? It must be their souls or bodies that led them there.

In 2003 Swara Srikandhi reached out to lesbians in Surabaya and established a group there. Though the group was short-lived, some former members of Swara Srikandhi, Surabaya, were still seeing each other informally by 2009 when the Kartini/ Transsign project started. By that time other small LBT groups had also appeared. They kept contact via internet chat rooms such as Klit and Lesbi and on Facebook. Their activities were mainly fun-based and most women joined to find a partner. Jealousies and quarrels often meant the end of particular groups. Due to the lack of a meeting space, they mostly encountered each other in malls or cafés.

In 2003 Bonny and Ade had established their own website, the Lesbian Forum. Strict rules were applied – no hate mails, no personal attacks. Another initiative of the group around Bonny and Ade was the Indonesia Queer Forum (IQF), consisting of themselves, Citra and two gay men (John Badalu and Rizal Iwan).[25] They brought out a CD-ROM on Indonesian lesbians. Women used the site for chatting, finding a friend, a lover or exchanging ideas. The participants were all middle-class women.

In a meeting we had in the Twilite Café, Bonny spoke passionately about doing something meaningful for the community.[26] They rejected labels: 'We are NL, no label lesbians', said Bonnie. 'I may be femme today and butch tomorrow. Why stick to one?' We discussed the split between them and the other members of Swara Srikandhi. The personality clash between Bonny – articulate, defiant and impetuous –and Wina, who is much more careful, played a major role. Wina used to reverse democratic decisions, complained Bonnie. And Bonnie did not agree to the way Swara Srikandhi was spending the money from MamaCash – renting and equipping an office, while people were leaving the organization.

KPI: Sektor 15

The euphoria following the downfall of the military dictator Suharto in 1998 led to many social and political initiatives. Through the cruel slander campaign against Gerwani, the third largest women's organization in the world at the time, any form of rights-based feminism in Indonesia had become suspect. Feminists had set up some women's organizations in the 1980s and 1990s, but as it was impossible to establish progressive mass organizations,[27] their reach was limited. Prominent women's rights activists, many of whom had been at the forefront of the mass demonstrations that led to the demise of the military dictatorship, came together to organize the first mass congress of women after the start of the Reformasi period, between 14 and 17 December 1998.[28] Nursyahbani Katjasungkana was elected chairperson.

I had just returned to Indonesia, after being blacklisted for many years, and was invited to attend the opening day. Together with Mrs Sulami, one of the most vocal surviving Gerwani leaders, we debunked the slander against Gerwani. The delegation of Aisyah, the women's wing of the conservative Muslim mass organization Muhammadyah, left in anger. The hundreds of other participants could not believe their ears. Had they been lied to all those years? Had the generals not been castrated by Gerwani members? I promised to make available the autopsy of the murdered generals' bodies which clearly showed that their genitals had been intact and that they had been killed by bullets.[29]

A delegation from Surabaya[30] proposed that sexual minorities would be included in the activities of the new organization, which was to be named KPI (Koalisi Perempuan Indonesia, Indonesian Women's Coalition).[31] It was decided that fifteen sectors would be established,[32] and that sexual minorities would be Sektor 15. Gayatri attended the congress, and Nursyahbani invited her to become a member of the presidium, as coordinator of Sektor 15. She declined for personal reasons. Instead, Syarifah Sabaroedin became Sektor 15's coordinator.

Ifa set herself the task of spreading the word outside Jakarta, as lesbians all over the archipelago did not have any idea about their rights. The KPI secretary in West Sumatra used her network to find jobs for the *sentul*, but that was the only region in which this type of work was successful. Ifa assisted her by providing advocacy on sexual rights via the *balai perempuan* (women's house).[33]

In 2000 Gayatri introduced Agustine to KPI, and she started to work at KPI in the secretariat. In September 2001 the organization's bulletin *Semai* (*Seedling*) devoted a whole issue to the problems lesbian women face.[34] The KPI chair set the tone with a column strongly arguing that the rights of LBT people are human rights which have to be protected under both national and international law. Syarifah contributed an article about compulsory heterosexuality, which in Indonesia is considered *kodrati* (natural) but which should be seen as a form of violence against women. Agustine herself chronicled the physical and psychological violence experienced by two lesbians.

Agustine invited all her friends from Perlesin, Lambda, Chandra Kirana, Swara Srikandhi and also from informal networks to join Sektor 15. I also obtained a membership card. The KPI leadership provided money for the first training programme for Sektor 15 members in October 2001, with Ifa as facilitator.

On 22 December 2001 a discussion on sex and gender was held in Jakarta, co-organized by KPI and the ILF, the Indonesian Lesbian Forum. Jack from Perlesin played an important role. From the ILF Bonnie attended. Swara Srikandhi was represented by Wina. The meeting was attended by twenty-two people and was facilitated by Myra Diarsi. This was one of the first public discussions on the differences between sex, gender and sexual orientation.

In 2002 KPI organized a two-week workshop on sexuality in Ciloto, for which Ifa, Gayatri, Nursyahbani and I were trainers. Some members of Sektor 15 joined. Topics discussed included genital mutilation (to which many women had been subjected, they discovered) and eroticism. On 9 February 2003 a discussion was held about sexual minorities in collaboration with Swara Srikandhi. This discussion was led by Ifa. One of the conclusions was that patriarchy hits women harder than gay men, as lesbians face a heavier burden of stigma and are often forced into marriages.[35]

Sektor 15 of the Jakarta branch of KPI tried to be the umbrella under which other groups of lesbian women could operate. In 2003 they had two groups, in Jakarta and in Padang, while in Ujung Pandang and Yogyakarta groups of lesbian women were coming together within the KPI but without the formal structure of a Sektor 15 status. Due to lack of funds the Jakarta-based national secretariat was unable to travel to cities outside Jakarta and to coordinate the groups. Setting up a Sektor 15 group in Yogya failed due to a lack of interest in political work and money. Another reason was that women did not want to be seen associating with Sektor 15, for fear of being outed.

Trying to avoid the shortcomings she had noted in earlier lesbian organizations, Agustine carefully built a community. This was not easy, as the various intersecting factors of class, education, identity and age always threatened to break up the group. She had picked up her leadership skills from KPI chair Nursyahbani Katjasungkana, who strongly supported Sektor 15. The philosopher Ifa had promised to write a proposal for funding but did not get round to it, so funding was scarce. The activists were attracted to KPI for various reasons, particularly the political discussions on gender and sexuality.[36] The *sentul* were desperate to find jobs, or small loans to set up a business (Dedi). Irfan, among others, wanted to learn about her rights. Lily joined because she experienced a lot of violence in her family. Why is my sexual orientation prohibited, she asked? Don't we lesbians have rights? Another reason to join Sektor 15 was to reflect on one's identity. And to be seen as full members of society. As Jack stated: 'I feel in KPI I have the freedom to speak out. KPI teaches me to be conscious about my rights as a lesbian. Therefore I hope Sektor 15 will not soon be dissolved, like other organizations have been.'[37]

Rights issues soon demanded attention. In February 2003 they received a letter from the vigilante group Forum Betawi Rempug in which these thugs announced they would attack places where LGBT people congregated during the coming Q!Film Festival (on 18 and 19 February 2003). The KPI chair, Agustine and colleagues decided not to reply to the letter, as that might lead to escalation, but just to inform the staff at those places. In further discussions they realized that their legal position was weak, though consensual homosexuality among adults was not formally prohibited. A major problem, however, is Article 240 of the (then) Criminal Code (KUHP) which disapproves of and warns against living together without being married. Particularly disquieting is the wording that such behaviour can be denounced if it is considered to disturb morality. This phrase can be used by homophobic people or groups to report LGBT couples to the police. The members of Sektor 15, therefore, decided that concerted action was needed and that a network would be set up, the Jaringan Kerja Warna-Warni (Multi-Coloured Network).

On 1 October 2003 a meeting was organized at the KPI office with members of the gay, lesbian and transpersons and *waria* community.[38] It was decided that the National Human Rights Commission (Komnas HAM), should be asked for a discussion and to explain the problems experienced by gay, lesbian, trans individuals and *waria* persons.[39] A declaration was composed which referred to the UN Declaration on Human Rights and the Constitution. Instead of the state guaranteeing the rights contained therein, the members of the lesbian, gay, trans and *waria* community complained that they were accused of being sick, abnormal, sinful, unnatural (*melawan kodrat*), and of spreading

HIV/AIDS. They were expelled from society and suspected of engaging in subversive behaviour and of committing immoral acts whenever they met. On several occasions they had been attacked by groups under the guise of religion and morality.

Komnas HAM, represented by Dr Taheri Noor (vice-chair, Commission of Monitoring) reacted by sending a letter to the Head of the National Police, exhorting the National Police Chief to follow up on the complaints that gay, lesbian and transpeople had made about violence committed against them, both in the household and in society at large.[40] After that more public statements were made, for instance, together with Dede Oetomo of Gaya Nusantara. In February 2005 they protested against a statement of Makarim Wibisono, then chief commissioner of Human Rights, who did not want to include the rights of LGBT people as part of his mandate.

Religion was another hot discussion topic at Sektor 15. The butches felt they could only pray or enter a masjid in *mukenah*, the prayer robe worn by women. For, they argued, we can trick humans into believing we are men, but Allah can never be deceived. But, I countered, you know that your soul is masculine, and that that is the most important innermost feeling for you. Don't you think Allah knows that? If your prayers are sincere, surely Allah will accept them? Do you really think Allah only cares for clothes? Agus and Reza felt I had a point. Why couldn't they pray as the other men did, full of respect, and sincerity, in the clothes they felt most comfortable in? Alvin was afraid that Allah would reject his prayers.[41]

Nursyahbani Katjasungkana, who had finished her term as chair of the KPI, had been elected to Parliament (2004–9). In the second KPI congress in 2005, Masruchah was elected as her successor. The members of Sektor 15 prepared well and they remained visible throughout the congress. Besides Agustine and Lily, Arif, Miki and Sherly also attended, Jack and Irwan came when they were free. Evi had her own stall with great *bakso*. Sri came from Sektor 15 Padang, with Linda and Fara.[42] Boy, a butch from Sulawesi, came with a KPI leader from the region. Among the 600 participants this small band of lesbian warriors stood out. Some participants were supportive, but there were also negative statements, that these lesbians 'hurt Islam'. Lily, Miki and Sherly spoke in the plenary, demanding that sexual orientation be included in the paragraphs on human rights. Their proposal was accepted. They were all delighted with their victory. This was the first time that lesbians had fought for their rights in a public forum.[43] After 2005, activities in KPI on LGBT issues decreased. The new leadership did not provide as much support as the previous presidium had done.

From around 2005 until 2010, when the space started to close again, openness around LGBT issues was at its highest point. On 27 August 2005, for instance, a discussion was held in LSA (Lembaga Sosial Agama, Social Foundation on Religion) on the beauty of same-sex marriage, arguing that *ayat* 21 of Ar-Rum in the Quran says that Allah has 'prepared for you a partner of your own kind'. This Quranic verse could be interpreted to be allowing same-sex marriage, the participants concluded.[44] Of course, this view was strongly opposed by others, such as the chair of Islamic Law at UI, Tahi Azhari.[45] Conservative media, such as *Republika*, vigorously rejected any attempt at legalization of this 'criminal behaviour', especially where it concerned 'professional lesbians' or promoters of lesbianism, such as Agustine who appeared again on TV on 13 June 2005, on Trans TV.[46]

Nursyahbani Katjasungkana started advocating in Parliament on LGBT issues. When at her instigation in 2006 the Bill on Administrative Matters was discussed, she proposed that changes should be made to the identity card that all people must have: a category for transpeople should be added.[47] Although she received no support from her colleagues in Parliament, the issue was hotly debated in the media. She always appeared at press conferences flanked by members of the LGBT community and saw to her satisfaction that members of the LGBT community had become courageous enough to fight for their rights. The political education she had given members of Sektor 15 of KPI had begun to pay off.[48]

In late 2005 the lesbian group in KPI decided to move out of KPI and set up the Ardhanary Institute. They asked Nursyahbani Katjasungkana and me to be their advisors.[49] Reflecting on this move, Agustine pointed out that during the 1998 congress KPI had accepted the importance of lesbianism. Yet she experienced many problems. Though she was a member of the secretariat, her colleagues found it difficult to accept that lesbianism was important. When regional leaders were known to be lesbians they were prevented from taking up leadership positions. She wondered when they would stop saying for pragmatic reasons that we have to downplay lesbianism, and when they would take up an ideological position, in line with the decisions taken in the 1998 congress, which is the highest KPI decision-making level. Without the strong support of Nursyahbani Katjasungkana they did not feel at ease any more within KPI.[50]

The KPI had stuck its neck out in these first years after the Reformasi. Mrs Murpratomo complained to Nursyahbani Katjasungkana: that the KPI has prostitutes and lesbians.[51] The resistance of these conservative, New Order women leaders made the alliance between LGBT and feminist organizations often difficult.[52]

Ardhanary Institute

The Ardhanary Institute was established on 14 November 2005 by RR Sri Agustine, Lily Sugianto, Afank Mariani, Yuyun Wahyuningrum and Erros. They immediately held their first seminar on the unconstitutionality of the discriminatory regional regulations that had been promulgated since 2001,[53] followed by four days of training on advocacy with media, religious institutes and women's organizations. Since the beginning Agustine assumed the position of director. Five divisions were set up: organization, research and publications, assistance, advocacy, and information and documentation. Based on their experiences in the KPI they became an umbrella for other LBT networks, such as Dipayoni in Surabaya, and groups in Padang, Lampung, Pontianak, Makassar, Surabaya and Yogyakarta.

The institute established itself formally, with by-laws which stated its aims. These were to eliminate all forms of discrimination against lesbians, bisexuals and transpeople (LBTs) in Indonesia by empowering LBT persons, building peer-groups and by advocacy for LBT rights. In line with the vision of their role model, Nursyahbani Katjasungkana, they based themselves on the 1945 Constitution, the Declaration of Human Rights and CEDAW, the Women's Rights Convention. Later they would advocate the Yogyakarta Principles, promulgated in 2006.[54] They also wanted to contribute to broader discussions on sexuality and sexual rights in Indonesian society. Issues they addressed included gender-based violence and the statements of the DSM 4 on homosexuality and SRHR (Sexual and Reproductive Health and Rights).[55] They were soon seen as a trustworthy organization and they managed to attract several donors to fund their activities.

Training and education were important components both for the development of the individual members of the Ardhanary Institute and for the growth and maturity of the organization. As many of the members had been evicted from their homes at a young age or had left their families, their formal education had been interrupted. This applied especially to the butches and the transmen, who realized it was hard to find suitable employment. Agustine herself, who came from a well-established family,[56] had lived on the streets, selling bottled tea on trains to survive. Since then she had enrolled at a university where she earned a master's degree in law and is now studying for her PhD. Agustine told me several times that they advised the young butches to try and live with their family if they support them through university, before coming out. Education is key to their future lives.

KPI had started providing training on issues related to gender and sexuality, and Ardhanary Institute activists followed the courses which they could join, for instance, provided by the Kartini Network, a two-week residential course in India coordinated by Abha Bhaiya and me on theory and research methodology.[57] In 2006 I found a small scholarship for Agustine to come for two months to the Belle van Zuylen Institute in Amsterdam, to which I was connected at the time, to pursue her studies on gender and sexuality. Slowly the activists developed an understanding of gender being fluid and contingent, not binary and stable, as the Indonesian *kodrat* prescribes. They shared this understanding with LBT activists all over Indonesia and, especially after 2010, were often invited to become trainers or resource persons at universities or major NGOs like the Rutgers Foundation.

The Ardhanary Institute team developed manuals and slides for these training purposes, as I experienced during a weekend in 2014 with the group Dipayoni in the mountains of Penanggungan around Modjokerto. It rained the whole time, so the young participants gladly huddled together in the central space, the only dry spot at the camping site, where they listened to a programme on the Yogyakarta Principles, reproductive and sexual rights and SOGIE.[58] They perked up by the end of the lecture, which dealt with sexual health. What should they do before making love, they wondered. The advice was to take a bath and cut one's nails.

The Ardhanary Institute made conscious efforts to integrate FTM transpeople into their organization. In Perlesin *sentul* incorporated a broad category of female-born persons who identified as more or less masculine. Gradually those who felt that their bodies and their gender were not aligned – and who did not identify as *sentul* but as men – no longer joined any LBT organization during the New Order, nor did they join Sektor 15. As a result they had no space to meet each other. Around 2010 the Ardhanary Institute started connecting with these people, at first, primarily through Facebook. This was not easy, as lesbian chat groups often rejected the members who came out as 'tg' (transgender), the popular abbreviation for FTM people at the time. In the Kartini/Transsign project several FTM transgender persons participated, both in Jakarta and Surabaya.

The Ardhanary Institute team successfully completed several research projects. Initially these were set up within the framework of the Kartini Asia research on heteronormativity (2005–9) and the Kartini/Transsign team's research on female masculinities (2012–14). After building up their capacity on research methodology and data analysis they themselves implemented research projects on violence against LBT persons,[59] conversion therapy and the five-gender system of the Bugis.[60] They received assistance from researchers at the UI (Universitas Nasional, National University). Several books were published by the team, which were used for training purposes and to make issues of gender and sexual diversity better known to university students.[61] They also produced leaflets and a comic book on issues lesbians faced – health, discrimination in society and the workplace, bullying at school, self-awareness, coming out and love in its many forms. They also provided counselling services and legal aid.

On 28 June 2009 I attended the launch of the compilation of chapters the team had translated from the book Evelyn Blackwood and I had co-edited in 1999.[62] This event showed how far they had evolved in the four years of their existence. Over 135 people registered. First the Ardhanary activists gave a show in which the diversity of several generations of women living with women were portrayed – the sturdy butch with two femmes on her arms, the younger androgynous women, all doing hip-hop movements. Seeing Tomi, one of the narrators of my research on b/f identities, in the role of strong butch moved me very much. Only a few years ago, when I interviewed him, he was desperate – no job, no lover, no future. Now Tomi had become very skilled with computers. He had joined Ardhanary as one of the core staff and had just given his first presentation at the university, as an example of an FTM transgender individual.

Nursyahbani opened the event, explaining the legal situation in relation to same-sex relations. Next, I gave an outline about the social environment at the time of my first meeting with Perlesin. How we had been unaware of the presence of other lesbians beyond our own communities. And how they tried to teach me how to live up to their idea of how a butch woman, which is how they classified me, ought to behave. A co-panellist expressed the solidarity of the Indonesian women's movement with the LBT movement. Other topics included the relation of human rights discourse with Islam and the existence of homosexual birds (such as certain penguins).

The Ardhanary activists built extensive national and international contacts. Internationally they linked up with the APWLD (Asia-Pacific Forum on Women Law and Development) network, to which Komnas Perempuan was linked (Nursyahbani Katjasungkana was a member of the board of APWLD). In 2011, they became a full member of APWLD. In that year a representative of the Ardhanary Institute became a board member of ILGA-Asia, after several members had already attended the network's congresses such as the one in Chiang Mai in 2008. By 2016, when the wave of political homophobia had spread, the Ardhanary Institute had built a broad network with women's organizations such as APIK and Komnas Perempuan, LGBT organizations such as Suara Kita, Arus Pelangi, Forum LGBTIQ and Pelangi Perempuan, crisis centres, healthcare providers, safe houses, and legal aid bureaus. They had also built relationships with law enforcement agencies to provide assistance to victims of violence against LBT persons. This included violence within LBT households.

The Ardhanary Institute has set up its own LBT crisis centre, at a secret location. They collaborate with lawyers from APIK and other legal aid bureaus to assist the victims of domestic violence. They also operate a hotline and provide psychological help. As for young LBT persons school is a very unsafe environment, the Ardhanary Institute collaborated with the One Vision Alliance in a programme to address bullying at school.

The SOGIE model which originated in UN circles was found to be very useful in training sessions with non-LBT persons. By 2010 the concept of LGBT had become common to denote people with a non-heteronormative gender or sexual identity. Societal, religious and political homophobia centred around that notion. Speaking about SOGIE allowed activists to avoid this inflammatory concept.[63] Together with the Yogyakarta Principles they became the core of training modules for the media (in collaboration with the collective of *Jurnal Perempuan*) and law enforcers.[64] Particularly in the period between 2010 and 2015 the Ardhanary Institute reached out to other non-LGBT organizations such as the feminist Muslim group Rahima and the progressive *pesantren* Fahmina.

At the time of writing this book, from 2021 till early 2023, staff members and volunteers from the Ardhanary Institute mostly work from home. Through prudent financial management they have bought a small office in a backstreet of a popular neighbourhood (the street is not accessible by cars, so the pickup trucks generally used in attacks by vigilante group cannot enter). Their public activities have almost stopped; events like the book launch discussed above cannot be held any more.

Contingent and fluid identities

The political experiences of LBT organizations and their members – particularly of activists belonging to the middle classes, and a developing global discourse on gender and sexuality – made the LBT persons in this research reflect both on the fluid nature of desires and identities and on the contingency of their own identities.[65] This section focuses on the period around the beginning of the Reformasi in 1998, when disenchantment with the dictatorship gave rise to new political freedoms which were accompanied with a proliferation of discourses on human and women's rights and on gender and sexual identities. In the 1980s the categories *kantil* and *sentul* were the most common identities available, and most female-bodied persons with non-heterosexual desires related to this terminology. From the mid-1990s, however, a larger range of categories gained currency and discussions on identities widened.

Identity formation is not always a linear process, from confusion about one's identity and one's feelings of sexual attraction to clarity and coming out. Fluidity means that neither gender nor sexual attraction are binary, neatly divided between the axes of female–male and heterosexual–homosexual. In a majoritarian Muslim country like Indonesia in which biological sex and gender identity are strictly divided in binary and hierarchical oppositions,[66] divinely sanctioned, this insistence on the instability of such categories is considered almost blasphemous in conservative circles.

Gender identities have to be negotiated in various social circumstances. Our narrators played with different layers of heteronormativity. If their passionate aesthetics in the 1980s were publicly aligned more or less along established heteronormative patterns, their relationships might blend in and they would not attract too much undue attention from their neighbours. This made it possible for these individuals to be 'proud and out, but not as lesbians'.[67] In the early 2000s this became increasingly difficult as the category of LGBT became more known publicly and as LBT persons themselves became more visible. Among LBT persons these developments led to intensive debates and soul-searching. What aspect of one's identity should one display in which setting? Out among one's friends, invisible at the workplace and in the family?

At the same time a proliferation of identities emerged. By the end of the first decade of the Reformasi the research conducted by the team of Dipayoni in Surabaya captured the diversity of identities among young urban women in same-sex relationships. Of the twenty-two male-identified respondents, three identified as *butchi*, eleven as male, two as lesbian male, two as transboy, and one each as in between, trans/TG, confused/butch, tomboy/FTM.[68] Their partners identified as lesbian (three) heterosexual (nine) or as same-sex (ten). In their relationships traditional gender patterns were dominant: eight classified their relationship as *hubby-wifi*, two as papa-mama and twelve as *suami-isteri*.[69]

Terms that were discussed but rejected by these respondents for public use were *belok* (twisted) and *wandu*, the traditional Javanese term used, respectively, for both male- and female-bodied transgender people. *Belok* was used internally though, as a marker of not conforming to heteronormative expectations. The terms *sentul-kantil* were considered old-fashioned. They also rejected the Bugis terminology of *calalai-calabai*, as too ethnically specific. Transboy or LGBT, on the other hand, were seen as too Western by some. Another term that male-identified LBT narrators were often called was *banci*. It is now mostly used for MTF transpeople. But again this caused confusion. As Agustine remembers:

> At school in Bandung I was called *banci*. My father called me to him and said our neighbours ask me, 'that child of yours, what is it? A daughter or a son? I am ashamed, I don't know how to answer them'. I was fifteen at the time. But I only felt like a *banci* when I was forced to wear a skirt, for instance when we went to church.[70]

One narrator suggested that the term *priawan* should be introduced, but the others felt it was too unfamiliar a term. This word, however, is now widely used. Yuni, a member of the research team of the same 2009 project in the Ardhanary Institute,[71] saw herself as a soft butch lesbian. Other terms used included *lesbong* or *les biola*, and in Surabaya *baloli* (femme) and *balola* (butch). Some felt these terms were derogatory.

The following fragments from interviews the Dipayoni team conducted with male-identified female-bodied persons provide an insight into the narrators' intense internal deliberations. What were they to do with the conflicting messages they received from their bodies, their souls and their surroundings?

Arya: [I consider] knowledge [of being a woman] as merely knowledge and do not internalize it. As long as it is not internalized, this knowledge will not hurt my soul … Soul calling is usually internalized into oneself, although discreetly. It brings a deep meaning to oneself and is harmful to one's soul if neglected.

Nick: I know my body is of a woman, but I don't want to be a woman. A woman has to be feminine and passive. I am masculine and active because I am a man … My soul revolts when people force me to do womanly acts … I am sure that I am biologically a man although other people say I am a woman. I don't care about what people say.

Bonnie: I found many terms for people like me. Some refer to me as *butchi*. On the internet, some categorize me as a transperson or as FTM. Some provide terms like transboy, or transmen. I consider all of them and feel transboy fits me well. It sounds cool although this term has not yet been popular in the [LBT] community.

Jack: Since my childhood I have felt I was a man. When I was in college, I read books about sexuality and suddenly I felt ambiguous about my (sexual) identity. I don't feel 100 per cent man. I am more 50 per cent woman and 50 per cent man. I find on the internet that my feelings have been defined as transgender … I know myself better now that I am a reversed *waria*.[72]

Rio was the only respondent who had wanted to change his body:

I believe that I am a man. I am economically independent now, and I could go to a doctor to help me to be a real man for which my inner calling craves. I have undergone surgery to get rid of my breasts and now control my male hormones under a doctor's observation … I grow a moustache and sideburns.

For most respondents the costs of surgery are prohibitive, but they are also held back by religious considerations. Their bodies are given to them by God, and tampering with their bodies means questioning God's gift. Yet the Dipayoni team reported that they perform their prayers as men and that at the time of death, they ask that their body be taken care of and prayed for as a male body.[73]

In 2022 the situation for Indonesian transmen has not improved substantially. They still face violence and stigma from society and their families. They are still the least understood and discussed members of the LGBT community, despite the efforts of the Ardhanary Institute and Dipayoni. Besides *priawan* they also use the term *transpria*. They have established a few organizations of their own, Transmen Indonesia (TI), founded in 2015; Persatuan Priawan Indonesia (Indonesian Transmen Association); and Transmen Talk.[74] According to Raiz Rizky, the president of Transmen Indonesia:

The fact that most transmen were raised from birth as girls contributes to the 'invisibility' of transmen in Indonesia … In this patriarchal system, people who are considered women are rarely given space … For example, they are vulnerable to rape, such as in the case of rape of a transman by his own family member with the purpose of 'turning' him back into a woman.

During an FGD in 2020 that TI held with fifty-six transmen participants from fifteen regions, the following issues were mentioned: bullying, workplace discrimination and religion-based conversion therapies, as well as open threats from public figures, such as one made by the sharia police agents of the Wilayatul Hisbah in Aceh in 2014, urging the arrests of individuals who wear clothing considered unaligned with their assigned gender at birth.[75]

Intersex?

In February 2010, the LBT community in Indonesia was confronted with a case of alleged forgery of identity. Alterina Hofan (Alter) had married Jane Deviyanti in Las Vegas on 9 September 2008. Alter was reported by his mother-in-law to the police, charged with sexual identity fraud and imprisoned.[76] In the press Alter was sometimes referred to as a tomboy or a lesbian. In the end a chromosome test proved that Alter was an intersex person with Klinefelter syndrome and could be classified as male. He was released. This case sparked great excitement in the LBT community, particularly among the FTM transpeople. Many hoped they might be intersex, so they could be easily classified as male and marry their lovers. The Dipayoni researchers reported that ten out of a group of twenty-seven FTM respondents believed they had male hormones. In an FGD with ten FTM transpeople three felt they had male hormones and one had it tested. As Rio happily explained: 'I checked it out in a hospital in Semarang. The results revealed that there are male hormones in my body. Therefore, I did hormonal treatment. The medical evidence shows that I'm really a man. I'm not a trans.'[77]

Among the FTM transgender persons linked to the Ardhanary Institute a similar excitement erupted. A few had themselves tested, but nobody was classified as intersex. The FTM trans individuals said that they did not want to be categorized as intersex, for the stigma against intersex and transpeople is similarly great. They preferred to claim they were actually biologically (perhaps partially) men.[78] This is an interesting observation, for usually the male-identified respondents in these research projects claimed it was their souls that determined their gender identity, not their bodies.

They tried to erase the most obvious female markers from their bodies, their protruding breasts. The ones lucky enough to have small breasts bandaged them, but this was uncomfortable for those with larger breasts. As Danny confided: 'I do not like my breasts, men don't have breasts. I feel very embarrassed with my wife during lovemaking. I underwent acupunctural treatment. It was expensive, but it was quite successful. My breasts are smaller and flatter when I bandage them.'[79] Their partners are no help. As Joe complained: 'The *pemmeh* (femmes) like *butchies* who have a flat chest. A *butchi* with big breasts will be ridiculed by them.'[80]

To have a manly voice was much appreciated among the male-identified narrators. Reza, the *suami* of Putri, considered himself to be a man. But he did not want an operation, as it would not make any difference to their lovemaking, he stressed. Putri said proudly that Reza often sings *dangdut* songs. But that though her man is so *cakap*, (handsome), he has such a womanly voice. All present burst out laughing, comparing the voices of the *sentul* and admiring Dani's voice, so deep, strong, manly. Agus's voice, they agreed giggling, is actually quite high, feminine, while Agus is such a tall butch.[81]

Three activist couples

The fluidity and contingency of the identities of LBT activists are illustrated by the stories of three couples, who were associated with Swara Srikandhi: Kris and Ree, Heni and Susan, and Mila and Wina. They portray the messy, often painful process of realizing one's sexual attractions, coming out to parents or not, finding a lover and locating oneself in the shifting world of sexual rights activism.

Ree realized she was a lesbian by the end of 1999, when she had just married and could not stand the marriage. Sexual interactions felt like torture. She had always been a tomboy but only when she met a woman at her office did she fall in love. They did not use the terms *sentul* and *kantil* for they felt that these were used by and referred to lower-class or grassroots women. Rather, they thought that they were 'no-label' lesbians. Or perhaps she was a butch? Butches are not as visible as *sentul*, she explained, who are really like men, almost transpersons. Her partner was very feminine. She learnt the words butch and femme in Swara Srikandhi.

Ree's partner Kris said that she already knew from the sixth grade at primary school that she liked women. She learnt the word lesbian from a book she read in junior high school. She had her first affair when she was in the first grade of senior high school, with a woman ten years older than her. Her first full sexual relationship was when she was seventeen years old and had just started university. Within a year her lover died of brain cancer, at the age of thirty. She then had a short relationship with a butch, but they soon broke up because Kris did not like or could not appreciate the male ego her butch lover displayed. At the age of eighteen she started a relationship with a 36-year-old teacher of hers who was already married. Kris ended that relationship as she felt her lover became too femme. 'She started nagging when she didn't get her way', Kris complained. Kris and Ree met in Swara Srikandhi. In 2004 they both identified as no-label lesbian tomboys.

Susan and Heni – in their early twenties, like Kris and Ree, when I met them – had a stronger butch-femme dynamic in their relationship than Kris and Ree. Susan only understood she was a lesbian when she heard a radio programme in 1995 in which some gays and lesbians featured. She then went to the library and found a book on abnormal psychology which discussed homosexuality but not lesbianism. That did not help her. She liked playing sports and boys' games and in junior high school she knew already that she liked women but did not understand her feelings and hid them from her parents. She only realized she was a lesbian after she was already married; she divorced as soon as she could. She started dating women from 1995 and in 1999 had her first full relationship with a femme. She also dated no-label lesbians and once a transperson.

Her partner Heni looks very butch. His mother strongly supported him and advised him to check his chromosomes. Susan was not happy with that: 'if Heni really is a man or becomes a man, does that mean I have a relationship with a man? I don't want that!' They often fought about that. When I met them, Heni had so far not yet dared to check his hormonal level. Already at the age of twelve, Heni felt he was a man and he had sex with a woman. When they were forcibly separated he was furious. His mother told him he was a lesbian. He then had many lovers till he met a woman who resembled his first love. But that woman betrayed him and had male lovers. Heni ended up in hospital after a suicide attempt. Heni was struggling to accept his body, a body that is only considered normal if he would make love to a man. But for himself he knew that was very wrong. 'Sometimes I think I am mad. So I want to be a man for then I will be perfect (*sempurna*) again'. And, he said: 'if God wants to give me a lover, let he be serious about that. My life is a mess. I hate my body. I only don't want to hurt my body because I promised that to my parents.' Heni was torn. Susan, whom he met at the end of 1999, does not want him to transition, yet that is what Heni himself wants, for then his body and sexual orientation would be aligned.

Mila and Wina have been a couple since 1995; both identify as lesbian. Due to family pressures they have not been able to live together. Their parents have always thought that they are just friends. At the time of the interviews, Wina did not even come to Mila's house. They only met at weekends. At work their colleagues did not know they were lovers either. Mila realized she was a lesbian at senior high school. She had a male friend who wanted to marry her. At first she agreed, but as she did not love him she called off the marriage. She was desperate: how to meet like-minded women? She heard about Chandra Kirana in 1994 via Gaya Nusantara and made contact with Gayatri. They had a nice conversation, but then she asked Gayatri not to contact her anymore as she was afraid of her mother.

Via Gaya Nusantara she found the name of another lesbian, who turned out to be Wina. After many letters, telephone calls and meetings they realized that they had fallen in love. On Valentine's Day at midnight in 1995 Mila asked Wina to become her lover. Wina said she had always been attracted to girls, but that she was confused – was she really a lesbian? To test herself and hoping to find a lover, in 1994 she posted an advertisement in the newspaper *Sinar Harapan*, looking for friends. She got hundreds of replies. She arranged to meet some of the men, but she did not feel anything for them, and the women she met just wanted to be friends.

Organizational matters and growing hostility

Managing the funds that became available after the Reformasi required accounting skills which were not always available. KPI had strict financial control mechanisms and the Ardhanary Institute followed in their footsteps. In Swara Srikandhi disputes about how to spend and account for the money led to major rifts. The entanglement of women's rights, sexual health and sexual rights under the banner of SRHR enabled collaboration between women's organizations and LBT associations. LBT activists became resource persons and later trainers in SRHR programmes in universities, the media, the judiciary and various government departments. Advocacy for policies to protect sexual minorities became a major focus for LGBT groups such as Arus Pelangi.[82] Other groups, such as the Ardhanary Institute, also worked on improving portrayals of LBT Indonesians in mainstream media. They collaborated with the prestigious *Jurnal Perempuan* (JP) to bring out an edition on same-sex issues in 2006. It covered issues like religion, human rights and media. Together with members of the JP collective Ardhanary activists visited the campuses of some of the major universities in Jakarta.

After the renewed campaign of political homophobia started, major donors to the LGBT community were forced to halt their LGBT-related programmes in Indonesia. The UNDP and USAID-initiated programme 'Being LGBT in Asia' was singled out as a foreign attempt to interfere with Indonesia's domestic affairs and was eventually forced to cease operations. Government agencies were obliged to place international funding agencies under close scrutiny and told them not to support LGBT organizations. As a result of these funding restrictions, many activities had to be halted and support for LGBT people, particularly for LGBT youth, was curtailed.[83]

The Dipayoni research team, for instance, had been able to assist many young LBT people at one of the most difficult moments of their lives, their coming out. This is a period that may be accompanied by much violence, including sexual violence. In 2012 the Dipayoni team published a collection of short semi-autobiographical stories with this theme.[84] Agustine wrote the introduction. Confusion and misery are dominant in these stories, but when the narrators experienced the power of love for another woman they knew this was the only way they wanted to live. They had to withstand taunts from their friends and the distrust and sadness of their family members. In only one story a mother supported her lesbian daughter. In the other stories the reaction of the parents varied from trying to marry off their wayward daughter to complete rejection and expulsion from the family.

The first major homophobic attack occurred in November 2000. An HIV/AIDS edutainment event involving drag shows in Kaliurang, Yogyakarta, was raided by around 150 men who called themselves the Anti-Vice Movement (Gerakan Anti-Maksiat) and members of the Gerakan Pemuda Ka'bah (Ka'bah Youth Movement).[85] In subsequent years, similar attacks occurred in other places. Two major attacks happened in 2010: an attack on a conference of the International Lesbian, Gay, Bisexual, Trans and Intersex Association Asia (ILGA) in Surabaya by a coalition of Islamist groups; and a raid on a workshop about transgender issues organized by Komnas HAM in Depok by the Islamic Defenders' Front (FPI).[86] The Q!Film Festival which had just started was also harassed.

The last two attacks happened when UN language on SOGIE began to be adopted by LGBT organizations because it was more neutral than the stigmatized category LGBT. In training sessions with women's and human rights groups on gender diversity, the picture of the so-called Genderbread person was popular, as it helped participants to understand the differences between gender identity, gender expression and sexual orientation.[87]

Attempts by parliamentarian Nursyahbani Katjasungkana to enact legislation to protect the rights of sexual minorities failed. With legislator Eva Sundari from the Indonesian Democratic Party (PDIP) she had tried to include protection for LGBT

people in the drafting of the Anti-Racial Discrimination Bill and the Citizens'
Administration Bill. Both bills passed into law without including the rights of sexual
minorities. Instead, homosexuality was criminalized in the 2008 Anti-Pornography
and Porno-action (APP) Law. In the campaign to stop this law, for the first time LGBT
groups received support from a political party, the PDIP.[88] The acceptance of this law
in Parliament demonstrated the hold of a narrow conservative Muslim definition of
morality on public discourse.[89]

The political struggle for LGBT rights continued. In 2008 Ratri M. discussed the
rights that LGBT people needed. She was afraid marriage equality would still be a step
too far, but without such equality the consequences might be, she wrote, that when one
partner who owns property dies, the other partner would be left without anything if
their house and possessions were not in both names.[90] When in 2012 Dede Oetomo and
Yulianus Rettroblaut, campaigned for their candidacy as members of the Indonesian
Human Rights Commission, Dede Oetomo formulated a vision which included the
controversial issue of same-sex marriage.[91] In March 2015, the Indonesian Ulema
Council (MUI) issued a *fatwa* that proposed punishment for individuals accused of
homosexual acts, ranging from imprisonment to death. Homosexuality was defined as
a serious disease that could be cured like other illnesses.

The attack on the ILGA conference in Surabaya had serious consequences for LBT
activists in that city. The Dipayoni group had to postpone many activities because their
terrified members decided to stay at home.[92] Since then they have mainly met on the
university grounds, avoiding their own private places and the public malls, such as
Crown Plaza, where they used to meet. Particularly the attitude of the police, who
accommodated the attackers and failed to defend the congress participants, made the
activists realize their existence was not protected in Indonesia.[93] Around this time also
the discourse spread that LGBT people are predators, out to seduce innocent, 'normal'
children.

While the hate campaign against LGBT communities and their organizations
intensified, the activists themselves built up support networks, both with other LGBT
associations and with women's and human rights organizations. After the Jaringan
Warna-Warni was established, Sektor 15 and later the Ardhanary Institute established
links with LGBT groups that sprang up all over the country, as mentioned above.[94]
Apart from these activist organizations, the Ardhanary Institute and Dipayoni also
reached out to the many informal networks of lesbians, who gathered in malls, public
parks and engaged in fun activities such as watching movies, partying, dating and
drinking.

IDAHO, the International Day against Homophobia,[95] was first organized by Arus
Pelangi in Indonesia in 2008 with a demonstration at the Bundaran HI in Jakarta.
Since 2016 it has not been possible to celebrate IDAHO in a public way. Besides the
long-standing contacts of the lesbian community with Gaya Nusantara, the Ardhanary
Institute also collaborated for a number of years with the GWL-INA (Gaya Warna
Lentera - Indonesia) Network, a national network of gay men, men who have sex with
men (MSM), and transgender women, established in early 2007.[96] The Ardhanary
Institute found the network offered little space for LBT activities and gradually
withdrew.

The collaboration with the *Jurnal Perempuan* and Komnas Perempuan consisted of shared training and workshops on sexual rights, lobbying together and collaborative research projects. Individual lesbians also joined women's organizations. Building trust was a slow process. Lesbians were eager to participate in the new democracy with its promised freedoms and rights, but feminists not always welcomed them.

Endang, interviewed for the Kartini project on heteronormativity in which APIK and the Ardhanary Institute participated, shared her experiences of when she joined women's groups. There was little attention to lesbian issues; the public role of women and harassment in the household were the main topics of discussion. Endang felt she was disliked because of her orientation. Senior activists suggested that lesbianism was a kind of disease and a sin. She even received a message on her mobile phone, reading, 'What is the difference between what you do with stealing, robbing, and raping?' During a workshop her colleagues refused to sleep in the same room with her.

Activists selectively adapted concepts and theories developed in the expanding gender and sexuality studies movement. They drew on international human rights documents that Indonesia had signed and ratified, in an effort to hold their government to account to fulfil its obligations to respect and protect human rights. The major document used for such lobbying is the Yogyakarta Principles, which addresses the broad range of human rights standards and their application to issues of sexual orientation and gender identity.[97] The Ardhanary Institute, Gaya Nusantara and other LGBT organizations actively promote the acceptance of the Yogyakarta Principles. So far, however, Indonesia has not shown itself to be particularly proud of being the country where these principles were formulated.[98]

Media strategies

LBT activists became media-savvy early in the new millennium. When in 2002 Swara Srikandhi's Ade was approached to take part in a TV programme, it was proposed that she would be accompanied by a psychologist for the discussions because the producers felt that lesbianism was a psychological illness. Ade protested and with some other lesbians decided to educate the public, to bring them up to date with modern theories on homosexuality. They wanted to explain that Indonesia has a long history of gender diversity and also to point out that one's sexual orientation is a human right. They managed to get an anthropologist invited alongside the psychologist and were able to present their views. This was the first time that lesbianism was seen in a positive light on TV.

In April 2004, the 45th issue of the influential weekly *Forum Keadilan* devoted its main discussion to the legalization of gay marriage. As the editorial concluded, 'every day gay and lesbian people are courageously stepping forward. Recently they asked for the right to marry officially. They hope that the present discussions on the Civil Registration Act fulfils their aspirations – who knows, maybe this is a time when this fact cannot be prevented or it is a signal of the [coming] destruction of the earth'.[99] The prevailing conservative view, however, remained that marriage equality is un-Islamic.[100]

The first time a gay relationship was portrayed in a positive way on screen was the 2003 film *Arisan* which dealt with the tribulations of upper-middle-class life.[101] However, the audience for this film was small and the content was so far removed from the everyday lives of ordinary *gay* and *lesbi* that they could scarcely relate to this distant wonderland. Meanwhile, references to homosexuality as being contagious and an illness continued to pop up regularly in the print media.[102]

Gradually more films with LGBT themes were produced, initially focusing on *waria*.[103] In 2018 the short film *Kado* appeared, portraying a masculine girl switching between women's and men's clothes – at home, expected to cook, and on the streets, a boy.[104] However, in the last few years there has been growing fear about offending radical religious groups, so the trickle of LGBT-themed films has almost dried up. Mia Dinata, the director of *Arisan* and its successor, *Arisan 2*, said that she received much more hate mail as early as 2011 after the release of *Arisan 2* compared to when the original *Arisan* film was released.[105]

The venues of the Q!Film Festival, which was organized annually between 2002 and 2017, were repeatedly raided by 'goon squads'. In September 2010 even the Goethe Haus in Jakarta where some LGBT-themed forms were shown was attacked by an angry mob of Muslim militants from the FPI.[106] The first versions of this annual queer film festival could be held with much less harassment. After 2010 screenings had to be cancelled in various cities. In order to avoid raids, activists advertised programmes only by direct text or instant messaging.[107] Danger was always present though and, therefore. in 2015 the Q!Film Festival was held at a Christian theology school in Jakarta. Islamic vigilante groups did not attack the event because religious intolerance might have sparked a mandatory police response. After 2017 it was considered no longer safe anymore to hold the festival.

Very few novels with an LBT theme appeared in this period. *Garis Tepi Seorang Lesbian* (The Margins of a Lesbian) by Herlinatien Suhesti appeared in 2003. It engages with the compatibility of Islam with homosexuality. For Paria, the nature of her love for Ri is akin to her love for God. However, she is separated from Ri, who remained in France where they had lived together. Paria, who is sometimes confused about reconciling her faith with her sexuality, has a supportive, *pesantren*-educated father who is familiar with the practices involving *mairil*.[108] After some confusion Paria returns to Paris, where Ri is diagnosed with leukemia. Supiastutik and Kusumayanti who examined some of these novels found that lesbians were generally portrayed as middle-class, well-educated and financially independent.[109] A rare publication about FTM transpersons was written by Yash. It presents two life stories focusing on their psychological development.[110]

Conclusion

While the democratic opening in 1998 initially enabled the growth of a human rights climate and the creation of media freedom, within two decades this atmosphere has changed; democracy is on the decline and political homophobia is rife. The government again controls the media, including social media, which has a detrimental impact on lesbian and gay activism. In this period LBT activism grew and organizations and activists managed to establish strong networks with women's and human rights organizations. From being small inward-looking groups during the New Order, LBT groups established themselves as actors in the wider field of civil society activism.

The 'success' of majoritarian Islamic groups in their campaign to get the Anti-Pornography Bill accepted can be seen as a form of postcolonial amnesia. Practices discussed in Chapters 2 and 3 of this book, such as transgender rituals and dances, all of a sudden were classified as potentially pornographic and liable to persecution. The rich variety of cultural and ritual expressions of gender diversity and same-sex practices was discarded in a historical waste basket in favour of the imposition of puritanical and patriarchal imported religious customs.[111]

During the democratic period, activists came out and LGBT organizations learnt from the experiences in the previous period and developed leadership and management skills. Foreign funding became available, initially mainly directed at gay men and *waria*, but under the banner of sexual health some LBT organizations could redirect their training activities to be included in these programmes. From the early 2010s the UN language on SOGIE began to be adopted by LGBT organizations as more neutral than the stigmatized category of LGBT and *gay* or *lesbi*.[112] While activists learned how to deal with internet and social media as tools for internal communications, information and advocacy, by 2017 the government began cracking down on internet sites, depriving LGBT youth and others from critical sources of information. Exposure to the growing body of international sexuality studies through study, training sessions and international contacts led to increasing reflections on identity, culture and embodiment. A plethora of self-definitions developed, particularly among male-identified persons, ranging from the accepted categories of male and *sentul* to tomboy, transboy, transgender, and *butchi*. While women identifying as lesbians (*no-label*, *andro*) started developing non-binary perspectives on sexuality, FTM individuals began organizing among themselves, following a binary gendered, yet non-heterosexual model. This led to intense internal debates in LBT circles, resulting in an awareness of gender and sexual fluidity.

Female masculinity as a pervasive but locally distinct phenomenon, firmly located in local patriarchies, deeply challenges Indonesia's construction of women's nature (*kodrat*), since 1965 reinforced by state ideology and religious conservative groups.[113] The non-normative female-bodied persons with a man's soul do not just hold up a mirror that reflects normative masculinity, but diffracts that normalcy, highlighting certain aspects (dress, behaviour), ignoring other aspects. The entanglement of the biological (genetic), psychological and socio-cultural aspects in processes of identity formation were the topics of fierce discussions. As Barad formulates, 'Neither discursive practices nor material phenomena are ontologically or epistemologically prior.... . Neither has privileged status in determining the other.'[114]

The early and consistent, though not always easy, alliance between the LBT and the women's movement is related to the realization that both groups are confronted with similar stigmas, namely that women are seen as the source of *maksiat* (immorality). The pressure to marry is less imposed on gay men and *waria*, as society is more tolerant of them, because men have a place in public life. All through this period homosexuality was labelled as a sin, a crime or an illness, or all three combined, by diverse conservative groups. LBT groups providing information were constructed to be promoting LGBT, seducing the nation's vulnerable youth.

Though Indonesia has ratified most international laws concerning human rights, and human rights are also enshrined in the Constitution and domestic laws, guaranteeing freedom of expression, organization and freedom of the media, LGBT organizations have found it hard to access those rights, especially since 2015.[115] Police did not protect them when they were attacked. But these attacks also created a stronger sense of solidarity, both among themselves and with other human rights defenders. In response to the aggressive verbal and physical assaults, activists adapted their strategies and programmes. Public events are now carried out underground, with dates, times and venues provided only to pre-registered participants very shortly before the event. The Covid-19 pandemic contributed to this way of working. Activists worked at home, avoiding their offices and malls.

The LBT organizations discussed here charted their own course, navigating between the Indonesian women's and gay-dominated LGBT organizations, and the Western hegemonic discourse of sexual rights. They battled with family pressures and invisibility, lack of funds and societal lesbo- and transphobia.

6

Superheroes and female playboys:
Butch-femme dynamics

Introduction

In this chapter I discuss the dynamics of b/f relations as they have developed over the past forty years. The focus is on the group that established Perlesin in the early 1980s and with whom I have kept in contact ever since. In 2003 and 2004 I held twenty oral history interviews with them in the midst of intensive participant observation. The interviews conducted in the Kartini/Transsign project, between 2009 and 2010 by researchers of the Ardhanary Institute in Jakarta and Dipayoni in Surabaya, are also included in the analysis. Although I comment on the differences in the ways the three generations of b/f lesbians discussed in this chapter shape their lives, I focus more on the similarities they share.

Although the gender expressions of *tomboi* are intelligible in Indonesian society, they are faced with enduring stigma.[1] *Tombois* can be understood as *bujang gadis*[2] and as such may be tolerated in their families and be left to roam about when they are young, but as they get older they may be forced to enter into a heterosexual marriage; upon refusal they may be thrown out of their homes. Femmes conform more to the stereotypical image of girls but face even greater pressure to marry when they get older (including corrective rape, as discussed in Chapter 8).

The butch-femme cultures described in the United States and Europe of the 1950s[3] came under pressure from the feminist-lesbian movement from the 1970s onwards.[4] The young students, intellectuals and activists of those years looked down upon the working-class b/f cultures. Whereas the lesbian subculture till then had been dominated by the bars, thereafter on the perfidious effects of patriarchy on relations between women were hotly debated in middle-class lesbian subcultures, in women's houses and university study groups. The lesbian bar culture was submerged and died out in many places, including in The Netherlands.[5]

Joan Nestle, reflecting in 1998 on her life as a femme, muses that her 'fem desire, …, expressed in the 1950s, can be explored in terms of performance as well as gut-wrenching need'.[6] The 1950s in the West were a hard time for those belonging to the b/f bar culture. Feinberg, after describing his torture by cops who arrested butch women who did not wear the required three pieces of women's clothing, shared his pain when confronted with the harsh arrogance of the new feminist lesbians:

We thought we'd won the war of liberation when we embraced the word *gay*. Then, suddenly, there were professors and doctors and lawyers coming out of the woodwork … We dressed up after work for the new meetings on campus, but they drove us out, made us feel ashamed of how we looked. They said we were male chauvinist pigs: the enemy. It was women's hearts they broke. We were not hard to send away. We went quietly.[7]

The young feminists ignored the courage of the butches who had faced cops, prisons and psychiatric wards, and the essentially subversive nature of femme desire – a non-heterosexual femininity.

In Indonesia the b/f culture charted a different course. Though some members of the budding lesbian-feminist movement after the start of the Reformasi also denounced b/f as copying heteropatriarchy, after long debates the b/f culture was embraced as one of the ways of living a same-sex-oriented life.[8] As much as b/f role-playing is about being rooted in a particular heteronormative regime, the b/f culture signifies an erotically satisfying passionate aesthetics and is an enduring non-heterosexual, though binary, social, cultural and erotic model. The role-playing, though ostensibly conforming to the heteronormative gender regime in Indonesia, is deceptive. For all their butch swagger, the sexual energy of the femmes is often the driving force.

Body or culture? Performance or deeply felt desire? The sex wars of the 1970s and 1980s in the West were ferocious. The work by Newton, Butler and Bourdieu on performativity became widely popular.[9] Yet it proved difficult to theorize butch embodiment,[10] while femme desire remained long enigmatic.[11] By attempting to push the 'dangerous desires' of the b/f culture into the feminist closet, the passionate aesthetics of this dynamic duo, the attraction of butch power for femmes and the desire for feminine sensuality that drives butches, is not recognized.

The stereotypical image of the Jakartan b/f community is that they copy heterosexual patterns and that the butches are violent and oppress their femme partners. This is not so different from what 'politically correct' lesbians in my own country in the 1970s said of the 'old lesbians' who preceded us.[12] But as Butler argued, the 'ritualized repetition' of prevailing gender norms allows for its simultaneous subversion.[13] A masculinity that is worn with stigma signals the pervasiveness of the 'original' at the same time that it reveals its central weakness: it is not tied to a male-bodied person.[14]

Femmes also disrupt the pervasive heteronormative passionate aesthetics, by demonstrating their desire for a masculinity that is not heterosexual. In most cases this meant that though they might be tolerated by neighbours and family, they nonetheless were never accepted fully. B/f couples lived liminal lives, in between 'normalcy' and deviance, their deviant lifestyle being made possible through their outward adherence to patterns of 'normalcy'. Yet at the same time they exposed these patterns for what they were: essentially unstable constructs.

In Indonesia's gender regime men are the providers for their families.[15] The butches take great pride in their role as providers if they can manage to do that, but due to the glaring discrimination they encounter in the labour market many of them are unable to do so, or have very low incomes. Their femmes stick with them even in cases when their 'husbands' face serious economic hardship. Often the femmes are the ones who secure the couple's economic well-being. Putri and Reza are good illustrations. To all appearances Reza, the 'man', is the provider, conducting the business of the family, while Putri stays around the house, bringing up the two children from her previous marriage. Yet Putri set Reza up, drawing him into the trading business she had established before they got to know each other.

During the long-drawn-out period of my fieldwork, I engaged with my narrators in their daily lives. For instance, in April 2003 I spent a day with some activists of Sektor 15 and members of the old Perlesin group, some of whom had joined Sektor 15. We had gone to the house of Dede and Endah.[16] It was small and well maintained with framed pictures, mostly of Endah and her daughters. The atmosphere was cosy, with sofas, pots of various kinds, painted cupboards, a big TV separating the space for guests and the dining table. Endah announced that she was the housekeeper. But Dede had done the cooking and served the food. The femmes kept to themselves, doing each other's hair, talking intimately. The butches did all the talking with me. They were very butch, with belted trousers, T-shirts and wide chequered shirts hiding their breasts. The colours they wore were masculine, black, or dark blue. They had short hair, apart from Dede who wore it in a greying tail, the way some artists do.

The femmes wore femmy trousers, with frills and in soft colours. Endah sported a pink shirt with a very low neck, which clearly showed her cleavage and the curves of her full body. She looked sexy, walking with slightly swaying hips, not with the determined stride of the butches. Diana was the youngest, slim, feminine, beautiful, with striking features and shoulder-length hair, which she kept fumbling with. Endah wore lipstick, the femmes were all adorned with various kinds of jewellery. The butches sported big wrist watches. The most striking b/f scene was during lunch. Diana was feeding Irfan, who sat with his jeans-clad legs spread wide, arms extended along the back of the sofa, while Diana kept her legs close together. They were completely relaxed, a beautiful couple.

Generational differences

Differences between the various generations of b/f persons can be illustrated by the choice of markers for their identities. While in the 1980s and 1990s *sentul* and *kantil* were most often used, younger generations nowadays hardly use them. Other terms in those years were the Javanese words *cewek* (woman) and *cowok* (man). These words are still around. Some male-identifying people would call themselves *laki* (man) rather than *sentul*. After the Reformasi, female-born people with a strong male identity would rather use the term FTM, trans or trannyboy. The youngest generation is most comfortable with the term *priawan*, a combination of *pria* (man) and *wanita* (woman) or transman.

The choice of appropriate terminology is a topic of great debate. When in 2009 two participants of the Dipayoni team who were between the ages of forty and fifty suggested the renewed use of the terms used in the 1980s and 1990s, *sentul, kantil*, instead of FTM, it was vehemently rejected by younger participants; they found it uncool and old-fashioned. Instead, they proposed the use of the terms *suami-isteri* (husband-wife) for b/f couples. The term *lesbi* became popular after the Reformasi, by the younger crowd of feminist lesbians, who identified as no-label or andro. Agustine recalled that when she met the first generation of butch lesbians, she thought they were *banci perempuan*. At that time (mid-1990s) she identified as *cowok* lesbian while the feminine women were called feminine lesbians. The term transgender she first heard in the KPI. Transsexual referred to *waria*.

During the Reformasi further distinctions arose among male-identifying lesbians. The term soft butch came up for feminist butches. Diana split from Irfan after the latter had hit her. Her new much younger butch lover, Ratna, didn't want to be called *suami*. So Diana learnt to see Ratna as a woman and address her as that.

Outside pressures

Media, society in general and religion are the most important outside pressures which b/f people experience and manage, while their own families rarely provide a safe haven. Many of these dynamics came together in one of the biggest and most tragic dramas in the existence of Sektor 15, the murder of Erly on 19 May 2004. I had interviewed both Erly and her partner Evi in the previous months and had got to know them better during numerous social events. Yet they had kept essential elements of their lives hidden.

Erly's murderer Iwan was the younger brother of Evi. The police said that Iwan hated Erly, for he had been having a relationship with his sister. This should have been no news to Iwan, however, for he had known this for some twelve years before the event. More so, Iwan was officially married to Erly. Evi also had an official husband. This was their cover in the heterosexual world, but very few people knew this in the lesbian community. Evi fled her house with the kids, afraid of what the neighbours would do. She lived in hiding for months and had to give up her flourishing catering business. Erly's family was furious and seized all of Erly and Evi's assets, house, car and money.

This was not an honour crime, however, a brother 'defending' the honour of his sister and family.[17] Erly and Iwan had set up an inter-island trading company together. As Iwan was a drug addict he kept taking money from the business. His original share was around seventy million rupiah, and that was fast dwindling. About one month before the murder they fought over money, and Erly paid him twenty million as a final payment. Iwan refused to acknowledge that with that payment he had lost control over the company, and he came to the house of Erly and Evi with a knife. Evi fled, Erly was killed. This story did not reach the media.

Over the following months it appeared that the situation was even more complicated and the role of Evi came to be seen in a more dubious light. She had pushed Erly to marry Iwan, as she herself was married to Bala, a sailor, and Erly was always jealous when Bala came home and claimed his wife. The idea was that Iwan would 'normalize' Erly. That did not work out and, frustrated, Iwan went back to his parents. Also, it turned out the money that Iwan had claimed was actually based on land, a part of Iwan's inheritance, which he had sold to his sister. Evi had refused to pay him his full share (100 million rupiah) and had tried to evade her responsibility by claiming that the money was used by Erly to pay a debt she had with KPI. She even approached KPI members to sign a declaration of debt. They refused. Due to these manipulations Iwan had become furious and went to the house of Erly and Evi. Evi, knowing this, fled, leaving Erly helpless. It turned out she had gone to the house of her secret lover that nobody knew about.

Sektor 15 was deeply shaken. They held prayer sessions for Erly and asked me for the photo that I had routinely taken of him. They knew the issue was not lesbianism as such, but that the murderer used that in the hope of getting a lighter sentence. The media played a dubious role, capitalizing on the stigma of lesbianism. And then there were the usual factors of discord in Indonesian society – drugs, a feud about an inheritance, money. The Sektor 15 activists were deeply troubled about the role of Evi, whom they had always held in high regard. How could her behaviour be explained?

The difficulty of coming out as lesbians plays a major role in the lives of b/f couples. Putri and Reza, for instance, seem to manage their relationship well. Yet Putri who tried to conform to social gender expectations, confided to me that though she attended many social functions and could thus be seen as a good wife, she could never tell her friends and neighbours that Reza was her partner. They knew Reza as Putri's younger brother. She had faced enormous pressure from her family to marry the man who was selected for her. Her brother had slapped her when she refused and stuck to Reza. She lamented that *sentul* did not have identity cards stating they were men. Those lucky ones who did acquire such a card by whatever means could indeed live with their wives unnoticed such as Ahmad and Wanda. They managed to get a family card stating they were husband and wife. They kept attending the meetings of Sektor 15 and the Ardhanary Institute, though Agustine warned them that they ran a risk – you are safe, coming to our meetings exposes you!

The psychological pressures of being rejected by one's family weighed heavily on our narrators. Budi, for instance, born in a high-placed family, told me that she was the fifth of seven children and was rejected by her parents, which had a devastating impact on her. Her siblings were all loved, so she hated her parents and revolted. She became rough but not criminal, she said. She ended up in a violent marriage, her husband forcing her to have sex, throwing her against the wall if she refused.

Rejection by one's family affects particularly our narrators born in patrilineal ethnic groups. Aris, for instance, was born into a Batak family in Medan. Though he was ultimately accepted by his family, due to the care he bestowed on his mother, he was excluded from a share of their patrilineal land in Tapanuli. When his mother was about to die she asked him to pay off any outstanding debts so as not to burden his younger siblings, which Aris did.

His father, an army officer, used to beat up his mother. Aris refused to become such a violent man himself, instead he always wanted to protect women, and in the end, said Aris, he began to love them. When Aris was eleven years old his father hit his mother so hard that she crumpled to the floor in front of Aris. When a furious Aris tried to shield her, her father shouted that this was his wife and that he was free to beat her and even to kill her. When Aris was eighteen years old he felt strong enough to stand up to his father. Even though his mother had suffered so much from her husband, she wanted Aris to marry. What for, Aris asked? To have a violent husband like you have? Aris left home.[18]

This was not the end of family trouble. When Aris finished high school his parents were broke. Because Aris had high grades their priest asked Aris's parents for permission to send him to the Netherlands for further education. The church would pay. But his parents refused – send one of our sons instead, they said. The priest explained that the sons did not have such good grades, so in the end nobody went. When he was around twenty, he had a friend called Boy. Both of them were *gagah, jantan* (valiant, manly). One day an uncle stormed into their rented room. He was a colonel in the army and shouted that his niece made the whole Batak family ashamed and that he had to be shot. After a while he relented and told Aris that if he agreed to marry a man, he would give him a car and jewellery. Aris refused.

Irfan was born in Ambon and had been a tomboy from an early age, climbing on the roof to put the tiles straight, playing war games with a catapult. His mother tried to force her child to learn how to cook which he hated, so he spoilt the dishes, putting too much salt in the sambal, turning the rice into porridge. When Irfan was fifteen years old, a marriage was arranged for him. He climbed into a tree and bellowed loudly his refusal, making the family ashamed. He was removed from high school, and he left home.

Tensions

The intense pressure under which most LGBT people grow up results not only in psychological trauma, but also in tensions within the b/f community and in their relationships. The *sentul* I met in the 1980s had a troubled relationship with the *kantil* in their group. They would talk to me about the femmes as being negative or imitation lesbians, classifying themselves as positive, or true lesbians. This speaks to the butches' great fear that their femmes might leave as soon as they found a man to marry.

The violence that the butches themselves had encountered in their natal families was sometimes internalized by them, giving them the idea that real men have to be strong, and violent. The activists of Sektor 15 were worried about this phenomenon and initiated a number of discussions on the topic. The *kantil* were happy that the violence some of them experienced from their butch lovers was openly discussed. I also joined the discussions on several occasions. It is hard to say whether or how much b/f relationships are more violent than either feminist lesbian ones (I heard of quite a few cases of domestic violence among lesbian couples) or 'normal' heterosexual relationships.[19] The femme partners participating in this research were silent about the acts of violence their husbands might have committed. I know of only one case in which domestic violence clearly erupted. Irfan was desperate because he had lost his job as a small trader in Bali after the Bali bombings of October 2002. No longer respected as the family provider, he found it hard to adjust. His partner Diana went to work, singing in a karaoke bar, leaving Irfan at home. Once, when she had stayed over in a friend's house and had been afraid to call home, Irfan hit her hard, in front of one of the members of Sektor 15. This became a big case, as the KPI is one of the major women's organizations in Indonesia fighting against domestic violence. Irfan apologized profusely but their relationship broke up shortly after. The general consensus among the b/f members of Sektor 15 was that it was fine to be a b/f couple and to play with heterosexual patterns, but that violence was not to be tolerated under any circumstance.

Though the more recent generation of butches generally has a higher level of education than the first generation, they are still faced with discrimination in the labour market and social stigma. As a result, half of the young butches interviewed by the Ardhanary Institute team in 2009 and 2010 were economically dependent on their girlfriends. The insecurity of the butches and their economic dependence resulted in domestic quarrels in which the femmes mostly had the upper hand, often also physically. They might threaten that they could always go back to their former husbands or find a new one, a 'real' man or a butch who was financially stable.

Messy family relationships, passionate love affairs and a social and legal climate, which condones heterosexual affairs but penalizes same-sex affairs in which one of the partners is underage, can lead to unwelcome encounters with the law. Yudi, for instance, who identifies as a 'true man' not as *sentul*, and whose lovers, he told me emphatically, are ordinary *cewek*, not lesbians, once ended up in prison. He had an affair with a fifteen-year-old girl from Cianjur who was very much in love with him and wanted them to marry. Yudi refused, but she said if you are a man, then you have to be a gentleman, you must be brave enough to take me with you. If not, you are a girl. With that challenge Yudi sold a necklace and took his lover to Solo. He got a job selling tickets for *ketoprak* performances. His money ran out and he asked his mother for money, but she never sent it. Instead, he was picked up by his elder brother who told him that mama was ill, so Yudi came home. The furious parents of the girl came to their house, and Yudi was taken to court in Cianjur. He found out that it was prohibited to elope with an underage girl. 'Wah,' Yudi exclaimed, 'It was not me who wanted to go away!' Fortunately, the girl was honest and told the judge that she pressured Yudi until he sold his necklace. So Yudi avoided a prison sentence but he had to give up his lover.

Identifications

The LBT movement has not always easily embraced the various identities that the acronym LBT suggests. I have already mentioned that in Perlesin the butches felt they were the true 100 per cent lesbians, and that their partners should not belong to the organization. After the Reformasi other problems arose. Sektor 15, initially consisting mostly of feminist lesbians, was wary of accepting bisexual and transpeople arguing that their sexual orientation was 'not clear'.[20] Agustine invited the old Perlesin group and slowly they became accepted. There were fierce debates on identities and labels. The categories used shifted over the research period, with the terms FTM, transman and *priawan* gradually replacing the category 'man' with which some of the older narrators identified.

Though the word Perlesin contains the word *lesbi*, this was such a novel term at the time that its members did not want to apply it to themselves. As Tomi told me, 'I call myself *sentul*, I heard that word for the first time in junior secondary school. *Sentul* means *jantan* (manly), so that felt good. I don't like the word *lesbi*, that is too harsh.' Before Dani learnt the word *sentul* she knew only one term for who she was, *wapendos*, *wanita penuh dosa* (sinful woman), a word created by her butch friend Dede.[21] Dani too felt most comfortable with the term *sentul* and never used lesbian, which he felt was derogatory.

For some persons of that generation identifying as male meant that they would not join an organization geared towards lesbians, for these are women. Reza said: 'I call myself a man. Some people would call me *banci* – let them. I don't want to be called *sentul*. If people call me *om* (uncle), or *pak*, that really makes my soul happy. But let nobody call me a lesbian.' Yudi discussed his hesitations about his identity: 'I pray to God that I never commit a sin. But I have already violated my *kodrat* by being born a woman but straightaway wanting to be a man.' I argued back: 'But your *kodrat* rests in your *jiwa* (soul)? And you tell me your *jiwa* is masculine? So then your *kodrat* is also masculine? Surely Allah would understand that?' Hesitantly Yudi responded:

> Iyaa, there is simply no womanliness in my soul. I am neither a *sentul*, nor an ACDC, like Agustine.[22] I am just a true man. All my lovers were *cewek* not lesbians. I once took my mother on the back of my motorbike and was called *banci*. I was so angry. The same thing happened when I was taking my child to school – 'hey your father is a *banci*, a *bencong*'. But the teachers are polite, they call me sir.

Jack, who also identifies as a man, told his family never to call him *ibu* but just *kak* (from *kakak*, elder sibling), for that refers to both women and men. He called his partner *meis* or *skat*.[23]

Some twenty years later, when Sektor 15 had organized its first gender and sexuality training sessions, feminist discourse was becoming commonplace among activists. The words *lesbi* or lesbian were more widely used. The older terminology of *sentul* and *kantil* was, however, also used by a younger generation of b/f lesbians. Irfan, for example, described himself as *sentul*. He had learned the term from a *kantil* lover. He also called himself a *lesbi*. Irfan stressed that his partner was bisexual but had identified as *lesbi* since they attended the KPI meetings. Both were proud Sektor 15 activists. Around this time the word bisexual was sometimes used for women who had had a heterosexual relationship. In earlier b/f circles the femme partner was always called 'just a woman' or *kantil*.

Among the femmes several terms were used. Endah said she was a '*kantil*, 100 per cent lesbian. I don't agree with those who think only *sentul* are lesbians.' Evi also identified as a '*kantil* who loves *sentul*, who are tomboy-like, who are romantic in love making and can stand up for themselves'. Lia, on the other hand, never called herself a lesbian. 'I am just a woman', she said, 'a housewife and my *sentul* partner is my husband. I don't understand what lesbian means.' Similarly, Rohmani told me that she did not feel lesbian. 'I am a woman, Yudi's wife. He is responsible the way a man should be, so in my view he is a man. He is handsome and cares for me. People around Yudi use terms like *kantil* and *sentul* but I don't. I am just a housewife, and happy to be called *ibu* Yudi – Mrs Yudi.' Irene sees herself as a woman, in no way different from a heterosexual woman: 'The only difference between my husband Aris and a man is perhaps his genitals. And maybe his attitude. Men like to beat women up, Aris doesn't.' Mia said it did not matter whether she was the partner of a man or a woman.

> To me Feri is a man – he just has to wear a skirt to work as he needs to make money. We are not *sakit* (sick)! We are normal! Some of us have been like this from a young age, and others become like us because they meet people like us. I hope our children don't become like us. I want them to be normal. God created us all. It is our *kodrat*.

Meuthia, who comes from a deeply religious high-class Acehnese family and who can recite the Quran beautifully, reflects that she is a real woman. 'I had to pleasure my husband sexually (*melayani suami*) and so it is the same with my *sentul*. I have to make sure my husband will not commit adultery. So in the morning I cook, and later in the day I go out to earn money [she has a thriving catering business]'. But the division of labour is different. 'My *sentul* is also a woman so he has to help me with cooking, like cutting the onions. Imagine if the wife is tired and the husband just sits there doing nothing.'

Dealing with neighbours remains a dicey problem, for this middle generation too, and this affects how they self-identify. Yuli wonders whether she can call herself a lesbian:

> We blend in well with our neighbours, we join the *arisan*, and the quranic lessons. I told them that Dani is my brother-in-law. But Dani doesn't join the quranic lessons or go to the mosque for he is confused about what clothes to wear. He joined the *siskamling* (neighbourhood watch), but the neighbourhood head said that he better not join, as he is a woman. Dani has a woman's body but from the outside he looks like an ordinary man. He is my husband to the outer world, for me he is a woman with a manly soul. He also sometimes cooks, makes coffee.

Dani is therefore presented alternately as a brother-in-law and as a husband, while all along everybody seems to be aware that he has a woman's body.

A topic of much debate was the spiritual or bodily location of their being different. Most butches said that they had a masculine soul (*jiwa*). Some also said it was God-given, so their *kodrat*. Again, others felt they should never lie to themselves for in their *hati kecil* (small heart, deep in their heart) they and Allah knew the truth. That is why Erly prayed in his women's *mukena* and why Dani could not join the Friday prayers in men's clothing. Others used the words *hati nurani* (usually translated as conscience). Both butches and femmes are concerned about their *hati kecil*. As Putri told me:

> Am I a lesbian? My *hati kecil* does not accept that. I am just a *kantil*, a woman, not a lesbian. Reza is a *sentul*. He is the head of our household. He takes care of the car. With sex he is on top of me. His soul is the same as that of a man, making love is the same only more pleasant. Sexually I am passive, as I was with my husband.

I am a full true woman, I receive. First Reza was not fully a man, but now he has learnt how to be a true *sentul*, for that is what I wanted.

An interesting statement, demonstrating that the *kantil* know exactly what they want in terms of lovemaking and that far from being passive, as they themselves state they are, they know how to turn their butches into well-performing *sentul*.[24] There is thus both a learned and an innate aspect to their b/f performance.

Three decades later another generation of b/f lesbians has become active in the LBT movement.[25] New words have appeared, new discourses have sprung up. The term *priawan* came into use from about 2011 onwards.[26] This is used by female-bodied persons with a masculine soul who do not want to have an operation. Transmen go for hormonal treatment and some want to change their bodies with an operation. They also use binders.[27] These are expensive, and you need minimally two to be able to wash them regularly. Poor *butchi* cannot afford two and their binders might smell – they are despised for that. The young crowd no longer identify as *sentul* or *kantil*, but as *butchi* or transboy, *treni* and other such terms.

A new issue is the intersex group. After the case of Alter in 2012, discussed in the previous chapter, some fifteen or sixteen of them have been meeting in the office of the Ardhanary Institute. They all live in ostensibly hetero-relationships. The Ardhanary Institute encouraged them to go to an intersex conference, but they were shy; they feel there is something wrong with their bodies and they do not want to attract attention. But they regularly search the internet for news about their condition and are happy to have found a place where they are welcome.

Some young butches hope they are intersex too, they told the Ardhanary team around 2012, but shy away from the test. One FTM felt he is genetically a male, the others recognized their female bodies. As some stated, they had a female body, but their *panggilan* or *keinginan jiwa* (call or wish of their souls) and their *perasaan* (feelings) are like men.[28] The terminology they used was *laki-laki*, *butchi*, transgender, *TG*, transseksual and intersex.[29] One respondent called himself *transboy*. He chose this term after searching on the internet. At school and at home they experienced similar problems as the older FTM people had – the obligatory school uniform; bullying; physical, sexual and psychological abuse in their families, pressure to marry. Many reported having run away from home at some stage.

Some saved money for hormones; others boasted that they do not menstruate, but it was known from their partners that they actually do. A few wanted to have a mastectomy. Only five were happy with their bodies and did not desire any form of gender affirmative operations. Two were undergoing hormonal treatment, while thirteen planned to have some form of operation. Five interviewees stated that religion, financial considerations and fear of the effects of transition made them hesitate to take hormones and undergo gender affirmative therapy. The young generation of transmen and *priawan* were also not keen to go for a sex-change operation.

Bhima underwent the first sex-change operations for an FTM person in Indonesia. In 1976 Bhima had started taking hormones. By then the first Indonesian gender transition team had formed and he had immediately enlisted for treatment. After the intake they realized he was serious. He went to the obligatory twenty sessions with a psychologist. Having completed those, he was eager to move on to the first operation. The doctors hesitated, however, when they saw on his identity card that he was a Muslim. They feared the wrath of conservative clerics. Bhima was desperate. 'Listen, I have come this far! I have saved up for this, sold my car, relatives have contributed, how can you do this to me? Tell me what other religion I should take up and I will immediately get my identity card changed.' However the doctors advised him to get a letter of recommendation from a noted Muslim scholar.

Bhima made an appointment with the progressive Muslim scholar Hamka. Bhima pleaded his case, upon which the teacher opened the Quran and pointed to a passage which read that when you are ill you must make all attempts to heal yourself. 'Are you ill?' Hamka asked. Bhima nodded vehemently. 'Fine, so then tell them that the Quran advises to heal your illness.' 'It is better, sir', Bhima suggested, 'that you write that down for them'. With that letter Bhima had no problem being accepted for the first operation, in which his breasts were removed.[30]

The second operation was performed in 1982. By then Bhima had changed considerably. If before 1976 Bhima was a dashing, rather androgynous looking youth, by the early 1980s his face had become more square, and with his moustache and beard he looked very masculine. At the back of his photo album he has a series of portraits of himself in which his progress into full masculinity can be seen from year to year. I met Bhima for the first time in 1982, when he was recovering from his operation. I brought him a letter from his former girlfriend, who lived in the Netherlands.

The vicissitudes of femme lives

The femmes I interviewed told their stories of femme power and courage with great pride. I soon learnt that for all the butch swagger, femmes are often the motor of the relationship, their active sexual energy the driving force. This is a reversal of the patriarchal gender regime which constructs women to be sexually passive. Though the performance of people's identities is largely learnt behaviour,[31] the femmes and butches I encountered stressed that their ways of living, loving, walking, talking and working seemed natural to them – tangible, essential, inherent and embodied parts of their lives.[32]

Joan Nestle defended the butch-femme lifestyle as a critical strategy of resistance: 'Butches were known for their appearances, fems for their choices.'[33] This does not ignore the fem ambiguity butches fear. Hiding their jealous insecurity, they at times overlooked the courage of femmes to stay with their butch lovers, and their resistance to the seductions of a life with a man, with economic and social stability. Butch-femme is ultimately all about desire and the female body. Sexuality is centred around femme pleasure; a good butch prides himself on pleasing his femme successfully. This sometimes leads to tensions, between the potential pleasures of reciprocity and hierarchical gender role stratification. An intense process of negotiation may be involved in the complex passionate aesthetics of these b/f couples.

Powerful femme writer Hollibaugh dreams: 'I am overtaken by a woman's hands, a man's cock, a lover's fever. I am possessed … ever since I saw a butch … I felt my own longing answered, knew for certain that I required this kind of woman with a hunger that would not quiet down.'[34] It requires an enormous amount of courage to live these desires, in the face of hostility, derision, violence, abjection, eviction. And often poverty, for the butches, due to their economic marginalization, sometimes struggled to provide.

Despite the strong erotic bond between them I heard many stories, particularly from butches, about *kantil* who had left their *sentul* because their family had forced them to marry. Or they themselves wanted to marry to have a child – then they would be respected socially. After that they hoped they could get back to their *sentul* or find a new one. The *kantil* I spoke to fought hard to resist the pressure from their families. An extra complication was that the *kantil* wanted to be seen as ordinary women. Marrying a man and having a child would be proof to society that this *kantil* was really a woman. Paradoxically this also helped their butch lovers. For if their lover was a 'normal' woman, should they also not be seen as a 'normal' man?

Maintaining the gender binary is a core aspect of b/f culture. When two femmes had a relationship with each other, it was called a Revlon relationship, as most of them were salesgirls for that brand of cosmetics.[35] This was not a compliment, and they were not very welcome at b/f gatherings. I once danced in a disco with a feminist friend whom they considered butch; they called us *hemong*, slang for homo, gay or *banci*.

Below are excerpts from interviews and discussions with four femmes: Irene, Endah, Lia and Putri. Irene recalls her dating period with Aris.

'We met in 1985. First we went to see a film and two weeks later we had sex. I was very much in love. My elder brother found out about us and was furious. He took me home. He had attended college in Australia, so when he saw Aris and me together, he realized what was going on. I ran away from home and went to live with Aris. Two years after we met I adopted an eight-day-old child from a hospital. Poor parents in those days who could not afford to pay the delivery costs sometimes left their child there, so whoever paid the bill could adopt the child. Aris was a driving instructor at the time. I was still at school. After I had adopted the child we had a future, so my parents were no longer angry with me. We have been together for eighteen years, our child is fifteen years old now, in the third form of junior secondary school. She calls Aris darling and me mama.

I never finished my studies, because Aris was jealous. I only had to write my thesis. Aris lost his job and now works as a taxi driver. I work in the family business doing the accounting, at home. My brother keeps criticizing me: 'Why did you choose this Aris? He hardly earns anything, not even enough for the household. There are so many men with degrees who would like you.' And I say, well, because I love Aris of course. He is a good person, full of attention, honest, but naturally he is jealous.

Irene keeps the peace with their neighbours, who call them *om* and *tante*.

Endah comes from a poor family and had to work hard as a child to help her divorced mother make ends meet. From the age of fifteen she worked in a night club. I use her own words to tell her story below.

There I discovered I was sexually attracted to women. I didn't know the words *kantil* and *sentul*. My first lover was a girl of my age. We kissed and that made my vagina wet, but we didn't really make love. I had sex for the first time when I was sixteen; I boarded with the girls of a club in Menteng. I seduced them. I was confused and asked myself why am I attracted to women so much? This question has haunted me till now. I will never forget the first time I had sex. It was wonderful. I took the initiative to touch her, I kissed her, I licked her all over, massaged her. She loved whatever I did and she also kissed and licked me in return till we both had our orgasms.

My mother realized there was something *tidak beres* (not in order) with me and became very angry. So I presented a male friend of mine to my mother. I was absolutely not in love with him, but I wanted to show my mother that I was 'normal'. We separated again when I moved to Cilacap to work. There I again seduced the girls I was boarding with. They were not lesbians, they had male lovers, I just seduced them. I didn't know any lesbians. But the world of lesbians was not alien to me for when I was in primary school a neighbour was a *sentul*, everybody called him *banci*.

My first serious woman lover was Rita. I was eighteen and she worked at the same night club. She was a drug addict. I loved her very much and realized I was 100 per cent lesbian because I really wanted to possess her. Rita was neither *sentul* nor *kantil*, she was like me. Our sex life was very nice, but because she needed money, Rita sometimes had a male lover. That made me furious. We separated because of that. I left Cilacap and worked in another night club. I liked to seduce the other girls and make love with them. I used the name Ricky then. If I were a man I would really be a playboy.

After a year I went back to Jakarta and met a *sentul*. My mother found out and married me off. I didn't feel any love for that man and told him I only wanted to stay married for four years until I had children. I never got any pleasure from sex with him. I managed to hold out for two weeks with him but then ran away with my woman lover. But I was pregnant. My mother was very angry as we had brought shame on the family. My husband was also very angry and jealous and called me insulting words. After that we hardly had sex, I always refused it; fortunately he worked out of town and only came home once a week. I had a second child and after that returned to my *sentul* lover. I lived with Agus for eighteen years. My kids called him papa. They only found out later that Agus was not a man but they continued to call him papa.

In a relationship with a *sentul* my role is that of a housewife. I like to make the bed up in a very romantic way, so that my *sentul* becomes sexually excited. I use sexy underwear, comb my hair, use perfume. But I take the initiative, I am very aggressive sexually, I always try to find a position that gives me most satisfaction. I hardly ever take the bottom position, for that does not work for me sexually. I can go on for a long time, from eight at night until five in the morning, having up to seven orgasms.

Another story from a femme is that of Lia, who as a child played with dolls, liked cooking and applying make-up.

When we played family I was always the housewife. When I was fifteen I fell in love with a *sentul*. We had a relationship for five years; we had great sex. He was the active partner. After sex he always indulged me and loved me. When my parents found out they were furious and I was sent away. I only attended school until the second grade of junior high school. The older sibling I lived with married me off to a man I didn't love. I consented to marry because my neighbours gossiped about my relationship with my *sentul*. I never liked lovemaking with my husband. I had a child with him. After my husband had had sex with me and had ejaculated he would just turn away and ignore me. Lovemaking with my *sentul* lasted much longer and I was always satisfied. I am a normal woman, I am happy to seduce, to cook, to look after the household.

Putri was brought up in a religious household. She still goes regularly to Quran study classes and usually wears a long skirt and *jilbab*. Her religious duties do not interfere with her life with butch partner Reza: 'I can still *sholat*. I have always been a good housewife and I have three children, so I fulfil my religious obligations. I would like Reza to go with me on the *haj*, but for *sentul* clothing is always a problem.' She told her story about meeting Reza:

When I was seventeen I married a man who was thirteen years older than me. I liked sex with him but left him when I met Reza. Reza was a family friend, he often visited our house, helped with cooking. I was then twenty-six and had three children. By that time my relationship with my husband had deteriorated. I was not allowed to leave the house and he often shouted at me. After having a relationship with Reza for one and a half years I divorced my husband. I could not have sex with him anymore after I had had sex with Reza. With Reza I felt happy, free. I have been together with Reza for fifteen years, I don't want to have a man ever again. I am not a lesbian. My *hati kecil* does not accept that. I am just a *kantil*, a woman.

Putri knows that there is nothing in the Quran about women making love with each other, only about men. Still, she feels uneasy:

I always pray to God that I will be allowed to liberate myself from Reza, but I cannot do that yet. For it is a sin. I am just sad that I am apparently born as a homo. I don't want my children to be like me. I will be with Reza for the rest of my life for I am already too far gone.

Good and bad butches

For an FTM or butch person, visibility as a man is both desired and tenuous.[36] When he is passing as a man, the FTM person risks discovery, by health workers, the general public, men in male toilets, their colleagues or bosses or their in-laws. In cases in which FTM people try to hide their bodies from their own partners, an elaborate game of deception and secrecy is required. I found that the partners of both butches and FTM people shared the burden of secrecy with their partners. For some FTM, gender-affirmative surgery puts an end to all this insecurity. As Green writes, who lived as a woman for the first forty years of his life: 'I remember what it was first like to feel that anonymity as testosterone gradually obliterated the androgyny that for most of my life made others uncomfortable in my presence … it was a joy to be assumed human for a change, instead of gawked at, scrutinized for signs of *any* gender.'[37]

In Indonesia few FTM people have had full gender-affirmative surgery. Yet they and the wider group of butches do want to be seen as manly. But what kind of a man? They need to be providers, good lovers and they also want to possess *wibawa* (power, authority). In this research I followed a number of butches and FTM people, some of whom, like Dani, Jack, Reza, Alvin and Agus, were seen as 'good' butches, and others, such as Feri, Dede and Yudi, as bad butches.

Butch insecurity is a great source of their anxiety. As Dani said: 'We *sentul* never know whether our *kantil* still wants to go with a man, if only for the money. In front of me they deny it, but before you know it they are married.' Yet Dani has been in a happy relationship for many years, bringing up a child together with his partner. Their insecurity is fuelled by the fact that most of them have lost the emotional and financial support of their families. They are lonely, their friends, their community, are the only anchors they have.

Alvin, a gentle handsome butch who joined Sektor 15 and became a staff member of the Ardhanary Institute, reflected:

> I had many lovers, but no one stayed with me. Perhaps their families pressured them. The longest relationship I had lasted ten years. Usually we broke up either because I was disappointed they would not understand my condition. Maybe I was too selfish? Always wanted to win a debate? Or because they were still young and wanted to live a normal life. I supported them. They want a normal life – for me that means sincerity, honesty. I could give them that. One and a half years ago I adopted the daughter of my younger sister. I want to look after this child and I am looking for a partner. I am lonely and desperate. It is nice to be in Sektor 15, we can share our feelings. This gives me a sense of community.[38]

One of the anxieties of b/f culture is to uphold the binary sexual division. The femmes cook and clean, while the butches play cards and smoke cigarettes, as I noted on numerous occasions. The butches also feel they are entitled to more leeway to *jajan* (infidelity, literally snacking) which is in line with the Marriage Law which allows polygyny, and sexist social customs. But there is a code of honour: a butch should never seduce the femme of another butch in the group.

Financial responsibility is a key issue. Dani told me: 'I am responsible for the finances. I also contribute to the household of my mother-in-law, so when I go there I am treated like a king.' And Jack said:

> For me being a man means that I can protect – then I feel strong, even if the woman is not close to me I want to defend her, like when I was still at school. I used to feel like a *jago* (literally cockerel, also thug) when I was still young. But now my source of pride is that I am responsible for our money, for our child.

Some femmes have little compassion if *sentul* fall short of these ideals, reflected in the words of Meuthia:

> They try to oppress us, to step on us. We have to get away as fast as possible from *sentul* who are creating trouble. They don't have the right to do that for they cannot maintain us and our children. Most of the *sentul* don't have a job. Therefore *sentul* have little self-confidence and they throw tantrums. If their wives have money they feel inferior.

Employment for the butches is therefore a major issue. They hoped that their LBT organization could provide economic support for them to set up a small workshop, where they could all work. Dede, for instance, deplored the fact that richer lesbians did not help them. He recounted approvingly a story about a rich lesbian in Bandung, who set up a *warnet* (internet shop) and some other small enterprises where butches could work.

But as in any good marriage, in long-term relationships the partners negotiate their roles, as the following accounts illustrate.

Aris: At first I had a lover who wanted to go back to her former male lover, so we fought a lot. In the end I moved out to a place where Irene also rented a room. But I fell ill for I didn't feel like eating. There was nobody to tell me to eat, you see. Ultimately Irene gave me food. I realized she really cared for me so I asked her whether she wanted to be with me. Now I have found the right one, my *jodoh*. I am not fooling around anymore. Irene understands my suffering. And perhaps she wanted to find someone to love her. I love her the way she wants to be loved. I have called myself *sentul* since I joined the group in Teuku Umar. I do the manly things in the house, like climbing in trees, fixing the lamps, carrying things. I am proud when my colleagues at work say this Aris is more manly than we are. When there is an accident on the road, I get out of my car and help the victims. I have been drunk at times, but never gambled. But since I have been with Irene I have never engaged in these activities.

Reza: I was always the goalkeeper when we played football but only when I became an adult I realized that my soul was masculine. I long felt like a superhero, possessing masculine strength. From primary school onwards I wanted to protect my girlfriends. I have always been attracted to women. When they shouted at me that I was a man, I thought this was just fine. But I was only courageous enough to date a woman when I entered university, for then I didn't need to wear a skirt anymore. I am proud that as a man I can protect my wife, make her happy and that I am never rude to her. I also take care of our finances, though my wife helps. We built our house together, it is in her name; the car is also in her name; everything is in her name. I am not active in Sektor 15 because that is about lesbians. I don't want to be called a lesbian, tomboy is ok. We don't have a lesbian relationship.

Agus also reflected on butch responsibilities: 'We have to be *gagah* (dashing) and not bow down to a woman. We need to be responsible financially, for only when we earn are we respected. If we cannot earn enough, it is fine if our partners help. But if she earns the money, what use is it to be a man?'

Another demand that butches have to meet is to be chivalrous. Aut, who had joined Lambda and Chandra Kirana, shared the following story.

My in-laws were very religious people. The father of my partner called me to him and said: 'It is fine you are going out with my daughter. At least it means she cannot get pregnant.' We used to sleep there, make love while only a bamboo wall separated us from her parents' bedroom. But after a few years her father called me to him again. 'Now my daughter has to get married. You have to let her go.' And I let her go.

Aut was proud of her consideration for her lover's interests. 'Yes, I let her go,' he repeated several times. 'I still see her. She has three children now.'

The butches were invariably disappointed and angry when they were addressed with female terms, such as *tante*. I once called my butch friend Daud, a short, dashing figure, *cantik* (beautiful). He was offended; I should have called him *ganteng* (handsome). Ideally, if a butch is good in bed, chivalrous, responsible with money and manly around the house, his femme will understand his cares, cook his food and be an ardent lover to him.

Some butches do not live up to this ideal. They may succumb to many vices such as cheating, gambling or drug addiction. Jack, a much-admired butch with a stable job as a driver at the Australian embassy, recommended his friend Yudi for a job with the ambassador's wife. Jack had told Yudi he was very lucky as his boss understood Indonesian, and Yudi did not speak a word of English. 'Don't let me lose face', Jack had warned. But that is exactly what Yudi did. He could not give up his gambling habit. When he forgot the time and was late, he mumbled, 'I was at the mosque, praying!' 'Nonsense', said his boss, 'I looked there'. So Yudi was fired. Jack said to me: 'You see, he is like that all the time. Borrows money, never pays it back. Lies to people. Gets very angry when he loses at gambling. So gradually people avoid coming to his house.'

Yudi went downhill. He lost all his money and his teeth and sometimes came to the office of Ardhanary begging for money. Their son blackmailed him. 'You are not my real father, you have no penis. I don't need to obey you.' So he grew up without Yudi daring to take stern action. The son ended up in jail, the first time for stealing, then later he raped a girl.

Feri did not live up to butch ideals either. He had a good job as a prosecutor in the court of Bekasi and also conducted some business, renting out cars. At some stage we had a party there, dancing, singing until late, with a real entertainer. Yet Feri proved unreliable. First he deceived Evi, Erly's wife, herself an astute businesswoman. He kept his wife Mia on a very tight leash, hardly giving her enough for the household, not paying properly for her children's education. Feri told nobody he was still fighting his drug and alcohol addictions. That was the reason why they still lived in a relatively cheap rented house. Feri ended up in prison, convicted of corruption. He told me his life story:

My mother beat me up for being a tomboy, told me I was ill and took me to see a psychiatrist when I was fourteen. I was also brought to a *dukun* (traditional healer) who sprayed water on me. I had to drink holy water and was bathed with flower water at midnight. I refused to wear a skirt and left home in the third grade of junior high school. My heart is that of a man but unfortunately I was born a woman. If it weren't a sin I would change my body. I often prayed: my whole heart is different from my body, why do I remain a woman who can bear children? When I left home I went to stay with a woman who accommodated street children and I continued my schooling there. We called her *emak* (mother). She let me wear trousers when I came home from school. I ended up in hospital because of my morphine addiction. My friends in the streets gave it to me.

Dede initially posed as a reliable butch:

This is our pride, isn't it? When we can maintain our wives, when they never have to go out to work. Some of us cannot even do that. They have to sell their wives. Their wives work for them in a night club or in a karaoke bar. You know what happens there. All kinds of men can touch them. I don't want that to happen to me.

But Dede was a scoundrel; he deceived both Nova and Yudi. He used the same trick – he would borrow their cars and then sell them. Yudi had lent him his younger brother's car. After that Dede disappeared. Agus went to search for him and was met by an angry house owner, because Dede had not paid their electricity bills for three months. Was Agus going to pay up? Everybody felt sorry for Endah. For Endah lost her house too, sold by Dede. Endah even lost all her jewellery to pay Dede's debts. The whole b/f community was furious with Dede: 'Endah was such a good wife, always cooking and looking after Dede.'

Sexual dynamics

In the b/f culture, where the gender and sexual binary between the partners is strictly monitored, butch and femme sexual performance is also divided along gender roles. But not according to the heteronormative passionate aesthetics, where male pleasure is central. On the contrary, butch performance is measured by the amount of femme pleasure. Aris said: 'When I pleasure my wife, I just follow her rhythm (*terbawa arus*). When she is satisfied, I feel manly, for then she will never leave me. If I cannot satisfy her well then it is soon bye-bye Aris.' In general the butches did not want to have their vagina touched, let alone penetrated.

Irfan explained:

I always take the initiative and penetrate my lover, I don't want her to enter me. I have an orgasm when my partner embraces and kisses me and when she talks in an erotic voice. My lover has had several male lovers, but only I was able to satisfy her, she says. A man should be sexually responsible. Women who have a husband told me that their men are selfish, never ask them whether they are satisfied. They can make love at the most for two hours and then they feel they are very masculine (*jantan*).

This is a topic of pride to the butches; their hands never become *loyo* (limp), the way a penis does, and are always strong enough to provide an orgasm to their partners, again and again. Alvin said: 'I once used a dildo but I felt sorry for my partner. It is better with your hands, for with a dildo you cannot feel what your partner experiences inside.'[39]

Butches pride themselves on taking the initiative with their partners, as Reza divulged to me. But later he admitted:

She kissed me first, for I had no experience. It was great. We started a love relationship straightaway. I felt my man's soul had been fully realized now that I had got a partner.[40] I learnt about making love from her from the first kiss to what we did in bed. But it was all spontaneous to me, for my soul was already like that. I held her, she never held me, I didn't want that. For I had to please her (*melayani*), that was my sexual pleasure, my orgasm.

Yudi concurred: 'As I am a man I satisfied her – didn't want her to touch me. When I stroked (*raba-raba*) her she was satisfied, and my *nafsu* (desire) became heated.'

Most butches were in awe of their partners' sexual energy. Agus said: 'We always had a good sex life. Endah is strong, she can easily have two orgasms or more. I am already dead after my first orgasm. But I always satisfied Endah.' Besides penetration with the hands, butches mentioned other techniques they used, like sucking, licking, rocking and stroking the clitoris. Rarely the participants also mentioned that they had an orgasm from rubbing their genitals against each other. Only Feri said they took turns on who was on top.

The middle generation of butches allowed for more mutuality. Erly explained:

With my lover I felt I was *cowok*, she *cewek*. I wore men's clothes; my lover would be angry if I wouldn't take the active role, she always waited for me to start making love. She had to have her orgasm first, unless I was very horny myself. I liked it very much when I was on top and our vaginas touched and we moved. I had to contain myself, for I could very easily have an orgasm. As foreplay we also entered each other's vagina or stimulated each other orally.

As femmes mostly identify as 'normal' women, they insist they uphold the sexual morale of 'ordinary' women, yet b/f pleasures may subvert that. Rohmani, for instance, explained: 'As a woman I had to serve my husband and I got no pleasure. Yudi always manages to satisfy me. Yudi is a woman yet he very much looks after me. My husband hardly looked after me.'

Mia had sex with Feri for the first time in 2001:

A real man, he stood out, his appearance, how he took decisions when we were talking. I wanted to feel near him. He seduced me. But later, we always negotiated.

He was always respectful. We had been going out for four times before we had sex – I was so aroused. It was the first time I enjoyed sex. I don't ever want to go back to having sex with a man. I was kissed by a boy and felt so disgusted I wanted to vomit. And then I married. When we had sex I covered my eyes with a pillow so he wouldn't see I was not aroused at all and he would not be hurt by seeing the empty look on my face. In our twenty-three years together I never enjoyed sex with him.

Evi was twenty when she got married. She screamed the first time her husband tried to have sex with her, and the next night it was the same.

After two weeks I was still a virgin. It hurt. So I went to a doctor who gave me an ointment which I had to apply to my vagina. In the end we had sex, but it still hurt very much and a lot of blood came out. I became pregnant. But I still hated the sex with him. Every time my belly became bloated (*kembung*); it was very painful.

They boarded with a tomboy who looked feminine and called Evi *tante*.

We became close friends and I found out that in the *pesantren* she had already had a woman lover. The first night we only kissed. The next night we had sex. That was the first time I really enjoyed sex. It felt so good. My husband knew it but he didn't care. He would have been jealous if it concerned another man. But I could no longer reject sex with my husband.

In a focus group discussion on b/f passionate aesthetics[41] we discussed the difference between *peluk* (embrace) which is what butches allow, and *pegang* (hold) which is what they do not want, for that might mean penetration. As Reza said: 'I don't want to be *pegang* for we are men who satisfy our women. If they do the same to us the passion disappears immediately – abhorrent!' Ellen agreed:

I once had sex with a *kantil* who called herself a lesbian and who had had a lesbian as lover before me; they would finger each other. So when we had sex she tried to hold my breasts – I got very angry, I wanted to hit her head. The most I want is to be embraced, and that we press our bodies against each other.

They agreed that the femmes deeply enjoy this way of having sex. Reza: 'she has become hooked on us having sex and she wants it again and again. But when my wife has an orgasm do I feel the same?' Tamara asked helpfully: 'Do you have convulsions in the part below your stomach?' Reza, relieved: 'Convulsions, yes. I don't want to be entered but if we both rub each other's vaginas against each other I have an orgasm.'
Tamara, who identifies as andro, shared her own experience:

The first time I made love was with a woman much older than I was. I only satisfied her, as I didn't yet dare to be touched. I was very afraid, my legs trembled. She asked me to grope her with my hands. I entered her vagina and I felt something extraordinary, something lovely, as if there were layers and layers of softness. When she had her orgasm I was very satisfied.

Other sexual techniques mentioned during the FGD included bodies and vaginas stuck together, oral sex or riding, having sex after watching blue movies or in a hotel. They all laughed, when Tamara remarked: 'Ah that is called 3C – check in – *cret* – check out.'[42] They all agreed that *sentul* are better at making love than men. Putri said: 'Men do not smell nice, don't behave nicely, they are ignorant,' and Diana added: 'Men – they sleep here they sleep there … They give us no orgasms, while we can get pregnant, and a sexually transmitted disease.'

Jealousy

Cemburu tanda cinta is a well-known expression in Indonesian: jealousy is a sign of love. Jealousy was a constant theme in their relationships and cropped up continually in the interviews and in all kinds of informal settings. However, it was hard to establish whether and to what degree this was a greater problem in b/f relations compared to 'normal' heterosexual relationships. The romantic love ideal that is a core aspect of the Indonesian model of passionate aesthetics is one in which both partners possess each other. Butches stress that they are possessive, as there are always too few femmes around. They feared that their *kantil* might prefer a man with a higher income. Jealousy was continually performed to emphasize mutual dependence and 'true love'. Somehow, I felt it was an act of mutual trust and reassurance, although it could go too far. The partner of Jack, for example, regularly handed over her mobile phone to her lover in order to have him check her messages and erase them. 'I don't know how that works', she explained to me. 'This way Jack can see that I don't receive any messages from other men.' By engineering dependence, and catering to the perceived jealousy of Jack, this femme performed femininity and reminded him that she was a loyal partner.

Butches were unhappy when their wives had to go out to work if they themselves had too little or no income. This was especially the case when this work involved the entertainment industry. Agus said: 'Sometimes I would be angry, because Endah worked in a night club, and she would return late.'

Femmes themselves could also be violently jealous. After a birthday party in the house of Feri and Mia, two femmes had come to blows in the kitchen, I was later told by Agustine. It turned out they had competed for the attention of their ethnographer, who had, however, scrupulously divided her attention among all the femmes present. I checked with Agustine. Had I been provocative? Could my attitude be misread, both during the party and the interviews so far? We reread the transcripts. It was clear I had not reacted to their seductions. The femmes show their sexual attractiveness, their daring, for the butches to keep control, to meet this challenge. Fortunately, I had kept the necessary *sentul* cool. But it is a dangerous game, and it also reflects particular heteronormative gender ideas, in which women have allegedly the passion, *nafsu*, which has to be kept in check by men who possess the *akal*, intellect. This makes butch jealousy a bit more comprehensible, for these femmes do flirt: with long glances, swaying hips appearing out of nowhere, suggestive silences, touching my hand, my arm, my knee.

Life as a b/f couple

However difficult their lives were in the 1980s and 1990s, the b/f framework also afforded them some safety. It was an intelligible model; the words *lesbi* and LGBT were not yet applied to them, and they were not evicted from their homes, as they are nowadays in certain fundamentalist neighbourhoods such as Depok. To a certain extent they were more out and proud than the middle-class feminist lesbians.

In the 1980s the *kantil* usually had more money as they could more easily find work. But the *sentul* had various privileges in the relationship. They felt they were the protectors, the ones who took the initiative. They tried to fulfil the stereotypical male roles. Love kept them together; it was the cement of their relationship. They tried to fit that love into the heteronormative model that they saw around them. The *sentul* were usually thrown out of their families and needed stability (*kenyamanan*), which they could only obtain if they had a *kantil*. The *kantil* strongly loved the sexual prowess of their *sentul*.

Irene was prepared to fight hard for her love for Aris. Her elder sisters were much better off. Aris and Irene lived in a simple house tucked away in a large lower-class neighbourhood. Aris said:

> The happiest thing in my life is that we have a daughter. This is very important for both of us. I am her father and need to protect her, love her, make sure she never wants for anything. The same goes for my wife. The child calls Irene mother and first called me daddy. I was confused. Suppose I die and I am called daddy and I go to the Lord and my body is that of a woman? So in the end she calls me darling. We have to be careful she is never mocked. When her friends come to the house she takes them to her room. Later, when she has grown up, she will be strong enough to confront the world and she can disclose to her friends then. Her mother is also active in the neighbourhood. I stay in the background. I would love to be married officially to Irene, so nobody would laugh at us anymore.

Even in a relationship with a rascal like Yudi, the femme partner is loyal. As Yudi himself admits: 'She is a good wife, she takes care of me. But I often stray from the right path, flirting with other women, gambling. I gambled away three motorcycles but now I have stopped.' This was in 2003, but Yudi had not stopped at all.

Agus and Endah lived together for seventeen years. They had met in Yudi's house. Agus looked back at that period with nostalgia. 'It was true love, we understood each other, our two hearts became one.' Yet they broke up after Agus had stayed with family for some time in Medan.

> Endah left our house to go into a rented room that Dede paid for. A younger sibling of Endah told me that they had struck up an affair. I knew very well of

course that if Endah likes someone she is reckless, she is not going to care about me and the children. So I let her go. I didn't want to have a huge fight. I buried it in my heart. I often stay over at the house of Dede. Sometimes the three of us sleep together, we are like siblings.

Jack, for all his butch economic success, never managed to live with his lover Lela:

First it was the husband who could not know, then the children were still at school and should be protected. Now they have finished their school, but I still live alone and am tired of that. I have to phone her again and again to tell her I want to eat this or that. Before she used to bring me food but now? And I have to wash my own clothes! She comes in the evening and leaves in the morning, we just sleep together. But I also want to talk. So I took another, younger lover. She chases after me, she wants to live with me and has one child.

Lela's husband was a bad man. He once kicked her hard in the stomach. Once he brought a woman home and had sex with her in front of Lela. Jack said:

When Lela met me and knew I had a job she became brave enough to approach me. Her husband said: 'I am the head of the household. I cannot be ordered around by my wife. If I want something she has to follow.' But I told him you cannot even pay for your wife's needs, how do you want to order her around? You tell her she is not allowed to go out but when there is no money you force her to go out to the streets [to find a client].

Yet shame about being a lesbian even pervades good relationships. Endah, who had long relationships with both Agus and Dede, and who was praised by all for being such a good wife to them, found out to her despair that her eldest daughter was having a relationship with a *sentul*.

She was boarding with a friend of mine who I considered my own child. She is a woman police officer. My daughter was like her little sister. She first denied it, but in the end, admitted that they were lovers. I was very sad, but my daughter defended herself by saying 'mami you are a lesbian yourself!' But I don't want my daughter to become like me. I want her to marry a man and have children. After that she can get divorced and become a lesbian.

When the old understandings about how a b/f relationship should be are contested by the younger generation, who are better educated, more feminist, conflicts can ensue between the partners. In 2009 the couple Tita, an FTM transperson, and feminine Rini, were interviewed.[43] One difference between them which soon created problems was that Tita thought that he was a heterosexual boy who had to educate his spouse based on religious principles, while Rini, who claimed herself to be a secular feminist, wanted to build a relationship with a woman in an equal atmosphere. Their vision on relationships and intimacy was also different. Tita accepted polygamy, while Rini was vehemently against it. Tita did not want to take off her clothes when they had sex, while Rini would like to enjoy the body of someone she loved. In the beginning, Rini let Tita control her life. She changed her appearance to become more feminine. Tita often checked Rini's emails and text messages on her mobile phone and restricted Rini's relationship with her friends. Sometimes Tita forced Rini to have sex. Rini compared it to marital rape in a heterosexual relation. She started rebelling, wearing sneakers instead of high heels and cutting her hair off without asking Tita's permission. Tita became angry. Ultimately Rini broke up the relationship. It had lasted three years.

In spite of the vicious politico-religious campaign against them, a subculture of LBT persons has sprung up which is more cosmopolitan and politically astute than the first generations of f/b lesbians I met. The gloomy fictional representations of lesbians (death, exile) have transformed into more nuanced depictions of lesbian life. For instance, the 2016 novel '*Tomboi versus Lesbi*' ends with a dream of future happiness.[44] The tomboy Rasya has fallen in love with Alisha. Their forbidden relationship ends when Alisha marries a man. After some adventures Rasya forms a relationship with Shandy, whose family help her to achieve economic success, proving her haters that a tomboy can achieve. Yet Rasya cannot forget Alisha. When he manages to set up a foundation to assist children with Down syndrome, he is reconciled with her suddenly proud parents. That allows him to dream that he will be able to create his own family, and have two children – with his lesbian lover.

Conclusion

The narrators in this research took up a wide range of subject positions, mostly within the b/f gender binary. Some *kantil* felt they were 'normal' women and some butches or FTM transpeople that they were 'normal' men. The butches presented themselves as responsible, honest men, and quite a few lived up to that ideal, but a number of them fell far short of it.

They grappled with the stigma imposed on them, as ill, or sinful. Religion was a great source of worry for them, as I discuss in Chapter 9. Jack reflected:

> There is nothing in the Quran about women making love to each other, not even an official *hadith* that denounces or prohibits women's same-sex relations, only an unofficial one. That man must have hated us. For only us butches are able to satisfy our wives. Those men just stick it in, move on top of their wives and when they are finished they roll off and turn around, dropping off to sleep. But with us there is not one woman who, once she has made love to a good *sentul*, desires an ordinary man. She might marry, that's all right. They are under such great pressure from their families. But they will always return to us.

Far from just copying the heteronormative passionate aesthetics of their surroundings with its masculine sexual aggression and feminine dependence, the narrators subvert it to become an eroticized, consensual pattern in which the femme's erotic energy is the motor of the relationship. This was recognized by the butches, who were quick to announce that they were the men in the relationship, but immediately agreed that usually they were seduced by their wives and that it was their honour to satisfy the desires of their partners.

Butch gender transgression was a common theme in the stories that the butches told me. All butches cited having experienced gender non-conformity at a very young age. As they phrased it, their subjectivity was built on the realization that they had a masculine soul. For most femmes, on the other hand, sexual attraction to a butch was their first experience of gender non-conformity. Because they felt that they were primarily attracted to the masculinity of their partners, they continued to identify themselves as 'women'. Sexual satisfaction was given as an important reason to stay with their partners.

The performance of masculinity is profoundly cultural yet complexly related to bodily desires. However convincingly male-identifying persons may perform their masculinity, the fact that they have female bodies renders their masculine swagger suspect to the outside world. In terms of partnership, courtship and parenting, a butch-femme couple embodies the falseness of the hegemony that heteronormativity projects. Finding a sexual partner and fighting for the right to love her is a difficult trajectory for our narrators. Yet many of our participants managed to negotiate these problems and lived happy sexual lives.

The couples from the first generation I interviewed live together, and their neighbours accept to a certain extent the particular arrangement they have forged. The butches are proud to be called *Om*, while their femme partners take care to share the activities expected of married women, such as participating in the women's neighbourhood associations. In one case a couple adopted a child so they could be a 'normal' family. Several of these couples looked after children, usually from the earlier marriages of the femme partners. In this liminal way, they have more space for manoeuvring than most self-identified lesbians of the more educated middle classes. These women, who engage in a much more direct way with the global gay/lesbian discourse, set up internet websites and chat rooms. But many are not publicly out and it is hard for them to live together. Paradoxically, it therefore seems that the secrecy and silence surrounding the b/f couples and their sexual practices affords them a more public life as a couple than out lesbians are able to carve out for themselves.

Members of the Jakarta b/f community have been negotiating their identities and subjectivities within a tight web of multiple and contradictory discourses, respecting some boundaries, rupturing others. The b/f culture has remained an integral part of lesbian life, with new generations of b/f lesbians joining their ranks.

7

Politico-religious homophobia:
The second sexual moral panic

Introduction

From late 2015 onwards a campaign of more intense politico-religious homophobia gripped Indonesia. The first national configuration of the criminalization of homosexuality was the 2008 Anti-Pornography and Porno-Action (APP) Law. The struggle for a revision of the Constitution and the Penal Code – and for marriage reforms, as well as the introduction of discriminatory regional regulations – created a climate of attacks on the perceived breach of morality that the LGBT movement posed. This climate needs to be understood. The increasing visibility of the LGBT movement and their presence at the campuses of prestigious universities was another factor that instilled disquiet among majoritarian Muslim groups. The convergence of political and religious interests, in a context of fierce competition for the support of the many millions of conservative Muslims, led many politicians and high-level bureaucrats to utter anti-LGBT statements.

In the first decade after the Reformasi the LGBT movement articulated demands for protection from discrimination and for equal rights. Activists protested against hate speech and incitement to hatred, and they demanded with some measure of success freedom of association and speech. However, the influence of conservative Islamic clerics which began to rise in the late 1970s accelerated in the open climate after the Reformasi.[1] Since regional autonomy was put into effect in 2001, a proliferation of regional regulations followed, many of them targeting same-sex practices. Even when these regulations were found to violate articles in the Constitution or in other laws, the responsible national authorities did nothing to force their retraction.[2] The first sexual moral panic took place after 1 October 1965 when Gerwani and by association the whole communist movement was defiled. From 2015 onwards both communism and the LGBT movement were debased, in the second sexual moral panic.[3]

The LBT community moves within Indonesia's heteronormative gender regime. Heteronormativity refers to a system in which sexual conduct and kinship relations are organized so that a specific form of heterosexuality becomes the culturally accepted 'natural' order. In this regime biological sex, sexuality, gender identity and expression, and normative gender roles are aligned in such a way that a dominant view on sexual and gender relations, identities and expressions is produced.[4] Power often works through the sexual. Sexual politics are about 'the moral, sexual, symbolic, cultural and political codes in which individuals, families and the nation are linked, and with the interplay between sexed and gendered bodies and the socio-political realm'.[5] Heteronormativity establishes the hierarchical heterosexual/homosexual binary, just as it institutes hierarchies among heterosexualities.[6]

Breaking down the pervasive power of heteronormative institutions requires the mobilization of different actors. By mid-2015 various LGBT organizations were preparing a campaign to demand that the government abolish all discriminatory regulations, enact legal protection against violations of their rights and provide safe spaces. They also protested against the discriminatory regional by-laws. This was as far as the political campaigning of the LGBT movement went, for these efforts were shelved when the homophobic politico-religious crusade took off later that year.

Fertile ground

The politico-religious campaign against the LGBT movement fell on fertile ground. The major moments of that campaign, the first phase of which lasted until mid-2016, have been analysed widely.[7] It was the culmination of a long process in which the secularism and rights-based approach of the nation's founding fathers was challenged by Muslim hardliners who wanted to establish a Muslim nation, ruled by sharia law.[8] In 1998 debates on morality constituted part of the drive towards the Reformasi, namely the condemnation of political and economic corruption and the mass rape of Chinese women in 1998.[9] Conservative Muslim groups, which had proliferated during the military dictatorship, managed to shift the focus from a secular human rights-based approach to supposedly Eastern traditional values. This discourse denies the universality of human rights principles, which are declared to be 'Western'. Not all Asian countries are averse to human, women's and sexual rights. Taiwan became the first Asian country to legalize same-sex marriage in 2017.

Indonesia defends its position by pointing to the limitation clause on rights, Article 28J(2), which states: 'In exercising his/(her) rights and liberties, each person has the duty to accept the limitations determined by law for the sole purpose of guaranteeing the recognition and respect of the rights and liberties of other people and of satisfying society's just demands based on consideration of morality, religious values, security, and public order.'

This clause is often used to justify anti-LGBT regional regulations or policies, invoking the need to protect 'religious or moral values'. It is also the basis of clauses in other laws which call upon society to report 'immoral' behaviour and it opens the door to vigilante violence.

Immediately after the Reformasi both human and women's rights activists and fundamentalist Muslims sought a revision of the 1945 Constitution. In 2000 the feminist lawyer and member of the Senate (MPR, Majelis Permusyawaratan Rakyat People's Consultative Council) Nursyahbani Katjasungkana introduced a proposal to extend the non-discrimination clause. Her inspiration was the South African Constitution, the most progressive constitution in the world. True to her responsibility as chair of the KPI, with its Sektor 15, she wanted to include sexual orientation as specific grounds for non-discrimination. Her proposal was rejected. This was the first time that sexual orientation was discussed in a public forum.

The struggle over the character of the Indonesian nation, secular or based on sharia law, came to a new height in 2002, when the MPR discussed the introduction of the Jakarta Charter as an amendment to the 1945 Constitution.[10] Islamist parties and Islamic militia such as the FPI and Hizbut Tahrir strongly supported this move. They were not successful and the Constitution remained secular. However, as the Pancasila is the preamble to the Constitution and the first *sila* states that belief in one God is the basis of the state, Islamist groups used that argument to fight for Muslim-inspired laws and regulations. In a TV broadcast the FPI pledged to fight for the introduction of sharia law at the regional level, for instance, by issuing regional regulations, which indeed later happened.

The opponents of women's rights and gender diversity won an important battle when in 2008 the Anti-Pornography Law was accepted by the national Parliament. Law No. 44/2008 on Pornography is the first national law to contain provisions on consensual homosexual relations among adults. Same-sex practices are called 'deviant behaviour' and the community is exhorted to report such behaviour. Article 1 of the law states: 'Pornography is pictures, sketches, illustrations, photos, writing, voice, sound, moving pictures, animation, cartoons, conversations, movements of the body, or other forms through a variety of communication media and/or performances in public which contain obscenity or sexual exploitation which violates the moral norms in society.' This definition is both vague and so inclusive that it may lead to widely divergent interpretations. Particularly troubling is that 'members of the community' are invited to play a role in enforcing the law. This is an open invitation to mob violence by right-wing vigilante groups. For the first time in Indonesian law the term 'deviant sexual relations' (*persenggamaan menyimpang*) is used, in Article 4.[11] The definition of deviant sexual relations includes sexual relations or other sexual activities with a corpse, an animal, oral sex, anal sex and lesbian and homosexual sex.[12]

In 2012 the feminist legal aid network APIK proposed to the Ministry of Women's Affairs that a Draft Law on Gender Justice and Equality would be introduced to Parliament. CEDAW and the Beijing Program of Action were the inspirations for this law. Even though the draft that was ultimately proposed by the ministry was less progressive than what APIK had produced, it led to violent negative reactions from conservative Muslim groups. The draft was never even discussed in Parliament, even though feminist parliamentarians such as Nursyahbani Katjasungkana and Eva Sundari fought for it. And although the draft never mentioned sexual orientation, it did mobilize misogynous and patriarchal sentiments among traditional Muslims, who wanted to keep their privileges, including the control over women's bodies.

From 2012 onwards APIK discussed revisions to the 1974 Marriage Law which allows for polygyny and in which men are classified as heads of households. As early and forced marriages are widespread problems, and the conditions to engage in a polygynous marriage are often flouted, APIK also advocated for the end of the legal pluralism in family laws inherited from the Dutch. It drafted a bill which would serve as an amendment to the 1974 Marriage Act. Proposed changes included the definition of marriage (Article 1) from husband and wife into the gender-neutral wording of partners, an end to polygyny and the removal of Article 31 on the husband being the head of the household. Even though the Bill on the Amendment of the Marriage Act had been included in the National Legislation Program of Parliament, it was not discussed. Hardliners suggested that the discussion about the amendment of the Marriage Law would prepare the way to a proposal to legalize same-sex marriage.

In the meantime, a far-reaching attempt to introduce gender equality in Muslim law had come from the usually conservative Ministry of Religious Affairs. The feminist Muslim theologian Siti Musdah Mulia, heading the foreign relations department of that ministry, contributed to the 2004 counter legal draft challenging Indonesia's Islamic legal code, recommending that it be amended to prohibit child marriage and polygamy, and allow interfaith marriage. Due to violent protests, particularly from the FPI, the redraft was ultimately dropped.[13] As a result of threats of violence Musdah Mulia had to leave the ministry. By that time not just polygyny but particularly same-sex marriage, about which both APIK's and Mulia's drafts were silent, were vehemently debated. So by 2015 same-sex marriage was already hotly debated in conservative Muslim circles, though it was never proposed by the LGBT movement or by feminist lawmakers or theologians. The hope by the beginning of the Reformasi that sexual rights could be protected had faded by the mid-2010s.

During the thirty-two-year military dictatorship of President Suharto, regional autonomy was limited. Suharto's successor Habibie, the first non-Javanese president, was fully aware of the high levels of regional discontent. In May 1999 Law No. 22 on Regional Autonomy was adopted (replaced by Law No. 32 of 2004). This allowed for the transfer of authority to the district level, but the drafters of this law neglected to make explicit that the regional regulations (Peraturan Daerah, Perda) had to follow the hierarchy of legal instruments in which the 1945 Constitution takes the highest place. The Perda are at the bottom of this hierarchy and cannot contradict laws and regulations higher up. This was reiterated in the Law on Regional Governance in 2014 (No. 23 of 2014).[14] Yet hundreds of discriminatory regulations and policies have been promulgated, criminalizing and controlling the lives of LGBT people, women and religious minorities. Most of these populist-inspired regulations are based on appeals to 'tradition, culture and religion'.[15] Violence and discrimination against women and LGBT people is now often considered to be enforcing morality instead of committing a crime.

A special apparatus is in charge of overseeing the implementation of these regional regulations, the Satpol PP (Satuan Polisi Pamong Praja, Administrative Police Units). Their uniforms resemble those of the police, but they are not trained as police officers.[16] Despite this, they have wide-ranging powers to arrest, fine and to hold people deemed to be violating the regulations.[17]

Yogyakarta Principles

A positive development, though not appreciated in political and religious circles, was the publication of the so-called Yogyakarta Principles. In 2006 a group of international human rights experts met in the Central Javanese city of Yogyakarta to consider the application of existing international human rights law to sexual orientation and gender identity. They elaborated a set of international principles based on already accepted international rights that most countries, including Indonesia, had ratified.[18] These twenty-nine 'Principles on the Application of International Human Rights Law in relation to Sexual Orientation and Gender Identity', clarify the existing international human rights standards with which all states must comply. The document recommends to states a series of activities that they should undertake to ensure respect for and the enjoyment of human rights by people of diverse sexual orientation and gender identity.[19] They were updated ten years later.[20]

The Yogyakarta Principles and the UN Sexual Orientation and Gender Identity and Expression (SOGIE) Declaration are seen as the key international human rights standards in terms of sex and gender diversity rights.[21] Human rights activists regularly refer to this document. Since it was developed the Indonesian LGBT community has used it as an important lobbying instrument.

The second sexual moral panic: Politico-religious homophobia

By the end of 2015 two campaigns emerged almost simultaneously: the whipping-up of a red scare in the country and a homophobic backlash. LGBT communities and a so-called New Style Communist Movement were targeted in what we analysed elsewhere as the second sexual moral panic in the country's modern history.[22] The present sexual moral panic is built on the post-1965 one and is impelled by the rise of conservative Muslim groups. High-ranking figures spearheaded a wave of homophobia, which began at the end of 2015. It started as a campaign to ban LGBT-friendly activities from Indonesian campuses and developed into condemnation of LGBT organizations generally. The conservative press and social media participated significantly in this campaign. Websites of LGBT organizations were accused of 'promoting LGBT', and the appearance of *waria* on TV was banned.

The first university to prohibit a seminar on LGBT rights was the Diponegoro University (Undip) in Semarang, on 13 November 2015.[23] The rector was quoted as saying that the notion of LGBTI went against religious teachings and that academic freedom would only be upheld by the university 'on the condition that it was conducted responsibly'.[24] On 3 December 2015, the rector of the University of Lampung in North Sumatra (UNILA) declared that both students and lecturers belonging to the LGBT community would be expelled.[25] Barely two weeks later, on 12 December 2015, the former rector of the Islamic State University Sunan Gunung Djati, in Bandung, opined that if LGBT people were allowed to exist, Indonesia would be cursed and punished in the same way as the Prophet Luth.[26] He warned that the recent attempts to reform the Marriage Law might open the path to marriage equality. By the end of 2015 the International Youth Forum at the Brawijaya University was prohibited as it was expected that LGBT issues would be discussed. On 24 January 2016, the rector of the University of Indonesia (UI) prohibited the presence on campus of the Support Group and Resource Centre on Gender and Sexuality Studies (SGRC UI).[27] The group had been conducting seminars on issues related to sexuality and gender. They had also collaborated with the LGBT Peer Support Network.

The Minister for Research, Technology and Higher Education, M. Nasir, supported the rector: 'A university campus must guard morality … the presence of an LGBT group on campus harms the morality of the people.'[28] He prohibited LGBT students to enter universities.[29] By the end of January 2016, discussions on homosexuality on campuses became prohibited and LGBT websites were banned. In February 2016, Administrative and Bureaucratic Reform minister Yuddy Chrisnandi said that there should be no homosexual civil servants.[30] Conservative political parties joined the chorus, including the moderate Muslim party PKB (Partai Kebangkitan Bangsa, National Awakening Party), associated with the pluralist and tolerant former president, the late Abdurrahman Wahid (also known as 'Gus Dur'). The same ex-generals who had been warning of anti-communist threats also featured in the homophobic campaign. Defence minister Ryamizard Ryacudu pompously declared in February 2016 that 'the emergence of a pro-LGBT movement among Indonesia's youth poses a larger threat than nuclear warfare'. The LGBT community is conducting a 'proxy war', he affirmed.[31]

The prominent PKS (Partai Keadilan Sejahtera, Posperous Juatice Party) politician Hidayat Nur Wahid[32] warned that the very basis of the State, the Pancasila, was at stake, as it was threatened by communists and LGBT (people).[33] A campaign started in which the so-called 'defenders of LGBT' were denounced. These included the progressive cultural centre Salihara, the LGBT organization Pelangi, the periodical *Tempo* and APIK, and specifically its co-founder chair Nursyahbani Katjasungkana, the director of the Jakarta branch Ratna Batara Munti, as well as Musdah Mulia.[34]

The Ministry of Women's Empowerment, which has LGBT issues in its portfolio, also presented a press release. Minister Yohana Yembise declared that 'the campaign to promote LGBT issues to our children must be stopped'. She pointed to foreign influences behind this apparently sinister campaign.[35] The powerful Coordinating Minister of Political, Legal and Security Affairs, Luhut Pandjaitan, conceded that LGBT people had rights but, he added, 'their condition is an illness involving a chromosome and LGBT people need curing'.[36]

On 17 February 2016 the navy admiral Ade Supandi ordered his sailors to look out for groups that wanted to support the LGBT community.[37] What was he expecting? An LGBT invasion? Other parts of the security forces followed suit. In 2020 military spokesperson Colonel Aidil explained that the Army Commander had issued a telegram No. ST/398/2009 on 22 July 2009, reiterated again through a telegram No. ST/1648/2019 on 22 October 2019, that LGBT is an immoral act. 'It is against the military discipline and a serious violation that must not occur within the army', Aidil declared.[38] The National Police announced that the force would hand out ethics punishments to personnel found to be engaging in LGBT activity, following the reports of alleged LGBT members in the military. Spokesman Brigadier General Awi Setiyono said that 'the police will take firm action, and sanctions awaits', referring to articles in the 2014 National Police Code of Ethics that stipulate that all personnel should follow moral, religious and legal norms as well as local wisdom.[39]

The campaign went on until mid-April 2016, when liberal and progressive media no longer reported LGBT hate speech on a regular basis. The conservative hate mongering daily *Republika*, however, held out somewhat longer. In this whole period LGBT people were portrayed as morally and socially ill. Sometimes they were to be banned or otherwise to be cured.

Creeping criminalization

Before the acceptance of the revised Criminal Code by Parliament in December 2022, a process of 'creeping criminalization' of the LGBT community had already been taking place in Indonesia.[40] This was fanned by the conservative Indonesian Council of Religious Scholars (Majelis Ulama Indonesia, MUI), Indonesia's top clerical body.[41] The MUI was established in 1975 as a means for the state to control the public expression of Islam.[42] It is an officially independent and non-governmental organization but derives part of its income from the state.[43] It received, for instance, 'socialization funds' from the Ministry of Religious Affairs to support the campaign to have the Anti-Pornography Bill accepted.[44] Its best-known function is to issue *fatawa* (singular '*fatwa*'), religious opinions on Islamic law that have no formal legal standing. However, some of these *fatawa* have a wide social influence.

On 31 December 2014, the MUI issued a *fatwa* (No. 57 of 2014) condemning homosexuality as immoral and a sin, suggesting that LGBT people be punished by caning or with the death penalty. Rather contradictorily, it also proclaimed homosexuality to be a disease and advocated the use of 'rehabilitation' centres to cure these 'perverts'. Many *waria* picked up at night have been sent to such centres.[45] In March 2015, when Ma'ruf Amin chaired the council, the MUI issued a warning that LGBT people should receive the death sentence. In 2016, a new *fatwa* was issued to ban Muslims from joining any groups promoting LGBT rights in Indonesia. In February 2016 the MUI called upon the government to draft a bill prohibiting LGBT activities.[46] Ma'ruf Amin concluded that LGBT activities were against the national ideology of Pancasila, the Constitution and the 1974 Marriage Law.[47]

The MUI has set itself the task of eradicating *maksiat* (sin) and moral deviancy from society. Fenwick argues that the MUI is 'entrenched, through law and practice, as the primary source of guidance to government on matters of Islamic religious interpretation … when Islam speaks to government, it is the voice of the MUI that is heard … MUI bodies are granted special status through law and regulation to deliver definitive interpretations of Islam in specific areas of administration'.[48] So, in spite of Indonesia's basically secular constitution, MUI, as the representative of Indonesian Islam, arrogates to itself the role of regulating particular 'Islamic' issues such as morality. This includes gender issues and homosexuality. Strikingly, corruption, arguably a huge moral issue in Indonesia, is not singled out for the attention of this body. The influence of MUI is also felt in the Marriage Law, where it opposes reforms that would ban polygyny. It is expected that the MUI will continue to push for a sharia-based economy, considering this is a very lucrative development for the council.[49] Such an economy will ultimately also need a sharia-based legal apparatus. This might be another route to the criminalization of behaviour that is deemed to fall outside of sharia-imposed norms.

Indonesia's Constitution provides for freedom of religion (Article 29) and is basically secular.[50] Yet religious values are injected into it by way of the Preamble. This Preamble contains the state philosophy of the Pancasila or 'Five Pillars'.[51] As already mentioned, the first *sila* (pillar) is Belief in One God. Other *silas* relate to social justice and democracy. In matters of religion and morality the first *sila* of the Pancasila relates more heavily to political and popular discourse than the other *silas*, and to the secular, human rights-based parts of the Constitution.[52]

The Indonesian Constitution, accepted in 1945, and revised between 1999 and 2002, stipulates that people have the rights to live, work and form a family. Children must grow up without violence and discrimination. People should be able to enjoy the benefits of health, education, technology and culture. Freedom of expression and of organization are guaranteed, including the rights to spread and receive information, to develop the self and the social environment. Citizens have the right to choose their domicile and should be safe from torture or humiliating treatment. The civil, political, social, economic and cultural rights in the Indonesian Constitution are in accord with international standards.[53] Based on the constitutional principle of non-discrimination, sexual minorities should also enjoy these rights. Yet these rights are regularly violated.

In a 2013 report the Forum LGBTIQ provided a long list of such violations, which included violations of the right to assembly, self-expression, security, education, as well as the right to choose one's life partner, the right to employment and the right to privacy. In 2016, seventy member organizations of the LGBTIQ Forum published a report on the situation of LGBT people in which the major violations of the rights of sexual minorities were listed: violations of equal protection before the law, of the rights to life, liberty and security of person, of freedom of expression, of effective remedy, of peaceful assembly and association, and the provision of adequate standards of living, free from discriminatory incitement. Special attention was paid to Aceh, the only province under sharia law.[54]

Transpeople in particular do not have a legal space for the recognition of their identities. The Law on Population Administration No. 23/2006 and the Presidential Regulation No. 37/2007 recognize only the identity of *waria* who have undergone gender reassignment. Their number, however, is much fewer than that of *waria* who have not undergone sex reassignment. Both laws do not acknowledge FTM trans individuals.

The Marriage Law only recognizes heterosexual marriage, while both a same-sex and a heterosexual relationship between adults and minors is a crime.[55] For heterosexual people, the age limits of the Marriage Law are often ignored, or dispensation is given, so this law in practice mainly applies to same-sex relations. Underage sexually active girls who have a homosexual relationship would thus be criminalized.[56]

The Health Law contains discriminatory phrasing. Following from Article 28B(1) of the 1945 Constitution, which states that 'every person has the right to form a family and to produce offspring via a legal marriage', the Health Law No. 36/2009 explicitly states that a healthy, reproductive and sexual life may only be enjoyed with a 'lawful partner' and without 'violating religious values'. Heteronormativity is thus enshrined in this law and religion is introduced in matters of health and reproduction.

LBT people have been evicted from their houses in several cases, just on the suspicion that they were lesbians.[57] Reports have come in from Depok, Bandung, Kupang and Padang.[58] In Padang the notorious Satpol PP arrested ten suspected lesbians.[59]

The Indonesian Criminal Code goes back to the Dutch *Wetboek van Strafrecht* (Criminal Code) of 1881, adopted in the Dutch East Indies in 1915 (No. 33). This Code was re-adopted after national independence as Law No. 1 of 1946.

Revisions to the Criminal Code have long been debated in the legislature. In 1963, a revision of the Criminal Code was discussed for the first time at a seminar in Semarang. Since then, fourteen revisions of the Criminal Code have been drafted between the years 1964 and 2013, prepared by different teams of legal experts.[60] In 2017 the president sent a new draft of the Criminal Code to the legislature. The length of this process reflects tensions within the drafting committees, with religious hardliner groups wanting to insert articles influenced by sharia law, including efforts to criminalize LGBT acts. Chief editor of *The Jakarta Post*, Endy Bayuni, concluded that 'the articles on sex, reflecting the obsession of controlling the sex life of individuals, are a throwback to British Victorian era puritanism that would almost guarantee a massive degree of hypocrisy'.[61]

The revised Criminal Code was ultimately adopted on 6 December 2022. It contains several contentious articles.[62] All forms of non-marital sex have been criminalized for the first time in Indonesia. This affects not only cohabiting couples but also those who cannot marry because of restrictions in the 2004 Marriage Law, and all LGBT couples because marriage equality is prohibited. Perhaps even more controversial is the clause on the possibility of using 'living law' to prosecute behaviour not explicitly mentioned in the code. This may mean that homophobic and misogynous clauses in the hundreds of regional regulations that have been promulgated in the past decades become elevated to the national level. The prohibition of the display of contraceptives directly targets programmes on sexual health and violates the principles of the right of expression, assembly and personal safety. This code strengthens the already discriminatory 2008 Anti-Pornography Law, in which homosexuality was included in the list of prohibited behaviours. Another problematic clause is the one that stipulates that all ideologies except Pancasila are prohibited. Homosexuality is often seen as a Western import and may be targeted as anti-Pancasila. Another problem is related to the prohibition of criticism of the president, high officials or state institutions. As there are many homophobic statements emanating from people in high positions, calling them homo- or transphobic may lead to prosecution.

Prior to the adoption of the revised Criminal Code, conservative elements in civil society made efforts to criminalize homosexuality. In 2016 a group of twelve conservative academics from the Family Love Alliance (AILA) petitioned Indonesia's highest court, the Constitutional Court, to review three articles in the Criminal Code, particularly Article 292 criminalizing same-sex relations between an adult and a minor. AILA is a conservative civil society organization which has a strong anti-gender equality and anti-LGBT profile.[63] It is one of the drivers behind the criminalization campaign against homosexuality. The applicants argued that Article 292 violated the religious values which were the moral foundation of the Constitution and the Indonesian state. They proposed that the phrase 'between an adult and a minor' should be deleted to make all forms of homosexuality illegal, regardless of age and consent, and suggested that such an offence should be punishable by up to five years in jail. The applicants also wanted Article 284 of the Criminal Code to be revised to ban all sex outside marriage, not just infidelity within a marriage. In December 2017 the Constitutional Court ruled that changes to the Criminal Code were a matter for parliament.[64]

During the hearings AILA 'expert' Dewi Inong argued that homosexuality was inherently immoral and went against Indonesia's founding principles: 'Is this in agreement with Pancasila? Are relations through the rectum a part of civilized humanity? It is a dirty thing and [now] we must recognise it as a human right. Is that normal?' Furthermore, she argued that homosexual acts should be criminalized because they were more likely to cause the transmission of HIV and other sexual diseases.[65]

Three other experts claimed that the LGBT movement waged a 'proxy war'. Another 'expert' claimed that the LGBT movement was historically initiated by Jewish people in the United States, and furthermore that the National Commission on Human Rights (Komnas HAM) and the National Commission on Violence against Women (Komnas Perempuan) were both promoting same-sex marriage.[66] Two of the witnesses denounced human rights as Western, to which one of the judges, Patrialis Akbar, agreed.[67]

LGBT groups were present during the hearings but could not defend themselves, afraid that that would trigger too many negative reactions. Komnas Perempuan had prepared an extensive statement, with the help of several lawyers from APIK, including Nursyahbani Katjasungkana. They argued that people's sex life is private and that extramarital consensual sex should not be criminalized.[68]

They further insisted that human rights are universal and non-derogable. They informed the court that in Indonesia non-binary gender systems such as that of the Bugis have existed for a long time.[69] Since 1992 the World Health Organization (WHO) had deleted homosexuality from the International Classification of Diseases, they reminded the court, concluding that one's sexual orientation is an intrinsic part of humanity.

Although mostly high-level academics, the AILA representatives position themselves as 'mothers', protecting the nation's families and children. They are supported by high-level politicians, including the present vice-president Ma'ruf Amin. Even though AILA's proposal was rejected, the group continues to agitate. AILA blamed the LGBT community for the many natural disasters with which God punished the nation in 2018, including deadly earthquakes and tsunamis.[70]

Just in case the revision of the Criminal Code did not result in the criminalization of homosexuality, several politicians had also argued for the adoption of specific anti-LGBT legislation. Saleh Partaonan Daulay, the leader of the Islamist PAN party, member of the Muslim mass organization Muhammadyah and Chair of Parliamentary Commission VIII, proposed that the government should draft an anti-LGBT law. 'The goal of this law is not to marginalize them as LGBT people but to protect the ordinary non-LGBT society', he explained.[71] A legislator from the fraction of the Islamist PKS (Partai Keadilan Sejahtera. Prosperous Justice Party), Nasir Djamil, promised to head the legislative process in parliament to 'contain the spread of LGBT issues and all other activities that might destroy the morality of the people'.[72] The content of the proposed anti-LGBT legislation remained unclear. 'LGBT people must be banned, just like we banned communism and drug trafficking', added the secretary general of political party Hanura (Partai Hati Nurani, People's Conscience Party) Berliana Kartakusumah in 2016.[73]

Hidayat Nur Wahid, the deputy speaker of the MPR and a PKS politician maintained that:

> LGBT people can be classified as waging an asymmetrical war, the kind of war that tries to influence people with the goal of destroying the moral foundation of society … It is a low-cost war, and therefore asymmetric. It is not a physical war … but when the morality of the people is destroyed, the country will have no morality anymore, no vision for the future; its glorious ideals will be destroyed so that the country collapses.[74]

In these discussions, the alleged growth of the LGBT community was attributed to unspecified Western influence. The image was invoked of the Indonesian nation (*bangsa*) as 'always already pure' and heterosexual, encouraging and also feeding off an ultra-nationalist and xenophobic discourse. The language used in these homophobic pronouncements is revealing. Instead of talking about lesbian or gay or transgender people, they use terms like *pelaku* (practitioners), or sufferers (*penyandang*), or *korban* (victims) of LGBT.

Aceh

The province of Aceh is an example of how a sharia-based socio-cultural and legal climate affects the LGBT community. After a vicious struggle of three decades between the national government and those who wanted autonomy and control over the region's rich resources, spearheaded by the GAM (Gerakan Aceh Merdeka, Free Aceh Movement), a Special Autonomy Law for Aceh (No. 18/2001) was signed in 2001. This created a degree of autonomy, allowing the province to make regional laws based on sharia, called *qanun*. The violence only fully stopped after the tsunami at the end of 2004.[75] In 2005 a Memorandum of Understanding (MoU) between GAM and Jakarta was agreed that gave Aceh regional autonomy.

Gradually the contours of the sharia-based provincial laws (by-laws) became more pronounced. In September 2009 the Qanun Jinayat (criminal by-law) was accepted, which allowed for the stoning to death of married adulterers and severe fines, imprisonment, or caning for paedophilia, rape, and homosexual or lesbian acts (respectively, *liwath* and *musahaqah*). After some controversies it was signed in 2014.[76] Since then the 'sharia police' (W*ilayatul Hisbah*, or WH), a civilian force whose mandate is to investigate and prosecute violations of *qanun* in conjunction with the police, has become more active. The WH had already been created in the 2001 law. They apprehend those who they deem to be contravening sharia, including lesbian women, gay men and *waria*.[77]

The raids by the moral police on lesbian women and *waria* have resulted in the out-migration of LGBT people from the capital of Aceh, according to Muhammad Nasir Djamil, who is an Acehnese member of the national Parliament for the PKS. He was happy with the success of the morality police because they had proven 'the problem' existed: 'At least now we know there are illnesses in society because of these raids.' The raids revealed there are hundreds of lesbians in the capital, he reported, some of whom are apparently now on the run.[78] If lesbians are caught, they might be sent to rehabilitation centres.[79] Identifying a lesbian or a gay man is not always easy. The *Qanun Jinayah* clearly stipulates there must be proof of same-sex conduct. The formulation of lesbian conduct is: 'Consensual behaviour between two or more women in which they rub each other's body parts or vaginas to get sexual stimulation.' A similar graphic definition is given for *liwath*, sodomy ('penis entering anus'). For this to be punished it must have been witnessed by two people. For adultery four witnesses are required. These witnesses are not allowed to spy.[80]

Aceh has the highest level of regional autonomy of all Indonesian provinces. Yet in the Memorandum which allowed this autonomy it is explicitly stated that the *qanun* must be in line with the major human rights regulations, such as the ICCPR. This is clearly not the case. The by-laws mentioned above flagrantly contradict the ICCPR. This is exacerbated by the behaviour of the officials in charge of security and public order. In October 2015 the provincial government of Aceh decided to enforce the implementation of the sharia criminal code which was passed in 2014, ostensibly 'to safeguard human dignity by prohibiting drinking alcohol, adultery, homosexuality and public display of affection outside of marriage'.[81] On 28 September 2015 two women, aged eighteen and nineteen, were arrested in Aceh, accused of being lesbians, after they were seen hugging.[82] They were detained for three nights and then sent to religious 'rehabilitation'. In 2016 Aceh announced that anybody belonging to the LGBT community would be caned.[83] In that year too employment for LGBT persons was restricted. In Bieureun, openly transgender people (i.e. *waria*) were no longer allowed to work at beauty parlours, which would lose their business permit if they violated this rule.[84] In May 2017 two young gay men were caned eighty-three times in Aceh for homosexual sex. Before dawn on 28 January 2018, police raided beauty salons, dragging twelve transgender women out on to the streets. The women's hair was shaved, they were taken into custody, and were forced to act as men. In 2020 a gay couple were caught by neighbours who had been spying on them in Banda Aceh. They faced a punishment of 100 lashes and ultimately received seventy-seven.[85]

Media campaigns and surveillance

The discourse of sexual rights that the LGBT community had carefully started to use after the Reformasi has opened up to public scrutiny the possibility of erotic intimacy among women. Women couples who previously managed to stay under the radar are now suspected of engaging in sexual acts. Hardliner periodicals such as the Islamist journal *Republika* mounted a vicious hate campaign. The anti-LGBT media used three methods to spread hatred – inflammatory articles, sensationalization of news on crimes committed by LGBT people and outright lies and slander.

On 24 January 2016, *Republika* published an inflammatory story with the headline 'LGBT is a serious threat' to the nation.[86] The Forum LGBTIQ Indonesia lodged a complaint of biased reporting and hate speech, but nothing much came of that.[87] On the contrary, the *Republika* article gave rise to the emergence of hashtags such as #*DaruratLGBT* (LGBT Crisis).[88] The journal continued publishing homophobic stories. They repeated the insidious suggestion of the Minister of Social Affairs, Khofifah Indar Parawansa, that gay men, by giving presents to poor families, seduce boys to become homosexuals – she had apparently heard of that happening in Lombok, where 'a son suddenly started applying lipstick …'[89] By fanning the flames of homophobia, the journal helped to push the National Broadcasting Commission to ban the appearance of *waria* on screen.[90]

Already before the second sexual moral panic erupted, the press had been publishing sensationalized stories of LGBT people. In 2008 the case of Ryan was widely publicized, in all its gory details. He had murdered his same-sex lover and chopped up his body. Even the respected journal *Tempo* cited the University of Indonesia criminologist Erlangga Mardiana who stated that people should not be surprised if gay men kill in such a sadistic way.[91] When both the Ardhanary Institute and Suara Kita put out a public statement refuting this kind of slander, they received dozens of death threats.

A common way of spreading homophobia is by associating homosexuality with paedophilia, such as the case of a prostitution network discovered in West Java.[92] When delinquent gay people are placed outside the moral framework of the nation, by implication the whole LGBT community is affected. This happened a few years later, when news broke about the mass rapist Reynhard Sinaga. He was convicted of having sexually assaulted and raped 159 people in Manchester, where he was studying. The focus on his sexual orientation, as if that was the cause of his horrible crimes, served to worsen the hatred of LGBT persons.[93] He was portrayed as having tainted the Indonesian nation. Muhammad Idris Abdul Somad, the mayor of Depok, a conservative satellite city of Jakarta, where Sinaga's parents live, called for more anti-LGBT raids to be conducted by the Satpol PP, to 'prevent the spread of LGBT'.[94]

Media that spread anti-LGBT news often complain that the LGBT movement spreads LGBT propaganda. The underlying ideas are that LGBT is an infectious disease and that unnamed foreign forces are behind the LGBT movement, trying to undermine the purity of the Indonesian nation. Ironically, the remedy they advertise hails from foreign countries such as communist Russia and China, even though in Indonesia communism is often as detested as the LGBT community. [95]

An early target of restrictions on the so-called LGBT propaganda was the portrayal of *waria* performers on TV. These artists performed comical characters in several popular TV shows in a stereotypical but also good-humoured way. Following a public outcry in early 2016 against this way of 'promoting homosexuality', the KPI (Komisi Penyiaran Indonesia, Indonesian Broadcasting Committee) produced a circular prohibiting shows which featured men who dressed and behaved like women.[96] KPI argued that such shows were not in line with the 'current social norms' of politeness, modesty and the protection of children and youth. Broadcasts with such content can 'push children to learn or to accept such incorrect behaviour as something that is customary in daily life'.[97] This ban violated the KPI's own 2012 Guidelines for Broadcast

Practices and Standards for Broadcast Programs, which prohibit programmes that stigmatize 'people of certain sexual orientation and gender identity'.[98]

Groups like the Indonesian KPAI (Komisi Perlindungan Anak Indonesia, Indonesian Child Protection Commission) clamoured for curbing the spread of information on LGBT people and their communities. The Ministry of Communication and Information reacted to this pressure by suggesting that a ban on websites containing LGBT-related issues would be included in the upcoming anti-LGBT legislation. The police urged the ministry to ban gay mobile phone applications after a case of the misuse of those applications for child prostitution in West Java emerged in the news. As a result, three gay apps – Grindr, Blued and Boyahoy – were banned.[99] On 11 February 2016, the ministry urged LINE Indonesia and WhatsApp to withdraw stickers and emoticons that displayed male same-sex affection from its platform as they might have a negative impact on children. Some companies complied, notably the messaging app LINE, which removed such emojis from their Indonesian service.[100] Altogether 477 websites with LGBT material were blocked by the ministry, as they were said to contain content on LGBT issues, pornography and radicalism.[101] In 2019, an Instagram account, @alpantuni, portraying comic strips about the lived experience of gay Muslim men, was accused by the government of promoting pornographic content and subsequently banned.[102]

The progressive press tried to counter the vicious attacks on the LGBT community by their intolerant media colleagues. Already in June 2015, when the anti-LGBT climate was heating up, the online history journal *Historia* published an article about a *waria* (FTM), called 'Si Putik' (The White One) who pointed the way for the legendary independence hero General Soedirman.[103] It was a dangerous situation, with the Dutch nearby, and no one else was courageous enough to lead the way. Interestingly, both the words tomboy and *waria* are used to describe Si Putih. The story portrays a female-bodied transperson in a highly nationalist setting, and as an exceptionally brave person.

The Alliance of Independent Journalists (AJI) awarded its yearly Suardi Tasrif prize to the Forum LGBTIQ and the IPT 1965, as two organizations that had been audacious enough to challenge mainstream opinion on two hotly debated issues, homosexuality and the 1965 genocide. On behalf of the Forum LGBTIQ, the award was accepted by two representatives from the Alliance, Abhipraya Ardiansyah Muchtar, a transman, and Kanza Vina, a transwoman.[104] She described how hard it was to grow up as a feminine boy in Bengkulu. She said her seniors in junior high school forced her to give them oral sex. She moved out from home at the age of fifteen and became a sex worker. Abhipraya told the audience that he had realized that he was born in the wrong body when he was still young.[105]

Supporters

Progressive sectors of civil society stepped up to protect the rights of the LGBT community. The women's movement has always been a strong supporter, particularly Komnas Perempuan and APIK. Students at university campuses, though heavily supervised, provided support as well. Human rights organizations followed suit. On

28 January 2016 a joint statement signed by 115 non-governmental organizations and hundreds of individuals urged the government to protect the rights of LGBTIQ people.[106]

On 5 February 2016, Komnas HAM, the National Commission on Human Rights, issued a strong statement. The commission urged public officials to put a stop to negative comments that violated the human rights of and incited violence towards the LGBT community. It also called on law enforcement agencies to curb abuse instigated by community organizations or individuals towards LGBT people. The commission referred to the Yogyakarta Principles and the only two government regulations that protect the rights of LGBT groups, namely the Social Affairs Ministry Regulation No. 8/2012 on minority groups and the Home Ministry Regulation No. 27/2014 on the guidelines for regional development in 2015 which includes the protection of the rights of gays, transpeople and lesbians.[107]

The liberal English-language journal *The Jakarta Post* regularly published articles supportive of LGBT rights. On 18 February 2016, an editorial strongly denounced the hate mongering.

> Panic is spreading about a 'movement' that seeks to convert heterosexual youth among those with apparently little exposure to lesbian, gay, bisexual and transgender (LGBT) people ... President Jokowi must remind the nation that Pancasila means equal treatment of minorities ... if 'belief in one God' means kicking out sexual minorities, Indonesia will be on par with Hitler's Nazi regime, which crushed perceived moral decadence and 'impurity'.[108]

The *Post*'s astute columnist Julia Suryakusuma, in her popular column Viewpoint, also sarcastically wondered whether: 'LGBT people [were] really so dangerous that they are put on par with that of crazy bomb-exploding radicals? It would be hilarious if it weren't so tragically pathetic.'[109]

Support also came from a group of lawmakers calling themselves the Pancasila Caucus. They included Rahayu Saraswati of the Gerindra Party (niece of chair Prabowo Subianto), Maman Imanulhaq of the National Awakening Party (PKB) and Eva Kusuma Sundari of the Indonesian Democratic Party of Struggle (PDIP). The group called on the government to protect LGBT people against all forms of discrimination and violence.[110]

These supporting voices to some extent mitigated the burden of the politico-religious homophobic campaign, yet the impact of this second moral sexual panic on the private lives of LGBT activists has been enormous. The few empathetic politicians of Golkar, Gerindra and the PDIP did not succeed in swaying their parties to support the idea that the LGBT community should enjoy the same human rights as other Indonesian citizens.

Consequences

The few months that this second sexual moral panic lasted, from November 2015 to April 2016, was a watershed for the LGBT movement. If before they had hoped that with careful advocacy, training and public events, they might gain a measure of sympathy from the wider public and fight for their rights, now they had to hide and hope that their allies in the women's and human rights movement would protect them. Since 2016 homophobic proclamations are routinely heard throughout the country by representatives of political parties, religious leaders and government officials.

LGBT organizations have made themselves less visible, by restricting access to their social media, or by no longer working from their offices. Individual LGBT people became depressed; not only they themselves but also their families were harassed. The FPI raided the Ardhanary Institute office in early 2016. The raid was coordinated by Fahira Idris, a member of the regional Parliament and a successful businesswoman. The Ardhanary Institute changed its name plate[111] and changed the setting of its website from closed to secret. They took down all pictures of their activities from their website, toned down its wording and deactivated their Twitter accounts. Another effect of the crackdown on LGBT organizations is that they find it increasingly difficult to conduct seminars or training programmes. Information on safe sex and reproductive rights and health can no longer be distributed via their own outreach programmes.[112]

When I met Ardhanary Institute activists in January 2018, they told me how their lives had changed after the campaign started. We met in Pejaten Village, one of the best-known malls in Jakarta, rather than in their office. The occasion was festive, Agustine had just become an attorney, after graduating in law the previous year. She had spent the years that she had to remain under the radar studying, determined to come back as a more qualified activist.[113] By the end of the lunch, Agustine bent over to me, asking: 'Why do they hate us so much? What have we done wrong? It hurts, though I try to ignore the mails.' She has two email addresses and two phone numbers – a new one for friends and colleagues and the old, by now public one. On the previous email address she has received hundreds of emails and messages expressing the loathing and hatred of mostly unknown people. We hate you, we will exterminate you and you don't deserve to live are among the mildest threats.

To the neighbours they are a regular women's group. The members of the Ardhanary Institute take care to speak softly, trying not to provoke their neighbours in any way. But whenever the *azan* sounds for Friday prayers, the women are afraid: will they come this time? 'They' are the members of radical Muslim groups coming to beat them up, chase them out of their office. From the mosques they know hate speech emanates. Not since 2003, when Agustine appeared on TV, had they received these kinds of hate messages.

They have withdrawn from public events. They hardly get any more funding. Even their auditor is being threatened and their bank enquired about a gift they had received from abroad. They subsist by delivering small training programmes which other organizations arrange, on gender awareness in media or on sexual health. The *Jurnal Perempuan*, with which they made a media guide, was told that if they did that again they might lose their printing permit. As an aside the narrators informed me that a new term has come up that they use among each other: j j – *jeruk makan jeruk* (orange eats orange) – after an advertisement some years ago which showed two oranges appearing to having fun.[114] This is at the same time a joke and a way of avoiding dangerous terms like *lesbi*.

The first raids were on 27 January 2016. For example in Bandung Kulon the FPI evicted lesbian women from their rented rooms, and the neighbours put up a banner saying 'Lesbi and Homo prohibited from entering our area.' Subsequently such banners appeared in many other neighbourhoods around the country.[115] Raids were also conducted on saunas frequented by gay men, and on private parties.[116] Human Rights Watch documented the major police raids on gay men.[117] Raids were often justified by alleging that the 'community' had voiced objections to the presence of LGBT individuals. However, these 'community members' often belonged to Islamist militias who accompanied the Satpol PP.

In February 2018 the administration of Depok announced it would set up a taskforce, including police officers and religious leaders, to 'anticipate the spread of LGBT among young people'. *Waria* and masculine-identifying lesbians were especially targeted, as they are the most visible members of the LGBT community.[118] Depok has long been dominated by the intolerant Islamist party PKS and is notorious for its anti-LGBT policy. On 10 January 2020, Idris Abdushomad, the PKS mayor, announced he would order the Satpol PP to conduct raids against the LGBT community and set up a crisis centre for 'victims of LGBT'.[119]

Much publicized was an attack in February 2016 on the only *pesantren waria* in Indonesia (and in the world) by the FJI (Front Jihad Islam, Islamic Jihad Front) in Yogyakarta. The coordinator of the *waria pesantren*, Shinta Ratri, went into hiding and the institution was closed. The pretext was that the community was said to be disturbed by its presence.[120] About a month later the *pesantren* resumed its religious instruction to *waria* in the house of chair Shinta Ratri herself.[121]

The influence of the politico-religious and homophobic campaign permeated the whole society. In 2018 Indonesia was struck by a particularly devastating series of natural disasters – a major earthquake in Lombok and a deadly tsunami in Sulawesi. As already mentioned, conservative groups blamed sexual minorities for provoking this *azab* (punishment by God) on their communities by their very presence.[122] In an anti-LGBT demonstration in Bogor on 9 November 2018, co-organized by HASMI (Himpunan Alumni Sunniyah Untuk Masyarakat Islami, Association of Sunni Graduates for the Muslim Society) and Forum Masyarakat Bogor, the following slogan was used *Homoseks Lesbian Seks Bebas Mengundang Azab Allah & Merusak Generasi Muda* (homosexuality, lesbianism and free sex invite the punishment of God and destroy the young generation).[123]

For many public positions a so-called fit and proper test is required. Organizations such as the broadcasting commission KPI and the KPAI made it clear that members of the LGBT community would not be accepted in their ranks. In interviews for positions at institutions such as these the candidates might be asked whether they support the LGBT community. If they answer in the affirmative they will not be hired. Students applying for scholarships abroad have to answer similar questions.[124]

Conclusion

From mid-April 2016, liberal and progressive media no longer reported LGBT hate speech on a regular basis. After the first wild statements had died down, most politicians and opinion leaders, apart from those in Aceh, were careful to stress that

LGBT people as Indonesian citizens were 'also' allowed to enjoy the human rights the Constitution guaranteed. But on the ground militias such as the FPI did not abide by these constitutional rights, and LGBT people have since been evicted from their homes, their work and their entertainment venues. Life for LGBT activists has become very difficult and it has become much less safe to come out of the closet. LGBT youth are particularly at risk. They are portrayed as 'victims' of LGBT influences which apparently has infected them through unspecified means, while most of them are growing up in staunchly heterosexist families. They are deprived of any support services that had previously been established with such care.

Though there are obvious parallels in the ways communism and LGBT have been scapegoated and stigmatized,[125] the sudden eruption of the second sexual moral panic was not triggered by something like a scandal or major event comparable to the actions of the 30 September 1965 movement. Yet several developments fed into the already toxic mix of Islamist politics: long-simmering religious intolerance and Wahabist *dakwa* (proselytizing) at universities and mosques. The virulent debate on marriage reforms was a contributing factor, as well as the growing social visibility of the LGBT community and LGBT-friendly events in prestigious universities. Above all, this campaign can be seen as the moral battlefield between majoritarian Muslim groups, some of which with links to earlier organizations that strove to establish a Negara Islam (Islamic State),[126] and more secular groups who want the nation to keep its secular and inclusive character, as meant by the nation's founding fathers.[127] By portraying LGBT as a foreign import as well as morally perverse, the anti-LGBT campaign appeals to a wide group of both ultra-nationalist and bigoted Muslims (as well as adherents of other religions). There are calls that the nation, the people (*bangsa*), are threatened, and particularly the nation's children, by this contagious illness called LGBT.

With communism, LGBT became a rallying point in the 2019 electoral campaign.[128] Both groups were used as an excuse to not focus on endemic problems in Indonesian politics, such as corruption, nepotism and the transactional nature of relations between politicians of all hues and military leaders and economic tycoons.[129]

A third category of abjection, besides communism and LGBT, is feminism, in the eyes of conservative groups like AILA and the PKS. But the ministry that is supposed to protect the rights of women, children (and LGBT people, always ignored in their statements), the Ministry of Women's Empowerment and Child Protection (WECP), also falls prey to the discourse of patriarchal heteronormativity in which 'deviancy', however defined, must be combatted. The ideology of gender harmony (an orchestra has a conductor and a player of the triangle, both are important for the outcome, the harmonious sound) and *keluarga sakinah* or the happy family (namely with a patriarchal father at the head), actively promoted by the Ministry of WECP, is inherently homophobic.[130]

As Rita Subagyo, prominent member of AILA, explains, though feminism has no direct link with this 'social illness', '[it] becomes the umbrella under which the existence of LGBT, prostitution, free sex and other deviant social behaviours can grow'. A widow may become feminist because of her biological needs, the consequence can be 'gender awareness, lesbianism and such things'.[131]

The discourse at community level (of sin, Sodom and contagious illness) is different to that of the academic hate mongers, such as the highly educated members of AILA. Their concern is with the family and the nation as a whole, and they mix and distort various pseudo-scientific Western arguments on biology, HIV/AIDS, psychology and psychiatry to support their position. Social constructivism, for instance, is (ab) used to 'prove' that LGBT is not related to inborn characteristics but is imposed from the outside. Therefore, the implication is that it can also be easily changed (as will be further detailed in the next chapter), if only the external influences are changed – for instance, through counselling and other forms of conversion therapy. Is not gender theory itself telling us that gender and sexuality are fluid? The apparent contradiction that LGBT and feminism are denounced as imports, alien to the 'pure' Indonesian nation, while the arguments to attack these two movements are derived from ill-understood or misinterpreted Western theories, seems to escape the AILA academics.

Apart from sin, deviancy, contagious disease and alleged violations of ethics and traditional culture, the discourse during this politico-religious campaign had several other characteristics. Human and particularly women's rights defenders were seen as a cover for LGBT groups. Meanwhile, the most targeted were LGBT organizations, although the effects of the campaign were also felt by many LGBT activists and other members of the community. They were portrayed as 'infecting' children and 'attacking' campuses and wider society. The campaign emphasized the alleged dangers of the so-called LGBT propaganda. Websites and other forms of social media were closed. A frequently heard accusation was that LGBT people preyed on the nation's youth. Conservative and particularly majoritarian Muslim leaders and preachers used an ultra-nationalist discourse declaring that LGBT was imported from the West. Western funding on sexual rights issues was targeted, Arab funding and Arab influence were not mentioned. Overall, the level of (feigned) ignorance, prejudice, outright lying and political opportunism was staggering. Its impact is still felt at the time of writing this book, and the same old arguments are repeated ad nauseam.

8

Family violence and conversion therapy

Introduction

LBT people are subjected to various kinds of violence in their families. One form of violence they experience is the conversion therapy which many of them undergo. Reports by Arus Pelangi and the LGBTQI Forum on violence against the LGBT community record hundreds of cases of violence against community members across Indonesia.[1] These findings do not reflect the prevalence, as there is widespread underreporting. LBT victims of different forms of domestic violence in general do not report these events to an organization, let alone to the police, as that would expose them and would bring shame upon their families. Ironically when they fall in love it is considered an offence against family honour and bitter sanctions may follow. The forms of persecution faced by the LBT community include intimidation; abuse; molestation; personal data dissemination; raids; destruction of goods; rape, including corrective rape; and extortion. Conversion therapy is widely used to 'cure' LGBT people of their perceived 'illness'. A common form of conversion therapy in Indonesia is *ruqyah* (exorcism).

Sexology

LGBT people in Indonesia are variously seen as sick, criminal or immoral; often all of these qualifications are combined. These attributes find their origin in various European traditions.[2] Dutch colonial morality imported its contemporary theories and sexual practices into the archipelago. Same-sex practices were widely criminalized in imperialist Europe. From the end of the nineteenth century onwards this legal regime was replaced in Europe by a medicalizing discourse which emerged in the wake of eugenic theories. Thus, during the heyday of imperialism, criminological and then psychiatric theories presided over the study of and state policy on sexual 'weakness', 'degeneration' and 'vice'. Freud's invention of psychoanalysis as a 'science of desire' in late nineteenth-century Vienna was a main contribution to the popularization of the assumption that humans are born with a sexual nature, and that there is a 'normal' course in the development of sexual subjectivity, in which male dominance and women's receptivity – naturalized as biologically determined – were eroticized.[3]

The new science of sexology set itself the task to uncover the 'laws of nature', to make sexual instincts intelligible. Sexual classifications became the object of a naturalistic approach imbricated with the construction of racial and ethnic traits. These medical and psychological theories became immensely influential. The works of European scientists like Havelock Ellis, Krafft-Ebing, Magnus Hirschfeld and other pioneers became popular in many corners of the globe.[4] Ellis described butches as inverted persons and femmes as 'normal' women seduced and perverted by 'inverts'.[5] Congenital sexual inversion was defined as the sexual instinct being turned by inborn constitutional abnormality towards persons of the same sex. This was a condition which was assumed to be comparatively rare. Ellis deemed homosexual attraction to be of 'universal occurrence among all human races', though (rather paradoxically) usually due to the 'accidental absence of the natural objects of sexual attraction'.[6]

In a similar vein Krafft-Ebing published the first edition of his sexological handbook that became widely popular. He divided the homosexual patients he treated between those whose inversion was inborn and those who had acquired it. He called the 'sexual inversion' of women who possessed a female body and a male soul 'gynandrous' or 'hermaphrodite', listing it as a congenital condition and a mental illness. As a psychiatrist he recommended treatment. His favourite method was hypnosis, but he had to admit that his success rate was very low.[7] The feminine partners supposedly entered into their relationship due to particular circumstances and were classified not as inverts but as perverts, who might return to 'normal' heterosexuality.[8] His ideas became the basis for the list of sexual perversions in the first, 1952 edition of the DSM (Diagnostic and Statistical Manual of Mental Disorders). Krafft-Ebing's essentialist perspective on sexuality also spread to various other colonized and modernizing countries.[9] Major sexological treatises were, for example, translated into Japanese.[10]

The philosopher Foucault maintained that the historical invention of sexuality was a disciplinary device. He argued that the deployment of sexual knowledge established a regime of knowledge whereby the 'normal sexual response' became the bedrock of public health and morality, naturalizing the social norms that regulated the distinction between licit and illicit desires and acts.[11] The constructivist revolution of the 1970s and 1980s turned the discourse on the perceived biological ('inborn') and psychological 'origins' of these inversions to a discourse of constructed desires and performativities, which was developed by feminist theorists such as Rich and Butler.[12]

Among sexual rights theorists a broad consensus has grown that the development of one's sex-gender identity is the result of a complex interaction between genetic, prenatal and postnatal endocrine influences and postnatal psycho-social and environmental experiences.[13] In 1987 homosexuality was removed from the DSM. However, gender dysphoria, a classification referring to transpeople, has remained in the *DSM 5*. The World Psychiatric Association, an organization of national psychiatric societies consisting of 138 member societies across 118 different countries, has denounced any attempts to turn LGBT people heterosexual through what they call 'reparative therapy'. They declared the practice is unethical and potentially harmful, while there is no sound scientific evidence that innate sexual orientation can be changed.

On 17 May 1990, the WHO removed homosexuality from their list of mental disorders. This action ended more than a century of medical homophobia. Since

2004 that date has been celebrated as the International Day against Homophobia, Transphobia and Biphobia (IDAHOT). Indonesia adopted the International Classification of Diseases (ICD) of the WHO and the DSM into their own Guide and Diagnosis of Mental Disturbances. In the third revised edition of 1993, point F 66 states that homosexuality is not a mental disease. Yet in February 2016 the Association for Clinical Psychologists of the Association of Psychologists Indonesia issued a statement promoting the healing of LGBT people.[14] The Indonesian Psychiatrists' Association also classified LGBT as a mental disorder in the same month.[15] Referring to the 2014 Mental Health Law, the Indonesian Psychiatric Association classified homosexuals and bisexuals as 'people with psychiatric problems', while transgender people had 'mental disorders', and claimed that both could be cured through proper treatment.

Alarmed, the president of the World Psychiatric Association, Renée Binder, sent a letter to Indonesian colleagues reminding them of research that proved that sexual orientation has genetic, hormonal and environmental components, is a normal variation of human sexual behaviour and not the outcome of free choice.[16] The letter strongly denounced reparative therapy on lesbian, gay, bisexual and transsexual people: 'There is no sound scientific evidence that innate sexual orientation can be changed. Furthermore, so-called treatments of homosexuality can create a setting in which prejudice and discrimination flourish, and they can be potentially harmful.' Therefore, any intervention purporting to 'treat' something that is not a disorder is unethical, it further stated.

The most vocal and influential proponents of the medicalization of homosexuality are professors Dadang Hawari and Fidiansyah from the Department of Psychology at UI. Professor Dadang is the founder of what he terms 'Islamic psychology' and sees AIDS as a punishment by God for homosexuals and adulterers. A complaint was lodged by members of Arus Pelangi at LBH Jakarta against Professor Fidiansyah when he proclaimed homosexuality a psychiatric disorder.[17] According to progressive psychologist Gunawan Wibisono, his homophobic colleagues not only base themselves on a particular interpretation of Islam but also on speculative Freudian theories. As Benny Prawira, who studied at the same faculty, noted, they do not use an evidence-based approach, they just proclaim what their clients would like to hear. The therapies they use include hypnotherapy and hormonal injections.[18]

It is difficult to assess how many official psychiatric wards or other centres offering psychological counselling engage in these unethical reparative therapies. Six clinics in Jakarta told Agence France Press in 2020 that they performed exorcisms that would 'cure' LGBT clients, although none openly advertised the treatment.[19] This is probably only the tip of the iceberg. We investigated the case of Ashok, a gay man from a prominent and very conservative family.[20] As a child he was bullied both at school and at home for being effeminate. He was sent to two conversion therapy centres by his older sisters, a Christian foundation[21] and a psychiatric hospital. Neither of them advertise this service on their websites. Their unease with this method, that they know is considered unethical, may explain why in the initial interviews they downplayed both the time Ashok spent in them and the kind of treatment he underwent. Only in subsequent interviews were the experiences that Ashok conveyed to us corroborated.

In 2002 he spent eight months in a so-called Christian rehabilitation camp, where he was sedated. He was subjected to a programme called '*pelepasan*' (release) which involved, three times a day, up to two hours of readings from the Bible and speeches that were meant to instil guilt and shame about his homosexuality. He left a psychological wreck but still as gay as when he went in. In 2004 his sisters again sent him to a conversion centre, this time a psychiatric hospital. When he refused to go along with the hospital nurses, security personnel sedated him. He stayed there for two years. He was diagnosed as schizophrenic and bipolar and forced to swallow medication. When he was finally released his trauma had increased, but his sexual orientation had remained the same. When Agustine asked the medical staff from the psychiatric hospital if they would treat an LGBT child, they conceded that they would.

Indonesian psychologists and psychotherapists should be assumed to be up to date in their scholarly literature. They know that conversion therapy is strongly rejected by their own international associations and considered pseudo-scientific, and that the Indonesian psychiatric association declared that homosexuality is not a disease, and thus cannot be cured either. Why they then still provide conversion therapy is unclear, but it is perhaps due to popular demand and financial considerations, because there is a market for these services in Indonesia. Most conversion therapy is paid for privately and so profit is a motive for providing it.

Religious groups of different denominations have called LGBT behaviour a 'social disease'. The Indonesian Ulema Council (MUI), the Indonesian Catholic Bishops Conference (KWI), the Council of Buddhist Communities (Walubi) and the Confucian Supreme Council of Indonesia (Matakin) released a statement in 2016 saying that LGBT people could be helped to 'get back on track to normalcy' if restrictions on the promotion of LGBT activities were applied. In this way 'deviant sexual tendencies' would be eradicated.[22]

Family violence

Family violence was frequently reported as the most traumatic form of violence by the narrators in this research. It takes the form of bullying, shaming, physical violence and psychological pressure to conform to the heteronormative binary pattern of gender behaviour. I also heard many stories of sexual violence in the form of the corrective rape of lesbian girls.[23] The LGBT organization Arus Pelangi found that almost 90 per cent of LGBT people had experienced violence.[24] In a follow-up research published in 2019, the organization produced a report on twelve years of persecution of LGBT people in Indonesia.[25] Most cases referred to intimidation; arrest; cruel treatment; murder; corrective treatment; raids; expulsion from family, jobs or housing; or the exposure of private data. Family violence was among the most common forms of persecution the victims reported. In some cases state or security personnel were involved; in other cases mass organizations were involved, most of them religious groups. The report concludes that the persecution of LGBT people in Indonesia is systematic.

Family violence usually becomes particularly acute around the coming out process. The collection of autobiographical stories by Daniel during the Dipayoni research project is full of accounts in which the protagonists are considered sinful or ill by their family members.[26] This puts enormous psychological pressure on them, out of fear of making the family ashamed in front of the extended family, their neighbours or other members of their communities, and it pushes them to fulfil the wish of their parents to get married. As a result they agree to marry, otherwise they usually leave home or are expelled from home, with all the misery and pain that entails. Paradoxically violence against LBT persons is usually justified because they are lesbian or FTM. On the other hand, violence is also often seen as the cause of them becoming LBT, both by LBT persons themselves, who explain that they hate the men who have abused them, and by therapists who want to cure them. Even corrective rape may be justified as a curing process – you have never had a good penis inside you.[27]

Sabarini, investigating family violence against LBT people with the Ardhanary Institute, wrote:

> Families can do twisted things on learning their daughter or sibling is a lesbian. A brother would force his butch sister to perform oral sex in an attempt 'to educate' her; a mother would hire a gigolo so that her daughter would know the 'pleasure of men'. The sexologist her mother brought her might grope her asking whether she felt any excitement. Families would force femme lesbians into marriages they did not want.[28]

For the narrators in my research, it was clear that home had been the most dangerous place to be. Males in their families might rape them to 'set them straight'. For a femme lesbian the greatest danger is to be forced into a marriage they do not want and to be raped by their husbands. In the rare cases LBT people report such violence to the police; they are cold-shouldered and told that it is 'no wonder you have been raped, you're a lesbian'. Some lesbians have considered entering into a fake marriage with a gay man. But they are afraid it will end badly, as the Marriage Law is biased against them and gay men enjoy the patriarchal dividend of their society. Gay men are also under pressure to marry – but they are usually older when this kind of pressure becomes intolerable, and refusing to make love is different from being raped. I also heard cases of suicide attempts after what seemed minor problems in a relationship. This may be caused by the deep fear that after losing their families they are now also in danger of losing their lovers.[29]

The following stories from my narrators illustrate the points made above. In some cases the abuses they experienced were not conveyed in the formal interviews I had with them but during parties or other encounters. This points to the traumas that haunt them.

Susy and Yoland are two of my best activist friends. As a dynamic couple they have been at the forefront of many of the activities described earlier. As a child Susy had been the victim of abusive incest with three men of her family, her father and two uncles. Yoland told me this in secret. Susy herself had only told Yoland after they had been together for six years. As a result of this childhood sexual abuse, Susy is disturbed, paranoid at times and deeply insecure. They were very young when they met and fell in love, in the early 1990s. Yoland, from a prominent Catholic family, was beaten up by her father and at some stage forced to move to Ambon, in the hope she would be 'healed' there. Susy used her savings to get Yoland back and then she herself was subjected to violence by her elder brother. The brother beat her and in self-defence Susy picked up a kitchen knife. He took her and Yoland to the police. At the station he beat them up before the officers' eyes, who remained passive. Ultimately the police advised Susy to report the brother for violence, but the girls were so afraid that they did not follow it up. Susy's brother reported their relationship to the office where both worked at the time and they were fired.

When she was twelve years old femme singer Diana was raped by her elder brother. She was blamed for it, for that brother was earning money for the family, and nobody wanted to offend him. She ran away from home to her father, in Kupang, who raped her as well. While pregnant from a foreigner who wanted her to have an abortion, she met Irfan, a butch who took good care of her; she almost lost her baby due to an illness. They lived together for some time happily, until Diana's brother abducted their two children, and brought them to live with him to Banyuwangi in East Java. He accused Diana of being a bad mother, and pictured Irfan as a devil (*setan*) who had seduced Diana. Due to the intervention of Nursyahbani Katjasungkana and the Ardhanary Institute they managed to get their children back. But already the eldest son believed Irfan was a *setan*.[30]

Irfan also had a traumatic past. When she was six years old her teacher put his finger in her underwear. It hurt very much. Her father raped her when she was in junior high school. He was big and smothered her. After that she revolted against him and slept in another room that she could lock. She could not tell her mother, who was often beaten by him. Instead, she tried to help her mother, but then Irfan received the beatings instead. Only when she had attended a training session in KPI did she learn to talk about this.

My narrators told me stories of parents who hired a man to rape them to 'heal' them, or fathers or brothers who would take that task upon themselves, or commit other forms of violence. Adom, a shy masculine butch with a baseball cap, said he was beaten up by his father and thrown through a glass cabinet door, into the gutter. He had hot water thrown over him. He ran away and lived on the streets for some years. When I met him, he was getting himself educated, and attended one of my lectures at the UI, where I discussed sexuality. He felt supported in that atmosphere; these were educated people who did not scorn people like him! When he walked beside me he touched my arm several times, proud, protective towards an older woman.[31]

With democratization and the growing visibility of LGBT lives, their pain also became more visible. In one of the first issues of *Semai*,[32] the journal of the KPI to which Agustine contributed, the physical and psychological violence experienced by some lesbians was chronicled. For example, Ina was beaten black and blue by her father when he found out she was a lesbian. Her jaw was dislocated so she could not eat for a week. She was sent to a psychiatric hospital and thought she deserved that as her elder siblings told her that lesbianism was an illness, a curse. Ina told Agustine she experienced hallucinations and even tried to commit suicide.

The Dipayoni research team also encountered numerous examples of domestic violence. Out of twenty-seven respondents, 48 per cent experienced physical violence,

26 per cent psychological violence, 22 per cent sexual violence, 15 per cent exclusion from family, and 4 per cent economic neglect. About 26 per cent of the respondents received multiple forms of violence. Most of these narrators had a middle-class background; losing one's family support if your parents knew that you were a lesbian was much feared. Riri, for instance, asked her interviewer not to come to her house: 'They will be able to identify us from our appearance, especially the butches … If my friends or family saw me among them woooo … I cannot imagine what might happen. I might be expelled and would not be able to go to university anymore.'[33] Some had turned to hurting themselves physically as a means to ease the pain. Ala showed her wrist and hand to her interviewer, marked with long scars: 'I do this anytime I feel desperate. [When I scratch] I move my painful feeling into physical pain. It is a relief.'[34]

In 2010 the Dipayoni team organized an exhibition of five photo narratives produced by their narrators. One of the stories was entitled Family Jail. The figures were all formally dressed, the men in suits and a *kopyah*, an oval head covering usually put on for religious occasions. The scene suggested a harmonious family. But for the protagonist it was a jail. At the end of the story, it was not clear whether the main character would follow her family's wishes or her own desires. In the latter case she had to give up her family. If she chose the family, she would sacrifice herself.[35]

This dilemma, being accepted by one's family or following one's own heart, is common, and can only be overcome when the LBT person becomes successful in some way. As Donny explained:

> After I finished my university studies and got a job, my parents finally accepted me. I stopped being beaten and scolded. My parents told me that I had to adjust myself in society so as not to be abused. [They said] I have to do good things to others, obey and worship God. The most important thing is being economically independent. Being accepted by both my beloved parents makes me proud.[36]

Financial independence is no panacea. In February 2022 *The Jakarta Post* published the story of Nyai. She thought she had managed to become independent from her parents after she graduated from college. She returned to Jakarta, found work and lived alone. At some point in 2017 she came out to her mother as queer and was 'pleasantly surprised by her warm acceptance. Things were tenuous, but there was at least a delicate balance.' Everything shattered on a dramatic day in September 2020. 'My mother asked if she could send some food over, so I shared my address with her', Nyai said. What arrived, though, was the 'worst day of her life'. An army of relatives and unknown men pounded her door and forcibly dragged Nyai and her partner – a transman – out of their beds. They were beaten up, verbally abused and physically assaulted. 'I was dragged from the fourth-floor staircase all the way downstairs by my own mother', Nyai recalled. 'She clawed my arms. My arms and legs were blue. They pulled my hair out.'

The horrifying ordeal did not end there. After a tense ride home, she was taken to a *pesantren* in a remote village in Central Java. For two days, she was subjected to conversion therapy. 'They bathed me and prayed over me', she recalled. 'There were my parents, my aunts … They told me to affirm my belief in God and drink something they had supposedly prayed over … They woke me up in the middle of the night and forced me to pray. They handed me a holy book and told me to hold it so I wouldn't be afraid.' Upon returning home, she found herself a prisoner. 'They took away all means of communication', Nyai said. 'I was kept in a room and forbidden to go out, except to the bathroom. They even delivered food directly to my door.'[37]

The fourteen autobiographical stories of LBT people by Daniel and others[38] present a rich picture of the perils of lesbian life for young middle-class women in Surabaya around 2010. Coming out and violence are important themes, as is the beauty of the discovery of the kind of love for which they sacrifice so much. The stories are full of violence and neglect from parents, if the women are tomboys, or with incredible pressure to marry, especially but not exclusively if they are more feminine lesbians. For example, although Riana's family knew she was a lesbian and had only fallen in love with women since she was in primary school, they tried to marry her off – seven times in total, to sons of friends of her father or family members. 'I felt like I was an object for trading.' In the end she decided to give in to her father's wishes to marry – as long as she herself could choose a gay partner. She was confident that with the help of insemination she could have a child. 'Status is very important for my family; they have a good name in the community which they want to sustain.[39]

Corrective rape is one of the most gruesome forms of violence that LBT people experience. The following three cases which took place in 2021 could have happened in any earlier period. Eliot is a 44-year-old FTM transperson, who was raped by his father when he was twenty-four. His father had left the household a few years earlier but returned and forced Eliot to wear women's clothes. He raped him to remind him he was a woman. Then he married him off. Eliot hated sex with his husband and would drink alcohol till he was drunk every time before sex. He had two children. He loathed himself and cut himself. After four years he managed to get a divorce. All his previous dreams of building a house to live in with his lover broke down. He remains deeply traumatized.

July was raped by her uncle when she was eighteen. She ran away to her father's house for protection, but then her father raped her. He threatened to kill her if she told her mother. As a result of the rape she became pregnant and had a baby. Not only fathers rape, mothers can organize a rape as well. The mother of Dewi paid for a gigolo to rape her when she was seventeen. Before that she had been taken to a sexologist who sexually harassed her. He would grope her, asking whether she had any sexual feelings. She only felt disgust. Ultimately her mother brought home a male sex worker who was to 'cure' her. Dewi ran away from home and managed to get into the shelter that the Ardhanary Institute had set up.[40]

To help victims of these forms of violence the Ardhanary Institute has set up a shelter at a secret location. Lawyers are available to provide legal assistance to those who come and stay at the shelter. Since 2012 psychological assistance has also been provided. Counselling can also take place via Facebook or email; sometimes house visits are made.

Conversion therapy

Conversion or reparative therapy can be defined as any intervention to change gender identities, behaviours or gender expressions, or to eliminate or reduce sexual or romantic attractions that are considered non-conforming.[41] Traditional healers, religious leaders and psychologists/psychotherapists – in private practices, in religious centres or psychiatric wards – pretend to be able to 'cure' LGBT people and make them 'normal' heterosexuals again. There is no record of anybody who has undergone such treatment of ever being 'cured'. On the contrary, most end up severely traumatized. This is corroborated by international studies on conversion therapy. Canada is one country which has recently prohibited LGBT conversion therapy.[42] The Human Rights Council in its 44th Session (from 15 June to 3 July 2020) declared that it is 'unethical for health-care professionals to purport to treat anything that is not a disorder'. These therapies violate the personal integrity of those treated. Instead, a gender-affirmative approach is advocated in which LGBT people learn to accept their orientation and how to deal with the social stigma.

The Independent Forensic Expert Group of the International Rehabilitation Council for Torture Victims, a group of pre-eminent international medicolegal specialists from twenty-three countries, declared that 'offering "conversion therapy" is a form of deception, false advertising and fraud'.[43] Among the consequences, they list the following: post-traumatic stress disorder (PTSD), chronic stress and negative health consequences such as stomach ulcers, skin diseases, migraines, sexual and eating disorders, vomiting and insomnia. They conclude that it is torture, not therapy. The practice violates several international human rights law principles, such as non-discrimination, the right to health and prohibition of torture and ill-treatment and the rights of the child. The organization calls on all countries to ban all forms of conversion therapy.

Horner has worked with people who underwent conversion therapy in the United States. Her clients experienced symptoms such as sexual and spiritual identity crises, depression and anxiety, hopelessness, sexual dysfunction and post-traumatic stress.[44] She recommends integrative solution therapies, grief work, community-based interventions and trauma work as healing strategies for treating LGBT clients after conversion therapy.

In 2020 the Asia Pacific Trans Network published a report on conversion therapy in Indonesia. They found that most of their respondents had been forced to undergo conversion therapy by their family. The Indonesian army is also involved in training transwomen and effeminate gay men to become 'real men' who embody a cisgendered and heteronormative masculine ideal.

The conversion therapy centres discussed in this chapter opened their doors after 2000. Stories I collected before the Reformasi suggest that parents would send their LBT children to individual psychiatrists or psychologists to be 'cured' or to *dukun* operating on their own for some sort of *ruqyah* process (ritual cleansing of evil spirits). Anya Sleebos, for instance, a well-known butch singer in the 1980s and 1990s, told me that she was sent to a psychologist when she was about twenty years old. The therapy had had no effect on her sexual orientation.[45]

In February 2021 several prominent LGBT activists received a notice about conversion therapy complete with a web address in their inboxes. Most were upset by the message, taking it as a warning. Others thought it might be a hoax, spread by one of Indonesia's ubiquitous intelligence services to make radical Islam look bad.[46] Being in Holland at the time, I opened the website terapiconversi.co and found that it was in Dutch, one of the many languages into which it had been translated.[47] The website contained the basic elements of conversion therapy as implemented in Indonesia. It listed a number of reasons for people becoming LGBT, including childhood sexual violence, Western media influence and being overpowered by an evil soul. I read on the website: 'Best for Indonesia is to exterminate this unnatural LGBT behaviour so we can protect our families and preserve traditional and cultural values.' A green picture (colour of Islam) showed the four kinds of services on offer: praying and fasting, electroconvulsive therapy, exorcism to expel the devil and sex therapy. Under the picture of a praying figure it said 'pray away the gay' and under the last picture of a man on top of a woman, the caption read 'corrective rape'. The service offered under electroconvulsive therapy was a form of aversion therapy: shock therapy or medication causing psychological distress when LGBT material was shown. The message (on Instagram and FB) the activists received read: 'It is not too late to return to God. God has not left you. Indonesia is a Muslim country, and we reject all sins. Let us help you drive Satan out from inside of you and you can become normal again.' The account name belonged to one Mohammad Susantu (@mohammadsusantu) who never replied when I asked for information.

For those who had undergone conversion therapy themselves, such as Acep Gates, seeing the website was a traumatic experience. He had undergone conversion therapy twice in his life. Before coming out of the closet, Acep went to *ruqyah* on his own initiative, because his religious family would not accept him being gay. That was in 2016. After he came out in 2017, his family forced him to undergo yet another conversion therapy for several months. The memories still haunt Acep. 'I hated myself even more afterwards. I was depressed and had to see a psychologist multiple times.'[48]

Hani Kumala, a psychologist from Atma Jaya University, criticized the website and said conversion therapy was pseudo-scientific. 'Forcing someone to see a psychologist without their consent is already a violation of human rights, let alone "corrective rape"', she said. The website's domain was registered in June 2020. Six pictures of people undergoing *ruqyah* were featured on the website which were credited to 'Persyarikatan Muhammadiyah', referring to Indonesia's second-largest Muslim group, Muhammadiyah. Muhammadiyah has denied any role in 'rape conversion' therapy, *ruqyah*, and the website. Sunanto, the chairman of Muhammadiyah's youth wing Pemuda Muhammadiyah, told *The Jakarta Post* that 'Muhammadiyah's method is not *ruqyah*. "We use modern healing methods, such as mentoring, counselling and psychology."'[49]

Perhaps this website was fake. It did considerable damage, tearing open the traumas of *ruqyah* survivors. It must have cost a lot of money to design and launch it, which raises the question of who paid for it. It is in general unclear which organizations are behind the various major conversion centres and how they are funded. Interestingly both fundamentalist Christian and Muslim institutions use roughly the same language, according to Benny Prawira Siauw. He suggests that the True Love Foundation from Hong Kong may partly fund Christian conversion centres, but there is no proof of that and their websites are silent on the issue. AILA, as discussed later, supports one of the largest Muslim conversion centres, Peduli Sahabat, but again there is no mention of any financial links.[50] The Islamist party PKS also supports them. Some financial assistance is provided through the Ministries of Health and Social Affairs which support conversion therapy.[51] Most conversion counsellors or institutions are privately funded and expensive. The profit motive is clearly one of the important triggers for psychologists to engage in this kind of therapy.

The Indonesian state is also involved in conversion therapy in several ways. The army runs a programme called Bela Negara (Defend the Country) which is a semi-military course that includes training on mounting a defence against homosexuality, which was classified as waging a 'proxy war' to destroy the nation by Defence Minister Ryamizar Ryacudu, as mentioned in the previous chapter. In 2008, Indonesian television ran a reality show called 'Be a Man' with 'effeminate men'. The idea was that they had to return to being 'true men' by being trained by the Indonesian military.[52] Tomboys were not singled out for this treatment.

Various ministries are also directly or indirectly involved in promoting or organizing efforts at counselling or converting LGBT people. The Ministry of Social Affairs, with its Directorate of Social Rehabilitation for Social Problems and Victims of Human Trafficking, runs a rehabilitation programme directed at people allegedly suffering from 'social dysfunction'.[53] *Transpuan* are categorized as 'People with Social Welfare Problems', which enables the Ministry, through its civil service police, to conduct raids to arrest them. These raids are usually conducted at night since the programme largely targets transwomen who work at night (as sex workers, for instance). The detainees are given psychosocial mental and spiritual 'guidance'.

In 2016 the Minister of Social Affairs, Khofifah Indar Parawansa, retraced earlier remarks about the efficacy of treatment in hot water spiced with lemon and herbs and put her trust in the so-called ESQ (Emotional Spiritual IQ) method, promoted in Indonesia by Ary Ginanjar.[54] This man was doing good business with eight training centres all over the archipelago and with over a hundred certified trainers in 2016.[55] So he was happy with the clients that the Ministry sent him. A journalist from the website Coconuts interviewed a person who had undergone this ESQ programme:

> I tried an ESQ program once and I know perfectly well how it works. Essentially they use scare tactics to get you to become devout followers of God. Most of their seminars are just showing cheap computer-generated imagery (CGI) videos of what it would be like to be tortured in hell. Then it's one guilt trip after another from there, and people actually cry when they're pushed to recount all their sins.[56]

Minister Khofifah herself promoted the ESQ method to 'cure' LGBT individuals: 'After going through ESQ, it appears that men then want to marry women. And so it is one of the options for redesigning social rehabilitation for LGBT (and drug users).'[57] In a flurry of activity Minister Khofifah had already been preparing a budget with Mr Ginanjar. He had this to say to defend his lucrative business model:

> The physics of LGBT people actually already conflict with their natural character (*fitrah*) as human beings. Once the *fitrah* is changed, there occurs an imbalance of the world ... both intellectual, physical and emotional [elements] may be

destroyed. ... LGBT violates religion that is also a part of human rights ... religious people also [have the right] to be free from human rights.[58]

When I visited the ESQ website again on 11 February 2022 there was no mention of LGBT healing. Instead, Mr Ginanjar offered a 'golden civilization' to those who attend the ESQ management school. It is unclear what happened to the LGBT people sent there by Minister Khofifah. In 2018 (she was by then governor of East Java), she still believed that LGBT people could be 'healed' through special therapies. 'In the Ministry we had a team that conducted counselling and testing.'[59] This team was called 'Bina Karakter' or 'Character Building'.

A glimpse into the practices that the ministry used to 'cure' LGBT people comes from the city of Padang. In November 2018, ten women were arrested for posting photos on Facebook, in which two women were seen embracing and kissing. The Satpol PP went searching for them for two days and rounded up the whole group.[60] In total, sixteen LGBT people were detained in raids in November 2018. The 'suspects' were handed over to the city's Social Services Agency. The head of the Social Services Agency of Padang, Amasrul, said that the sixteen were given guidance by both psychologists as well as religious figures. According to Amasrul, Social Services would follow up at the home of the 'perpetrators' to make sure they did not repeat their actions. So state and family are collaborating in an effort to transform LGBT people into heterosexual cisgendered persons. Muslim militias are also mobilized. According to the news website Coconuts, Amasrul said that the government had agreed to work with certain civil society organizations (*ormas*) to perform *ruqyah* on LGBT people in the area. As Lucky Abdul Hayyi, a member of Padang's Majelis Mujahidin (Mujahidin Council), one of the *ormas* the government is working with, explained, his group had prepared *ruqyah* experts for the Social Services Agency, to turn *waria* into 'real men'; the help of the army was also invoked.[61]

The Ministry of WECP, which has LGBT in its portfolio, is also involved in conversion practices. All over the country it has set up centres for the protection of women and children.[62] Some of them are equipped with psychologists and spiritual counsellors for LGBT youth.[63] The Muslim counsellors use *ruqyah* practices to 'cure' these youth. Under the previous minister, Yohana Yembise (2014–19), this ministry steered a strictly patriarchal heteronormative line, promoting a so-called Gender Harmony programme.[64] Neither she nor the minister since 2019, Bintang Puspayoga, have ever spoken out to protect LGBT people, rather they denounced 'LGBT propaganda'.[65]

The Ministry of Religion also promotes the 'guidance' of LGBT youth. The director of Information on the Religion of Islam, in the Ministry of Religion, Khoirudin, declared that the LGBT movement can be compared to a terrorist group, as the LGBT movement works in secrecy. The ministry advocates both religious and psychological 'guidance'.[66]

The Ministry of Health has a Haji Health Centre, directed by Dr Fidiansyah, a psychiatrist who calls LGBT a mental illness. He is also an advisor of the organization Peduli Sahabat, which has the objective to make LGBT people walk the 'straight' path. The video in which he produced this opinion was shared hundreds of thousands of times and used as ammunition by anti-LGBT groups. Another psychiatrist, Dr Andri, tried to mitigate the harm from this video by pointing to the 1993 Directory of Psychiatric Illnesses of the Ministry of Health. The response of Dr Fidiansyah was weak, to put it mildly. He declared on TVOne on 16 February 2016, in the programme Lawyer's Club, that the book he used was 'much thicker' than the guidebook used by LGBT activists.[67] In spite of their own 1993 directory, in 2018 the Ministry of Health declared that LGBT is a mental illness.[68]

Both Christian and Muslim methods of conversion therapy attempt to do similar things: to bring the LGBT person back on the 'sacral, right path' to Jesus or Allah.[69] Those who have undergone conversion therapy recount stories of physical and psychological violence. Yoland was sent to a psychiatric ward by her brothers. She resisted so much that they gave her injections all the time, so many that she had hallucinations. She had no idea what they injected. She saw a psychiatrist twice but refused to say a word. She got friendly with the nurses, helping them with bringing food around. They advised her to stop resisting the injections if she did not want to have them anymore. So she did. After two weeks she was released, because the nurses spoke to the doctors.[70]

Conversion therapy can also be imposed by the police as an alternative to incarceration. In 2006, the doomed love relationship between Wahyu (aged twenty-two) and Desi (aged thirteen) in Solo, Central Java, reached headlines. Wahyu sold snacks in front of an alley in which the house of Desi stood. Wahyu was poor, had little education and looked masculine. Desi came from a much richer family and looked very feminine. She seduced Wahyu, who was shy because of the great class difference. Their affair was discovered and they ran away but were finally caught and brought back to Solo. Wahyu was imprisoned and charged with having sex with an underage girl. The parents of Desi did not press charges on condition that Wahyu would go to be 'cured'. She was brought to the Yayasan Keluarga Rumah Damai in Semarang, for mental rehabilitation. If she had refused to go, she might have faced a life sentence, the police told her. Desi was kept at home by her parents and brought under the supernatural influence of an *orang pintar* (witch doctor). She was bathed in a ritual manner, her hair was cut and her parents held a *slametan* (ritual, as a cleansing ceremony). She was not allowed to go out of the house unless accompanied by a male family member and those who saw her said that she had an empty look in her eyes.[71]

The shelter of the Ardhanary Institute assists victims of conversion therapy. Another initiative is a youth suicide prevention community, established in 2013 after the founder, a young psychologist, had read a story about a gay man who had committed suicide after undergoing conversion therapy. On the website it is not mentioned that it caters to LGBT youth, to prevent undue attention from authorities, which might result in the website being closed.[72] But the site is well known among LGBT activists who refer LGBT youths who have ended up in deep depression after conversion therapy.

Thus far from being in decline, the conversion therapy of LGBT people, including the practice of *ruqyah*, is thriving, largely due to the rise of majoritarian, conservative Islam, supported by political leaders hoping to gain political support or out of sheer bigotry. Complicit are rogue psychiatrists who violate the basic tenets of their profession.

Conversion practices: *Ruqyah*

One of the most common practices of conversion therapy in Indonesia is *ruqyah*. This ritual is used for various forms of the cleansing of evil spirits. Though of pre-Islamic origin it is fully integrated into conservative Muslim practices. For how long the ritual has also been used to evict the *jin* or *roh* with which LGBT persons are supposedly afflicted is unclear. Traditional tribal animist and shamanist beliefs included exorcist rituals, ranging from curing mental illnesses to ritual cleansing of villages to cast out evil spirits. Scholars agree that exorcism has remained popular in the country thanks to the rise of religious conservatism in Indonesia since Reformasi, when conservative Muslims suddenly enjoyed greater freedom after being repressed for more than thirty years. According to Dina Listiorini, who conducts extensive research on discrimination against the LGBTQ community:[73] 'the 2000s pop culture justified this notion. Islamic TV shows were everywhere, and at the same time the media started to depict LGBTQ public figures as outcasts'.[74]

Since late 2015 several prominent political and religious leaders have been proclaiming that the sexual orientation of LGBT people is a contagious disease. It is no wonder that all kinds of quacks and unscrupulous professionals see business opportunities.[75] Dedi Natadiningrat, a cleric and practitioner of *ruqyah* at Cirebon Al Quran Therapy in West Java, told Nikkei that he had received 'seven LGBTQ patients wishing to be cured' since he started his business in 2010. 'By the grace of Allah, I can say that one person I treated now has changed his orientation by 60 percent', he said, without specifying how he measured that healing process.[76] The pressure under which LGBT persons live is intense enough to make some members of the LGBTQ community request exorcisms of their own accord. Ailsa, a Jakarta-based exorcism therapist, said that every week one or two 'patients' commit themselves to her centre to 'fix' their sexual orientation.[77] Usually people are being sent to *dukun*, or *kyai*, to get healed. They are threatened that if they do not repent, they will no longer be considered part of the family, losing family protection and inheritance rights. This applies particularly to LBT persons.

Ruqyah has been traumatic to most who have undergone it. It can even lead to a person's death. In the village of Temanggung, Central Java, a seven-year-old girl was murdered by her parents. She had been subjected to *ruqyah* as her behaviour had been considered unruly. On the advice of a *dukun* she was drowned in a water tub. The parents believed that she was possessed by a *genderuwo*, an ugly, hairy and frightening ghost. After the ritual, the parents laid their daughter's body in a room in the house because the *dukun* told them that the girl would be resurrected. In 2018 in Trenggalek, East Java, family members killed an elderly mother during a *ruqyah*. She died of suffocation after her children poured water down her throat to get rid of the evil spirit that allegedly caused her stomach ache.[78]

Few Muslim leaders speak out against the practice. Arif Nuh Safri, however, a cleric with the transgender Islamic boarding school Al Fatah in Yogyakarta, said the practice of *ruqyah* has nowhere proved to be effective. 'I heard from fellow clerics about *ruqyah* for LGBTQ. I said "please prove it. You can come to Al Fatah anytime if you can prove it", but nobody has come yet.' He heard from some of the students at Al Fatah how traumatized they were after undergoing *ruqyah*: 'It was torture and inhumane.'[79]

The *ruqyah* ritual rests upon the notion that the gendered body is porous and unstable.[80] The belief that *jin* (spirits) can enter the permeable body leads to the idea of exorcism, to drive them out. As Hegarty maintains in a study on *waria*, the notion that gender and sexuality are shaped by forces beyond the individual body reinforces popular opinion that homosexuality is something which can penetrate from the outside. In this view homosexuality is seen as an illness with which people can be infected.[81] This illness is associated with *jin*. Together with *syaitan* and *iblis* (devils) they were created by Allah from fire. Allah then shaped Adam from clay and ordered all other *makhluk* (creatures), so the *malaikat* (angels), *jin, syaitan* and *iblis*, to prostate themselves before Adam. *Jin, syaitan* and *iblis* refused – we have been created from fire, how can we bow to a *makhluk* created from clay? Only the *malaikat* obeyed the order of Allah and since then they have helped human beings. But *jin* attempt to draw everyone to the fire of hell where they abide. *Jin* position themselves in one's body so one commits mistakes and does not follow the right path. With the help of a *ruqyah* ritual it is possible to exorcise the *jin* that causes one to become a homosexual person.[82]

A 2016 report of the Ardhanary Institute contains a profile of Dani (pseudonym), a feminine gay man who underwent conversion therapy. Law student Dani wanted to become a solicitor. As a feminine gay man he was always bullied and ridiculed. To be considered 'normal' he married a woman, though he was not sexually interested in her. He tried to bury his homosexuality by going into traditional counselling, hypnotherapy, and visited a specialist in *ruqyah*, who was said to be able to drive out his *jin*. In 2014 he learned that a religious teacher, Abdul Maliq, a member of the group Komunitas Peduli Ruqyah Syari'ah, (Community Concerned about Syaria Ruqyah) could cure homosexuals. His method to conduct '*ruqyah syariah*' was to read verses form the Quran and *hadith*. The idea is that the *jin* becomes afraid of the Quranic verses and leaves the body of the patient. Dani was told to sit on a mat facing the religious teacher. He read verses from the Quran in a loud voice and beat Dani's back and thighs. The preacher pressed his hand on his thighs, and finally on his throat, which is the place where the devil resides according to the preacher. The *jin* hides in the blood vessels he explained, so he had to draw it out by massaging those vessels. It hurt very much and Dani wanted to vomit. The *ustadz* said this was a sign that the *jin* was about to leave Dani's body. After this treatment Dani had to bathe in water mixed with salt and *bidara* leaves. After the treatment Dani felt nervous, sinful, afraid, angry and he wanted to inflict harm on himself. He hated himself. Ultimately Dani divorced his wife and went to live in Bangkok.[83]

The following harrowing stories provide more details of this unethical method. The parents of Syifa took her to an Islamic conversion therapy centre, which has thirty-two branches across Indonesia, where she realized how traumatic the exorcism process can be. She heard screams and people being whipped from the room next door.[84] Slapping, painful massages and bathing in blessed salt water are other methods of *ruqyah*. In extreme cases 'sex therapy' is offered, a euphemism for rape.[85] A common method used in a *ruqyah* ritual is to press the tender flesh between thumb and hand with such pressure that the patient screams. This is seen as a sign that the *jin* is leaving the body.

Tuasikal observed a method of 'self *ruqyah*' used in the Darun Ni'mah mosque in Lebak Bulus, Jakarta. Scores of people, old, young, men and women follow the instructions on how to expel the bad spirit (*roh jahat*) from their own bodies. According to the trainer, Muhammad Hafidz, LGBT are possessed by an evil soul or black magic (*sihir*). He said that these LGBT people must be pitied, they did not choose this lifestyle. The participants are taught the so-called *ruqyah mandiri* (self-*ruqyah*) method. They spread out pieces of paper with words from the Quran in the palms of their hands and then rub their hands all over their bodies. Then the evil soul starts to be expelled. They do it for hours, some of them vomit. Muhammad Hafidz claims he has cured many gay and lesbian people in this way.[86]

Halim recounted the story of FTM transgender Andin, who, for two decades, endured harassment and abuse as his family desperately tried to 'cure' him. Treatments ranged from being 'bombarded with quranic verses while trapped in a locked room for days, to being doused with freezing water by an *imam* promising to purge the 'gender disease'. Once he was taken against his will to a religious teacher near his hometown of Medan, North Sumatra. The teacher showed him a burial shroud and prayed over him. He was then given a stark choice: 'Relinquish life as a man, or go to hell.' Andin is haunted by the horror of that memory. He has not changed, but his parents have not given up hope – they sacrificed a goat for that purpose.[87] Organizations like the Ardhanary Institute and Arus Pelangi warn of the dangerous consequences of conversion practices. Yet the practice is thriving. The Ruqyah Association has a website and Facebook account but does not openly advertise anti-LGBT therapies.

Ruqyah centres

The MUI and AILA provide support to two well-known *ruqyah* centres, Peduli Sahabat and the Abu Albani Centre. Using rights language AILA proclaims on its website that LGBT people have the right to be healed. The text explains that LGBT defenders claim that LGBT people suffer from intimidation from society, causing depression. But, they insist, many LGBT people find they are tested by Allah and they need guidance to find a normal life. From the Foundation Peduli Sahabat, represented by Agung Sugiarto (also called Kak Sinyo), AILA members have learnt that the healing process is not easy, as their patients are intimidated by the many pro-LGBT propaganda campaigns.[88] On their website they also rail against radical feminism which they see as threatening the family.

AILA set up AILA Care for 'guidance' on family matters. Conversion therapy seems to be the major activity of AILA Care.[89] In a 2019 book published before AILA Care was established, the authors recommended that religious counselling be provided to LGBT people.[90] According to them the vital mechanism to control sexual orientation is religious counselling. They received this advice from specialists who have already been doing this for over thirty years, they claimed.[91] Chair Rita Soebagio explained in a press release that AILA Care provides non-profit guidance which consists of Psychological First Aid (PFA) to family members who experience problems.[92] This is a very careful way to announce that they are supporting or giving counselling to LGBT people and the families with LGBT kids, to 'heal' homosexuality.

When I accessed the website of AILA Care on 24 February 2022, registration with a photo ID was required. Mention of counselling for LGBT people was nowhere to be found any more. This is not surprising, because AILA consists of highly educated women, many of them university professors, who know well that conversion practice is regarded as torture.[93] They are also aware that in July 2020 Instagram had blocked content on conversion therapy in Indonesia.[94]

In a book by a prominent member of AILA, Professor Euis Sunarti from the prestigious Agricultural Institute of Bogor, the same theme is covered.[95] The (heteronormative) family must be protected from the dangers that the growth of the LGBT movement allegedly forms, and LGBT people have the right to enter into conversion therapy to become heterosexual again. This form of therapy is recommended with references to articles on brain plasticity. This insight from gender theory, that gender is not static but fluid, as well as recent discoveries in neurology, are twisted into a fake theory that LGBT people can be converted to become 'normal' heterosexuals again. Professor Sunarti is also associated with a volunteer group that defends the family, called GiGa (Penggiat Keluarga, Family Activists), established in 2014. Their hundreds of volunteers all over Indonesia are called to 'assist' families who harbour cases of social and sexual deviation. The volunteers (teachers, psychologists and the like) offer preventive and curative care.

AILA helped Agung Sugiarto to establish Peduli Sahabat.[96] The idea is that people who experience same-sex attraction must be assisted not to become *pelaku* LGBT (practising homosexuals). In 2018 Ferena and Estu Fanani conducted a preliminary mapping of the links AILA has with like-minded individuals and organizations. These links involved a political party (PKS), the MUI, various Islamic centres for higher education, and *pesantren*, the influential Wahabist Dewan Dakwah Islam Indonesia (DDII), Masyumi, Muslimat Hiyadatullah, the Komunitas Pencinta Keluarga and various lawyers and psychologists.

Peduli Sahabat has a group called Menanti Mentari (Waiting to Dance) to assist people who are married to LGBT people.[97] In 2014 Peduli Sahabat published a book *Anakku Bertanya Tentang LGBT* (My Child Asks What LGBT Is).[98] It has the same message as the website of AILA – through self-discipline people who are attracted to people of the same sex can rewire their attraction towards heterosexuality. Dr Fidiansyah is one of their advisors. On their website they provide the following steps to transform homosexual to heterosexual desire:

1. *Taubat Nasuha.* To demonstrate deep remorse about sins, in this case the sin of being LGBT. In this phase and all through the therapy the client is required to read all kinds of religious texts that promise destruction and moral decay in relation to LGBT, and that tell the client that the only way to be a good Muslim is to give up the evil ways of engaging in LGBT behaviour.
2. *Menghapus Kontak dan Konten.* The client is requested to totally cut him or herself off from his or her previous life. LGBT friends and contacts must be

removed from all social media, and the LGBT person must promise never to contact these people again.

3. *Menguatkan Rasa Malu.* At this stage, totally isolated and miserable, and brainwashed into believing the depth of the LGBT sins they have committed, their feeling of being ashamed must be strengthened. They must be told to consider how they put their family to shame, how they have hurt their community, nation and religion.

4. *Mensugesti Diri.* A phase of hypnotherapy may follow, in which the client is brought to believe sexual attraction can be redirected.

5. *Perbanyak Perbuatan positif.* The client may then be directed to do good deeds, to redirect feelings into ways that are more profitable for society and to build up a form of self-esteem not tied to sexual attraction but to social usefulness.

6. *Persiapan Menikah.* The therapy is considered successful if the client can be steered into preparing for a heterosexual marriage.[99]

The Peduli Sahabat Foundation is associated with the Abu Albani Centre which openly advertises its conversion therapy.[100] This institute claims that same-sex desire is the result of the person being possessed by an evil spirit (*jin*). Gay men are considered to be possessed by a female spirit and lesbian women by a male spirit. They promote their services with the stories of people they allege to have healed. Such stories detail that the 'patient' suffers from mental problems which enable the evil *jin* to enter the body. One such case is that of a masculine lesbian woman who had been sexually abused by several village leaders and even her own uncle, from the age of five until the end of her primary school days. The diagnosis made by the centre was that she suffered from mental problems which facilitated the *jin*'s possession of her body. The therapist therefore proposed to mentally heal the woman. She was told that God had wanted to test her and that the only way for her to enter heaven was to forgive her rapists.

Their *ruqyah* technique involves the incantation of the Quran so that the *jin* will be exorcised. Verses from the Quran are read until the patient vomits out the *jin*. The idea is that by stimulating the nerves in the brains, the 'sufferer' will become heterosexual. The therapy can be augmented by acupuncture (through a cupping method) which is supposed to have a similar effect on those nerves, as well as hypnotherapy, religious spiritual training and physical exercises. The healing method also includes Thibbun–Nabawi, which is supposedly derived from the Quran itself and which involves pinching, rinsing, herbal medicine and various spiritual techniques to improve the organic functions of the client. The therapy is considered successful if the 'patient' goes back to 'normally' desiring a person of the other sex.[101]

Conclusion

Indonesia has a wide variety of individuals and institutes involved in the conversion therapy of LGBT people. They range from village healers who provide holy water, or a flower bath at midnight, to invasive and humiliating, psychologically and physically hurtful practices. These practitioners speak about *jin* or *roh* which have to be expelled via *ruqyah* techniques. These practices are also offered in specialized conservative Muslim institutes. Christian institutes are also involved in these so-called spiritual healing practices. Not only village quacks advertise their services but highly educated arch-conservative religious individuals and institutes also promote the possibility of the 'healing' of LGBT people. They are aware that the international world denounces these techniques, but they link up with similar conservative groups in the United States, copying their terminology.[102] The criterion these groups use for the 'success' of their therapy is that the individual concerned has married heterosexually or expressed the intention to do so. It is of course possible that somebody has found a heterosexual partner, but in most cases this concerned a forced marriage, leading to deep unhappiness, as only the behaviour, not the sexual orientation, has changed.

The effects of conversion therapy can be very traumatic, declares Lina Zurlia, who has supported many LGBT people who were forced to undergo such therapy and were heavily traumatized.[103] She has never come across a person who has become cisgendered or heterosexual because of undergoing reparative therapy. LGBT conversion therapy is driven by the 'shame culture' of Indonesia, concludes the APTN in its 2021 report.[104] As one of their informants declared, the religious teacher who lectured him, told him, 'There are no *bencong* in our ancestors, *bencong* is the devil.'[105]

9

God's creatures: Religion and sexual rights

Introduction

Indonesia has a secular Constitution, yet its national character is defined by adherence to religious practices, due to the emphasis on the first *sila* (pillar) of the preamble to the Constitution, the Pancasila. This *sila* stipulates the belief in one God.[1] Other *sila* uphold democratic principles and social justice. Fierce debates have been and are being waged on both the relative importance of and the interpretation of the Pancasila as well as on the dominance of the first *sila*.[2] The growing influence of Wahabi and Salafi interpretations of Islam stimulates the spread of an orthodox version of Islam, intolerant of the country's wide ethnic, religious and gender-based diversity.[3] Practitioners of diverse (Muslim) practices may be called *syirik* (polytheist) which can lead to societal disapproval or even unwelcome attention of Islamist vigilante groups. Yet polytheist Hinduism, the majority religion in Bali, is included in the list of accepted religions.

President Sukarno tried to balance nationalism, communism and Islam, but his successor took a different course. He eliminated progressive and communist groups from Indonesia's social, cultural and political life and initially repressed fundamentalist Muslim groups. The later rise of fundamentalism was a protest movement against the New Order regime.[4] When Suharto's power waned, he sought to shore up his control over society by cultivating Islamist groups, particularly the *dakwah* (proselytization) on university campuses.[5] When Indonesian society opened up after the collapse of the regime, these Wahabist groups were already well established and were able to expand their grip on society.[6] They claimed the right to define a new moral order, based on their interpretation of religion and history, introducing or strengthening a homophobic discourse. Through the introduction of anti-woman and anti-LGBT regional regulations in particular, they managed to change Indonesian society, down to the way streets and public places look. When I first stayed in Indonesia in the mid-1970s, women would often wear regional, batik or Western dress, and few had their hair covered; schoolgirls wore knee-length skirts. Currently, however, the panorama is dominated by women wearing a *jilbab*, while many, including schoolgirls, wear long flowing robes copied from the styles of Arab countries. Fundamentalist men have started wearing long robes as well, over trousers that end several inches above their ankles, Salafi style.[7] As Mulia summarized, 'A turn to Islam has been a return to a static, historical, exclusive, patriarchal ideology, rather than a return to the authentic vision of Islam, which is dynamic, critical, rational, inclusive, appreciative of pluralism and plurality and accommodative to changes and reforms.'[8]

How do members of the LBT community negotiate their religious lives? Three overlapping dimensions can be distinguished: the spiritual, the social and the political realms. Spiritual aspects touch on questions of sin and one's relationship with Allah/ God. The social domain is related to how one presents oneself to the community and how one is seen to practise one's piety. Foucault's notion of 'technology of the self'[9] can be applied here, in the sense of one's ethical self-understanding as a good Muslim, including dress codes, manners of praying and other forms of behaviour. In the political realm I look at how LBT people relate to the state, how they strive to be considered good citizens and how they uphold their human and sexual rights. In contrast to the West where sexual rights are associated with secularism,[10] an important part of the struggle for sexual rights in Indonesia is the production and dissemination of progressive interpretations of religion.

The world of Islam

Indonesia has the world's largest Muslim population, some 205 million people, over 88 per cent of the country's inhabitants. Most are Sunnis and follow the Shafi'i school.[11] There are two mass Muslim organizations. The rural-based Nahdlatul Ulama (NU) controls tens of thousands of *pesantren* (Islamic boarding schools), the *kyai* (leaders) of which are highly revered. Their version of Islam is considered moderate and contains many traditional Indonesian elements. The Muhammadyah is a more orthodox organization, adhering more strictly to Quranic teachings and is influential in cities; it focuses on Islamic teaching, from kindergarten level to Islamic universities.[12]

Though the vast majority of Muslim scholars and leaders denounce homosexuality as un-Islamic, sticking to the heterosexist interpretation of the story of the Prophet Lut, there are vast differences in opinion about the position of the LGBT community in Indonesia. The NU contains both conservative and more liberal streams. While young Muslim leaders such as Aan Anshori[13] argue for a greater understanding of issues related to gender and sexual orientation and posit that nobody can take away the basic rights of another person, conservative figures denounce the existence of the LGBT community. These include the Rais Aam (president) of the NU, Ma'ruf Amin (who, since 2019, has also been the vice-president of the nation) and the General Chair Said Aqil (until the end of 2021). These representatives of the NU leadership declared that the LGBT community disavows the natural disposition of humanity (*ingkari fitrah manusia*).[14] The NU Central Board (PBNU) urged the Parliament to criminalize LGBT[15] and to rehabilitate LGBT people to become 'normal' again.

The family of the late president Abdurrahman Wahid still wields considerable influence both within the NU and the PKB and in wider Indonesian society. His eldest daughter, Yenny, heads the Wahid Foundation. She has publicly supported the LGBT community stating that they have the same rights as other Indonesians and are entitled to state protection. She argued: 'LGBT people existed around the time of the prophet Muhammad fifteen centuries ago. They were called *khuntsah*.'[16]

Muhammadyah denounces homosexuality, which they consider to be at odds with the true Islam faith (*akidah*).[17] Only the former (until 2015) chair of Muhammadyah, Din Syamsuddin, called upon the people not to express hatred towards the LGBT community.[18] Both the NU and Muhammadyah support counselling, confident that homosexuality can be healed somehow. But while major segments of the NU see a place for the LGBT community in Indonesian society, Muhammadyah wants to ban them altogether.

Interestingly, the anti-LGBT movement uses rights language against the LGBT community. The Wahabi *dakwah* (proselytizing) movement has been particularly active on university campuses since the Suharto era and has given rise to a surge of Islamist student movements. For example, the chair of the Front Mahasiswa Islam (Islamic Student Front FMI), Ali Alatas, stated that the LGBT community advocated that homosexuality is related to genetic factors. 'But that would imply that they blame God.' He referred to the American Psychological Association as political and corrupt. Just as the LGBT community fights for their rights, 'we also have the right to refuse the existence of the LGBT community to protect the family and society', he concluded.[19]

Islamist homophobia

Given the widespread belief in evil spirits and black magic in Indonesian society, the accusation uttered by an anti-homosexual cleric during the ILGA conference in Surabaya in 2010, that the existence of homosexuality was a sign sent by God announcing the end of the world, which was widely spread in the media, produced fear in the LBT community.[20] Similar statements were heard after a series of natural disasters which Indonesia experienced in subsequent years. Being held responsible for such catastrophes because one does not perform the only religiously correct sexual practice, and being considered abnormal, has led to severe psychological problems such as depression and (attempted) suicide among members of the LBT community. Being LGBT and Muslim is often seen as incompatible. Even the right to pray to God is often violated and transgender people may be evicted from mosques or religious institutes.[21]

At the grassroots level the pure hatred that hard-line militias shout out is illustrated by a 2010 pamphlet produced by the FPI in Jakarta. It is entitled *Ayo ganyang* (eliminate) *homosex and lesbi*. It went viral on social media. Quoting selective *hadith* and various verses of the Quran, which do not actually mention lesbian or gay sex,[22] the document screams that homo and lesbian behaviour is *terkutuk* (cursed) and *terlaknat* (damned). The gist of the argument offered is that LGBT has nothing to do with human rights so it can never be protected under that banner; Indonesia is not an Islamic state, but neither is it a Devil's state; liberal unbelievers are an intellectual mafia, who rape religion with their arguments based on human rights, and they are supported by foreign funding and try to legalize same-sex marriage.[23]

Progressive voices defending the sexual rights of LGBT people are few, but they are a great support for the LBT community. Particularly, when the Covid-19 pandemic struck from the first months of 2020 onwards, dialogues, webinars, interfaith discussions, and internal (secret) discussions on religion and homosexuality mushroomed. Activists are empowered by these debates and though they are not in a position to strike back, they know they have some allies and this increases their self-worth.[24]

Islam and homosexuality

Are Islam and homosexuality incompatible? Feminist Muslim scholars such as Fatima Mernissi, Amina Wadud and Musdah Mulia stress the sex-affirmative statements in the Quran, a sign of God's mercy and generosity towards humanity, characterized by such valued qualities as love and beauty. Based on similar interpretations of the Quran, several scholars stress there is no incompatibility between human and sexual rights and Islam. The story of the Prophet Lut, always cited as evidence of the Islamic and Christian God's condemnation of homosexuality, is in this interpretation related to sexual violence and disobedience.

Hard-line Muslims insist that homosexuality is prohibited in Islam. Yet the word 'homosexuality' does not exist in classical Arabic. What does exist is *liwath*, sodomy, which includes heterosexual anal intercourse and excludes lesbianism. The word associated with lesbianism is *sihaq*, rubbing, the word does not appear in the Quran and there is no punishment associated with *sihaq*. The only punishment stipulated in classical Islamic law (*fiqih*) is for *zina*, adultery, which carries the death sentence. Although *liwath* is considered a sin, it carries an unspecified sentence, as it does not involve the penetration of a vagina by a penis, and there is no danger that a pregnancy may follow. Proving *liwath* and *zina* is equally difficult since four live witnesses must testify. If someone denounces another person for *zina* or *liwath* and proof is insufficient, he or she can receive eighty lashes with the whip.

So homosexuality as such is not prohibited in Islam, only anal sex, and it is prohibited in a heterosexual context as well.[25] Sexual orientation is not discussed in *fiqih*. While many consider homosexuality an illness, it cannot at the same time be a sin, for in the Quran illness is not criminalized.[26] In important periods of Islamic history homosexuality including women's same-sex practices was seen as part of the human sexual repertoire. The 2004 edition of the Perfumed Garden, a classic sixteenth-century Persian book on the delights and secrets of erotic love, contains illustrations of Mughal India.[27] While most of the pictures show sometimes complicated heterosexual erotic positions, at least two pictures refer to women's same-sex intimacy. On page 79 two women are shown in an erotic embrace while on page 178 five women are portrayed in a bath, two of whom are captured in an intimate hug.

There is much evidence of medieval Muslim texts on male homosexuality, but there is very little on women.[28] Habib presents Ahmad Tifashi's thirteenth-century book *Nuzhat*,[29] which contains a chapter on tribadism – called grinding (*musahiqat*). The women refer to each other as 'witty women' (*tharifa*), stressing their intelligence and charms.[30] As Habib maintains, 'The sexual process seems to be both a pleasure and an art form to be taught and learned; to be given and received beyond the binary of active-passive.'[31] Habib notes that Al-Tifashi distinguishes between 'inborn grinders', described as a malady, and those who have been converted to the practice. While Habib interprets the text as indicative of the widespread use of same-sex techniques and pleasures, Al-Ghafari stresses that this discourse is straddled with heterosexual overtones, in which the penis is endowed with superior powers of providing pleasure. However, the active, 'witty', desiring grinders, such as Warda in Al-Tifahi's text, are not portrayed as engaging in a practice that is only second-best to heterosexual practices.[32]

Leemans notes that *sihaq* is not mentioned in the Quran nor in the most accepted collections of *hadith*, while *zina* and *liwath* are frequently mentioned. She maintains that though references to women's same-sex love are scarce, and usually written from a male-dominated perspective, love between women is recognized, as the following quotation indicates: 'They engage in a passionate love for each other, as men do, but even more intensely.'[33] In many more fragments the sexual lust women feel for each other is described as greater than that for men, so all-encompassing in fact that this can lead to *fitna*, strife, moral destruction of the *umma*, the Muslim community.[34]

As discussed in Chapter 2, in some precolonial Southeast Asian societies women and sexually diverse people played a leading role in rituals and communications with the spirit world. The monotheistic world religions, on the other hand, promote an idea of female spiritual and intellectual weakness.[35] By the end of the eighteenth century, Islam had been fairly well established in the region. Watson Andaya asserts that though spirits, and spirit mediumship still provided the means whereby women could gain recognition as healers and seers, a long line of Islamic teachers saw such practices as unacceptable polytheism. [She observed] … 'a growing concern with … maintaining the male-female distinction as a heightened sense of 'being Muslim'. As Andaya suggests, this trend was accompanied by the condemnation of feminized men and male homosexuality.[36]

Imam Syafi'i (the revered founder of one of the four schools of Islamic thought) maintained that only sodomy which is carried out in public can be judged. Only after the death of the Prophet, during the rule of Abu Bakar, a couple who committed sodomy were put to death. The Quran only mentions two genders/sexes, men and women. Mulia recalls that in the *fiqih* literature four gender variants are mentioned: women, men, *khunsa* (effeminate men) and *mukhannit* or *mukhannat* (manly women).[37]

The prominent Islamic scholar and former chair of the NU, Said Aqiel Siradj, wrote an article in 2009 in which he did not denounce homosexuality but portrayed the relation between Islam and homosexuality in a positive light. He acknowledged that homosexuality has always existed in history and that Muslims have also practised it. During the Omayad and Abbasid empires, drinking liquor and practising various forms of sexual relations was common, he reminded his readers. Only in *fiqih* was homosexuality considered a major sin and a punishable offence. *Fiqih* considers homosexuality the same as *zina*; the Syafi'i, Maliki and Hambali schools opine that it must be similarly punished. Only the Hanafi school differs and considers homosexuality less than *zina*. He ended by quoting Malik bin Anas, the founder of the Maliki school: 'If someone says you are a follower of Luth then he himself should be caned.'[38] These and other topics related to religion and lesbianism were hotly debated in many seminars, both public ones, and internal, sometimes even secret meetings.

Progressive interpretations of monotheistic religions

Although progressive religious leaders and academics are rarely able to modify the positions of their conservative colleagues, their lectures and writings are critically important for the LGBT community. Their insistence on the compatibility of human rights, compassion and empathy in their religions touches the hearts and minds of LGBT people. Spiritually they feel relieved that their God will not condemn them, socially they feel strengthened in insisting their form of piety is accepted, and politically they can argue that their struggle for their rights as citizens in Indonesia is legitimate.

References to homosexuality in the Bible or the Quran are few. Progressive interpreters of these texts point to the central ethical tenets such as compassion and empathy. They argue that the condemnation of sexual acts does not apply to committed relationships founded on love. The major text used by conservative Christians is Leviticus 20.13, which states that if a man lies with another man as with a woman, both partners are to be executed. Women lying with each other is not discussed. Other sexual acts such as adultery and incest are likewise prohibited. The most virulent statements against homosexuality are made by Paul (Romans 1.18-32 and Romans 2.14-16).

For Jews, Christians and Muslims alike, the story of the destruction of Sodom and Gomorrah is central to the traditional condemnation of male homosexuality. The cities are said to be destroyed because of homosexuality. As recounted in Genesis 19, however, this is not a story about love or consensual sex between men: it is about rape and inhospitality. Mulia, Abdullah and other progressive religious scholars who studied the text agree that both in the Old Testament and in the Quran the crime which aroused God's wrath was not homosexuality.[39] Rather, progressive interpretations of the story of the Prophet Lut indicate that Allah deemed a plurality of other practices sinful, including idol worship, adultery, prostitution, forced sexual slavery, tyranny and robbery.[40]

When the crowd demands that Lut give up their visitors, he offers his two virgin daughters in their stead. This leads to the possibility of attempting to avert homosexual rape, besides all the other crimes the inhabitants of Sodom had already committed (Genesis 18.16-33). The fact that the guests are male is not emphasized. After the visitors (angels in human form) rescue Lut and his family, God rains down fire and brimstone upon Sodom, Gomorrah and other cities nearby. Lut's wife is not spared, yet there is no indication that she is a lesbian. In other references to Sodom homosexuality is not mentioned.

As Abdullah maintains, the Quranic Lut argues with the men of Sodom over the merits of abusing his daughters or his guests (11: 78–79; 15: 67–69). The wrath of Allah is not so much caused by homosexuality but by violence. There is no mention about same-sex practices that are not violent. God is even more wrathful about the depraved people of Noah, who are not known to have engaged in sodomy. The only righteous people in the story are the Prophet Lut and his daughters, while his wife probably adhered to the old goddess worship.[41] Abdullah also studied the verse in An-Nisa, which is widely used to denounce lesbianism. The verse reads in English (translation by Dawood): 'If any of your women commit a lewd act, call in four witnesses from among yourselves against them; if they testify to their guilt confine them to their houses till death overtakes them or till God finds another way for them.' This verse is usually interpreted to mean that women who engage in unlawful sexual intercourse will be punished. The word used however is *fahishay* which is a very ambiguous term generally translated as violence or sexual obscenities – not specifically homosexuality – but acts such as bestiality, debauchery or orgy. Abdullah explained that in these and other verses on relations between men, the Arabic words used are *fahisyah, sayyiat* (cruelty), *khabaits* (indecency) and *munkar* (deviation), and not *liwath* (sodomy).

For many years the Islamic scholar Musdah Mulia has been a staunch ally of the feminist and LGBT movements in Indonesia. In 2008 she stressed that in the eyes of God people are valued on the basis of their piety and that homosexuality is created by God and therefore natural.[42] In an article in 2010 she noted that in the *fiqih banci, khunsa, mukhannit* (feminine men) and *mukhannath* (masculine women) were mentioned and she wondered why if the ancient *ulama* found space for homosexuality, the contemporary ones could not do the same. Her hunch was that it would upset the theocracy and dominant received opinion too much, because then woman-unfriendly interpretations of Islam would also be subjected to a similar process of reinterpretation.

Mulia advocates Islamic humanism, based on equality and peace, virtue, wisdom, compassion, pluralism and human rights. These Islamic core values are contrary to fundamentalism which resembles a rigid theological sect, she asserts. Islamic fundamentalists are groups espousing the belief that sharia is an everlasting and eternal set of rules, which do not have to be reinterpreted and adjusted to changes over time. True to its type, Indonesian Islamic fundamentalism lays claim to an 'essential or sacred truth' and they readily use Islam not simply to legitimize but to sacralize their political agendas, with far-reaching emotional, psychological and cultural consequences. No area of personal and social or public life is spared from fundamentalists' control and their totalitarian regulations, according to Mulia.[43]

Mulia maintains that the imposition of the fundamentalist sharia that Islamists want leads to 'intellectual impoverishment' due to their literal interpretation of the Quran. This has plunged them into the 'dregs of absolutism', trying to impose their own wishes on others.[44] She stresses that Islam prioritizes the importance of safe and responsible sexual intercourse, and condemns all violence, including bestiality, incest and paedophilia. There is a place in Islam for transgender people, intersex persons and for gay men or lesbian women. Islam is not concerned with sexual orientation but only with sexual behaviour, she argues. The major criterion is that this behaviour cannot be violent or irresponsible. Both hetero- and homosexual persons are condemned if they engage in violent or cruel sexual acts. In general, Allah is more interested in people's piety than in their sexual orientation, and only Allah can judge the quality of that piety, not human beings. In this interpretation there is no place for discrimination and hatred.[45]

In an interview with the progressive online publication *Magdalena*, Mulia criticizes the religious education system in Indonesia. She argues that most people only learn from their *ustadz* (religious teachers) and that schools do not emphasize critical thinking. Without using critical reasoning students accept everything as dogma. Religious teaching is based on fear, she maintains, whereas God is the most loving, most merciful, most beneficent, as stated in the phrase Muslims say every day, '*Bismillaahirrahmanirrahim*'. These characteristics should be rooted in us, so there would be no stigma and prejudice. She insists that the government should take a strong stand and ensure that the only religious teachings accepted in Indonesia are those that are compatible with the principles of democracy, Pancasila and the central tenet of Islam as *rahmatan lil alamin* – the blessing for all humankind. Only sexual behaviour that is irresponsible, that hurts people and makes people sick or by which they are tortured, regardless of their sexual orientation, is prohibited in Islam.[46]

An interesting group that espouses similar ideas is the already mentioned Gusdurian network. This consists of young progressive leaders in the Muslim mass movement Nahdlatul Ulama (NU), who follow in the footsteps of their revered former leader, Gus Dur, former president Abdurrahman Wahid. Co-founder Aan Anshori argues that the classical interpretation of the Quran is patriarchal and heteronormative.[47] He is a frequent guest at all kinds of LGBT-themed events, where his views and those of his colleagues reverberate widely. He is also a member of the Islamic Anti-Discrimination Network, which fights for the acceptance of religious, sexual and gender diversity. As a younger activist, he is very active on social media.

The protestant church also has a progressive branch, for instance, the Centre for Gender and Sexuality Studies of the Jakarta Theological Seminary, founded by the late reverend Stephen Suleeman. Engaged with the queer community since the 1990s, Stephen was a strong ally of the country's LGBTIQ movement. He has also been responsible for including sexuality studies in the formal education of new pastors and theologians in Jakarta, Bandung and other major cities in Indonesia.[48]

Ga asserts that progressive church leaders and theologians do not feel or think that homosexuality is a sin or an illness, but simply a fact of life.[49] And though Jesus never seems to have spoken on the topic, there are references in the Old Testament that point to the existence of deep friendship relationships, erotic or otherwise, between women (Ruth and Naomi) and men (David and Jonathan). She agrees with Muslim theologians who stress that the most important issue is to love God.

The Roman Catholic priest Helminiak studied biblical scholarship about homosexuality. While cautioning against viewing biblical teaching as 'the last word on sexual ethics', he stresses the need for an accurate understanding of what the biblical 'facts' are and concludes that 'the Bible supplies no real basis for the condemnation of homosexuality'.[50]

There are other progressive thinkers. Ade Armando, a communication expert from Universitas Indonesia, has challenged Islamic clerics who see homosexuality as '*haram*', by asking about the source of sexual desire. He suggests that all desire and love come from God, and thus also desire towards the same sex must come from God. People can plan a marriage – but not whom they love.[51]

The debate about the sinfulness or not of homosexuality is ultimately also about an interpretation of God. Is S/he merciful, forgiving and tolerant of its own creatures, or punitive, revengeful and rigid? Musdah Mulia, Ga, Aan Anshori and scholars like them stress the first interpretation, fundamentalists the second.

Practices

The story of Sandy from the staunchly Muslim Minangkabau region illustrates the anxieties a lesbian woman can experience in a conservative Muslim family.[52] When Sandy was twenty-five years old she was on the verge of committing suicide. This crisis brought her closer to God.

> In our little heart we know it is not allowed. It is a sin. My hobby is reading religious books just to look for a term for us. We already know from religious teaching and also from our parents about the prophet Lut ... I am *butchi*, ... manlike ... my relationship with Mira is against religious belief, ... an illness, because we follow our lust. If we try to contain our lust as religion teaches us, we would never be like this ... it is '*sunnah nabi*' – what prophet Mohammad does, that we should marry and have children. It is already obvious from the *hadith* that God creates anything on the earth as partners, such as night and day, sun and moon, man and woman. But I feel nothing for men ... I have to change ..., because I am God's creation and will come back to Him. [If I don't have a male partner] ... I will have to wait in the hereafter. Although there is no punishment for lesbians explicitly stated in the Quran or *hadith*, what it says is 'what we get in the hereafter is what we do in life' ... So now I isolate myself from lesbian life ... But I feel insecure, dizzy, lonely. I don't know the meaning of life anymore ... I have a friend who wants to have a specific marriage law for us. She just enjoys life on earth ... She should have a moment for her soul. Her soul is empty. What they know about Islam is only praying five times a day, fasting in the month of Ramadhan, but they don't know about the world. The world is just fake. God created Satan and we are influenced by Satan. Just remember the conversation between Adam and Satan. Satan is forced to honor Adam's feet, but Satan refuses. Satan stated that he would try to seduce Adam and his grandchildren in every way necessary. I have been used by Satan and I follow him.

This abridged version of Sandy's account encapsulates the inner turmoil of a person who wants to live a good religious life, but is taught to be afraid that her God will not accept her if she remains a lesbian.

During my fieldwork with LBT people, religion was a frequently discussed theme. In a discussion in April 2003, Anton, one of the butch leaders of the b/f community since the early 1990s, told us that he had converted to Islam after being a very devout Christian. He had gone on the *hadj* three times. At the time he regularly attended *pengajian* sessions. He had to go to the *pengajian* in female attire, with a head scarf, otherwise he was not allowed in. He felt deeply emotional about it. All participants agreed that the Quran clearly says that women should never dress in male attire. Dian kept repeating that you can lie to others, but never to Allah, who will always know. Yet they also felt that because Allah had created them they should be allowed to exist as they are.

Anton had also stopped making love to his partner, he revealed in another discussion, and was more like a mother than a lover to her. This conflict, between the inner desire to get close to Allah and to learn about Islam, and one's outward persona, was a source of major tension for the butches in my research. The femmes seem to be more relaxed about religion and their sexual choices. Surely, if Allah had wanted them to love men, they would have been able to do that? But instead, he had given them this manner of loving, which they found very satisfying.[53]

To be accepted in one's religion as an LBT family is a major issue. Yohan is proud that he managed to get his family of three accepted in his church. They are Catholics. Initially there was gossip about them, but he told them that in the afterlife it is God who decides what has been a sin. God is almighty; it is impossible that somebody has not been created by God. 'Every year we get a Christmas card from the church. We can be buried together. The church sees us as a family. When a younger sister of mine fell ill and died, the pastor came to visit and she was buried here. So it means we are accepted, doesn't it?'[54]

Male-identified Irfan said that in his church the pastor talks all the time about Sodom and Gomorra and accuses people like him of committing a major sin. 'But I read the Bible and why Jesus came to earth. To me it is a sin when you lie to yourself. So hypocrites are sinners. I never hurt my partner, I don't rape her, I don't force her. I love her, you know!'[55]

Like Anton who called lesbians *wapendos, wanita penuh dosa* (women full of sin), Dani had stopped having sex. He feels that if he loves women, that is not so much a sin, but seducing them and having sex definitely is.

> My sin was seducing women. Now I have a stable partner and for a long time now I have not sinned anymore. We are like sisters. We don't have sex anymore. That is how religion sees it. Isn't it? The story of Lut is about sex? Isn't it? Allah is called generous; he will certainly forgive those who repent. Hopefully I will be received [in heaven]. But as long as I live I will live with a woman. God and the people know I am a woman but also that my soul is that of a male. God knows everything. Now I never go there anymore, I pray at home. We both perform our *sholat* with a *mukena*. I cannot do that in the open.[56]

Reza also negotiated between his private belief and his public persona:

> I pray with a *mukena*. Though my soul is male, religion tells me I must dress like a woman. For I don't live alone, I live in a community and they think I am a woman, though they call me *om* and my wife calls me papa. *Sholat* is to link up with Allah. But my clothing has to do with my surroundings. If I use a *peci* and *sarong* they will think I deride religion. But Allah knows everything. I am reading the Quran in both Indonesian and Arabic and would like to study further. I always ask Allah why I have not been made fully into a man. When there is a *pengajian* I cannot come dressed as they are, with a *jilbab*. I want to search for knowledge, whatever the opinion of society, but I have to do it privately. When I worked with the Canadian embassy, I once brought my *mukena* to the mosque – I was thrown out, they shouted that I was a man. But in the mosque here they know I am a woman. They tease me – here is *om*, in women's clothes. My children also get confused, how come you use a *mukena* and crouch down when you pee?[57]

Agus, a somewhat older butch, said that he now wanted to get closer to God. Brought up in a strict Muslim family he realized that

Allah brought me into this world as a true woman so when I go back to Him I must also be *murni* (pure). My soul is that of a man but when I approach Allah I have to get back to being a woman. If not, I am afraid my *sholat* will not be accepted. Religion taught me one can better become a sex worker than loving another woman. So now I repent, I want to return to the right path, in line with the teachings of Allah.[58]

These inner conflicts vary in extent, and with stages of the life course. As Jack confided, 'I want to enter heaven but for the moment I want to live heaven on earth first.'[59] Feri prayed in *mukena* the regular four or five times per day:

Allah knows everything. If we do not try to be close to Allah, Allah will not be close to us. But it is not fair that I am given a heart like this. In the Quran they say it is a sin. I read the Quran regularly in Arabic but I never go to the mosque, for I feel awkward in these clothes. I would like to go on the *haj* but I have to change first to become like the other women, with a *jilbab*. Perhaps if we really try with all our heart, we will be able to change.[60]

Evi told Allah every time she prayed that she loved her *sentul*, and asked for forgiveness.[61] Endang, another femme, said she did not care that religion does not allow same-sex relationships. 'For me love is the most important. I never prayed to God about my feelings for women. You don't need to talk about such things, I feel, for God anyway already knows all that. I am not afraid God is angry with me for, well, it is a nuisance if I have to stop loving women.[62]

Some turned to God for help. When young Agustine realized she was a lesbian she prayed: 'God, give me a sign, so I know the direction I must take. If you don't allow me to live a lesbian life, then show me heterosexual love. But within a week I met Grace who taught me about lesbian sex. Now wasn't that a clear sign from God?'[63]

LBT people are encouraged by the fact that there is nothing in the Quran about lesbian love, and not even one official *hadith* that denounces or prohibits same sex relationships between women, only an unofficial one.

For *transpuan* and *waria* the issue of what to wear while performing the *sholat* is equally important. Many of them want to be able to do that in a *mukena*. As with the *priawan* discussed above, their clothing is an expression of their spiritual relationship with God, and a manifestation of their social selves as women. They can express both aspects of their religious selves in the unique institute of the *pesantren* for *waria*, Al-Fatah, in Yogyakarta, described in more detail below. Unfortunately, there is no such public space for *priawan*. Al-Fatah was initially also attended by lesbians, but due to the immense media attention that the *pesantren* received, they withdrew, not happy to be so exposed.[64]

The story of Amar Alfikar, the co-founder of the Indonesian Transgender Network, illustrates the benefits and happiness that come from a surrounding that accepts one's identity, in this case a transman. Amar's activism led him to fight for a spiritual space to worship Allah. As a child he felt that he was in the 'wrong box' and was later diagnosed with gender dysphoria. As a child of an Islamic preacher who led a *pesantren*, he had a hard time accepting himself, inflicting self-harm and questioning his religion. Because he understood that Islam does not accept transgender people, he was afraid that his family would say that transgender people would burn in hell and do not deserve God's love and heaven. However, his father and mother accepted him. Amar recalled that in a tense three-hour discussion his mother said: 'Never leave this family. You are still my child. I love you more and more,' and that,his father said: 'This is my child's destiny. My child's nature is like this ... The owner of the heart is Allah. We have made our efforts (*ikhtiar*), so now, we support him and his choices.'

His brother took Amar to Habib Ja'far Assegaf for *ruqyah*, hoping that he could return to being a woman. But Habib Ja'Far chided him: 'Are you forcing your brother to live not according to his nature? Allah created the unusual among the common people.' In February 2022, Amar joined the Queer Islamic Studies and Theology (QIST) group led by Amina Wadud. This is a platform that promotes research on sexual diversity as both a component of human knowledge and an integral aspect of Islamic teachings.[65] Amar reaches out on social media with the message that the human rights of LGBTIQ should be protected. He has a YouTube channel, and its main message is: God sent the Prophet to spread love to the universe, so that means that love should be practiced by everyone.[66]

Mairil

Despite the outright rejection of same-sex love by the Islamic authorities, the occurrence of same-sex activities in the country's hundreds of *pesantren* is a well-known phenomenon. Both boys and girls can be *mairil* to either *kyai* or other lecturers or to (elder) students. What is remarkable about this rather hypocritical position is that religious leaders usually condone this behaviour as temporary, not related to an LGBT orientation but as a natural outlet of sexual desires. This clearly contradicts the philosophy behind many conversion therapies, whose success is measured in terms of changing people's sexual behaviour and getting them heterosexually married. In the latter view the sexual orientation can be accepted, but same-sex practices are sinful. In the case of *mairil*, the reasoning is turned upside down, the behaviour is not sinful, as it is assumed that it is unrelated to same-sex orientation. Indeed, it seems many *mairil* marry a heterosexual partner after leaving the *pesantren*, but not all, and intimate friendships between former consensual partners is common.

In many cases a *mairil* relationship between male partners involves the absence of consent. It is not possible to gauge the depth of trauma *mairil* experience in what amounts in many cases to rape. In January 2004 I met Ahmed, a male staff member from KPI Yogya. He told me that as a child he was sent to a *pesantren* close to his home village Wonosobo, Central Java. He was a baby-faced youth liked by older men. He was repeatedly and violently raped by his teacher. He cried a lot and was comforted by an older friend of his. 'Yes, that's what he does all the time; for a *guru ngaji* (religious teacher) this is normal, we have to accept this.' Ahmed had nowhere to complain and left the *pesantren* heavily traumatized. He now finds it very hard to build a lasting relationship.[67] That was the first time I heard about the *mairil* phenomenon. For though apparently widespread, it is also an open secret. All religious scholars I spoke to admitted that this was a common phenomenon.

In women's *pesantren* also the phenomenon of *mairil* occurs, though even less is reported about this. It seems these relationships are more equal and the age gap between the partners is less. Nurish described erotic relationships between older girls (*kakak,* elder sister) and their *adik* (younger sister), in which the *kakak* played the protective role and donned male clothing while her *adik* was dressed in more feminine clothes. As the women would be expelled if they were caught in any form of erotic contact, they kept their relationships hidden.[68] Kholifah reported that sexual attraction and even behaviour between two *santriwati* (female students) was not considered a problem, as long as it was not considered lesbian – which is as an overt sexual activity.

When Nyai Hindun Aisyah, a well-known progressive women's leader, visited the Ardhanary Institute on 9 January 2013,[69] she was accompanied by a leader of the *pesantren* Hasyim Asyari.[70] The venerable *nyai* told the LBT activists that they had known lesbians all their lives:

> In our *pesantren* there were lesbians, called *mairil.* When it was known they didn't yet have a lover they were teased and we tried to find one for them. We only punished those who had heterosexual relations; they would be evicted. But sexual relations between *mairil* was not a big deal. They were warned but they were still allowed to study at the *pesantren.* It is the prerogative of Allah to decide what is a sin. *Amal* (good deeds) and *ibadah* (devotion) are the only important issues.[71]

The *mairil* phenomenon (called *alaq dalaq* in Madura) is widespread.[72] The word homosexuality is carefully avoided in religious circles; when *santri* mention it, they refer to onanism.[73] Both in traditional and in modern *pesantren*, *mairil* relationships occur. These relationships may continue after one or both of the partners have left the *pesantren.* As Dzulkarnain maintains, intimacy between a same-sex couple in a *pesantren* can thus lead to an alternative family constellation, as the extended families of all partners are involved in regular meetings.[74]

The word *mairil* seems to be derived from the term '*mar-ah fil lail*', an Arabic expression that means 'wife in the night'; this assumes a temporary sexual activity in order to reach physical satisfaction. While Islamic teachings require Muslims to abstain from sexual activities and to control their sexual desires, it is socially accepted that this is 'too hard', particularly for young boys and men. As heterosexual activities without being married to the other person are sinful, practising '*mairil*' is the lesser evil from the perspective of Islamic law. It is just a 'small sin'. Not only in Islam, but also in Christianity and Buddhism, same-sex relations occur in sex-segregated settings, suggests Muhyidin, as a compromise between religious imperative and existing reality.[75]

A typical male–male *mairil* relationship involves an older *santri* who has sexual contact with a younger *mairil*, often while he sleeps. In that case the activity is done in the dark, and called *nyempet* (from *sempit*, narrow), and consists of interfemoral (between the thighs) contact until ejaculation. Some authors make a distinction between a more loving *mairil* relationship and *nyempet*, which they consider just a covert activity for sexual release.[76] Religious leaders often portray the phenomenon of *mairil* as situational, denying the genuine attractions and desires underlying many of these relationships. What does transpire is that the *mairil* relationship among men is hierarchical and age-differentiated and is often fuelled by the sexual desire of the older *santri*.[77] Same-sex relations in the *pesantren* are sometimes referred to as *amrot-amrotan* (to play woman) between adolescent male pupils and *musyahaqah* to describe same-sex relations between adolescent female students. *Musyahaqah* is derived from the Arabic term *tassahouq* which refers to the act of grinding.[78] Among girls it seems the *mairil* relationship starts with friendship and then may evolve to become a sexual relationship. It resembles a b/f relationship.

As most authors agree, the younger partner in a male–male relationship is usually an androgynous looking boy, such as Ahmed. Such baby-faced boys are typically the preferred objects of affection of older boys who sometimes compete for their prospective partner's attention.[79] As these boys grow up, they in turn will take on other younger boys as *mairil*.[80]

The erotic relationships may be temporary, the partners experiencing a combination of love, romance, friendship and eroticism. In other cases, in which teachers and much older students are involved, force and sexual violence may occur, as Ahmed experienced. In the hierarchical atmosphere of a *pesantren*, in which *kyai* and other religious teachers are highly revered, it is difficult for a young student to complain when (s)he experiences violence.[81] With the heightened attention on homosexuality and debates about the criminalization of the LGBT community, attitudes in modern *pesantren* are shifting, as Iskandar already observed in 2006, and a greater intolerance and even denial of homoerotic relations within the student community has become more common.[82] Although most sources insist that the partners in a *mairil* relationship are not LGBT and the whole phenomenon has nothing to do with homosexuality, and is temporary, Enha said that a friend of his who had attended a *pesantren* in Bandung, and then got married but quickly divorced, presently heads a network of homosexual *pesantren* alumni.[83]

Syaifuddin's novel *Mairil* contains a chapter on the intimate relationship between two female *santri*, Jamilah and Maryati, whose bond raises mixed feelings from the *pesantren* community, varying from alarm to complete nonchalance. Their romance is suggested in a long love letter that Maryati writes to Jamilah about the future of their relationship after Jamilah has left the *pesantren*. Maryati confesses she constantly imagines them together again in an erotic embrace. However, Jamilah, who is due to marry a man, has had a change of heart since her time in the *pesantren* and receives the love letter with feelings of shame, anger and disgust.[84]

Piety as practice

Sartorial choices to exercise one's religious obligations were an important topic for the LBT narrators. Wearing a *jilbab* or a *hijab* in public are markers of a Muslim identity. Some LBT activists have started wearing a *jilbab*, demonstrating their piety and their

wish to belong to the Indonesian nation. For *transpuan*, the *jilbab* is a symbol of modest
womanhood and the desire to present onseself as a 'good Muslim woman'. Wearing a
jilbab is also a protection. Vigilantes will not readily attack or mock a veiled woman; it
bestows dignity and respect on her.

Some people gingerly move between various spaces of the family, the community
and one's friends. They present contingent identities, as obedient children, good citizens
and pious Muslims or Christians, as well as LGBT people.[85] Others try to present a
more coherent self in which their spiritual and their sexual orientation apparently are
not in conflict, while navigating their heteronormative surroundings. In both cases
demonstrating one's piety is critical. In Islam there are strict rules on how one should
perform one's *ibadah* (religious obligations) and outward behaviour is an important
aspect of one's piety.[86]

At the family level Islamic injunctions play a major role with behaviours, and this
also applies in lesbian families. Husbands in the so-called *keluarga sakinah* (happy
families) model are supposed to be guardians and guides for their wives.[87] Sartorial
choices, behaviour within one's family and the choice of partner(s) are all aspects of
the aesthetics LBT people navigate in their heteronormative surroundings, in efforts to
present themselves as pious Indonesian citizens, and good Muslims.

A good example of this modification of the self is the *pesantren* for *waria*, Al-Fatah,
in Yogyakarta.[88] Their main challenge is to be recognized as pious persons, of moral
integrity. It was founded after the 2006 earthquake in Yogyakarta, which caused great
loss of life and damage. The LGBT community, both Muslims and Christians, gathered
to pray for the victims. Aside from organizing these inter-religious prayers, Mariani
and her best friend Shinta raised money from many *waria* all over Java to buy food
to be distributed among the victims. They also provided free hairdressing services in
the shelters. Due to the success of their charitable efforts Mariani and Shinta held a
pengajian twice a week, every Monday (*Senin*) and Thursday (*Kamis*). They invited
Kyaj Haji Hamrolie, an open-minded religious leader who always invited Mariani to
attend his *pengajian*. They took the name of Hamrolie's large *pengajian*, Al-Fatah, in his
honour (The Opener, the Revealer, the Granter of Success, one of the names of Allah).

The *kyai* asked some of his students to teach *waria* about Islam, in particular about
how to perform the *sholat*. The *waria* can choose whether they use a *sarong* or *mukena*
to perform the *sholat*. As Safitri observed, those who opted for a *sarong* 'behaved in a
more "masculine" manner', for example speaking in a baritone voice, reducing their
effeminate conduct, and removing their make-up. Once they were finished with their
prayers, they returned to their feminine behaviour.'[89] The *pesantren* was originally
located in Notoyudan, a heavily populated kampung in Yogyakarta. It occupied a small
house in a narrow street, where Mariani had established a salon. She paid the rent and
other expenses.[90] Mariani maintained that Allah created all human beings and that
Allah is the only one to judge people on their *takwa* (piety). Humans were created
differently, espousing differences in skin colour, race, language, sex, sexual orientation
and gender so that the people can get to know each other in all their diversity, to create
mutual understanding. She had faith in Allah's justice only, not in the interpretations
of the *ulama*. Al-Fatah is thus a unique institute, where *waria* can negotiate their
religious subjectivity. It offers them flexibility in choosing a religious identity outside

of the public gaze, where they can explore their own truth about their bodies and their relationship with Allah. Mariani did not undergo surgery as she felt she did not have the right to change what God had provided, but in the early 1990s when silicone injections became available she injected herself directly into the skin of her breasts and face. This practice is visible in the swollen faces of the older *waria*. Younger *waria* prefer hormone injections.

Mariani herself had first worked the streets as a sex worker and later as a singer in a popular *dangdut* group. From there she started cleaning a beauty salon and worked her way up to own one. The land in Notoyudan belongs to the Sultan who, with his queen Ratu Hemas, is known to support women and minorities. On our visit several *waria* performed classical dances; the older, dignified Ibu Yayu, dressed in a magnificent yellow gown over a red dress, gave a moving rendition of the evergreen Bengawan Solo. A younger *waria* recited Quranic verses.

Ibu Mariani passed away in 2014, after which the *pesantren* moved to nearby Kotagede, to the house the co-founder Shinta Ratri had inherited. By that time the school was supported by the Nahdlatul Ulama University of Jepara. Students could learn about the issues related to transgender and Islam and engage in Quran readings and reciting prayers.[91] The previous year Mariani had managed to go on *umrah* (minor haj) to Mecca, dressed as a woman. After her first attempt failed, a friendly village head in Yogya gave her a card stating she was a woman so she could get a passport identifying her as female.

The place is a refuge for young *transpuan* who have been rejected from their families and schools, as well as a place for human and sexual rights advocacy. As Rere, a young *waria*, told Di Ilio in 2019, 'I'm a responsible student, a good Muslim. Never mind if I'm a girl or a boy, I'm part of this nation and I'll fight to claim my rights.' She prays five times a day. 'Making peace with Allah, having a place where you can pray openly in women's clothes, and deepening your knowledge of Islam, all of this is a liberating experience.'[92] Due to its fame the school has also attracted unwelcome attention. In February 2016, it had to be closed for four months after an attack by a local vigilante group calling itself Islamic Jihad Front (FJI). The *pesantren* received wide support, including from the local police.[93]

From the start, members of the Al-Fatah *pesantren* buried deceased *waria*, who had either no family or whose families had rejected them, and tended their graves. In 2019, the Waria Crisis Centre was founded by Rully and Shinta Ratri. Initially they only aimed to assist victims of violence; after the attack of the FJI, many *waria*, already traumatized, felt even more unsafe. Presently the Waria Crisis Centre is also open to older and sick *waria* and those who face economic, social and legal issues. They can stay for free, with food, medicine and other basic needs provided by the centre, which was badly needed during the Covid-19 pandemic.[94]

Conclusion

Religion may discard us, but God never will, is a feeling widely shared among LGBT activists familiar with the views of progressive religious scholars. Despite widespread rejection of their sexual orientation by hardliner Islamic leaders, the confidence to be accepted by God is enormously empowering. It boosts their spiritual morale, helps them negotiate their social selves and stimulates them to fight for sexual rights and to be accepted as full Indonesian citizens. Yet their adversaries use the rights discourse as well. MUI deputy secretary general Amirsyah Tambu opined that homosexuality has nothing to do with human rights. Human reproduction is a much more important human right in his view, which is thwarted by free sex and homosexuality. He sees LGBT people as performers of abnormal sexual behaviours which betray human nature because in the long run it could 'eliminate the next generation'.[95]

Contrary to what Mulia, Armando and other progressive thinkers assert, conservative religious leaders such as Ma'aruf decree that homosexuality is not created by God, but a psychological disorder, and therefore curable. He argued that God created good and bad behaviours and told humans to choose the good behaviours. Benny Susetyo of the Indonesian Bishops' Conference agreed with him.[96] Fundamentalist groups claim that they possess the authority to purify the religion, to steer it away from progressive interpretations. Typically, women and sexual minorities are targeted. In their condemnation of an alleged moral crisis, they return to the basic texts of their religion. Yet even that resurrection of the presumed sources of divine authority is open to interpretation, as we saw in the section on the Prophet Lut. The interpretation favoured by conservative groups like the Wahabi is patriarchal, hierarchical and intolerant.

Progressive religious leaders and scholars like Musdah Mulia and Kyai Hamrolie and the young NU scholars of the Gusdurian network provide enormously important political support for the LGBT community. This in turn helps LBT Muslims become more at peace with their spiritual and social personae. In spite of this support, LGBT people are faced with stigma and have to negotiate their contingent identities between family, workplace and private life. They also navigate their religiosity, moving in between their spiritual selves and their public performance as Muslims. How to perform the *sholat*, based on the bodies in which they were born, or on their trans souls, is an important issue. The few *waria* who belong to the Al-Fatah *pesantren* have found a solution for themselves, but many others face major dilemmas. We have seen how the butches face difficulties, because they felt they could only pray or enter a mosque in *mukenah*. For, they argued, we can trick humans into believing we are men, but Allah can never be deceived. Clothing is an expression of spirituality, an attempt to come closer to one's God, and a performance of the social self.

Belief in the afterlife, thought to be a return to Allah in the form they were born, strongly influences the sartorial choices of transpeople while performing their *ibadah*. How deeply this belief is felt is illustrated by the burial of Dorce Gamalama. This gifted and popular performer, banned from TV due to the post-2016 restrictions, died in early 2022 from Covid-19 complications. She had clearly expressed her wish to be buried according to the procedures for women. Yet ultimately her own family decided she had to be buried as a man, near the mosque she had built herself for the community. 'I have become a woman since the surgery, so I should be bathed [and buried] as a woman,' she had declared publicly.[97] This decision sparked enormous controversy, with the MUI insisting that Dorce be buried as a man, and the NU proclaiming that her personal choice had to be respected. It will be a long struggle before the spiritual, social and political aspects of the religiosity of LGBT people can harmoniously be aligned, when they will be accepted by their communities, and the country's religious leaders, just as they themselves know their God accepts them for their piety and their charity.

10

Heteronormativity revisited

Introduction

The trajectory that the Indonesian LBT movement has taken from its inception in the early 1980s until now, as analysed in this book, gives rise to several reflections. The concept of heteronormativity proves useful to analyse the homophobia,[1] violence and stigma that LBT people experience. It also allows the analysis of their resilience, ranging from the symbolic subversion of b/f couples – a model that persists to this day – to the courage of gender justice warriors. Elsewhere I have defined heteronormativity as a 'double-edged sword that not only marginalizes those who fall outside its norms but also patrols those within its constraints'.[2] The nature of heteronormativity in Indonesia, permeated by an Islamist conservative, binary ideology, informs its current form of homophobia: to be a member of the happy (*sakinah*) Indonesian family one has to despise LGBT people. This is both state policy and proclaimed from the mosques.[3] At the same time heteronormativity determines the particular forms of its symbolic subversion by the LGBT community. To strive to be a good Indonesian citizen, a good Muslim and to have a 'normal' family, when one is not expected to aspire to any of these, is a direct confrontation with the current form of heteronormativity.

The workings of heteronormativity, its passionate aesthetics, help us understand the specific forms of resistance in which LBT activists in Indonesia engage. Symbolic subversion, defined as acts involving 'secrecy, partial acceptance of the codes of normalcy, denial of personal needs, and the secret search for sexual pleasure' as well as 'hard work, sacrifice and defiance', applies to many of the tactics LBT persons deployed.[4] The ways that the various generations of b/f couples and other activists have negotiated their involvement with their communities and the nation, in view of the harsh heteronormative reality in which they live, are prime examples of such subversions. This discourse thus goes beyond a narrow sexual rights paradigm which focuses on the public, legal realm, inhabited by rights-bearing individuals. Symbolic subversion also takes place at the family and community level, and when negotiating intimate relations, and is always political.

Although heteronormativity is restrictive, because it closes off many options in life that our narrators would like to see opened and defines them as abject beings, it is critical to understand subversion as enabling. It opens up possibilities which are not only related to particular practices, such as earning one's own income and forming a family. It also offers a personal quest to shed the mental and moral restrictions of abjection. It requires a different way of looking, of seeing the straight, heterosexual model as not the only way of being and relating. And it necessitates a reorientation of normality: to accept the legitimacy of one's own embodied desires, to get rid of the shame and guilt produced by the passionate aesthetics of heteronormativity. Subversion incorporates both visible, physical and public manifestations of resistance or (self)destruction, from suicide to the struggle for women's and sexual rights. Those struggles may be seen as the manifest forms of resistance.[5]

There are important ways in which the Indonesian LGBT movement has charted its own course. For instance, the increased visibility of LGBT people after the democratic opening of society did not lead to greater acceptance, better protection against violations and to more rights, but rather turned public opinion against them.[6] Also, while in certain countries in the West a form of homo-nationalism appeared, in which accepting LGBTIQ rights was seen as a positive development for the nation,[7] in Indonesia public discourses of lesbian and gay activists have been seen as a threat to national security and in need of overt regulation and criminalization.[8] They have been accused of waging a proxy war against the nation and as forming a threat to the national philosophy of the Pancasila and Islam.

When the 'new' lesbian movement got under way in the 1970s in the West, the b/f communities were ridiculed as 'old lesbians'. But in many countries like the United States they did not totally disappear.[9] The persistence of b/f patterns and the relative ease with which FTM transpersons are accepted in the midst of LBT organizations are important characteristics of the Indonesian movement. This is also due to leaders such as Agustine who in their turn were supported by the growing Indonesian feminist movement. B/f patterns are found in other Asian contexts as well, such as China, Taiwan, Thailand and Hong Kong.[10] B/f relations, though not always accepted by more radical feminist lesbians, have never posed a big challenge to the LBT movement. To this day the Ardhanary Institute consists of an interesting mix of radical, androgynous activists (no label), b/f couples (of three generations now) and *priawan*, while young activists have started identifying as queer. There have been huge debates around these formations, but no major rifts have occurred.

Another characteristic of the Indonesian LBT movement is that the focus of their struggle has not been so much in terms of rights-bearing individual identities but in community and family acceptance. This is linked to the fact that (extended) families play an important role in the lives of LBT persons in Indonesia. Expulsion from the family means financial stress, loss of social support and loneliness. Both family violence and the culture of family silence pose major problems. Silence means that parents and siblings do not need to know things that are not spoken about openly. And as long as they do not 'know', they do not have to reject an LBT family member. This culture of silence both facilitates a range of socially accepted norms, as long as any divergences are not too great, and also hides underlying power relations and masks violence and discrimination.

The b/f couples I worked with negotiated their identities within the margins of heteronormative harmony (*rukun*), outwardly accepting some established gender patterns (butches occupying the 'public' space, their 'wives' being responsible for the household), internalizing other characteristics (jealousy, possessiveness, romantic passion, butch economic responsibility) and again rupturing others (feminine sexual passivity, women's emotional dependence). LBT people may assume an identity that is more suitable for acceptance in the family, while being openly out towards friends. This projection of contingent identities is not limited to Indonesia. It has been analysed in other Asian contexts such as Sri Lanka.[11] It is more or less accepted that the 'truth' about oneself may differ according to circumstances.

Outward appearance (short hair, masculine clothing in the case of butches and *priawan*) has always been an important marker of one's gender. Unisex clothing has been introduced rather late in Indonesian society and has remained restricted to progressive members of an educated urban middle class. Dressing in masculine clothes was thus a significant public statement. But it also meant that for bystanders the 'truth' of the choice of clothing signified the 'truth' about that person: they were accepted as men. This has, however, differed over time. While in the 1980s a b/f couple could more easily remain under the radar provided they exhibited 'normal' heteronormative behaviour, the label LGBT that came into use after the Reformasi has increased the suspicion with which this kind of couple is viewed.

Indonesia's LGBT activists have been struggling to resist the criminalization of homosexuality. Though some may dream of marriage equality, the reality is that such a demand would only incite homophobia. The fear of and hatred towards homosexual people, combined with misogyny, affect both lesbian and heterosexual women, though not in the same way. Political homophobia is omnipresent. It not only directly affects all LGBT persons but also makes the alliance between LGBT and feminist organizations difficult, because it weakens feminist leaders who may be accused of being lesbians or 'lesbian defenders'. The concrete effects of coming out as LGBT may mean the loss of status, of employment, an end to a political career or it can lead to vigilante attacks. LGBT people may feel impelled to modify their behaviour, politics, ambitions and dress. It may make lesbians who might be strong leaders or prominent, productive citizens to suppress their personal lives, or withdraw from leadership positions altogether.[12]

In the West the dominant discourse on homosexuality in the first half of the twentieth century was the medical model of deviance, superimposing an earlier judicial regime in which homosexuality was criminalized.[13] In Indonesia same-sex practices were never prohibited in precolonial times. They came to be seen as sin, crime or mental illness as the Dutch expanded their imperial regime and as Islamic reform movements have come to dominate earlier more inclusive forms of Islam. Support for gender pluralism and diversity faded away. After Indonesia's independence, a process of what I called elsewhere postcolonial amnesia became evident; the new rulers copied the moral systems they had inherited, particularly in relation to gender and sexual relations, while they were proclaiming a return to the values of a precolonial past.[14]

Without idealizing or homogenizing precolonial archipelagic social structures, it is clear that, as advanced in Chapters 2 and 3, at several periods in time and in particular communities, acceptance of gender pluralism and diversity and same-sex practices was known. Indonesia was not alone; as the bio-archaeologist Geller maintains, gender flexibility has been a general and cross-cultural phenomenon that was once widespread.[15] This situation of gender pluralism and diversity existed, while homosexual people were persecuted in Europe. The colonial imposition of a narrow, patriarchal and blatantly heteronormative morality, its continuation in the postcolonial period, as well as the homogenizing forces of nationalism have deeply changed this disparate pattern. In certain cases this meant a narrowing of the possibilities for expression of people's capacities for non-heteronormative desires and practices.[16] In Indonesia, with the growing influence of a bigoted, fundamentalist interpretation of Islam, this process leads not only to enormous pressure on people living non-heteronormative lives, but it has also almost erased the historical consciousness of gender variance. Under the present heteronormative regime, the gender binary is considered to be traditional and natural.

Besides the demand for rights, the (symbolic) subversion of the heteronormative order has antagonized the adversaries of the LGBT community. Upsetting to conservatives has been the gradual breakdown of the model of belonging in which same-sex people were expected to blend in with the heteronormative world, for example, by accepting (if temporarily) the obligation to marry or by silently enduring their inferior status in society. Their apparent accommodation to the tenets of heteronormativity did not undermine the contemporary regime of hegemonic heteronormativity. When LGBT people became publicly visible it became clear that gender had to be seen as more fluid and flexible than previously assumed. At the same time, the wider circulation of terms like gay and *lesbi* drew attention to the isolated *wandu* or *banci* living under the radar in the countryside and to the women's same-sex couples living hitherto-inconspicuous lives in neighbourhoods or boarding houses, leading to their outing and in some cases eviction. Public debates on homosexuality on television, in the print media or on social media gave Islamic clerics and other conservatives a platform to argue that LGBT people were living an immoral lifestyle.

From slandering to criminalizing

Though LGBT organizations such as Perlesin and Lambda were pioneers in raising the consciousness of gender and sexual minorities in New Order Indonesia, they were not able to sway public opinion in their favour. As far as LBT organizing was concerned, only with the support of women's rights organizations, initially mainly the KPI, were they able to formulate their demands and integrate them into a wider social and political agenda. Hate mongering against communists inspired the 1965 sexual slander against Gerwani, and this first sexual moral panic established a pattern in which 'deviant' sexuality came to be viewed as a threat to the nation. To further its own political interests, the New Order regime imposed uniformity on society, insisting on 'traditional' gender and sexuality norms. Heteronormative familial tropes – Suharto as the Father of Development, and family principles (*asas kekeluargaan*) as the basis of the state – suffused public discourse.[17]

During the New Order small activist groups were operating mostly under the radar. Human, women's and sexual rights language was eschewed – it was too dangerous. Media coverage, generally inquisitive in the early 1980s, quickly became mostly negative, framing gay and lesbian persons as sick and morally abject. Yet it brought issues of same-sex love into the open. Through training, magazines and awareness raising, the idea of an LBT identity began to be harboured.[18] The LGBT communities that sprang up after the 1998 democratic opening gradually started using the discourse of human, women's and sexual rights – particularly after the Yogyakarta Principles were promulgated in 2006. After 2015 a politico-religious homophobic campaign destroyed all careful advances the LGBT movement had made in terms of protection against discrimination. President Jokowi, who came to power in 2014 with a human rights-oriented agenda, did nothing to stem the rise of anti-LGBT hate speech.

Alongside people associated with the banned Communist Party, LGBT people have become a scapegoat in the political arena. In the absence of debates on the serious political and socio-economic issues the country faces, political parties play the moral card and compete in their aversion to both groups, hoping to gain votes from a conservative electorate.[19] Public acceptance of homosexuality in Indonesia is notoriously low. The Pew Research Centre conducted a survey among 38,426 people in thirty-four countries from 13 May to 2 October 2019. The study was a follow-up to a 2013 report which revealed that in Indonesia 93 per cent said homosexuality was morally unacceptable and only 3 per cent said it was morally acceptable. In the Asian region Indonesia scored low. In Malaysia 9 per cent of the population felt that homosexuality was morally acceptable, for South Korea the figure was 39 per cent, Japan 54 per cent and the Philippines scored even higher with 73 per cent.[20] The 2019 survey showed that Indonesia's score for acceptance of homosexuality had increased to 9 per cent, South Korea went up to 44 per cent, Japan to 68 per cent while the situation in the Philippines remained the same.[21] Indonesia's score was just above the score of Nigeria (7 per cent) which was found to be the most homophobic country in this survey.[22]

Homophobia thus has wide support, and uttering homophobic statements increases one's electoral capital. It is not surprising, therefore, that particularly in election campaigns homophobic sentiments escalate. The major support the LBT movement receives to counter the attacks on their community is from the feminist movement, such as Komnas Perempuan and APIK, and from the wider human rights community such as Komnas HAM. Unfortunately, the human rights movement was split during the 2019 presidential electoral campaign.[23] Since then civic space has been declining even further, and social media are being more intensely monitored.[24]

In the last decade of the New Order the idea of an LBT identity began to take hold through their organizations which held training and awareness-raising sessions and through the attention media paid to LGBT issues. After the Reformasi and assisted by the growing influence of feminist organizations, LBT people tried to fight publicly the discrimination and violence they experienced. Hope was expressed that the state would end the discrimination they had experienced at schools and in the workplace. This hope was smashed when the Anti-Pornography Bill was accepted in 2008, the first law that includes a clause against LGBT people. LGBT organizations never voiced a demand for a marriage equality law, aware that that would antagonize conservative forces. They watched when feminists formulated a draft for a reform of the Marriage Law and noticed that any proposal for reform was struck down by shrill voices which accused feminists of wanting to introduce free sex and same-sex marriage. Since then, all they have been able to do is try to stem the tide of growing support for anti-LGBT legislation.

The acceptance in Parliament of the revised Penal Code on 6 December 2022 ended a period of long public debate on the criminalization of homosexuality. It criminalizes all forms of non-marital sex and opens up the possibility of using 'living law' or local communal values and norms to prosecute behaviour not explicitly mentioned in the code. Patriarchal customary laws, or the new homophobic regional regulations, may be imposed under this provision even if they violate the human rights provisions enshrined in the Constitution. This revised Code also strengthens the 2008 Anti-Pornography Law. The display of contraceptives is also prohibited, and safe sex and sexual health campaigns may be prohibited. Other controversial articles of the revised Penal Code are that all ideologies except the Pancasila are prohibited, and that criticizing the president or state institutions, for instance, by calling them homophobic or transphobic, can be seen as a criminal offence.

The Family Resilience Bill (RUU Ketahanan Keluarga) is another effort to further criminalize LGBT people. It has also been dubbed the 'Bedroom Bill' as it purports to regulate people's private sexual lives.[25] It is a deeply patriarchal, Islamist-inspired law. Like the Anti-Pornography Law it defines homosexuality as a 'sexual deviation'. In Article 85 of the draft bill it is stipulated that a state body responsible for 'family resilience' would be required to handle 'family crises due to sexual deviation' through spiritual guidance and social, psychological and medical rehabilitation.[26] This is the language AILA also uses, and for which GiGa is established. Article 86 reads: 'Families experiencing crises due to sexual deviation are required to report their members to agencies handling family resilience or rehabilitation institutions to undergo treatment.' A clause on families reporting their members considered 'deviant' to the authorities is also already within the Anti-Pornography Law. If this Family Resilience Bill became law it would open the door for hostile families to send their LGBT members to a psychiatric ward or to some other conversion centre. AILA, the MUI, the PKS and the enormous political and social network they have been building over the years are campaigning hard to make this happen.

The Anti-Sexual Violence Law on the other hand is welcomed by the LBT community. After a long struggle it was finally accepted in May 2022.[27] The original proposal by Komnas Perempuan in 2012 included nine types of sexual violence.[28] Hardliner groups including AILA protested loudly against this draft arguing it promoted free sex and homosexuality, though the bill said nothing about those two issues. Several civil society groups strongly supported this bill, including the LGBT organizations Suara Kita (Our Voice), the Ardhanary Institute and Gaya Warna Lentera Indonesia (GWL INA), in the hope that violence against LGBT people would be recognized more easily if the bill was passed.[29]

The law stipulates prison terms of up to twelve years for crimes of physical sexual abuse, both within marriage and outside; fifteen years for sexual exploitation; nine years for forced marriage, which includes child marriage; and four years for circulating non-consensual sexual content. Convicted abusers must pay restitution and authorities have to provide counselling to victims. In principle, LBT persons who are forcibly married or have been subjected to 'corrective rape' should be protected under this law (though rape is also included in the Penal Code). In practice, there are many obstacles to the implementation of this law on behalf of LGBT victims of sexual violence.

LGBT people have specific concerns. One of these is the difficulty of having one's trans status publicly recognized so as to get an identity card which accepts this status. The Covid-19 pandemic made clear the predicament of LGBT people who do not have an ID card; the government provided various schemes of social support, for which an ID card was necessary. Also, people can only access health facilities through the government's health support system with an ID card. But many LGBT people do not have an ID card, as they have been evicted from their homes and cannot lay claim to the Family Card which is the basis of an individual ID. The Home Ministry realized this and promised to ensure that an electronic ID card would be made available for transpeople. This seems sympathetic but it does not mean that a third category is added to the card – a T (trans) or an X (non-binary). The gender/sexual binary is strictly maintained. The sex of the persons is determined by the sex assigned at birth, as contained in the birth certificate and stated in the Family Card.[30] Only a court decision based on sex reassignment surgery can open the possibility of being registered in the desired sexual category.[31] This formal route is awkward and expensive and involves psychological testing and operations. Poorer and less-educated transpersons cannot access these services and some of them engage in identity fraud, which if discovered, for instance, by suspicious in-laws, can lead to a prison sentence.[32]

Apart from Aceh, which is governed by homophobic sharia law, in other parts of the country hundreds of regional bylaws have been implemented, many of which contain anti-women and anti-LGBT articles, such as in Palembang, South Sumatra, Cianjur and Bogor.[33] Satpol PP and Islamist vigilante groups are employed to make sure that these regulations are abided by. The anti-gender movement in Indonesia is getting stronger, with a number of groups coming out forcefully against feminism and the LGBT community. Since December 2020 GiGa, established by AILA board members, is asking for volunteers who are anti-LGBT to protect traditional family values.[34] The view of their trainer, Professor Euis Sunarti, on Indonesia's families, is that they are naturally religious, hierarchical and harmonious.[35] The Centre for Gender Studies, a think tank of AILA director Dr Dinar Dewi Kani, associated with AILA's communication department, spreads the idea that feminism comes from Western women's hatred of men. Western feminism is portrayed as a Man-Hating Movement, which sees all men as rapists. While in Islam, the centre proclaims, there is no gender bias as Islam is based on the concept of justice.[36] AILA and other hateful Islamist groups are saturating Indonesian society with what Lies Marcoes calls 'radicalism without violence'.[37]

Continuing stigma and violence

The marginalization and abjection of LGBT people continues. By the beginning of the second sexual moral panic in 2015, universities were the major objects of surveillance, and academic institutions tried to impose bans on their student body and staff. In 2023, the year of completing this book, many state institutions are imposing discriminatory methods. Adding to the long list of prejudices faced by the LGBT community in Indonesia, some government institutions are refusing to recruit those they say possess 'deviations' of sexual orientation and behaviour. For many positions so-called *fit and proper* tests must be administered. These usually contain a question on LGBT issues. The same applies to fellowships abroad. If one confirms one does not hate LGBT people, one has failed the test.[38]

The following case demonstrates the entanglement of political and homophobic concerns. As part of a drive to weaken a major icon of the Reformasi – the Anti-Corruption Committee (KPK) – in 2019, the Indonesian Parliament (whose members are notoriously high on the list of people convicted for corruption) adopted a law that stipulated that the KPK should be under the control of government, thus losing its independence. As a result, all KPK members had to become civil servants and had to conduct a test. This test did not deal with their competencies as corruption fighters, but with their moral standards. It included questions on the alleged cruelty of the Japanese, religion, Western culture (as destroying the morality of Indonesian people) and homosexuality (should LBGT people have rights, or receive physical punishment?). One also had to write an essay on such organizations as the PKI, the FPI and on homosexuality. Some of the most prominent progressive investigators answered honestly and failed this test.[39]

Not much support can be expected from the president. In 2024, his second, final term ends, but he is building a dynasty, and he knows that voicing anti-LGBT sentiments will gain his sons and son-in-law political capital. His son-in-law was newly elected as mayor of Medan; he called on Medan to become an 'anti-LGBT city'.[40] Others, such as the governor of Riau concurred; he demanded that LGBT people repent as the cases of HIV/AIDS in the region increase.[41] Even in Makassar, in South Sulawesi, the home of the Bugis with their five gender system, the regional council (DPRD) is planning to introduce anti-LGBT laws, as other regions already have done, according to the chair of the DPRD, Andi Hadi Ibrahim Basso.[42]

The nation

The wave of homo-and transphobia engulfing the archipelago since late 2015 conveys a deep concern – what bodies belong to the nation? How are 'normal' citizens imagined? What kind of conduct is permitted and what movements around sexuality are accepted? Who can define the characteristics of the nation? In this process both colonial and postcolonial legacies must be incorporated.[43]

Regional regulations that contain conservative gender norms and anti-homosexuality clauses are typically justified by linking them to alleged traditional and religious norms. I discussed previously how 'tradition' was reinvented to deny gender diversity and how progressive interpretations of Islam and Christianity allow for a discourse of sexual and human rights. This begs the question of how far the present postcolonial model of belonging is based on authentic notions of citizenship in the huge and diverse archipelago. For while the nation is redefining itself as a homophobic entity, its history is rewritten. Both tolerant religious traditions and the occurrence of gender diversity are being erased. This erasure continues. At the annual celebrations of Bone's anniversary in 2022, for the first time in the history of South Sulawesi, no *bissu* were allowed to participate. The *arajang* were not cleansed in the ritual way and the *maggiri* dance was danced by women, and not by *bissu* in traditional clothing, now considered feminine. The *bissu* had long negotiated about their participation, offering to wear different pieces of clothing, but the governor was adamant.[44] This heteronormatization of tradition is also evident in the *reog* dance in Ponorogo, where the role of the *gemblak* has been taken over by girls, and in the *gandrung* dance of Banyuwangi. The transgender aspects of these cultural and religious traditions are being destroyed, replaced by heteronormative patterns.

Izrahuddin, reflecting on what an authentic Indonesian national identity might entail, asserts that a genuine member of society would be expected to uphold the Pancasila or Five Principles of the state: belief in God, humanity, unity, democracy and justice. This is in keeping with a sense of Indonesian exceptionalism, defined by Sukarno in 1959 as the 'national personality' (*kepribadian bangsa*).[45] This special Indonesian character is different from the Western situation and is built on its own wide variety of cultural and ethnic systems. But as discussed earlier in this book, certain customs are ignored, and instead important elements (sartorial, religious, cultural and behavioural codes) have been imported from the Middle East and from the West. Democracy and justice are also considered much less important than belief in God, all elements of the Pancasila.

LBT people claiming their identities as Indonesian and wishing to belong to the nation have to overcome the heteronormative logics of nationhood which construct non-normative sexualities as perversions and subversions which are deemed threatening to national authenticity. The backlash against the LGBT community then must be seen as part of a broader agenda to diminish secularism, pluralism and liberalism. Ultimately issues of gender and sexual identity relate to the character of the nation – does it want to be a liberal democracy, in which the rights of all its citizens are recognized, true to its Constitution and its national slogan Unity in Diversity? Or does Indonesia want to be seen as a bigoted nation in which minority rights are subjugated to those of the adherents of a majoritarian Islam? LGBT activists support their claims to be 'authentic' Indonesians with accounts of precolonial histories of homosexuality, civic participation in democratic processes, linking up with other human and women's rights organizations and with participation in educational, religious and cultural activities.

LGBT people also want to be good Muslims. Giving charity is one of the basic requirements of Islam. To emphasize their citizenship, LGBT persons have been actively involved in administering charity.[46] Back in the 1980s Perlesin members sought to raise money to help prisoners. During the Covid-19 crisis LGBT organizations engaged in charitable activities, while vulnerable members of their communities, such as *waria*, sex workers and street singers were hard hit by the lockdowns. As Rodriguez and Sivianita noted, LGBT people have been supporting citizens impacted by Covid-19 measures across the archipelago.[47] In Yogyakarta, members of the Al-Fatah *pesantren* for *waria* distributed food every Friday to destitute *waria* and other poor people, like *becak* (pedicab) drivers. Similar activities have been taking place in Maumere on Flores, with

LGBT organizations distributing food and face masks, and even assisting vulnerable people to pay their rent. To finance these activities, they asked for donations.

The potential power of social movements in the form of the ghost of a resurrected communist movement has continued to haunt the Indonesian nation, ignoring the history of violence of hardliner Islamic groups, or absolving them from blame. The hatred towards the LGBT community seems to be directed especially at its organizations; in the process science is distorted to confuse homosexuality with paedophilia and contagion, and sexual orientation with behaviour. There is a widespread view in society that the nation has to be defended against threats to its integrity and morality, defined as attacks on the Pancasila and Islam. In conservative eyes these are the same, as they only recognize the first *sila* of the Pancasila, belief in one God.

Defenders of human, women's and sexual rights who do not specifically proclaim (mainstream) religious values are seen by conservative Muslims as 'liberals' who do not uphold Islamic values but, instead, spread LGBT propaganda and communist ideas.[48]

All over the country civic education based on the values associated with the Pancasila is a compulsory topic. One of the aims of these courses is to instil an anti-LGBT attitude among the students.[49]

The proliferation of identities within the LGBT movement threatens the supposed stable sex/gender binary on which Indonesia's heteronormative regime is based. Those who cannot be captured in this binary mould are excluded, as happened to a student who claimed to be gender neutral at an event at their university.[50] The university later apologized, but then that apology was again condemned for promoting LGBT.[51]

Words count. When the acronym LGBT became popular, it was immediately associated with a deviant Western phenomenon. Homosexuality is also a tainted term. The introduction of the UN-based SOGIE discourse on sexual and gender identities by activists was intended to deflect those negative and stigmatizing connotations. It became widely used for training purposes in the field of SRHR.[52] At the moment educated young activists, exposed to the internet and other social media, often self-identify as queer. When people self-identify as queer I follow that usage in relation to them. But in my view using the term 'queer' as an umbrella term runs the risk of ignoring the specificity of the trajectories of lesbians, bisexual women and FTM transpersons, compared to gay men and MTF transpersons, who are mostly the topics of discussion and in studies.[53] In addition, such an umbrella term, coined in the Western LGBTIQ rights movement, tends to foreground the experiences of those middle-class Western rights activists, while neglecting the specificity of movements in other locations.

Sexuality and gender relations now function as a battlefield between those upholding democracy and human rights on the one hand and conservative forces including armed forces and religious fundamentalists on the other hand.[54] The latter forces dominate both the present government and the political opposition, and in this arena civic space is shrinking. Conservative forces like AILA are becoming more influential, spreading hatred and influencing public opinion. In the process gender binaries are reaffirmed and sexuality essentialized. In a Foucauldian turn of events, the more Indonesia tries to censure what it deems sexually perverse behaviours, such as free sex and LGBT, and accuses the human, women's and sexual rights warriors of betraying the nation, the more the nation defines itself in sexual and gendered terms, showcasing its bigotry.

Conclusion

In Indonesia's clientelist political system, where protection depends on patronage networks of economic tycoons and military leaders, the LGBT community is in a particularly weak position. In the absence of mechanisms to enforce the rule of law universally, railing against perceived LGBT immorality provides cheap political capital to a wide range of opportunistic, Islamist and populist groups.[55] The LGBT community has few allies; the women's movement is their strongest supporter, but even that relationship is wrought with difficulties. Particularly Muslim women's groups find it problematic to openly support LGBT groups. Whereas in the West support for the LGBT community can gain one the approval of anti-Muslim groups – homonationalism – no such mechanism exists in Indonesia. However dubious this form of conflation of an Islamophobic discourse (inspired by white supremacy) with an LGBT discourse appears, it has helped gain large public sympathy for members of the LGBTIQ community in the West (though the battle is far from over). In Indonesia among the broader social movements, such as organizations of farmers or workers, there is little explicit attention to the incorporation of sexual rights. Yet LGBT workers experience significant workplace discrimination.[56]

It is striking that the rise of anti-LGBT hate speech appeared during the presidency of the supposedly reformist Jokowi. Prior to this time, such harsh moral judgements had usually been carried out by conservative Islamic organizations, such as Muhammadiyah, and the MUI. The fact that Jokowi has made no effort to restrict hate speech espoused by influential religious and political leaders has had a disastrous impact on the lives of LGBT Indonesians. Though anti-LGBT hate speech has been specifically associated with the long campaign for the 2019 presidential election, it has not disappeared since the election was over. Jokowi's agenda is characterized by a campaign to curb Islamic radicalism. Perhaps to strengthen his Muslim credentials he still condones pronouncements by his allies about detesting homosexuality.

In an anthology discussing Indonesia's record of democratic transition after 1998, the authors conclude that Indonesia's democracy has regressed. They point to restrictions of freedom of speech and organizations, the unchecked rise of right-wing vigilantism, the weakening of critical democratic institutions, such as the KPK, and the erosion of checks and balances on executive power.[57] The abuse of the 1965 Blasphemy Law[58] and the draconian 2008 Electronic Information and Transactions (ITE) Law, under which, for instance, WhatsApp chats can lead to one's arrest, is a formidable weapon.[59] Political analyst Power calls this 'executive aggrandisement'.[60]

In spite of outrageous accusations that the LGBT community is waging a 'proxy war' against the Indonesian state, the threat of violence comes from radical and jihadist groups. This strand of violence dates back to the early days of the republic, when the new state had to fight the Darul Islam and its military wing, the TII (Tentara Islam Indonesia).[61] Although it is Islamist terrorists who have killed people, the mainstream, increasingly conservative Wahabist and Salafist Islamic groups have had a pervasive influence on Indonesian society. They have firmly planted a climate which is intolerant of diversity and imposed dress and behavioural codes.

So where are we after forty years of LBT activism? Earlier studies of the Indonesian LGBT movement such as by Blackwood in 2010 and Boellstorff in 2005 pointed to a globalization of *lesbi* and gay identities. However, what we have witnessed more recently is the globalization of heteronormativity and homophobia, with majoritarian conservatives taking their cues from Russia, China and conservative Muslim countries. To support their case, they point to 'Eastern values', ignoring the fact that Taiwan, for instance, has adopted marriage equality, and that countries like Thailand, the Philippines and South Korea have far higher scores for the acceptance of homosexuality. They also ignore the fact that while in Europe homosexuals were persecuted, gender diversity and same-sex relations were never criminalized in the precolonial archipelago and in some communities these people had high status.

And yet, although their activities have to be conducted with greater vigilance, a new generation of internet savvy activists has grown up who know how to deal with government surveillance. They are faced with a new set of questions. How to reclaim an authentic same-sex and gender diverse space which is both inherently Indonesian, rooted in its complex histories and cultural contexts, yet that is open to outside influences without being dominated by them? They need resilience, creativity and courage to operate under the present repressive conditions. Though the anti-LGBT campaign was ostensibly directed against LGBT organizations, out of fear LGBT people might collectively claim rights restricted to heterosexual people, in practice the backlash has seriously affected individual members of the community as well – depriving them of housing, jobs, social protection and exposing them to discrimination, violence and stigma. Perhaps their history of organizing may support them and continue to give them the hope of living a life without discrimination.

Notes

1 Introduction: Now we just whisper to each other

1. This meeting took place on 31 October 2018. The two other participants were Dian and Wulan.
2. See Katjasungkana and Wieringa (2016).
3. For more details see Chapter 7.
4. See: 'LGBT Crackdown Feared in Indonesia'. https://www.theguardian.com/world/2017/sep/06/lgbt-crackdown-feared-in-indonesia-after-12-women-evicted-from-home. Accessed 23 January 2021. A village official was quoted as saying: 'It's not acceptable to have female couples living together. Some have short hair, acting as the males. Some have long hair, acting as the females. It's against Sharia (Islamic law). It's obscene.'
5. See Wieringa and Katjasungkana (2018) for an analysis of the stigma both communists and members of the LGBT community face and how these stigmas are related.
6. See Mietzner and Muhtadi (2019) on how intolerant Islamist views are spread. The research of Rumah KitaB, coordinated by Lies Marcoes, investigated the spread of fundamentalist ideas among the wider Muslim public. Results are forthcoming.
7. b/f refers to butch-femme. See the discussion later in this chapter.
8. *Waria* are usually defined as MTF transpeople. Another, more pejorative term, is *banci*. It is important to understand the *waria* position as a gender identity, not as a specific sexual orientation. The men who have sex with *waria* or *banci* do not see themselves as gay. See Oetomo (1996: 261) for a discussion.
9. They had also protested when Mrs Sulami, a former leader of Gerwani, and I spoke on the fate of the socialist women's organization Gerwani, which was destroyed after a campaign of sexual slander in 1965, as part of the coup that brought General Suharto to power. See Wieringa (2002) and Wieringa and Katjasungkana (2018). In protest the representatives of Aisyah, the women's wing of the conservative Muslim mass organization Muhammadyah, walked out of that session.
10. Named after a visit I organized to the National Museum, where we studied statues of Ardhanary, the deity who combines male and female characteristics. See Chapter 2.
11. She is presently enrolled on a PhD programme.
12. The Jakarta Post (2016c).
13. The T in this book mostly relates to FTM transpersons, though where relevant a discussion on MTF transpersons is provided.
14. At present a more correct terminology is used, assigned female at birth, but I find it so unwieldy that I prefer in the interest of the readability of the book to use female-bodied (or male-bodied, where relevant).
15. See Wieringa (1999) for a discussion on this topic.
16. See, for instance, Wieringa, Blackwood and Bhaiya (2007). See also Sinnott (2004) and Wang (2021).

17. BIN, Badan Intelijen Negara, National Intelligence Service, formerly called BAKIN, Badan Koordinasi Intelijen Negara, National Coordinating Intelligence Body.
18. From *pria* (man) and *wanita* (woman).
19. See, for instance, Boellstorff (2005, 2007) and Wijaya (2020). On *waria*, see Hegarty (2019a, 2019b) and Toomistu (2019).
20. A term introduced in global HIV/AIDS campaigns, men who have sex with men.
21. ASTREA and MamaCash (2020). See also Hildebrandt and Chua (2017).
22. See, for instance, Brenner (1998), McGregor, Dragojlovic and Loney (2020), Suryakusuma (2011) and Wieringa (2002). An exception is Bennett and Davies (2015).
23. See Wieringa (2016a, 2020a) for a discussion on heteronormativity and passionate aesthetics.
24. For analyses of similar autoethnographic experiences, see also Blackwood (1995), Dahl (2010), Newton (1993, 2000) and Wekker (1994).
25. See Vance (1999).
26. As feminist anthropology students, we set up this group in 1974. It organized the first feminist anthropology conference in the Netherlands and became the basis of LOVA, Landelijk Overleg Vrouwenstudies Antropologie (LOVA, National Council of Women's Studies Anthropology), which still exists. Other members were Anna Aalten, Lenie Brouwer, Britt Fontaine, Marijke Mossink and Marion den Uyl.
27. See Wieringa (1992) for a discussion of the shift from biological determinism to social constructivism and Wieringa (1999) for the relevance of this discussion for Jakarta's b/f community. See Rubin (1975).
28. See Wieringa (1987).
29. See Wieringa and Blackwood (1999).
30. See the account of her daughter in Bateson (1984).
31. On constructivism, see Foucault (1978, 1985, 1988) and Weeks (2010).
32. See Wieringa (2009) for a discussion on postcolonial amnesia.
33. See Wieringa (2016a) for a discussion about how 'unruly bodies' are created.
34. Braidotti, following Deleuze, calls those potentialities 'pure flows of energy capable of multiple variations' (2011: 158).
35. See Wieringa (2020: 291) for a definition of 'passionate aesthetics', which I define as the dynamics, motivations, codes of behaviour and presentation, subjectivities and identities that together make up the complex workings of erotic attraction, sexual relations and partnerships patterns. For an in-depth discussion of heteronormativity and passionate aesthetics in Indonesia, see Wieringa (2016a: 33–4).
36. The Foucauldian term bio-power refers to the numerous and diverse techniques for achieving the subjugation of bodies and the control of populations and is a constitutive component in the government of both colonial territories and postcolonial nation states. See Lemke (2001).
37. Gerakan Wanita Indonesia, Indonesian Women's Movement, a progressive socialist-feminist organization which became the third-largest women's organization in the world in the early 1960s.
38. See Wieringa (2002). Gerwani members were accused of castrating and killing the generals who were abducted by the 30 September 1965 Movement.
39. See, for an analysis of the propaganda behind these campaigns, Wieringa and Katjasungkana (2019). For an account of one such attack, see Wieringa (2018). Only in January 2023 did the Indonesian president Joko Widodo officially acknowledge the mass murders committed in 1965/6 as a crime against humanity.

40. My first academic article on the Indonesian b/f culture is Wieringa (1999).
41. See Wieringa (1999, 2007a, 2009a).
42. See subsequent chapters. Sektor 15 is the fifteenth interest group of the Indonesian Women's Coalition established in 1998. It dealt with sexual minorities.
43. Consent was recorded on the tapes. These tapes are in Jakarta, in the archives of the Ardhanary Institute. The research materials also became the basis for various training and discussion sessions with LBT and feminist women.
44. On my use of English pronouns see below.
45. From fieldnotes dated 5 February 2004:

> Another butch, with a well-paid job, was still living in a rather modest house. I wondered about that when I interviewed her but didn't ask this question. At the time she didn't tell me she was fighting her addictions. Her femme partner told me she was really tight with money, giving her every day just enough for their daily needs, begrudging her the school fees for her children. I only found out many years later, when she (the butch partner) was arrested for corruption, how dependent she had been on drugs and alcohol and how desperate she was to get enough money to pay for them.

46. The butch partner was murdered by the femme's brother in mid-2004. Although the reason seemed to be financial, the media blew it up as a lesbian murder. See Chapter 6.
47. Halberstam (1998) calls this kind of eclectic methodology 'scavenging'.
48. See Butler (1993).
49. See Halberstam (1998) for a discussion of female masculinity in Western history.
50. Fieldnotes, 15 April 2004.
51. Fieldnotes, 12 May 2003. There are several important publications on the theme of sexuality and fieldwork. The introduction to Gloria Wekker's fine analysis of Surinamese *mati* women is one of the most impressive texts on the topic (Wekker 1994, 2006). See also the essays in Lewin and Leap (1996).
52. Its intersecting themes are women's/gender studies, fundamentalisms, livelihoods, conflict and violence against women and sexuality. Founder members include Abha Bhaiya, Kamla Bhasin, Sister Manalansan, Bernadette Resurrection, Thanhdam Truong, Amrita Chhachhi, Nighat Said Khan, Nursyahbani Katjasungkana and Saskia Wieringa.
53. See Vargas and Wieringa (1998).
54. Based on the Kartini conference in Bali, the edited volume *The Future of Asian Feminisms* was produced (Wieringa and Katjasungkana 2012).
55. APIK presently has eighteen offices in the country. It was established in 1995. They provide legal assistance and lobby for gender-sensitive laws or policies.
56. In Indonesian there is one word for widows and divorced women, *janda*, though sometime the added information *mati* (dead) or *cerai* (divorced) is used.
57. See Bhaiya and Wieringa (2007).
58. The International Association for the Study of Sexuality and Culture, established in Amsterdam in 1997. I am a co-founder and past president (2001–3). Abha Bhaiya is the current acting president.
59. See Kristeva (1982: 4).
60. See Butler (1993).
61. See Wieringa (2012, 2016, 2020a).

62. Riek Stienstra was a prominent lesbian activist and organizer and the director of the Schorer Foundation, best known for its AIDS-related work. She passed away in 2007. Her estate was dedicated to international research and training for lesbian rights organizations.
63. Namely English, Afrikaans, Hindi, Marathi, Bengali, Malayalam, Telugu, Kannada, Tamil, Sinhala, Russian, Indonesian, Setswana, Tagalog; only in a very few cases were translators used.
64. The final report was finished in 2011 (Wieringa 2011). The next year two Dipayoni team members published an edited version of their own research in Mazdafiah and Widaningrum (2012).
65. General Suharto crushed the movement in a day and declared this to be a communist coup, ignoring the fact that military personnel were heavily involved. The CIA and the British secret services who were wary of Sukarno, whom they considered left-leaning, played a supportive role in the affair. See Robinson (2018).
66. The 30 September Movement consisted of a group of military men and a few top leaders of the Indonesian Communist Party (PKI). The whole Communist Party was blamed for the affair; see Roosa (2006).
67. See Robinson (2018), Wieringa (2002, 2003) and Wieringa and Katjasungkana (2019).
68. See Melvin (2018), Robinson (2018) and Roosa (2006).
69. This is not the first time the association between communism and homosexuality has been made in Indonesia, see Wieringa (2000). For an analysis of the two sexual moral panics, see Wieringa and Katjasungkana (2018) and Wieringa (2022b).
70. See Buehler (2016), Kersten (2015) and Wieringa (2020b).
71. See Aspinall and Mietzner (2010), Hadiz (2017) and Wieringa (2020b).
72. See, for instance, Bourchier (2015). See also Power (2020) and Setiawan and Tomsa (2022).
73. See Gerlach (2018).
74. See Bennett (2005), Blackburn (2004) and Brenner (1998).
75. See Wieringa (2003) and Wieringa and Katjasungkana (2019). As I argued elsewhere, this model has made a comeback in recent years. See Wieringa (2015a).
76. See, for instance, Wieringa (1995, 2003, 2015a) and Suryakusuma (2011).
77. See Kendall (1999) and Wieringa and Blackwood (1999).
78. See Wieringa (2007a).
79. 'Jenderal Polisi diduga LBT diperiksa Propam Polri'. https://www.cnnindonesia.com/nasional/20201020161738-20-560596/jenderal-polisi-diduga-lgbt-diperiksa-propam-polri.
80. See also Blackwood (2005) on the difficulties to be consistent with naming the various gender-transgressive identities (and ritual practices).
81. This is stipulated in the 1974 Marriage Law.
82. See also Murray (1999).
83. LGBTTSIQQA: Lesbian, gay, bisexual, transgender, transsexual/two spirited, intersex, queer, questioning, asexual.
84. See Butler (1993), Fernandez (2020) and Puar (2007). In Indonesian studies of the LGBT movement the term queer is also used; see Izharuddin (2013), Arisah (2008) and Wijaya (2020).
85. Newfield et al. (2006) define an FTM transgender person as an individual who was 'labelled female at birth and chooses to identify as male, whether or not s/he receives transgender medical treatment' (2006: 1447-8).

86. Terminology is still being debated. Many transgender people, for instance, prefer the term gender incongruence to gender identity disorder.
87. As a beautiful boy he aroused the desire of the female water nymph Salmacis who embraced him with such passion that they fused.
88. See Grewal and Kaplan (1994) and Povinelli and Chauncey (1999).
89. For instance, in Adam, Duyvendak and Krouwel (1999).
90. IDAHOT was the acronym used for the last march.
91. See also Sedgwick (1990).

2 The twilight of the gods

1. The idea was to have a history tour about Indonesia's sexual politics. After the museum visit we went to Lubang Buaya, where they could study the bronze mural in which Suharto's version of history is portrayed, including the scene of the so-called Dance of the Fragrant Flowers in which Gerwani members had allegedly seduced the abducted generals, after which they had castrated them on 1 October 1965. See Wieringa (2002, 2003).
2. See Chapter 7 for a discussion on these regional regulations.
3. *I La Galigo* describes the epic creation myth of the Bugis people in South Sulawesi. Based on oral tradition, it was put into manuscript form from the eighteenth century onwards and runs to over six thousand pages. It is the world's longest epic text. In 2011 it was inscribed in Unesco's Memory of the World list. See Koolhof (2017).
4. The Bugis adopted a five-gender system, with male/masculine and female/feminine on the outer edges, and male/feminine, female/masculine and *bissu* (intersex or fusing all sex/gender positions) in the middle. See Davies (2010), Pelras (1996) and Sugianto (2015).
5. See Davies (2010) and Lathief (2004).
6. See Blackwood (2005).
7. See Andaya (2000: 29).
8. See Blackwood (2005: 857).
9. The term 'androgynous' was often used, conflating a terminology for hermaphroditism and homosexuality; Boswell (1995).
10. See, for instance, Foucault (1978).
11. See Bleys (1995) for a discussion of such texts.
12. See Peletz (2009) and Clarence-Smith (2012).
13. See, for instance, Peletz (2009).
14. There is an abundant literature on these topics, for instance: for the Philippines, see Garcia (1996) and Johnson (1997); for Thailand, see Aldous and Sereemongkonpol (2008), Jackson and Sullivan (1991), Käng (2012), Sinnott (2004) and The (2002); and for Indonesia, see Boellstorff (2005), Hegarty (2019a, 2019b) and Toomistu (2019).
15. See, for instance, the discussion in Ong (1991: 21).
16. The impressive opening carving of Candi Sukuh, representing the meeting of yoni and lingga (Parvati and Shiva), stands in contrast with the mermaids in the popular seaside resort of Ancol, the upper halves of which are now covered up, as are the many statues of nude women in the presidential palace in Bogor, inherited from the days of Sukarno. Present-day artists can be prosecuted for portraying genitals in such an open fashion, under the stringent 2008 Anti-Pornography Law.

17. See, for instance, Parker (1992).
18. See McClintock (1995).
19. Dutch women were also considered responsible for preserving the unpolluted whiteness of the European community; see Clancy-Smith and Gouda (1998) and Stoler (1995).
20. See Carey and Houben (1987).
21. See Gouda (1995) and Tiwon (1996).
22. See Conner et al. (1997: 67), quoting Daniélou (1992).
23. See, for instance, Nihom (1986) and Kinney, Klokke and Kieven (2003).
24. See Daniélou (1992); see also Pande (2004).
25. See Mookerjee (1988). See also Kinney, Klokke and Kieven (2003: 131).
26. See Andaya (2006: 47).
27. In this form she is still very popular in India. The capital of Bengal, Kolkata, is named after her (Kali Kota).
28. See also Ariati (2010). In Javanese mythology she is called the queen with the flaming womb (*niriswari*).
29. There are several statues of Durga Mahishasuramardini, such as in the Central Javanese temple of Sambisari (near Yogyakarta), or the East Javanese Candi Jawi; this statue is now located in the Surabaya Mpu Tantular Museum. In both these statues Durga is standing on the defeated buffalo, from which the dwarfed demon Mahisha emerges.
30. See Heraty (2006: 1).
31. See Heraty (2006: 41–2).
32. See Ariati (2010: 369).
33. See Ariati (2010).
34. Halfway between Denpasar and Gianyar in Bali, the temple of Kutri, Dharma Bukti, has a fine statue of the goddess. It is situated on a hilltop, from which a large part of South Bali is visible.
35. See Andaya (2006: 29).
36. This happened in our own village in East Java. Before 1965 this and other rituals were alive, accompanied by a *gamelan* orchestra. The *gamelan* is in disrepair, only some old people still know how to play it and they hardly do that, for fear of antagonizing the fanatical Muslims in the area. The only cultural activities at present are related to the many mosques.
37. See Andaya (2006).
38. See Andaya (2006), based on the *Pararaton*, the Book of Kings. But, as Krom mischievously wonders, why did the first husband of Ken Dedes, Tunggul Ametung, not become ruler of the world? See Krom (1926: 313–14).
39. The novel *Pramoedya Ananta Toer* wrote about this story, for example, does not stress the sacred powers of Ken Dedes; see Toer (1999).
40. See Andaya (2006: 232).
41. The goddess's name comes from *prajna*, true wisdom, and *paramita*, perfection. See Kinney and Marijke Klokke (2003).
42. 'History of Women in Buddhism'. http://awakeningbuddhistwomen.blogspot.com/2015/02/history-of-women-in-buddhism-indonesia.html.
43. See Andaya (2006: 58).
44. See Kumar (2000).
45. The south coast of Java is particularly dangerous. The story goes that when Ratu Kidul needs a new pillar for her undersea palace, she sends dangerous waves to the shore, where fishermen or other bathers are trapped.
46. See Andaya (2006: 13).

47. See 'Avalokiteshvara'. http://www.britannica.com/EB checked/topic/45363/ Avalokiteshvara. Accessed 4 June 2015.
48. See Wieringa (2007c).
49. See Honig (1985) and Topley (1975).
50. See Baroni (2002).
51. See note 47.
52. See, for instance, Wieringa (2007b).
53. See Balzer (1996), who refers to the ethnographer of the Chukchi in North-Eastern Siberia, Bogoras (originally 1909). In North-Eastern Siberia, shamanistic practices have been widely documented, e.g. among the Chukchi. Practices varied widely, from males who were braiding their hair in a woman's way, to healers cross-dressing fully and pursuing all activities a woman usually does, forsaking hunting and herding reindeer. In this process the shaman is assisted by spirits (Balzer 1996). The transformation may be so complete that the shaman also has psychic changes, losing his 'brute courage and fighting spirit' (Balzer 1996: 166). As such, the 'soft man' takes a male lover who s/he marries, according to the proper rituals. This marriage often lasts until one of the partners dies. Female shamans going through a similar process are more rare, but the ethnographer Bogoras heard of a case of a woman healer who was ordered by the spirits to become a man and who learnt how to use a spear and a rifle. She too engaged in a same-sex marriage, with a younger woman. In their lovemaking they made use of a 'gastrocnemius' (dildo) made from a reindeer leg (Bogoras, in Balzer 1996: 167). These shamans were thought to be guided by extraordinarily powerful spirits. Though the shamans were highly respected, even feared, the transformation process was not easy, and involved 'great personal sacrifice' (Balzer 1996: 168). Balzer cites another ethnographer working in the same region among the Nivkh or Gilyak communities, Shternberg (1904), who collected a great diversity of cases. This researcher concluded that 'the power of sex and sexual transformation lay at the heart of shamanism'. In the 1920s and 1930s these transgender shamans were persecuted under the Soviet regime, both because they engaged in shamanism and because they were classified as sexual deviants. Similar practices have also been recorded in Korea (Kendall 1985).
54. See Wilken (1912).
55. In a collection edited by Hooykaas (1947).
56. The bird is called *bangau* in Indonesian, similar to a heron. *Boerake* is the old spelling for *boerakee*.
57. A kind of junglefowl.
58. See Lathief (2004: 48–9).
59. Paraphrased from Hooykaas (1949: 13–16). I used the same article to comment on the way the famous trans entertainer Dolce Gamalama was denied her last wish, to be buried as a woman (Wieringa 2022). See also Gamalama (2005).
60. See Schärer (1963), quoted in Blackwood (2005).
61. See Kroef (1954: 259).
62. See Perelaer (1870).
63. See Berkusky (1912), cited in Bleys (1995: 180).
64. See also Kroef (1954). The male God Mahatala created two young men, Sambaja Sangir and Sambaja Sanggiang, who lived together for a very long time, before they went their separate ways and each married. From Sambaja Sangir humankind was born. Sambaja Sanggiang's offspring were called the Sanggiang. Both groups started fighting. The humans threatened to conquer the Sanggiang, after which the last group retreated to Sanggiang island in the sea of clouds, taking a group of *basir* with them.

65. See Schiller (1991: 415). See also Sutlive (1992) and Sutlive and Appell (1991).
66. Conner, Sparks and Sparks (1997: 224).
67. See Kroef (1954).
68. See Schiller (1991: 427), based on fieldwork between 1982 and 1984.
69. See Karsch-Haack (1911: 197–206).
70. See Hupe (1846) in Karsch-Haack (1911: 197).
71. See Schwaner in Karsch-Haack (1911: 198).
72. See Karsch-Haack (1911: 189–99).
73. See Karsch-Haack (1911: 189–99). Perelaer, who worked for the civil service, collected interesting information on the income of *basir* and *bilian*. The *basir*, the high priest of the Dayak, was rewarded f 2.50 for his services, while the eldest *bilian* received only f 1.25 and ordinary *bilian* f 0.75.
74. See Perelaer in Karsch-Haack (1911: 19); he calls it 'greuliche Sittenlosigkeit'.
75. See Perelaer in Karsch-Haack (1911: 200).
76. Perelaer did not detail what kind of sexual conduct was concerned for girls, heterosexual or same-sex acts; for boys it can be assumed he means same-sex acts.
77. See Perelaer in Karsch-Haack (1911: 200).
78. See also Wilken (1912: 352).
79. See Karsch-Haack (1911: 489).
80. Paraphrased from Hardeland (1859: 53–4).
81. See Andaya (2006: 57), quoting Sandin.
82. From 'Manangism' by the Venerable Archdeacon J. Perham (undated), quoted in https://en.wikipedia.org/wiki/Transgender_people_and_religion. Accessed 25 July 2021.
83. The story is well known. See for a popular version: https://tropaws.wordpress.com/2018/06/23/iban-gods-in-the-sky-menjalara/.
84. See Graham (1983) for an overview of the literature on the Manang of the Sea Dayak.
85. See Sutlive (1992).
86. See Karsch-Haack (1911: 203), citing the Bishop of Labuan.
87. No details are given about what this violation might entail.
88. Tuak is an Iban liquor made from cooked glutinous rice mixed with home-made yeast containing herbs for fermentation.
89. See Henry Ling Roth in Karsch-Haack (1911: 203).
90. See Karsch-Haack (1911: 203), quoting Henry Ling Roth.
91. See Karsch-Haack (1911: 203).
92. Andaya (2000), Davies (2004, 2010) and Pelras (2006).
93. See Chabot (1950) and Kroef (1954).
94. See Chabot (1950), quoted in Kroef (1954).
95. The ceremony was called *irebba*.
96. See also Suliyati (2018) and the interesting documentary on *calalai* by Kiki Febriyanto, who collaborated with the Ardhanary Institute. See also Sugianto (2015).
97. See Matthes (1872: 23).
98. See Pelras (1996: 97). See also Andaya (2000).
99. See Karsch-Haack (1911: 211–15), citing the Dutch Indologist Matthes.
100. See Wilken (1912: 376). See also Hardeland (1859: 53).
101. See Matthes (1872: 23).
102. See Matthes (1872: 24).
103. See Davies (2004: 188–9).
104. AC–DC is a widely used pun, referring to the switching between two electric currents, and is used to denote someone of uncertain sex or gender.

105. See Lathief (2004).
106. In the 2008 article by Ariyanto, the words *calabai* and *waria* are used interchangeably.
107. As told by the *bissu* Puang Temmi, in Thamaona (2003: 33).
108. See Pelras (1996).
109. Andaya (2000), Pelras (2006), Graham (2004, 2010).
110. See Koolhof (2017). The text achieved world fame only from 2004 onwards when Robert Wilson produced an opera based on the text of the *I La Galigo*. It was performed only once in Indonesia, in July 2019. https://seleb.tempo.co/read/1188 361/i-la-galigo-kembali-dipentaskan-di-jakarta.
111. In Part 1 of the *I La Galigo*, Batara Guru descends from heaven and becomes the first inhabitant of the middle realm, the Earth. He is accompanied by the *bissu* Lae-Lae who helps Batara Guru to arrange life on Earth, establishing rules and traditions, culture and language. When the twins Sawérigading and Wé Tenriabéng are born, *bissu* have to assist. The birth is extremely difficult, and after several days it is clear that *bissu* blood must flow. Several *bissu* are sacrificed but after the successful birth they are revived. Wé Tenriabéng, who is a *bissu* herself, has to discourage her brother from marrying her and advises him to marry I Wé Cudaiq, the youngest daughter of the king of China, who resembles her closely. She herself departs to the Upper World. As a *bissu* she has knowledge of the mystical sword with which the heavenly tree can be cut and that must be felled to become a boat for her brother. The queen of China also has *bissu* who inform her that the suitor of her youngest daughter is on his way. They marry and *I La Galigo* is born with the help of *bissu*. When I Wé Cudaiq is pregnant again Sawérigading hopes it will be a girl so she can become a *bissu*. And indeed Wé Tenridion is born complete in *bissu* costume, but she remains in a coma from which she can only be revived if *bissu* symbols are brought to her. These belong to Wé Tenriabéng and thus derive from heaven. She left them when she went to heaven so they have to be brought back from the country of origin. The land there has known many misfortunes, harvests have failed and trade has declined since she left. *I La Galigo* brings the *bissu* symbols to his sister who recovers. Summarized from Koolhof (2017: 28 a.f.).
112. See Pelras (1996: 166–7), referring to the merchant and missionary Paiva (1545). See also Chabot (1950).
113. The Dutch colonial servant Friedericy, who spent many years in South Sulawesi before the Second World War, wrote a few insightful novels on the region's history. In *The Last General* he describes the Dutch conquest of Bone. The brilliant Bone general Mappa (called Bontorio by the Dutch after the name of his feudal estate Bontorihoe) is served by several *bissu*. The guardian of his house's *arajang* is described as follows: '[the priest] was dressed in the loose red robe of the virgins, sported a black shining girl's haircut, on its fringes – forehead and temples – painted with black lacquer, his lips were painted purple-red. He moved like a young woman, for he was a *wandoe*, a man with a female soul in his body' (Friedericy [1947] 1965: 13). This priest, elsewhere described as 'a friendly old woman with a deep hoarse voice', becomes one of Mappa's closest friends (Friedericy [1947] 1965: 32). The main *arajang* of Mappa's house are a *keris* that has been in the family for forty generations, and a magical spear, La Badoe. Before Mappa's battles the priest performs all the proper rituals, and these *arajang* are carried with him. Only in the last battle they were left behind, and the Dutch conquer the Bonese army.

In another novel situated in the 1920s, a *bissu* is still guarding the ritual objects of the now powerless queen such as the *gaoekang*, a golden *keris* preserved in white cloth, only to be opened under the correct prayers and the burning of incense (a ceremony the queen herself performs). Other symbols of power consist of weapons, special stones, gongs and antique Chinese porcelain (Friedericy 1958). See, for his career, Friedericy (1961).

114. See Budiarti (2007).
115. See Andaya (2000).
116. See, for instance, Hakim (2014).
117. See, for instance, Ad'han and Mabrur (n.d.).
118. (DI/DII): Darul Islam/Tentara Islam Indonesia. See Van Dijk (1981).
119. See, for instance, Lathief (2004: vi).
120. In some sources the term Operasi Taubat refers to the next wave of persecution, the anti-communist purge. See, for instance, Hakim (2014).
121. See Boellstorff (2005: 39). See also Davies (2010).
122. See Thamaona (2003: 32–9).
123. See Thamaona (2003).
124. The rumour at the time was that if someone saw a lady-boy or transgender person, for seven days their good deeds would not be accepted by God.
125. See Graham (2004).
126. Kate Lamb, 'Indonesia's Transgender Priests Face Uncertain Future'. http://america.aljazeera.com/articles/2015/5/12/indonesias-transgender-priests-face-uncertain-future.html. Halilintar Lathief is an anthropologist from Hasanuddin University who has studied the *bissu* phenomenon for decades.
127. See Lathief (2004). At present the number may have changed.
128. See Andaya (2000), Ariyanto (2008), Lewi (2012), Pelras (1996) and Hakim (n.d.).
129. See Hakim (2014).
130. See Ariyanto (2008). Namely, in Bone there are forty *bissu*, in Soppeng eight *bissu*, in Wajo twelve *bissu* and in Pangkep twenty-two *bissu*.
131. This is the usual way of dissolving events which those in power do not like. See Hajramurni (2017).
132. See Hakim (2014).
133. See Lathief (2004).
134. Ichon, pages 15–18 in *OUTZINE* Newsletter, Arus Pelangi, Edisi XII/Juni, 2008. Jakarta: Arus Pelangi.
135. 'Makassar Mulai Godok Raperda Anti-LGBT'. https://www.cnnindonesia.com/nasional/20230108161415-32-897620/makassar-mulai-godok-raperda-anti-lgbt, 8 January 2023.
136. See Andaya (2006: 230).
137. See Blackwood (2005) for a discussion on sacred gender.
138. See Peletz (2009: 16).

3 Liminal spaces: Court and village culture

1. See Blackwood (2005), Gouda (1995), Peletz (2009), Wieringa (2010) and Garcia (1996) for numerous examples.
2. See Gouda (1995) and Kerkhof (1992).

3. See Aldrich (2002) and Boellstorff (2005).
4. *Ludruk* is a popular dance form which originated around the turn of the twentieth century in East Java. See Peacock (1987). In East Java the *ludruk* theatre groups depicted stories from daily life. On *reog*, see Boellstorff (2005) and Wilson (1999). See also Hughes-Freeland (2008a and 2008b) and Pigeaud (1938).
5. See Wieringa and Katjasungkana (2018) and Wilson (1999).
6. See Oetomo (2001b).
7. This is not so much about a 'lesbian' identity. In the Western world self-defined lesbians appeared only around the early twentieth century (Vicinus 1992). In Indonesia I locate the emergence of a political lesbian identity in the 1980s (though the word was around earlier).
8. See Van Baal (1984: 140). See Wieringa and Blackwood (1999) for a discussion on these so-called sapphic silences.
9. See Sawitri (2001: 44).
10. See Sawitri (2001: 44).
11. The *Manusmriti*, the Laws of Manu, written in Sanskrit, was produced between the second century BCE to the third century CE. See Thadani (1996) for a discussion on the *Manusmriti* and women's same-sex practices in India. This code was highly influential in pre-Islamic Java as well, until well into the fifteenth century. But no information is available as far as I know on its application in daily life.
12. I could not find a definition of podication, though I consulted various dictionaries including the Shorter Oxford. Specialists who I consulted had no idea either. It possibly refers to the practice of rubbing the penis between the thighs of the lover (intercrural contact), but anal intercourse may also be meant.
13. An older form of *gamelan* orchestra in Bali than is used today.
14. See Jacobs (1883: 13–14, 134–6).
15. See Andaya (2006: 192).
16. See Karsch-Haack (1911: 490). See also Wieringa (2012) for a discussion on dildos in precolonial societies.
17. Creese (2008: 9): 'If a woman touches the genitals of a maiden without reason, the fine is 8 pana = ma 10 = 4,000 and she must pay for the medicines; if she is betrothed the woman who assaults her must pay three times the bride price and her clitoris is sliced; if the woman is already married and seizes the genitals of a maiden, her vagina is cut and also two of her fingers cut off.' There is no record of this rule ever being applied.
18. See Winter (1902), describing court life in 1824.
19. See Winter (1902: 25).
20. Whether the women actually used dildos for their love making or that Winter could not think of any other way in which women could please each other is not clear.
21. See Gayatri (1993). See also Faderman (1980) for a discussion of such female friendships in the West.
22. See Mangunwijaya (1988). Scenes of women's intimacy, bathing and dressing are also portrayed on the so-called 'hidden foot' of the Borobudur, its base (Badil 1992). Photos of the base of the Borobudur, covered up after investigation, are to be found at the Leiden National Museum of Ethnology.
23. See Carey and Houben (1987: 19–20).
24. See Kumar (1980).
25. See Carey and Houben (1987: 20).
26. See Okado (2011).
27. See Andaya (2006: 60).

28. See Carey and Houben (1987: 19).
29. Cited in Murray and Roscoe (1997: 257).
30. See Verse 91 in the *Nâgarakertâgama*, for example in Pigeaud (1963: 70–1). See also Brandes (1920: 34–5).
31. Centini herself is a *cethi*, an attendant, companion, of Princess Tambangraras, wife of Seh Amongrogo, one of the protagonists.
32. I read the Indonesian version produced by Santoso (2006). In its most complete Javanese version it counts almost 30,000 stanzas making up over 700 cantos. See also Anderson (1990).
33. See Santoso (2006: 19).
34. For instance, Santoso (2006: 25, 98, 291–3). See also Wieringa (2016a) for a discussion on these dancers. Hughes-Freeland (2008a and 2008b) noted their decline during the New Order. See Hefner (1987) on *tayuban* in East Java.
35. Wilken provides an astute observation relating to sex work and respect among these female dancers. According to him, among the Olo-Ngadju Dayak the female *basir* engage in prostitution, while among the Olo-Manjian these women are highly respected. These shamans are thus associated both with sex work and with respect. As *taledek* and *ronggeng* dancers originate from shamans and shamanistic dancers, this combination – sex work and respect – also applies to them (Wilken 1912: 390). See also the literature on temple prostitution in India, for instance, Soneji (2012).
36. See Santoso (2006: 64).
37. See Santoso (2006: 162).
38. See Santoso (2006: 165).
39. See Santoso (2006: 163); Mas Cabolang and Nurwitri have sex with seven girls.
40. See Santoso (2006: 166).
41. See Santoso (2006: 177–80).
42. See Santoso (2006: 119, 154).
43. Not only unmarried girls but also young widows who have already had a taste of sexual love, desire Mas Cabolang (Santoso 2006: 85–6).
44. See Santoso (2006: 288–91).
45. The Panji cycle belongs to an oral tradition and has many versions. Leiden University Libraries houses the greatest collection of Panji manuscripts in the world. The collection consists of over 260 manuscripts in eight languages, the majority written on palm leaf or paper. They are a combination of historical tales and mythical elements. The cycle is recognized in UNESCO's Memory of the World Programme.
46. See Santoso (2006: 323–5).
47. Andaya (2006: 192). Andaya here points to a methodological issue. The pornographic male gaze of the authors of these courtly accounts as well as of their intended audiences might influence their descriptions of what women exactly were doing with each other.
48. See, for instance, the version of Meyboom-Italiaander (1924).
49. See Rosjidi (1983).
50. See Kumar (2000), for an account of how colonial administrators downplayed the women's armies at the courts of Java, and Wieringa (2002), for the way the women guerrilla fighters who joined the national liberation war against the Dutch were ignored in present day historiography. Gerwani, the Communist-oriented women's organization, consciously drew upon the model of valiant womanhood and frequently invoked Srikandhi's name.
51. See Florida (1996).

52. The *Mahabharata* is one of the great Hindu epics, the other being the *Ramayana*, which are very popular in Indonesia. The *Mahabharata* tells the story of the struggle between the five Pandawa brothers and their numerous Kurawa cousins. Bhima is the strongest Pandawa, renowned for his courage. Arjuna is the most ascetic and revered Pandawa brother. He is known for his inner strength and sexual prowess.
53. In Indonesia Srikandhi is mostly used, in India Shikandhi. As the story with the *yaksha* is mostly found in India I use Shikandhi in this paragraph.
54. See Gayatri (1993), citing Wiryoatmojo.
55. See Ras (1976). I joined the *gamelan* group Raras Budoyo which performed this *wayang* play in the 1980s in the Netherlands. Artistic director was Elsje Plantema. See also https://www.discogs.com/artist/8458827-Elsje-Plantema.
56. Bhima is such a shining example of manly strength and honour that he is widely popular. President Sukarno likened himself to this *wayang* hero.
57. See also Carey and Houben (1987) and Tiwon (1996).
58. According to Cok Sawitri, Balinese kings were known to have male lovers. An example is King Kania of Klungkung (personal communication). See also Vickers, who remarks about the seventeenth-century king of Northern Bali, Panji Sakti, that he surrounded himself with transvestites and was 'a great sodomite' (2012: 37). He quotes the noted Bible translator Leydekker.
59. See Pucci (1992: 59).
60. See Chapter 5 on Sektor 15 and the KPI.
61. The 1938 collection of Javaanse Volksvertoningen (Javanese Popular Performances) by Pigeaud contains many references to various popular art forms in which male-bodied or female-bodied dancers or performers are portrayed.
62. See Pigeaud (1938) and Peacock (1987: 197–208). See also Ong Hok Ham (1972) and Sunardi (2009).
63. See Foley (2015).
64. See Kartomi (1976). *Reog* dances were performed in many places in Central and East Java; see Pigeaud (1938).
65. See Lyon (1941), Oetomo (1991), Wilson (1999) and Wachirianto (1991).
66. See Ishomuddin (2019).
67. See also Tohari 1982, on the fate of a *ronggeng* dancer.
68. Pebrianti Charolin. 2022. detikjatim, 'Menguak Hubungan Gemblak-Warok di Reog, Seperti Apa Sebenarnya?' *detikjatim*, 13 April. https://www.detik.com/jatim/bud aya/d-6030946/menguak-hubungan-gemblak-warok-di-reog-seperti-apa-sebenarnya.
69. See Groenendaal (2008) and Rapoport (2018).
70. See Wieringa (2003).
71. See Peacock (1987).
72. *Wandu* is Javanese for *banci*. It was also performed as a stand-alone dance.
73. The *ngremo* dance was created by a former *gemblak* dancer from Ponorogo, Cak Mo, in Jombang, and later brought to Surabaya. There it became the opening dance for *ludruk* performances. The *ngremo tayub* is danced by female-bodied dancers and the *ngremo putri* by male-bodied dancers. At present, the dance is often performed to welcome important guests, as I witnessed during the seventy-year anniversary celebration of the cultural group Sapta Darma (on 7 January 2023 in Lawang). Two cross-dressing female-bodied dancers performed the dance in a vigorous masculine style, with big strides, high arm positions and strong head movements. They had a moustache pencilled on, but their hair was feminine. They had broad ankle bracelets on their right feet, accentuating their forceful steps. These were village dancers. On

YouTube several videos circulate of professional dancers performing the *ngremo*, sometimes by a group containing both female- and male-bodied dancers.

74. Marhaen was the name of the typical Javanese peasant who inspired Sukarno to model the Indonesian nationalist movement. He called his populist ideology marhaenism.

75. See Wieringa and Katjasungkana (2019) for a further analysis of these cultural wars in the first half of the 1960s.

76. See Setiawan (2016).

77. See Oetomo (2001b).

78. Dorce Gamalana was a very well-known transgender TV actor. See also Wieringa (2022a).

79. See Anoegrajekti (2003: 110–13). *Jajan* literally means snacking, and is a common term for men having extramarital affairs.

80. See also Soelarto and S'Ilmi (1976).

81. See Anoegrajekti (2007: 53).

82. See Blackwood (2010: 54–5) for an analysis of the transformation of the Minangkabau *randai* dance drama. In 1939 Islamic leaders issued a *fatwa* on the transgender practices in which both male-bodied and female-bodied dancers were involved. All-female performances where transvestite girls might sport moustaches were prohibited. Since the 1960s cisgendered girls have taken over the roles of the transvestite boys (Kirstin 1998).

83. See Larasati (2013: 69–77).

84. See Thamrin (2019) for more details about how these popular art forms disappeared after 1965: https://nationalgeographic.grid.id/read/131715339/ketoprak-jawa-pernah-dibunuh-dua-kali?page=al. *Rebana* or *terban* are hand-held drums.

85. See Soelarto and S'Ilmi (1976: 4–5). The *seblang* was still performed in the village of Bakungan, Cungking. It is also a shamanist trance dance, they report, but there is no attempt at the penetration of a *keris*. With the help of incense the spirits (*roh*) are called. There are also Shivaaist influences. The authors maintain that the *seblang* resembles the *srimpi* and *legong* dances. The *seblang* dancers circle around the dance floor making erotically suggestive moves with their shawl, enticing men to come and dance with them (Soelarto and S'Ilmi 1976: 15). The *srimpi* is a Javanese court dance, and the *legong* is a Balinese dance.

86. See Soelarto and S'Ilmi (1976: 14–20).

87. See Soelarto and S'Ilmi (1976: 24).

88. 'Politik Ormas ini lagi; Festival Gandrung sewu pun Ditolak – Besok apa lagi?'. https://seword.com/politik/ormas-ini-lagi-ini-lagi-festival-gandrung-sewu-pun-dito lak-besok-apa-lagi-bErQn0RRG.

89. See Ardian (2018).

90. Also by Raffles (1817), in *The History of Java*, and Pigeaud (1938).

91. See Andrianto (2014).

92. *Rejeki* means good luck; *jodoh* means one's life partner; *kematian* means death.

93. *Jiwa sang Penari*, a TV documentary, broadcast on Metro TV on 8 January 2020.

94. See: 'Lengger Dance from Banyumas'. https://www.historyculture.my.id/2011/12/leng ger-dance-from-banyumas.html?m=1.

95. See: https://regional.kompas.com/read/2019/12/11/06070021/kisah-rianto-penari-lengger-lanang-banyumas-perjalanan-hidupnya-diangkat-di?page=all. Kisah Rianto Penari Lengger Lanang Banyuman; Perjalanan Hidupnya Diangkat? The Indonesian title is Kucumbu Tubuh Indahku.

96. In 2015 Rianto participated in the SoftMachine project by the Singapore artist Choi Ka Fai. Amongst other dance forms he performed a dance with a mask of Sekar Taji. He also performed a masked masculine dance. Rianto says he embodies both femininity and masculinity and expresses that through his art: 'I can't think of myself only as a man. I feel it won't do justice to my body.' See the documentary: https://www.youtube.com/watch?v=sNEk-R0_R6I and https://twitter.com/bbcworld/status/1219410100001157120?lang=en.

97. I used some of the materials presented below in a blog posted on the website FORSEA.co. See Wieringa (2021); https://forsea.co/gay-couple-caned-in-aceh-indonesia/ (Gay couple caned in Indonesia).

98. In Section 9, chapter 33 of this regional Islamic Criminal Law, it is stated that: (1) Every individual intentionally involved in *liwath* and *musahaqah* will be punished with 100 lashes at the most and a fine of 1,000 grams of pure gold at the most or 100 months in jail at the most. (2) Every individual who intentionally 'promotes' *liwath* and *musahaqah* will be punished with 80 lashes at the most and a fine of 800 grams of pure gold at the most or 80 months in jail at the most.

99. Two men were arrested in Banda Aceh in November 2020 after a raid by a vigilante mob on their apartment. Accused of having sex, they were handed over to the police. They were convicted by a sharia court and administered seventy-seven lashes each with a rattan cane. The public flogging on Thursday 28 January 2021 was watched by dozens in the city's Tamansari Park. This was the third public flogging of gay men. In 2015 two women were detained who had been caught embracing each other in a public park. See, for instance: https://www.abc.net.au/news/2021-01-29/two-men-caned-77-times-for-having-sex-in-indonesia-aceh/13101764, or https://www.hrw.org/news/2021/01/28/77-lashes-gay-couple-indonesia#.

100. On her Twitter account in 2012, accessed 15 October 2019. See also: https://twitter.com/knightktm/status/1354808059298598922?lang=ar.

101. See Kruyt (1877). See also Wilken (1912).

102. The term was used more widely. At the other end of Sumatra, in Lampung, boys aged between nine and twelve who waited on men and entertained them by dancing were also called *sedati*. Karsch-Haack (1911) considered it a form of institutionalized prostitution.

103. See Jacobs (1894, vol. 1: 112; vol. 2: 222–3, 235–7, 328).

104. See Snouck Hurgronje (1906: 221–2).

105. See Jacobs (1894: 41).

106. See Praag (n.d.).

107. See Karsch-Haack (1911: 489).

108. See Atkinson (1990). There is also a record of a woman marriage in Sumatra, in Alahan Panjang in 1939. Rakit, a widow, and Tinoer asked the village headman of Alahan Panjang if they could get married. Instead of being issued a certificate, the two were sent to a doctor in Solok, according to the journal *Sin Po* of 21 February 1939. Interestingly, the article is titled *lesbische liefde* (lesbian love). So the word was around at that time but how widespread it was, or the practices it referred to, are not known. They had been together as husband and wife for eight years which apparently had not aroused any suspicion. The masculine character of Tinoer was described as 'like a male duck' (Boellstorff 2005: 47–8). Thanks to Tom Boellstorff for this information and photocopies in an email to me dated 28 March 2010. The photocopies are of a local newspaper *Persamaan*, 13 February 1939. See Budiman (1979).

109. Examples from Wieringa and Blackwood (1999: xxxv).

110. See Karsch-Haack (1911: 211).
111. See Karsch-Haack (1911: 208–9).
112. See Bloembergen (2011).
113. See also the interesting autobiography written in the 1920s by a homosexual man, Sutjipto, who asserts that paedophilia was widespread within Dutch communities (Sutjipto 1992: 114–15, 131).
114. See Kerkhof (1992). See also Aldrich (2002) and Boellstorff (2005).
115. See Budiman (1992: x–xi).
116. See Aldrich (2002), Boellstorff (2005), Budiman (1992) and Gouda (1995). This prohibition would remain in force until December 2022, when a revised penal code was adopted in Parliament.
117. See Bleys (1995) for a further discussion on terminology and the theories on which Western observers in the nineteenth and early twentieth centuries based themselves.
118. See Andaya (2006), Blackwood (2005) and Kroef (1954). See also Peletz (2009).
119. See Andaya (2000: 29).
120. See Andaya (2006: 230). In our book on heteronormativity in Asia I discussed this process in more detail (Wieringa 2016a).
121. Beynon, analysing the letters of Lady Mary Wortley Montagu and her visits to Turkish harems, notes that sapphism was generally associated with the lasciviousness of Oriental women in harems. Orientalist heterosexist fantasies of an East where sex was freely available and all sorts of 'vices' proliferated, titillated Western audiences (Beynon 2003).
122. See Peletz (2009).
123. See Bhabha (1994) on hybridity and mimicry in a colonial and postcolonial context. On the association of communist phobia and homophobia, see Wieringa and Katjasungkana (2018).
124. https://www.ugm.ac.id/en/news/21556-students-explore-values-of-traditional-cross-gender-dance-lengger-lanang. 19 August 2021. There are at present only twelve *lengger* dancers remaining.
125. Fieldnotes, 20 January 2018.
126. See also Sedgwick (1990).
127. See Wieringa (2020a) for a further discussion on the intelligibility of norms.

4 Delicious sins: Growing visibility

1. See Wieringa (2002). In 1965 Gerwani was the third largest women's organization in the world, with at least 1.5 million members.
2. See Robinson (2018) and Roosa (2006).
3. See Melvin (2018) and Wieringa and Katjasungkana (2018). The extent of Suharto's involvement with the abduction and killing of the generals is still not known. According to a 'passive' scenario he knew of the plans but failed to protect his superior officers. In a more 'active' scenario he may have had much more influence behind the scenes.
4. On the classification 'genocide', see the final report of the IPT 1965 (IPT 2017) and Wieringa, Melvin and Pohlman (2019). Often a figure of 500,000 murders is used. We estimate a total of one million may be closer to the truth (Wieringa and Katjasungkana 2018). Sarwo Edhie, one of the architects of the killing, boasted of having murdered three million people.

5. See Wieringa and Katjasungkana (2018).

6. See Herlambang (2013), McGregor (2007) and Wieringa and Katjasungkana (2018).

7. The song was composed during the famine towards the end of the Japanese occupation. It tells of a mother cutting weeds that grow at the edges of rice fields. It became very popular around the beginning of the 1960s, and was sung by school children all over the country. See Wieringa and Katjasungkana (2018) for an analysis of this song and how it was used by the New Order's propaganda machinery.

8. For details of this media campaign, see Wieringa (2002, 2003).

9. See Anderson (1987).

10. See Wieringa (2003).

11. See Katjasungkana and Wieringa (2003).

12. See Blackburn (2004).

13. See Wieringa (1993, 1995, 2002).

14. See Wieringa and Katjasungkana (2018).

15. A phrase I coined, Wieringa (2002).

16. See Wieringa (2000). I was unable to interview Tris Metty, as I only learnt of her story after she had already passed away. She was the first chair of Gerwis.

17. Interview by Augustine, in an email to me sent on 7 February 2011.

18. See Hegarty (2019a and 2019b). The community discussed here refers to those who were not a part of the cultural or religious contexts where transgender people could be found, as discussed in Chapters 2 and 3.

19. See Anonymous (1930s) in Hooykaas (1947: 12).

20. See Blackwood (2010) and Wieringa (1987).

21. See Boellstorff (2007).

22. See Boellstorff (2005), Davies (2010) and Ediati (2014). *Wandu* is the Javanese term for a transgender person.

23. See Boellstorff (2005: 95) and Wieringa (2015a).

24. Thanks to the Queer Indonesia Archive, who sent me this material. The first letter is in *The Ladder* of June 1964 (vol. 8, no. 9). Ger van Braam is of mixed Javanese, Spanish and Dutch heritage.

25. Ger contributed a short story about a meeting at an airport in the August 1964 issue of *The Ladder*.

26. A photograph of Ger seated on a bed, in front of a wall of bamboo sticks, adorns the cover of the November issue of *The Ladder*. She looks straight at the camera, with a melancholy look.

27. This she shared in her first letter, in June 1964. The tale about her husband is in the November 1964 issue.

28. So far not many traces of Ger's life in Holland have been found. Presumably, she lived in Breda.

29. Interview with Gayatri, 23 April 2003.

30. The FGD took place on 23 May 2003, at the house of Reza. Present were Agustine, Jack, Dian, Agung, Retno and Yudi.

31. Magnolia champaka.

32. They profit from what Connell calls 'the patriarchal dividend' (Connell 2009: 142).

33. State Minister of Women's Affairs from March 1993 to March 1998, she was sometimes called Waria Agung (High Waria), because as a former beautician she always applied heavy make-up.

34. Interview with Gayatri on 23 April 2003. Statements in *Pos Kota*, 18 June 1994. See also Gayatri (1996).

35. See Hegarty (2019a, 2019b).
36. See the article '"Wanita-Adam" – Sebuah Persoalan', in *Kompas*, 16 January 1969, by Arief Budiman (in Hegarty 2019a). See also Boellstorff (2005: 56–7) and Budiman (1969 and 1982).
37. So using the umbrella term *waria* for MTF transgender people is actually incorrect, but for reasons of consistency I sometimes do use *waria* as a general term. Nowadays the term *transpuan* is also used.
38. See Hegarty (2019a).
39. See Hegarty (2019a) and Boellstorff (2005).
40. See Hegarty (2019a: 73). Khunsa are variously seen as hermaphrodite, intersex or transsexual. See Chapter 9.
41. See Hegarty (2019a: 76).
42. See Wieringa (2016a: 62–3).
43. Participants included doctors in reproductive health as well as religious leaders and legal experts. They reasserted the biologically deterministic binary division between two sexes and two genders and concluded that only those with ambiguous genitals (intersex persons) should be medically treated. Six hospitals were assigned to carry out such operations.
44. See Hegarty (2019b).
45. Generations of lesbians grew up with this tragic tale of the 'invert' Stephen Gordon.
46. There is no date of publication given, but references contained in the book itself (to a popular actress Cheng Pei Pei and to the well-known lesbian club Gateways in London) make it seem likely that the novel was published in the late 1960s.
47. See *Tempo* (1981a).
48. See *Tempo* (1981b). Within two years they had already separated. Bonnie took a male lover who she later married. Joice Erna, a lesbian film actress, disparagingly commented that Bonnie was only looking for a thrill, while Jossie was truly in love with her (*Zaman* 25 Juni 1983).
49. In Chapter 8 I will continue the discussion on conversion therapies.
50. See the letter by Keith Foulcher, *Gay Community News*, May 1982.
51. *Tempo*, 48, 30 January 1982. Title: 'Sungguh Normal' (Truly Normal).
52. *Tempo*, 6 and 13 March 1982.
53. In personal letters to me, including a few letters from men who assumed I was a man and wanted to establish contact.
54. Published in *Tempo*, 7 August 1982.
55. This is a term coined by Adrienne Rich (1980), which was widely discussed at the time.
56. Oetomo (2007).
57. Dated 6 August 1982.
58. See Boellstorff (2005) and Oetomo (2007). The Kelompok Kerja Lesbian Dan Gay Nusantara (Task Force for Gay-Lesbian Nusantara) was founded on 1 August 1987.
59. In 2007, Yulianus Rettoblaut (Mama Yuli), chair of the All-Indonesia Waria Forum, ran to become commissioner of Komnas HAM. She only received one vote from the Parliamentary Commission on Law and Human Rights that had to decide on membership. This vote was from MP Nursyahbani Katjasungkana. In 2012 both Mama Yuli and Dede Oetomo tried again, and failed.
60. 'Inilah 11 Anggota Komnas HAM 2007–2012; Sang Waria tak Lolos'. Detiknews, 27 June 2007. https://news.detik.com/berita/d-796362/inilah-11-anggota-komnas-ha m-2007-2012-sang-waria-tak-lolos.

61. Joice was in a relationship with her butch lover Erna. She joined their names and was called Joice Erna.
62. *Zaman* (1983a), 18 June.
63. *Zaman* (1983b), 25 June. 'Heavy class' presumably refers to what earlier sexologists called 'true perverts', butch lesbians.
64. These older richer women were called STW, short for *setengah tuwa*, (half old).
65. For similarities with such cultures in Western countries, see, for instance, Kennedy and Davis (1993), Nestle (1984, 1992, 1998), Onstenk (1983) and Schuyf (1994).
66. Interview with Syarifah, 10 May 2003, and my own observations.
67. From numerous conversations with Ifa, including a formal interview on 10 May 2003, and my own conversations with other *sentul* at the time.
68. I reported on this meeting in a fictionalized short story in my travelogue *Yours Sincerely Dora D* (Wieringa 1987). See Chapter 6 for a fuller analysis of b/f relations.
69. Focus group discussion on 13 April 2003 in Pondok Gede, in Dedi's house.
70. See Boellstorff (2005) and Hegarty (2019a) for similar sentiments among gay men and *waria*.
71. According to Dedi, during a focus group discussion in Dani's house in Bukit Duri in 2003.
72. Abbreviation for Jakarta, Bogor, Tanggerang, Bekasi.
73. He was known to be gay himself and was sympathetic to lesbians. A Mr Smith from the United States also contributed.
74. Focus group discussion held on 30 April 2003 in Aris's house, who had attended all Perlesin and most Sappho meetings.
75. See Agustine (2008).
76. Interview with Aris, 30 April 2003.
77. COC is the largest LGBT+ organization in the Netherlands.
78. Ifa, in an interview on 10 May 2003, told me that she never trusted this Angky, and therefore never joined Sappho.
79. He even invited three pimp friends who worked in Tambun. They ran one house in that prostitution complex. They had five girls working for them, all from Cirebon, who rented rooms per hour. Otje said that she had once visited them, and they just sat there drinking all day.
80. Focus group discussion at Dani's home on 28 December 2003.
81. Focus group discussion on 13 April 2003.
82. Interview with Gayatri on 23 April 2003.
83. Focus group discussion on 13 April 2003. The network was first called Jaringan Kerja Chandra Kirana. In 2003 the name was changed.
84. See also Gurning (2003) and Murray (1999).
85. According to Gayatri, the upper classes did not want to build an organization with the lower classes. Djuna herself said she was afraid to lose her job.
86. Pseudonym, so for reasons of anonymity I cannot give the name of the channel she worked for either.
87. Nursyahbani Katjasungkana, chair of KPI, had offered Agustine a job in the secretariat of the KPI's bulletin, *Semai*.
88. The International Lesbian Information Service (ILIS) was founded by ILGA in 1980 and became an independent organization in 1981. ILIS organized several conferences and also published its own newsletter. Activities ceased in the late 1990s. ALN was an offshoot of ILIS.
89. In 1973 homosexuality was deleted from the WHO list of mental illnesses, and in 1983 from the list of the Association of Psychiatrists in Indonesia.

90. Focus group discussion with former members of Chandra Kirana, 15 April 2003.
91. See Wieringa (2003).
92. There is abundant literature about this. See, for instance, Bennett (2005), Blackburn (2004), Brenner (1998), Wieringa (1995, 2002, 2003, 2016a), Wijaya and Davies (2019).
93. See also Gayatri (1996).
94. Wieringa (1987).
95. See, for the ALN, Zimmerman (2000).
96. Zimmerman (2000). After the second ALN conference in Saitama, near Tokyo in 1992, which was attended by two Indonesian lesbians, Gayatri and Rosawita, the next conferences were held in Taipei (1995) and Quezon City (1998).
97. Letter to me dated 28 January 1986.
98. One of Kalyanamitra's trustees, Fauzi Abdullah, a well-known progressive lawyer working on labour issues, remarked: 'With another Ifa, Kalyanamitra is in danger of being labelled as a lesbian organization.' Interview with Gayatri, 23 April 2003.
99. Name withheld. She passed away in 2011.
100. My letter was dated 24 March 1982.
101. Name and function withheld.
102. Interview with Yang Suwan, 13 October 2001.
103. At the time Gayatri made a living as a consultant while she only had a bachelors (undergraduate) degree. Her competitors had a masters or a PhD. She was a local specialist for a USAID project and always had to prove that someone with her sexual orientation could work well.
104. Interview with Gayatri, 23 April 2003.
105. Fieldnotes, 28 October 2001,
106. Focus group discussion at Dani's home on 28 December 2003.
107. There was a common perception at the time that lesbianism is infectious.
108. See Chapter 8.
109. See Gayatri (1993).
110. Monique Wittig was a very influential French author in the 1970s and 1980s. See her collection of essays *The Straight Mind* published in 1992, but containing much earlier work. See also Sabaroedin (2001 and 2006).
111. See the following articles: https://regional.kompas.com/read/2008/11/11/2319464/tubuh.perempuan.quotlocusquot.politik. And https://tirto.id/hari-ibu-mengenang-sang-feminis-radikal-syarifah-sabaroedin-dcqT.
112. Blackwood (2010) and Boellstorff (2005) emphasize the influence of the global LGBT movement on Indonesia's LGBT movement. I am more inclined to stress the indigenous aspects, while not ignoring the relevance of the global movement.

5 Shadows in the night: Post-Reformasi identity politics

1. See Sawitri (2001).
2. See Suara Ibu Peduli (1999) and Wieringa (2002). In the historiography of that transition the role of the student movement who took over after the women is usually emphasized.
3. See Yulia (2012). See also Wijaya and Davies (2019).

4. See on other specific Asian LBT movements: Engebretsen (2014) and Wang (2021) on mainland China, Chao (2010) on Taiwan and Sinnott (2004) on Thailand. See also Chiang and Wong (2017).

5. See, for instance, Boellstorff (2005), Hegarty (2019a) and Rodriguez (2018).

6. The dilemma about which direction the LBT movement should go made Jeumpa and Ulil (2002) proclaim that in the gay movement lesbians are treated like the second sex, while the women's movement sees them as stepsisters, 'we become like garlic among the onions'(Jeumpa and Ulil 2002). In a bitter poem they wonder: 'How happy I would be to know you do not see a leper before you / Nervously groping with her rotten finger / Making a space between us / Or perhaps I am just a flower eater to you / With savage passion devouring every breast or thigh I see / So you can do disgusting things next to me.'

7. See also Wieringa (2007a).

8. Fieldnotes, 8 May 2003. Swara Srikandhi set up the first lesbian website in Indonesia: www.swaraSrikandhi.cjb.net.

9. The number of followers on the website is not known; they did not collect web statistics.

10. Focus group discussion on 24 May 2003 with Swara Srikandhi members.

11. Email letter signed by Terkupas on 16 September 2002. Also the post of Arya on the website, 11 September 2002.

12. I have not seen this show (with Bonnie, Ade, Arua Kingkong, Mungil and Kris), only the one on 4 March 2003. I do have printouts of the website conversations.

13. Bonnie in a letter to me dated 31 May 2003.

14. For instance, Ivana used the term *kecoa blekekek* (dirty cockroach) about Bonnie who had refused to return the books to Swara Srikandhi, on 7 November 2002.

15. *Darah lesbian halal untuk diminum, dagingnya halal untuk dipotong* (literally: It is permitted to drink lesbian blood and to cut up their meat).

16. Email to me from Agustine at the KPI, 18 March 2003, and focus group discussion on 22 May 2003.

17. Kalijodo was a well-known prostitution area in Jakarta.

18. In the course of that one month I counted sixteen death threats from Iman Prasetyo or his followers.

19. Over the next week she found out Mas Imam used various aliases, including the (women's) name Ita. She became furious and regretted her invitation.

20. As discussed in a focus group discussion on 24 May 2003.

21. Emails dated 14 and 15 April 2003.

22. Transgender FTM was described as a foreign term for a female-bodied person who feels he is a man. FTM transpersons are not lesbians, and the concept lesbian transgender that we often hear is not correct, the article warned. A butch is a lesbian who may be dressed in a similar fashion to an FTM transperson, but still identifies as a woman.

23. Discussion at the office of Swara Srikandhi on 26 April 2003, with Wina and Arya.

24. See also Agustine (2008).

25. John Badelu is the co-founder of the LGBT film festival.

26. On 23 April 2003.

27. Law No. 8 1985. Under this law all civil organizations had to be registered with the Ministry of Home Affairs. The ministry could dissolve mass organizations (ormas) without legal process or right of appeal if they were seen to be a threat to the nation,

to promote communism or did not accept the state ideology of Pancasila as their abiding principle.

28. Some 600 women attended from all over the archipelago. Members of the preparatory committee included Wardah Hafidz, Chusnul Mar'iyah, Agung Ayu, Agung Putri, Debra Yatim, Kamala Chandrakirana, Myra Diarsi, Ratna Batara Munti and Umi Lasmina.

29. See Anderson (1987). The autopsy was signed by both President Sukarno and General Suharto.

30. From the KPPD (Kelompok Perempuan Pro-Demokrasi) chaired by Eva Sundari, a prominent politician of the PDIP, who later served several times as an MP.

31. Some of the members of this group had been working with *waria* on the streets of Surabaya.

32. The fifteen sectors of the KPI: older women; women living in care homes and disabled women; professional women; women working in the informal sector; urban poor women; rural poor women; young women; secondary school and university students; sex workers; workers; widows/divorced women; women heads of households and single women; marginal girls; peasant women; fisherwomen; housewives; lesbian, bisexual and transsexual women.

33. Interview with Ifa, 10 May 2003.

34. Chief editor was Nursyahbani Katjasungkana. She got some funding from the Dutch funding agency NOVIB, so the bulletin looked professional, printed in four colours. See U (2001) and Agustine (2001).

35. Extensive minutes of these discussions are available.

36. Focus group discussion on 13 April 2003, Pondok Gede.

37. Focus group discussion on 13 April 2003, Pondok Gede.

38. Besides members of Sektor 15, Ade Kusumaningrum of Swara Srikandhi, and representatives of Sektor 15 of West Sumatra, Srikandhi Sejati, Qmunity, Yayasan Pelangi Kasih Nusantara, Pelangi Nusantera Yogyakarta were present. Non-LGBT organizations also supported the initiative, including Forum LSM Jabotabek, ADHAM, Yayasan Pemantau Hak Anak, Centre for Reproductive Rights and Policy Yogyakarta, LBH-APIK and several individuals, including myself.

39. The acronym LGBT was not used at the time.

40. KomnasHAM letter No. 6.732/SKPMT/XII/03, 16 December 2003.

41. Fieldnotes, 24 June 2004.

42. Sri was conducting research on the butch-femme community in Padang together with Evelyn Blackwood.

43. The congress decided to change the name 'sector' into 'interest group'. This worried the members of Sektor 15, for the title Sektor 15 is less obvious than announcing one attends a meeting of the 'interest group on sexual minorities'.

44. LSA was set up by students of IAIN Semarang.

45. Letter from Nursyahbani Katjasungkana to me, 11 October 2005.

46. See Husaini, Adian (2005). http://www.republika.co.id Thursday 30 June 2005, Homoseksual dan Umat Islam.

47. Nursyahbani Katjasungkana also proposed to add religious beliefs, to accommodate the many traditional religious belief systems (other than the recognized official six religions).

48. Email from Nursyahbani Katjasungkana, 7 December 2006.

49. Other advisors: Masruchah (then chair KPI), Evelyn Blackwood, Ester Mariani, Suma Mihardja and Evilina Sutrisno.

50. *Lokakarya dan TOT tentang seksualitas dan HAM*. By Kartini Asia Network. Jakarta 6–10 September 2006. Mimeo 213 p.
51. Influential chair of the Women's Veterans' organization and former minister of Women's Affairs. See Suryakusuma (2011) and Wieringa (1993, 1995) for an analysis of the Indonesian women's movement in the New Order.
52. See Khanis (2013), Rinaldo (2019) and Wieringa (2015a).
53. See Chapter 7 in this volume and Katjasungkana and Wieringa (2016).
54. From their website: The Yogyakarta Principles address a broad range of international human rights standards and their application to SOGIE issues. On 10 November 2017 a panel of experts published additional principles, the Yogyakarta Principles plus 10.
55. On the DSM (Diagnostic and Statistical Manual of Mental Disorders) of the American Psychiatric Association, see chapter eight.
56. She carries the title RR, Raden Roro, which is given to a female descendant in the fifth line of a king.
57. Abha Bhaiya and I were the coordinators of the Kartini sexuality theme. This workshop was the start of the big project on heteronormativity in Asia.
58. SOGIEB: Sexual Orientation, Gender Identity and Expression and Bodies. This term was coined by the United Nations. Originally it was called SOGIE, the B was added later. UN (2008).
59. See Agustine and Sari (2021).
60. Lily Sugianto was the main researcher from the Ardhanary Institute team. A film was produced on *calalai*.
61. The first book was a compilation of translated chapters from the book *Female Desires* that Evelyn Blackwood and I had co-edited (Blackwood and Wieringa 1999). The Indonesian version came out in 2009. The second book was co-edited by Agustine and Evi Lina Sutrisno in 2013.
62. See Wieringa and Blackwood (2009).
63. See also Wijaya (2020).
64. See Agustine, Arivia and Candaningrum (2015).
65. See for discussions on this topic Butler (1993) and Wijewardena (2007). See also Blackwood (2010).
66. See Blackburn (2004) and Brenner (1998).
67. See Wieringa (2007a: 75).
68. See Wieringa (2011: 321, table 11).
69. See Wieringa (2011: 329, table 12).
70. Conversation on 5 November 2003.
71. Teams from both Dipayoni and Ardhanary participated in this research project on female masculinities.
72. Interview fragments from Wieringa (2011: 320–4).
73. See Wieringa (2011: 325).
74. These groups are very active on social media, on Twitter, Facebook, YouTube. On Transmen Talk, see, for instance, 'Am I Man Enough?': Diskriminasi terhadap Identitas Transpria Muda (Studi Analisis Video YouTube Trans Men Talk Indonesia), July 2021. DOI: 10.22146/studipemudaugm.65214.
75. See Wijaya (2020).
76. See Wieringa (2015b). Violation of Article 266 of the Criminal Code on forgery of identity, in conjunction with Article 263 of the Criminal Code and Article 378 of the Criminal Code on fraud.
77. SeeWieringa (2011: 326).

78. See Ediati (2014).
79. See Wieringa (2011: 327).
80. See Wieringa (2011: 328–9).
81. Meeting at the house of Surya and Nuri on 21 January 2004.
82. See Davies (2010).
83. See UNDP/USAID (2014).
84. See Daniel (2012).
85. See Oetomo (2001). See also Boellstorff (2004). It was a violent attack; twenty-five participants were injured.
86. https://lifestyle.kompas.com/read/2010/06/29/18482431/~Nasional Komnas HAM: Aksi FPI Langgar HAM. Kompas, 29 June 2010.
87. See also Wijaya (2019). The gender bread person is an infographic in human shape that graphically illustrates four components of human identity: assigned sex, gender identity, gender expression and attraction.
88. See Ariyanto and Triawan (2008).
89. In March 2009 a coalition of human and women's rights groups and activists filed a judicial review with the Constitutional Court; it was rejected in March 2010.
90. Among other issues she also noted that single women could not have a pap smear, so lesbian women could not get access to this service either. See Ratri (2008).
91. The Netherlands was the first country to accept marriage equality, in 2001.
92. See Wieringa (2011: 269).
93. See Yulia (2012).
94. The Institute Pelangi Perempuan (IPP) was established in 2006 by Kamilia Manaf. https://www.takebackthetech.net/connect/institut-pelangi-perempuan.
95. Now called IDAHOBIT: International Days Against Homophobia, Biphobia and Transphobia.
96. It started with eleven organizations; at present eighty-three GBT organizations are linked up.
97. See http://www.yogyakartaprinciples.org/principles_en.htm.
98. See Chua (2019).
99. See Sumbogo (2004).
100. For instance, in *The Jakarta Post* of 23 February 2011, the Religious Affairs Minister Suryadharma Ali warned against 'liberal thinking' including the demand for marriage equality.
101. See for a discussion Murtagh (2013).
102. See Boellstorff (2005); Wieringa (2015a).
103. See, for instance, the YouTube documentary *The Rise and Fall of Queer Cinema in Indonesia*' in which the media specialist Lisabona Rahman is interviewed. Films produced in this period include *Madame X, Lonely Man, Sun Moon Hurricane* bv Andrew Chung, and *Arisan 2*.
104. A fifteen-minute film by Aditya Ahmad.
105. Other films about sexual diversity include *Sanubari Jakarta* (April 2012) which carries ten stories of lesbians, gay, *waria* and transsexual and *Lovely Man* (May 2012) which tells the story of a daughter's quest for her father who has become a *waria*.
106. http://metrotvnews.com/index.php/metromain/newsvideo/2010/09/28/114 019/Q-Film-Festival-Diprotes-FPI. I attended that event and noted the fear produced by the shrieking militants outside the gate.
107. See Arisah (2008b) and Paramaditha (2018).

108. See Chapter 9. See also Izharuddin (2013).
109. See Supiastutik and Kusumayanti (2008).
110. See Yash (2003).
111. See Peletz (2009) for a discussion of the influence of modernist Islam on gender diversity.
112. See, for instance, Gayatri (2015) and Wijaya (2019).
113. The term female masculinities was coined by Halberstam (1998). On Asia, see Blackwood and Wieringa (2007). For Indonesia, see Wieringa (2002, 2003) and Suryakusuma (2011).
114. See Barad (2006: 26).
115. See Katjasungkana and Wieringa (2016). See also Wijaya and Davies (2019).

6 Superheroes and female playboys: Butch-femme dynamics

1. On the intelligibility of *tomboi*, see Blackwood (2010). See also Wieringa (2007a).
2. The word *bujang gadis* derives from *bujang* (an unattached (loose) young man) and *gadis* (young girl, virgin).
3. See Kennedy and Davis (1993) and Kooten Niekerk and Wijmer (1985).
4. The denunciation of the b/f bar culture was initiated by the San Francisco-born collective the Daughters of Bilitis, also called the DOB or the Daughters. It was established by a small group of upper-middle-class women in 1955, at a time of anti-gay and lesbian witch hunts. The Daughters strove to acquire respectability for lesbian women within the women's movement by erasing butch-femme behaviour, dress codes and lifestyles. See Case (1993). The group lasted until 1995. *Bilitis* is the name given to a fictional companion of the Greek poet Sappho.
5. See Loulan (1990) and Kennedy and Davis (1993). The lesbian bar culture died out in the Netherlands. In the United States it survived much longer, especially in Black and Latin communities. Kooten Niekerk and Wijmer (1985), Nestle (1998), Schuyff (1994), Wieringa (1999). See also Dahl and Volcano (2009).
6. See Nestle (1998: 128).
7. See Feinberg in Nestle (1992: 107).
8. I attended a number of those debates and shared my disappointment that the b/f bar culture in the Netherlands had died out due to the arrogance of us young lesbian-feminists. See also Wieringa (1999).
9. See Newton (1972, 1993); Blackwood and Wieringa (1999).
10. But see Halberstam (1998).
11. For femme power, see Dahl and Volcano (2009).
12. See Wieringa (1987, 1999).
13. See Butler (1993).
14. See Halberstam (1998).
15. See, for instance, Brenner (1998).
16. 13 April 2003.
17. See, for instance, an article in the *Lampu Merah* of 20 May 2004, *Istri ketahuan lesbi ditusuk suaminya sampai mati* (A wife who was known to be a lesbian was stabbed to death). The article was accompanied with a photo of the naked body of Erly, stab wounds clearly visible.

18. Agam Siregar from Pangkalan Brandan in North Sumatra experienced the same problem. He never got the share of ancestral land that his brothers received.

19. Komnas Perempuan regularly publishes reports on domestic and other forms of gender-based violence. The majority of the cases APIK deals with are related to domestic violence. See, for instance, Komnas Perempuan 2014b and 2019.

20. Agustine, in an email to me, dated 21 August 2001.

21. This is the only time I heard this word mentioned. It must have been created in the late 1970s. For gay men they used *lapendos, laki-laki penuh dosa* (sinful man). I do not know if those words were used elsewhere as well, or whether it was just used in a very small circle of friends.

22. ACDC was a term used in those years for a lesbian who was neither butch nor femme. The b/f couples were confused – how would you know who was the butch or the femme in that relationship? I never heard non-b/f lesbians apply that term to themselves. ACDC is a term related to electrical supply – alternating current and direct current. Here it means switching sexual/gender roles.

23. Derived from the Dutch words for girl and darling.

24. I myself also went through this learning process, see Wieringa (1987).

25. This section is based on the Kartini/Transsign research, carried out by both the Ardhanary Institute and Dipayoni in 2009 and 2010. Both teams conducted intensive interviews with around twenty participants. I had trained them and held numerous discussions in the following years with the researchers and edited their reports (Wieringa 2011).

26. *Priawan* from *pria* (man) and *wanita* (woman), so FTM transperson. *Transpuan* from trans and *perempuan* (woman) is a more fashionable term for MTF transpersons, formerly clubbed together under *waria*.

27. Binders are mostly imported via Hong Kong, with which they have a connection with the large group of women migrant workers in same-sex relations, who have set up the Spidershop; see Lai (2020).

28. See Wieringa (2011: 55).

29. See Wieringa (2011: 56).

30. Bhima had heard that the first female-to-male operation was done in China, before 1965. His first two operations were performed by the gender teams of Dr Harman in the Ciptokusumo hospital in Jakarta. Dr Harman was a psychiatrist.

31. See Bourdieu (1990) and Butler (1993).

32. See also Blackwood and Wieringa (1999) and Wieringa (2020a).

33. See Nestle (1984: 233).

34. See Hollibaugh (2000: 253–4).

35. See Wieringa (1987).

36. In Indonesia the distinction between FTM and butch has been so fluid, in particular during the early years of the FTM movement, that I use both terms here.

37. See Green (2004: 182).

38. A few years later Alvin had found the true love he had been looking for.

39. On the use of dildos, see Wieringa (2012).

40. The word often used was *pendamping*, literally companion, soulmate.

41. Focus group discussion on 8 February 2004.

42. From *ceret* (diarrhoea), but also slang for orgasm among lower-class lesbians.

43. Interviewed by Bernadet Sinta Situmorang in April 2005.

44. See Samudera (2016).

7 Politico-religious homophobia: The second sexual moral panic

1. See Buehler (2016) and Kersten (2015).
2. See Katjasungkana and Wieringa (2016). In Pariaman (West Sumatra) homosexuality is illegal for all citizens, in Palembang (South Sumatra) for Muslims.
3. See Wieringa and Katjasungkana (2019).
4. See Wieringa (2016a, 2020a) for a discussion of heteronormativity in Indonesia.
5. See Wieringa (2003: 71–2).
6. See Wieringa (2020a).
7. See Pausacker (2021) and Katjasungkana and Wieringa (2016).
8. There is an enormous literature on this struggle; see Wieringa and Katjasungkana (2018) for an overview.
9. See Platt, Davies and Bennett (2018).
10. The Jakarta Charter is a clause that stipulates that Muslims must follow sharia law. After long debates this clause was not added to the Constitution in 1945. Since then, however, fundamentalist Muslim groups have tried to add this clause to the Constitution.
11. It reads: 'Everybody is prohibited to produce, make, reproduce, multiply, spread, broadcast, import, export, offer, sell, rent or make available pornography; sexual violence; masturbation or onany; nakedness or that gives the impression of nakedness, genitals; or child pornography.'
12. Thus far *penyimpangan seksual* was not used to refer to same-sex activities. For instance, in a section with that title in the book on Javanese sexuology (Endraswara 2002), the term refers to heterosexual deviations. What is meant by *penyimpangan*? The author suggests that it means 'far from *kebiasaan naluri manusia* (natural, instinctive human behaviour)'. He gives an example: a young man presents himself at a boarding school for girls and when the door opens, he opens his fly and swings his *burung* (bird) in front of the astonished women. The author also refers to a case of bestiality in the Serat Centhini.
13. See Mulia (2004).
14. Article 251(2e) states: 'Regional policies are not allowed to contradict higher level regulations and common interests, nor can they be allowed to discriminate on the basis of ethnicity, religion, belief, race, gender and relations among groups.' Sexual orientation, gender identity and gender expression (SOGIE) are not mentioned, but it could be argued that they fall within these categories.
15. See also Buehler (2016). See also Katjasungkana and Wieringa (2016).
16. Instead, the Satpol PP receives training by the army.
17. Their powers, which combine those of the police, prosecutors and judges, derive from those of the *baljuw*, a colonial officer (similar to a sheriff), a position which was introduced by the VOC (Vereenigde Oost-Indische Compagnie, Dutch East Indies Company). See for the implementation of their function, for instance, Darmawan (2018).
18. Available at www.yogyakartaprinciples.org/.
19. See O'Flaherty and Fisher (2008).
20. See O'Flaherty (2015).
21. See Sauer and Podhora (2013).

22. Wieringa and Katjasungkana (2018). See also Wieringa (2000) for the association of communism with homosexuality.
23. See 'Universitas Diponegoro Tolak Diskusi Soal Gay'. 13 November 2015. http://www.cnnindonesia.om/nasional/20151113140504-20-91469/universitas-diponegoro-tolak-diskusi-soal-gay. Accessed 13 November 2015.
24. See Sinuko (2015).
25. See Tribun Lampung (2015).
26. See 'Mantan Rektor UIN Jika LGBT Dibolehkan Indonesia Bisa Dikutuk Kayak Kaum Luth'. 12 December 2015. http://m.hidayatullah.com/berita/nasional/read/2015/12/12/mantan-rektor-uin-jika-lgbt-dibolehkan-indonesia-bisa-dikutuk-kayak-kaum-luth. Accessed 12 December 2015.
27. See Yulius (2016).
28. See http://www.cnnindonesia.com/nasional/20160123211552-20-106213/menris tek-sebut-lgbt-tak-bolehkan-masuk-kampus. Menristek Sebut LGBT Tak Bolehkan Masuk Kampus, 23 January 2016, See also Wijanarko (2016) and *The Jakarta Post* (2016d).
29. See 'Indonesian Minister of Education Calls on Universities to Refuse LGBT Students'. http://www.lgbt-education.info/en/news/local_news/160211-indonesian-minister-of-education-calls-on-universities-to-refuse-lgbt-students.
30. Teuku Muh S. Guci. 2016. 'Menpanrb Yuddy Chrisnandi: PNS Tidak Pantas LGBT'. http://jabar.tribunnews.com/2016/02/12/menpanrb-yuddy-chrisnandi-pns-tidak-pan tas-lgbt. Accessed 12 February 2016.
31. See 'Menham: LGBT Bagian dari Proxy War Harus Diwaspadai', 23 February 2016. http://www.republika.co.id/berita/nasional/umum/16/02/23/o2zwbx219-men han-lgbt-bagian-dari-proxy-war-harus-diwaspadaiSelasa.
32. Former chair PKS, vice-speaker of the MPR.
33. *Riau Daily* (2016).
34. Email correspondence with Feni and Nursyahbani Katjasungkana, 8 February 2016.
35. See Menteri PP dan PA: tolak kampanye / promosi LGBT terutama kepada anak-anak. Press Statenent: 16 /Humas KPP-PA/2/2016 Jakarta (16 February 2016).
36. See *The Jakarta Post* (2016e).
37. See Okezone (2016).
38. See Adyatama (2020). According to the military spokesperson, the legal process will be strictly applied and there will be an additional sanction of dismissal through a military court. Aidil said the Law No. 34 of 2004 on the TNI noted that soldiers can be dismissed dishonourably if they are found to have a personality or commit acts that are harmful to the TNI discipline.
39. See Adjie (2020).
40. See Katjasungkana and Wieringa (2016).
41. Though the *fatawa* of this council have no legal standing, some have been considered binding by the courts, as Lindsey (2019) argues.
42. See Hooker (2003).
43. The MUI also earns income from the lucrative issuing of *halal* certificates and the rest from its involvement in the sharia economy. See Nadzir Ibnu (2019), 'Is MUI Beyond Reform? Don't Be So Sure', Indonesia at Melbourne. https://indonesiaatmelbourne.unimelb.edu.au/is-mui-beyond-reform-dont-be-so-sure/.
44. See Katjasungkana and Wieringa (2016: 82).
45. See Arus Pelangi (2013).

46. See *The Jakarta Post* (2016c).
47. *The Jakarta Post* (2016b) 'Indonesian Clerics Declare LGBT Groups Haram', 17 February. http://www.thejakartapost.com/news/2016/02/17/indonesian-clerics-decl are-lgbt-groups-haram.html.
48. See Fenwick (2018: 272).
49. See Fealy (2019).
50. Only six religions are accepted: Islam, Catholicism, Protestantism, Buddhism, Hinduism and Confucianism, while religious naturalism and 'deviant' sects face discrimination. In practice, the majority religion, Islam, dominates the social, cultural and political life of Indonesia, and members of accepted minority religions can face restrictions. A positive development is the 2017 decision by the Constitutional Court which declared that 'traditional belief' (*aliran kepercayaan*) can also be mentioned on identity cards. See Marshall (2018).
51. The Five Pillars are the following: (1) the belief in one God, (2) just and civilized humanity (3) Indonesian unity (4) democracy under the wise guidance of representative consultations and (5) social justice for all the peoples of Indonesia.
52. Wieringa and Katjasungkana (2018).
53. For example, both the rights contained in the ICCPR (International Covenant on Civil and Political Rights) and the ICESCR (International Covenant on Economic, Social and Cultural Rights) are ratified by Indonesia. Each country's performance in relation to the ICCPR is assessed in Geneva every four years, in a process called the Universal Periodic Review (UPR). Article 26 of the ICCPR reads:

> All persons are equal before the law and are entitled without any discrimination to the equal protection of the law. In this respect, the law shall prohibit any discrimination and guarantee to all persons equal and effective protection against discrimination on any grounds such as race, colour, sex, language, religion, political or other opinion, national or social origin, property, birth or other status.

This is further reinforced in General Comment No. 20 on Non-Discrimination (Sauer and Podhora 2013: 137).
54. This report was prepared for the Universal Periodic Review of Indonesia according to the ICCPR.
55. Article 292 of the Criminal Code prohibits a same-sex relationship between an adult and a minor and article 293 of the Criminal Code prohibits sexual relations between an adult and a minor without consent.
56. This criminalization is exactly what happens. At present APIK, the women's legal aid institute, is dealing with several of those cases.
57. See the report Lembaga Bantuan Hukum Masyarakat, *Aturan Hukum Mengenai Razia dan Persekusi terhadap Kelompok Minoritas*: https://lbhmasyarakat.org/wp-content/ uploads/2020/12/Pilu-Pemilu-Kelompok-LGBTI-dalam-Politik-Omong-Kosong-Laporan-Mondok-2020.pdf
58. See Kupang.tribunnews.com (2018), *'Pasangan Sejenis Digerebek: Begini Pengakuan Mereka Kenapa Memilih Menjadi Lesbian'*, http://kupang.tribunnews.com/2018/11/19/ pasangan-sejenis-digerebek-begini-pengakuan-mereka-kenapa-memilih-jadi-lesbian.
59. See Batam.tribunnews.com (2018), *'Satpol PP Kota Padang Tangkap 10 Wanita Lesbian'*, http://batam.tribunnews.com/2018/11/06/viral-satpol-pp-kota-padang-tang kap-10-wanita-lesbian-media-asing-ikut-memberitakannya. 11 June 2018.
60. See Najih (2018: 149–50).

61. See Bayuni (2018).
62. See 'Indonesia's Parliament Passes Repressive New Penal Code'. https://thediplomat.com/2022/12/indonesias-parliament-passes-repressive-new-penal-code/. Accessed 10 December 2022.
63. See AILA (2019).
64. See Butt 2019. See also Mahkamah Konstitusi RI (2016a and 2016b).
65. Coconuts Jakarta (2016). See also: https://news.detik.com/berita/d-3356989/hakim-konstitusi-patrialis-akbar-soal-lgbt-zaman-nabi-luth-dibinasakan.+Hakim Konstitusi Patrialis Akbar: Soal LGBT Zaman Nabi Luth Dibinasakan. 28 November 2016.
66. Pawestri (2016).
67. Email from Nursyahbani Katjasungkana to me on 29 August 2016. The three witnesses were: the chairman of Indonesian Child Protection Commission, Asrorun Ni'am Sholeh; a legal expert from Padjajaran University, Atip Latipulhayat; an expert in constitutional law from Indonesia University, and Hamid Chalib.
68. Komnas Perempuan also argued that couples whose marriages could not be registered would be criminalized.
69. Executive Summary. Permohonan Komnas Perempuan sebagai Pihak Terkait Dalam Perkara Nomor: 46/PUUXIV/2016.
70. See Hidayatullah (2014). AILA members presented seminars on God punishing Indonesia for the presence of an LGBT community, such as the one held in my own neighbourhood in Depok on 26 October 2018.
71. See 'RUU LGBT Penting Untuk Melindungi Rakyat Indonesia'. http://www.republika.co.id/berita/nasional/umum/16/03/10/o3sw24361-ruu-lgbt-penting-untuk-melindungi-rakyat-indonesia. 3 October 2016.
72. See Republika (2016).
73. *The Jakarta Post* (2016a).
74. 'Waspadai LGBT Sebagai Perang Asimetris'. 21 March 2016. https://www.beritabanjarmasin.com/2016/03/waspadai-lgbt-sebagai-perang-asimetris.html. Accessed 21 March 2016.
75. See Jauhola (2010).
76. See Amindoni (2019).
77. Human Rights Watch (2016a).
78. See 'Di Razia Ketat para Lesbi Mulai Keluar dari Banda Aceh'. 12 December 2015. http://m.hidayatullah.com/berita/nasional/read/2015/12/1285228-dirazia-ketat/para-lesbi-mulai-keluar-dari-Banda-Aceh. Accessed 12 December 2015.
79. See 'Suspected Lesbians in Indonesia to Undergo Rahabilitation'. 10 March 2015. http://www.thejakartapaost.com/news/2015/10/03/-2-suspected-lesbians-in-indonesia-to-undergo-rehabilitation. Accessed 10 March 2015.
80. See http://www.benarnews.org/indonesia/berita/Qanun-11102015145139.html.
81. See 'Indonesian Aceh Province Enacts Sharia Criminal Code'. http://www.abc.net.au/2015-10-24/ Indonesian-aceh-province-enacts-sharia-criminal-code/6882346. Accessed 24 October 2015.
82. See 'Police Urged to Release Women Accused of Being Lesbians'. 4 October 2015. http://www.the jakartapost.com/news/2015/10/04/police-urged-to-release-women-accused-of-being-lesbians. Accessed 4 October 2015.
83. *The Jakarta Post* (2016c).
84. Simanjuntak and Junaidi (2016).
85. See '77 Lashes Gay Couple Indonesia'. https://www.hrw.org/news/2021/01/28/77-lashes-gay-couple-indonesia#.

86. See Republika (2016).
87. See 'LGBT Makin Unjuk Gigi Republika Disomasi'. http://www.tarbiyah. net/2016/02/lgbt-makin-unjuk-gigi-republika-disomasi.html and 'Republika Disomasi Soal LGBT'. 2 March 2016. http://nasional.republika.co.id/berita/nasional/ umum/16/02/03/o1z30f257-republika-disomasi-soal-lgbt.
88. See Human Rights Watch (2016a: 16). See also Wijaya (2020).
89. Mursid (2016), '*Mensos: LGBT Sasar Keluarga tidak Mampu*'. http://www.republ ika.co.id/berita/nasional/umum/16/02/16/o2mj41366-mensos-lgbt-sasar-kelua rga-tidak-mampu. 16 February.
90. Rostanti (2016).
91. *Tempo*, edition no. 21, 27 July 2008. Accessed 21 June 2021.
92. *The Jakarta Post* (2016), 'Busted Prostitution Ring Sparks Fears of Child Trafficking Network in W. Java', 4 September. http://www.thejakartapost.com/news/2016/09/04/ busted-prostitution-ring-sparks-fears-of-child-trafficking-network-in-w-java.html.
93. See also Marching (2020).
94. See Syakriah (2020).
95. See 'Russia Law Banning Gay Propaganda'. 11 June 2013. https://www.theguard ian.com/world/2013/jun/11/russia-law-banning-gay-propaganda. It concerns the amendments to Article 5 of the Russian Federal Law No. 135-03, 'For the Purpose of Protecting Children from Information Advocating for a Denial of Traditional Family Values', enacted on 30 June 2013, criminalizing the distribution among minors of materials 'promoting' non-traditional relationships.
96. Circular by the KPI No. 203/K/KPI/02/2016, issued on 23 February 2016. It stated that men would be banned from TV shows if they showed the following traits:

   1. Dress like women
   2. Apply make-up as women do
   3. Have a feminine bodily expression (including but not limited to style of walking, of sitting, of moving hands, or other forms of behaviour)
   4. Speak like women
   5. Demonstrate the correctness or promote [the idea] that a man can behave in a womanly way
   6. Demonstrate a greeting to a man in a way that women should use
   7. Utter terms and expressions that are often used in circles of women.

97. See Harsono (2019).
98. *The Jakarta Post* (2016), 'Broadcasting Commission Chided for Prohibiting "Feminine Men"', http://www.thejakartapost.com/news/2016/03/01/broadcasting-commission-chided-prohibiting-feminine-men.html. See also Komisi Penyiaran Indonesia (2016). 1 March.
99. Listiorini and Davies (2017). See also *The Jakarta Post* (2016), 'Govt Mulls Banning LGBT Applications after Child Abuse Probe', 10 September, http:// www.thejakartapost.com/news/2016/09/10/govt-mulls-banning-lgbt-appli cations-after-child-abuse-probe.html. See also, 'Government Moving Forward with Plans to Block Grindr and Other "Gay" Apps', 15 September, http://jaka rta.coconuts.co/2016/09/15/government-moving-forward-plans-block-gri ndr-and-other-gay-apps. See also Afiie (2016).

100. See 'Gay Muslim Comic Artist Alpantuni Talks Us Leaving Instagram Recent Return'. https://coconuts.co/jakarta/features/exclusive-gay-muslim-comic-artist-alpant uni-talks-us-leaving-instagram-recent-return.
101. See 'Ini Dia Bentuk Promosi Line Terkait'. http://www.nbcindonesia.com/2016/02/ ini-dia-bentuk-promosi-line-terkait.html. Accessed 15 February 2016.
102. See 'Indonesia Pressures Instagram to Take Down Gay Muslim Comic Strips'. 13 February 2019. https://www.euronews.com/2019/02/13/indonesia-pressures-instag ram-to-take-down-gay-muslim-comic-strips. Accessed 13 February 2019.
103. Isnaeni (2015).
104. Forum LGBTIQ (2016), 'KANZA VINA: Pidato Penerimaan Penghargaan Suardi Tasrif dari Aliansi Jurnalis Independen', 26 August. http://forumlgbtiqindonesia. org/2016/08/26/kanza-vina-pidato-penerimaan-penghargaan-suardi-tasrif-dari-alia nsi-jurnalis-independen. Kanza Vina Pidato Penerimaan Penghargaan Suardi Tasrif dari Aliansi Jurnalias Independen
105. Yosephine (2016c).
106. Sapiie (2016).
107. Yosephine (2016a).
108. Editorial (2016), 'Stop Provoking Stigma', *The Jakarta Post*, 18 February. http://www. thejakartapost.com/news/2016/02/18/editorial-stop-provoking-stigma.html.
109. See Suryakusuma (2016).
110. Salim and Parlina (2016).
111. Name withheld.
112. See Haynes (2018). He cites a 2017 Human Rights Watch report that HIV prevalence rates among gay Indonesian men have increased fivefold, from 5 per cent in 2007 to 25 per cent in 2015.
113. At the time of writing this book she is completing her doctorate in law.
114. Fieldwork notes, 28 January 2018.
115. See https://nasional.tempo.co/read/news/2016/01/27/058739964/cari-kaum-lgbt-fpi- sweeping-rumah-kos-di-bandung, '*Cari Kaum LGBT, FPI Sweeping Rumah Kos di Bandung*', 27 January 2016.
116. Human Rights Watch (2018).
117. See https://www.hrw.org/node/376306, 7 September 2020: 'Indonesia: Investigate Police Raid on "Gay Party"'. See also Human Rights Watch (2017 and 2018). On 30 April 2017, fourteen men were arrested at a gay party in Surabaya. They were sentenced to between eighteen months and thirty months in prison under the Anti-Pornography Law. On 21 May 2017, the Atlantis Spa in Jakarta was raided; 141 people were arrested, and ten were charged for holding an alleged sex party under the Anti-Pornography Law. In October 2017 a club popular with gay men in Jakarta was raided and fifty-eight men were arrested. The case went viral, but ultimately no charges were made against them. On 15 December 2017 they were sentenced to between two and three years in prison. In January 2018 police raided a home in Cianjur, West Java, and arrested five men, who were accused of holding a 'sex party'. Condoms and lubricants were presented as evidence.
118. See Topsfield (2017). See also *The Jakarta Post* (2018).
119. See Tan (2020).
120. See: https://m.tempo.co/read/news/2016/02/25/058748325/pesant ren-waria-di-yogya-dipaksa-tutup. Pesantren Waria di Yogya Dipaksa Tutup. 25 February. No one had even noticed that the neighbours were unhappy with the presence of Al Fatah. See Chapter 9 for more on the *pesantren waria*.

121. Readers Forum (2016), 'Yogyakarta LGBT School Resumes Operations', *The Jakarta Post*, 10 March. http://www.thejakartapost.com/news/2016/03/16/yogyakarta-lgbt-school-resumes-operations.html.
122. Irsyad (2018).
123. See 'Ormas Gelar Aksi Tolak LGBT di Balai Kota Bogor'. https://www.merdeka.com/peristiwa/ormas-gelar-aksi-tolak-lgbt-di-balai-kota-bogor.html. Accessed 22 November 2021.
124. This information is based on many informants who do not wish to be named. See also https://www.konde.co/2016/07/lgbt-dagangan-moral-pemilihan-komisi.html/, 'LGBT, Dagangan Moral Pemilihan Komisi Penyiar an di DPR'. Accessed 20 July 2016.
125. See Wieringa and Katjasungkana (2018).
126. Particularly the Darul Islam in West Java.
127. The nation's motto is Unity in Diversity, *Bhinneka Tunggal Ika*.
128. See Wieringa (2020b) for an analysis of the impact of the 2019 elections on the human rights community.
129. See, for instance, Setiawan and Tomsa (2022).
130. See Wieringa (2015a).
131. See http://www.cintakeluarga.id/gaya-hidup-yang-diedukasi-doktrin-femini sme-jadi-pendorong-lahirnya-perilaku-lgbt/, *'Gaya Hidup yang Diedukasi Doktrin Feminisme jadi Pendorong Lahirnya Perilaku LGBT'*, Posted 3 July 2014.

8 Family violence and conversion therapy

1. See Arus Pelangi (2013, 2019) and Forum LGBTQI (2013).
2. See Robinson (1989), Fausto-Sterling (2000), Foucault (1978) and Richardson (2000b).
3. See Jeffreys (1996) and Wieringa (2002).
4. See for a discussion Bland and Doan (1998), Drucker (2014), Robinson (1989) and Bauer (2006).
5. See Ellis (1913).
6. See Ellis and Symonds ([1897] 1994).
7. The first edition was published in 1886. In the fourteenth edition of 1911 he could only boast of one case in which he considered his treatment to have yielded some measure of success. This edition was published posthumously by Alfred Fuchs and contains more than 200 case studies. See also Weeks (2010).
8. See Von Krafft – Ebing (1912). His contemporary, Magnus Hirschfeld, did not believe in the possibility of curing homosexuals by whatever means, including hypnosis.
9. See Wieringa (2009).
10. See Frühstück (2003).
11. See Foucault (1978, 1985, 1988a). See also Halperin (2002) and Weeks (2010). Brooten (1996), however, maintains that the medicalization of homoerotic activities in the West did not follow the trajectory Foucault established but had taken place already in antiquity.
12. See Butler (1993) and Rich (1980). See also Wieringa (1989).
13. See, for instance, Ahmed (2006), or the website of the American Psychological Association: https://www.apa.org/topics/lgbtq/orientation.
14. See Republika (2016), *'Himpunan Psikolog Menentang Kelompok yang Halangi Pemulihan Penyandang LGBT'*, 6 February 2016. Http://nasional.republoka.co.id/nberita/nasional/umum/16/02/06/

o23v6y330-himpunan-psikolog-menentang-kelompok-yang-halangi-pemulihan-penyandang-lgbt.

15. Yosephine (2016c).
16. On 8 March 2016; the letter was directed at Dr Tun Kurniasih Bastaman.
17. Republika (2016), https://www.republika.co.id/berita/nasional/umum/16/03/23/o4hkwh365-guru-besar-ui-lgbt-penyakit-gangguan-jiwa, 'Guru Besar UI: *LGBT Penyakit* Gangguan Jiwa', 23 March. The claimants received many death threats via social media. The claim ultimately fizzled out.
18. Interviews with Gunawan Wibisono on 25 December 2021 and Benny Prawira on 26 December 2021.
19. See Halim (2019).
20. Ashok is a pseudonym. Co-researchers were Nursyahbani Katjasungkana and Agustine. The research was carried out in 2021. The name of the hospitals are also withheld, to protect the privacy of 'Ashok'.
21. A Christian organization that runs a hospital and a theological school.
22. See Yosephine (2016d).
23. See Agustine (2021).
24. See Arus Pelangi (2013).
25. See Arus Pelangi (2019).
26. See Daniel (2012).
27. See also Yolandasari (2015).
28. Prodita Sabarini (2010), 'Lesbians Face Double Discrimination', *Jakarta Post*, 4 October. See also Agustine and Sari (2021).
29. Fieldnotes in April 2003.
30. Interview on 5 February 2004.
31. Fieldnotes on 25 January 2014.
32. The issue gives only the year, 2001.
33. See Wieringa (2011: 259).
34. See Wieringa (2011: 267).
35. See Wieringa (2011: 287–90).
36. See Wieringa (2011: 334).
37. See Ibrahim (2022).
38. Daniel (2012).
39. See Daniel (2012: 60).
40. See Agustine (2021).
41. Asia Pacific Transgender Network (2020).
42. See 'Canadian Lawmakers Pass Bill Criminalizing LGBT Conversion Therapy'. https://www.reuters.com/world/americas/canadian-lawmakers-pass-bill-criminalizing-lgbt-conversion-therapy-2021-06-22/. 22 June 2021. Internationally, the following reports are among the most recent documents on the negative consequences of conversion therapy: Ashley (2019) and (Lee et al. 2021).
43. See 'It's Torture Not Therapy', 23 April 2020. https://irct.org/media-and-resources/stories/article/1027. IRCT. Accessed 26 June 2022.
44. See Horner (2019).
45. Interview on 6 June 2003.
46. This is not a strange idea. Recently it transpired that this was a method used by the British intelligence agencies around 1 October 1965. Selected intellectuals received fake newsletters in which Sukarno and his foreign minister Subandrio were targeted. See Lashmar, Gilby and Oliver (2022).

47. When I opened the website on 15 February 2021, I saw that it was in 100 languages. When I opened it again on 10 February 2022, the website was empty (just having three blocks: herbal, psychometric and narcissism) and a notice appeared that the domain name could be bought for 1999 US dollars.
48. See Amahl (2021).
49. See Amahl (2021).
50. Interview with Benny Prawira Siauw on 26 December 2021.
51. This funding is minimal, via the regular health insurance programme BPJS kesehatan (Badan Penyelenggara Jaminan Sosial), the national health insurance scheme, and the programme for social assistance for youth (PKSA, Program Kesejahteraan Sosial Anak) of the Ministry of Social Affairs.
52. Asia Pacific Trans Network (2021).
53. Ministry of Social Affairs, '*Rehabilitasi sosial tuna social dan korban perdagangan orang*', Law No. 11 of 2009, Article 7, Paragraph 1, https://intelresos.kemsos.go.id/.
54. See https://m.tempo.co/read/news/2016/02/28/173749009/menteri-khofi fah-lgbt-bisa-sembuh-melalui-pelatihan-esq (2016), 'Menteri Khofifah: LGBT Bisa Sembuh Melalui Pelatihan ESQ', *Tempo*, 28 February.
55. See http://www.esqway165.com/solution/training-schedule/. Accessed October 23, 2016.
56. See https://coconuts.co/jakarta/lifestyle/social-affairs-minister-we-wouldnt-treat-lgbt-boiling-water-and-spices-just-drug-users/ Coconuts Jakarta, 14 March 2016. Social Affairs Minister We Wouldn't Treat LGBT Boiling Water and Spices Just Drug Users. She said it worked well for drug users.
57. Khofifah as quoted in http://redaksikota.com/2016/02/28/mensos-punya-solusi-rehabilitasi-lgbt-dengan-direbus-air-panas/#.VuTAFdIrKUk, 'Mensos Punya Solusi Rehabilitasi LGBT Dengan Direbus Air Panas', by Masibnoe. 28 February 2016.
58. See Nathan (2016).
59. See 'Peristiwa Khofifah; LGBT Bisa Disembuhkan'. 15 October 2018. https://www.merdeka.com/peristiwa/khofifah-lgbt-bisa-disembuhkan.html. Accessed 15 October 2018.
60. See 'Posting Foto Ciuman di FB 10 Wanita Diduga Lesbian Ditangkap'. 5 November 2018. https://news.detik.com/berita/4287826/posting-foto-ciuman-di-fb-10-wanita-diduga-lesbian-ditangkap Senin. Accessed 5 November 2018.
61. Coconuts Jakarta (2018), 'Indonesian City Says It'll Work with Exorcists That Expel Female Genies from Men to "Cure" LGBT Behavior', 21 November, quoting the West Sumatran portal Covesia.
62. P2TP2A, Pusat Pelayanan Terpadu Pemberdayaan Perempuan dan Anak (Integrated Service Centre for the Empowerment of Women and Children).
63. See pekanbaru.tribunnews.com/2018/02/11/jangan-jauhi-korban-lgbt-risdayati-bawa-ke-p2tp2a-tempat-berobat-dan-bertaubat. Accessed 10 April 2018. Jangan Jauhi Korban LGBT Risdayati Bawa ke P2TP2A Tempat Berobat dan Bertaubat. This message details the situation in Pekanbaru, where Muslim religious leaders are involved in the P2TP2A to 'cure' LGBT people. The ministry's website is silent on the issue. It is unclear how many of these centres in the country follow a similar practice.
64. See Wieringa (2015a) on this programme, and how the ministry slipped back from a women's rights-based approach to gender harmony ('no two captains on a ship').
65. See, for instance, Harahap (2021).
66. See Teresia (2019: 17).
67. See http://sains.kompas.com/read/2016/02/19/16141561/Nyatakan.LGBT.Gangguan. Jiwa.dr.Fidiansyah.Dituding.Menutupi.Kebenaran, Kompas (19 February 2016),

'Nyatakan LGBT Gangguan Jiwa, dr Fidiansyah Dituding Menutupi Kebenaran', 19 February. And 'Dr. *Fidiansyah diminta mengkoreksi ucapan kelirunya yang semakin mengekalkan kebencian terhadap LGBT'*, posted by Kabar LGBT on 20 February 2016.

68. See 'Kemenkes LGBT Masalah Jiwa'. 1 February 2018. https://www.republika.co.id/berita/nasional/umum/18/02/01/p3flrg440-kemenkes-lgbt-masalah-jiwa. Accessed 1 February 2018.

69. Interview with Benny Prawira Siauw on 6 December 2021.

70. Interview on 1 April 2003.

71. Criminal charges were prepared against Wahyu, based on Article 292 (same-sex relation with a minor). For LBH APIK Jogja, this was a difficult case. Usually they defend victims, and the victim in this case, according to the Criminal Code, was the thirteen-year-old girl. Wahyu was accused of abduction and sex with a minor – both crimes. After long consultations with a feminist organization, the Lembayung Institute, the lawyers of LBH APIK Jogja decided that they would defend Wahyu as well, for this was also a case in which a woman was accused of committing a sin, of being abnormal, mentally ill. Report Workshop Strategi Advokasi *'Hak-Hak Seksual dan Pemberdayaan Perempuan" Bagi Lesbian, Janda dan Pekerja Seks'*, Kartini Network Bekerjasama Dengan LBH APIK Jakarta. Jakarta, 2 August 2006. Mimeo: 25–30.

72. Name of website and founder withheld for security reasons.

73. Lecturer at the Department of Communication at Atma Jaya University in Yogyakarta. See Listiorini (2020).

74. Cited in Adi Renaldi (2021), 'Indonesia's LGBTQ community angry at rise of conversion therapies'. 13 March. https://asia.nikkei.com/Spotlight/Society/Indonesia-s-LGBTQ-community-angry-at-rise-of-conversion-therapies. Accessed 24 July 2021.

75. See, for instance, Waidzunas (2015) for a critique on conversion therapy in the West.

76. See 'Transgenderism Mental Health Disorder Says Indonesian Psychiatric Association', LGBT. 22 February 2016. http://www.theguardian.com/society/2016/feb/22/transgenderism-mental-health-disorder-says-indonesian-psychiatric-association-lgbt.

77. Evan (2020).

78. See 'Central Java Parents Charged with Murder of Daughter in Islamic Exorcism Case'. 22 May 2021. https://www.thejakartapost.com/news/2021/05/22/central-java-parents-charged-with-murder-of-daughter-in-islamic-exorcism-case.html.

79. Cited in Adi Renaldi (2021), 'Indonesia's LGBTQ community angry at rise of conversion therapies'. 13 March. https://asia.nikkei.com/Spotlight/Society/Indonesia-s-LGBTQ-community-angry-at-rise-of-conversion-therapies. Accessed 24 July 2021.

80. See Geertz (1960) and Keeler (1990).

81. See Hegarty (2019a, 2019b).

82. This belief is widespread in Java. I was told this story by several people who are knowledgeable about Javanese culture.

83. Ardhanary Institute (2016: 10–14).

84. Evan (2020).

85. Yuniar (2021).

86. See Tuasikal (2016).

87. See Halim (2020).

88. Accessed 15 February 2020. https://cintakeluarga.org; info@cintakeluarga.org © AILA Indonesia | Aliansi Cinta Keluarga Indonesia 2021.

89. Email from Ayu Yolandasari dated 21 February 2021.
90. AILA (2019). The book is called '*Transformasi Menuju Fitrah: LGBT dalam Perspektif Keindonesiaan*' (*Transformation According to One's Natural Character*). This book also contains the logo Dompet Dhuafa, the Muslim charity that divides the considerable income from *zakat* (religious taxes). This institution is managed by Muhammadyah.
91. AILA (2019: 97).
92. RILIS AILA INDONESIA; Perihal Launching Layanan AILA Indonesia 22 Desember 2020, No. 01/G.3/SEKJEN/AILA/XII/2020.
93. Co-founder Rita Soebagio posted an opinion article on 31 January 2022, titled 'If homosexuals come into power the events around the prophet Luth may return'. She regrets that in the DSM 4 homosexuality is no longer seen as a mental disease, and expresses fear that soon homophobia may be classified as a mental disorder.
94. See 'Instagram Blokir Kontan Terapi Konversi LGBT?'. 7 November 2020. https://www.suara.com/tekno/2020/07/11/102324/instagram-blokir-konten-terapi-konversi-lgbt?page=all.
95. Sunarti (2021). The launch of the e-book on 27 February 2022 was attended by more than one thousand people. The book also details the efforts of Professor Sunarti, her colleagues at AILA and Peduli Sahabat, when they brought a case to the Constitutional Court demanding that homosexuality be criminalized.
96. See the website pedulisahabat.org, which states that the Foundation Peduli Sahabat was established in 2015 with the help of AILA. Accessed 21 February 2021.
97. Email from Ayu Yolandasari dated 21 February 2021.
98. See Sinyo (2014).
99. See also the anonymous and untitled research paper: http://repository.umy.ac.id/bitstream/handle/123456789/29417/8%20BAB%20IV.pdf?s. Accessed 17 June 2022.
100. See website pedulisahabat.org, in which they acknowledge the assistance of AILA and the support of the Islamist party PKS.
101. See 'Rehabilitasi Kelainan Orientasi Sexual'. http://www.abualbanicentre.com/rehabilitasi-kelainan-orientasi-sexual. Accessed 25 February 2016.
102. For example, the NARTH (National Association for Research and Therapy of Homosexuality) group. See for a critique: https://www.splcentre.org/fighting-hate/intelligence-report/2012/narth-becomes-main-source-anti-gay-%E2%80%98junk-science%E2%80%99.
103. Budiman (2020), '*Ruqyah Terhadap LGBT, Bisakah Dibenarkan?*'. 21 July. https://www.voaindonesia.com/a/ruqyah-terhadap-lgbt-bisakah-dibenarkan-/5511203.html.Ruqyah Terhadap LGBT Bisakah Dibenarkan. Lina Zurlia is a member of the ASEAN SOGIE caucus. See also Galih J. Pangestu (2019), 'Rukiah Terhadap Kelompok LGBT Adalah Tindak Kekerasan'. 29 June. https://magdalene.co/story/rukiah-terhadap-kelompok-lgbt-adalah-tindak-kekerasan. Accessed 17 May 2021.
104. Asia Pacific Transgender Network (2021: 7).
105. Asia Pacific Transgender Network (2021: 8).

9 God's creatures: Religion and sexual rights

1. Indonesia has six recognized religions, and everybody has to adhere to one of these. These are Islam, Protestantism, Catholicism, Hinduism, Buddhism and

Confucianism. Only Islam and the two Christian religions are monotheistic. Atheists face severe discrimination. Only in 2017 could traditional beliefs be mentioned in one's official documents.

2. There is a wide literature on the topic; see, for instance, Buehler (2016), Fealy (2019), Kersten (2015) and Van Bruinessen (2013).
3. See, for instance, Hefner (2011).
4. See Hefner (2000), Mulia (2012) and Van Wichelen (2010).
5. See also Katjasungkana (2012) and Van Wichelen (2010).
6. As Wee (2012) maintains, Wahabi influence stretches back at least two centuries. Their efforts to purify Islam were accompanied with violence. Their influence grew because the religiously diverse sultanates were destroyed by the Dutch, accelerating the development of an anti-colonial, uniform, Wahhabi-influenced interpretation of Islam. See also Peletz (2009).
7. These trousers are called *cingkrang*. Often the wearers also sprout some hairs on their chins.
8. See Mulia (2010b).
9. See Foucault (1988b).
10. See Puar (2007) and Rodriguez (2018, 2019).
11. See https://en.wikipedia.org/wiki/Islam_in_Indonesia. Accessed 6 January 2022. They cite the latest population census.
12. See, for instance, Buehler (2016), Bruinessen (2013) and Kersten (2015).
13. He is inspired by the brilliant intellectual and progressive NU leader Abdurrahman Wahid, Indonesia's third president, popularly called Gus Dur. Aan Anshori co-founded the group GurDurian, after the words Gus Gur and *durian*, a foul-smelling but sweet-tasting fruit. This is the most progressive group within the NU. See Rappkler.com (2016).
14. See http://www.rappler.com/indonesia/123810-nahdlatul-ulama-lgbt-ingkari-fitrah-manusia '*Nahdlatul Ulama: LGBT ingkari fitrah manusia*', 6 February 2016.
15. In a letter dated 22 February 2016.
16. See 'LGBT People Have Right to Live Equally with Others: Yenny Wahid'. News Desk, *The Jakarta Post*, 2 August 2016. http://www.thejakartapost.com/news/2016/08/02/lgbt-people-hav/e-right-to-live-equally-with-others-yenny-wahid.html.
17. See #darurat LGBT #LGBT Abnormal #PP Muhammadiyah #Yunahar Ilyas; see also Muhammadiyah Dukung Media Massa Lawan LGBT dengan Edukasi, 9 Februari 2016, 16:52:01. https://hidayatullah.com/berita/nasional/2016/02/09/89072/muhammadiyah-dukung-media-massa-lawan-lgbt-dengan-edukasi.html.
18. *The Jakarta Post* (2016), 'LGBT People "Not a Security Threat"', 7 March, http://www.thejakartapost.com/news/2016/03/07/lgbt-people-not-a-security-threat.html.
19. See '*FMI: Kita Juga Punya Hak Menolak LGBT*', 18 February 2016. http://www.suara-islam.com/read/index/17201/FMI--Kita-Juga-Punya-Hak-Menolak-LGBT.
20. Wieringa (2011: 246-7).
21. For instance, Mohamad Safiq, aged twenty-five, was expelled from a *pesantren* in Brebes regency, Central Java, after a teacher found out about his sexual inclinations, as the *Jakarta Post* reported. See H. Halim (2016), 'Minorities Denied Entry to Mosques, Schools', *Jakarta Post*, 2 June, http://www.thejakartapost.com/news/2016/06/02/minorities-denied-entry-to-mosques-schools.html.
22. See the Quranic verses: An-Nisa 15-16, Al-Araf 80-84 and Al-Ankabut 28-35. See below for an alternative interpretation of the story of the Prophet Lut, as contained in Al-Araf and Al-Ankabut.

23. This is an abridged version of the pamphlet *Ayo Ganyang Homosex & Lesbi*, 2010. Habib Rizieq Syihab, the chair of FPI held a lecture expressing similar opinions on 5 October 2010. He specifically denounced Ulil Abshar, a prominent liberal reformer.

24. See also Rodriguez (2019, 2022), who stresses the agency of transpersons and the liberating potential of progressive human rights-oriented interpretations of Islam.

25. Based on the interpretation of Al Baqarah (222–3). The *sura* Al-Baqarah is the second and longest *sura* of the Quran.

26. For a further discussion on homosexuality and *fiqih*, see Homoseksualitas dan Fiqih. 18 February 2016. https://azisaf.wordpress.com/2016/02/18/homoseksuali tas-dan-fiqih/.

27. See Dunn (2004). See also Vanita and Kidwal (2000) for some translations of texts on same-sex love in this period.

28. The 1997 collection on *Islamic Homosexualties* by Murray and Roscoe contains only one chapter on woman-woman love.

29. Full title: *Nuzhat al-Albab Fima La Yujad Fi Kitab* (The Diversion of the Hearts by What is Not to Be Found in Any Book).

30. Grinding is more often used for a particular sexual technique. I heard it used in Singapore, as a term for lesbian women – tofu grinders. Habib mentions this as well.

31. See Habib (2007: 78); see also Habib (2009).

32. See Al-Ghafari (2013).

33. Translated from the Dutch translation of Al-Tifashi, quoted in Leemans (1995: 63–4).

34. See Mernissi (1985) for a further analysis of the association of *fitna* with femininity and the dangers that women's sexual lust represents in Islam.

35. See Andaya (2006).

36. See Andaya (2006: 93).

37. See. S. M. Mulia (2009), *Understanding LGBT Issues in Islam: Promoting the Appreciation of Human Dignity.* Istanbul: CSBR Sexuality Institute.Another feminist Muslim scholar, Suad Joseph, translates *khunsa* as intersex, and *mukhannath* as bisexual or effeminate (Joseph 2003: 419). See also Zuhrah (2021) who found that during the time of the Prophet Muhammad three terms were used to denote gender diversity, *mukhannas*, male-bodied; *mutarajjilah*, female-bodied transpersons; and *khunsa*, what we would now call intersex.

38. See Siradj (2009). He recalled debates which were waged about what kind of *khunsa* might attend the Friday prayers and how they should be dressed.

39. They are not the first ones to point this out. As Siradj (2009) reminds his readers, Ibn Hazm in the eleventh century had already stressed that the people of Lot were hit by stones, were infidels and that their major sin were their attempts at violence, to rape their guests (an angels sent by God to guide Lot out of Sodom).

40. On the story of Lut, see also Jamal (2001) and Shannahan (2010).

41. Correspondence with Imam Daayiee Abdullah, a US-based legal scholar and imam, who then used the pseudonym Brotherman, and who has carefully studied the Arabic text of the Quran (email 31 May 2001). See also an interview with him in *The Conversation*, 'Friday Essay: The Qur'an, the Bible and Homosexuality in Islam', 16 June, https://theconversation.com/friday-essay-the-quran-the-bible-and-homosexual ity-in-islam-61012.

42. See Khalik (2008).

43. See Mulia (2012: 291). See Katjasungkana (2012) for an elaboration of these developments.

44. See Mulia (2012: 293).

45. See Mulia (2010): 'Understanding Sexuality in Islam; Promoting the Appreciation of Human Dignity', www.asiapacificforum.net/issues/sexualorientation. Accessed 9 April 2010.

46. H. Diani (2014). 'In the Land Where Everyone's God: Interview with Musdah Mulia', 8 August, http://magdalene.co/news-215-in-the-land-where-every one%E2%80%99s-god-interview-with-musdah-mulia-.html.

47. A colleague of his, Roy Murtadho, teaches at the ecological *pesantren* Misykat Al-Anwar in Bogor, where gender diversity is honoured. Haris Prabowo in Tirto. id, 9 March 2023, '*Di Pesantren Misykat Keragaman Ditanam*'. Di Pesantren Misykat Keragaman Ditanam.

48. See A. D. Udampo (2021), 'Obituary. Reverend Stephen Suleeman Standing for LGBTIQ Affirmation', *Jakarta Post*, 20 November, https://www.thejakartapost.com/opinion/2021/11/19/obituary-rev-stephen-suleeman-standing-for-lgbtiq-affirmat ion.html.

49. See Ga (2008). She is widely known as *pendeta* Ester, a feminist theologian who strongly supports the women's movement.

50. See Helminiak (2000).

51. See S. Bahri (2015), '*Ade Armando: LGBT Tidak Haram, Rasa Suka Sesama Jenis itu Diciptakan Tuhan*', 17 March, https://www.dakwatuna.com/2015/07/05/71274/ade-armando-lgbt-tidak-haram-rasa-suka-sesama-jenis-itu-diciptakan-tuhan/. See also Armando (2015).

52. The story is based on interviews conducted in from September to November 2005, by Ratna Batara Munti. I used parts of the profile Ratna produced for our book on heteronormativity (Wieringa 2016a). For present purposes I return to the original profile. I have summarized the original thirty-page mimeographed text.

53. Fieldnotes, 13 April 2003.

54. Interview on 27 December 2003.

55. Interview on 25 December 2003.

56. Interview on 28 December 2003.

57. Interview on 21 January 2004.

58. Interview on 23 December 2003.

59. Interview on 30 December 2003.

60. Interview on 5 February 2004.

61. Interview on 15 April 2003.

62. Interview on 14 April 2003.

63. Interview with Agustine on 4 May 2003. Grace is a pseudonym.

64. Interview with Mariani, founder of Al-Fatah, on 11 October 2011. See also Safitri (2013).

65. See A. Wadud (2022), 'The Launching of Queer Islamic Studies and Theology (QIST) (video)', Youtube: The Lady Imam channel. https://www.youtube.com/. See also Wadud (1992 and 2006).

66. Ismoyo and Alfikar (2022).

67. This story was told to me during the second KPI congress, on 14 January 2004. Ahmed is a pseudonym.

68. Nurish (2010). See also Kholifah (2012) and Mustaqfiroh (2014).

69. A *nyai* is a woman leader of a *pesantren* or the wife of a male leader. Nyai Hindun Aisyah led the Pondok Pesantren Putri Aisyah Kempek Cirebon.

70. One of the most famous *pesantren*, founded by her grandfather, the founder of the NU.
71. Fieldnotes from a visit to the Ardhanary Institute on 10 January 2013.
72. See Syarifuddin (2005). It occurs even in the Muslim part of South Thailand; see Kosem (2017).
73. In an email to me from Gaya Nusantara, dated 1 December 2009, quoting the research on *mairil* by Iskandar Dzulkanain.
74. See Dzulkarnain (2006).
75. See Muhyidin (2013).
76. See Izharuddin (2013).
77. See Iskandar (2006); Oetomo (2001a); Saifuddin (2006). See also the novel *Mairil* by Syarifuddin; it is written by a former student of a *pesantren* who offers an 'insider's' perspective on these erotic practices in non-moralistic terms.
78. See Oetomo (1996: 264).
79. See also Khumaini (2014a), '*Fenomena Mairil: Menyingkap Tirai Bisu Pesantren*', https://www.qureta.com/post/fenomena-mairil-menyingkap-tirai-bisu-pesantren. And Khumaini (2014b).
80. See Oetomo (1996).
81. See, for instance, the story told by Enha, who is asked by his son who returns to his *pesantren* whether there was this phenomenon called *mairil* in his father's time? For a friend of his is a victim and does not dare tell anyone. Enha (2015), 'Budaya Mairil', *Kompasiana*, 1 July, https://www.kompasiana.com/www.istanayatim.net/559351bba 2afbd650704dce2/budaya-mairil.
82. See Iskandar (2006). See also chapter ten.
83. Enha (2015).
84. See Syariffudin (2005: 51).
85. See also Blackwood (2010) and Wijewardena (2007).
86. Foucault coined the term 'technology of the self' for this phenomenon, which requires the discipline of 'certain modes of training and modification of each individual, not only in the obvious sense of acquiring certain skills but also in the sense of gaining certain attitudes' (Foucault 1988b).
87. See Wieringa (2015a) for an analysis of this phenomenon.
88. There is a lot of literature on this unique *pesantren*; see Hegarty (2019a); Rodriguez (2018, 2019); Sa'dan (2020); Safitri (2013); Toomistu (2019),
89. See Safitri (2013: 93).
90. I visited them at the *pesantren* in October 2011.
91. See https://gaya.tempo.co/read/news/2013/11/24/205532048/pesantren-waria-yog yakarta-satu-satunya-di-dunia. 24 January 2013. 24 November 2013. Pesantren Waria Yogyakarta Satu-Satunya di Dunia. Editor Evieta Fadjar Pusporini.
92. Di Ilio (2019).
93. Muryanto (2016 and 2020).
94. Ulung (2022).
95. Marbun (2014).
96. See NU Online 'Religious Leaders Say Homosexuality Not from God', *Jakarta Post*, 1 April 2008. https://www.nu.or.id/news/religious-leaders-say-homosexuality-039 not-from-god039-cWua0. Accessed 3 November 2023.
97. Fikri (2022). See also Wieringa (2022b).

10 Heteronormativity revisited

1. I follow Reddy's definition of homophobia as a 'discourse of power, dominance and control ... a kind of performative communication ... a persuasive discourse engineered to arouse emotion around the object which it despises'. (Reddy 2002: 165).
2. See Wieringa (2016a: 27).
3. On state policy, see Wieringa (2015a).
4. See Wieringa (2016a: 35).
5. See Wieringa (2016a; 2020a) for a more extensive discussion of symbolic subversion.
6. See Wieringa (2019: 128).
7. See Puar (2007). An example is the Netherlands.
8. See Wijaya and Davies (2019).
9. See Gopinath (2018) and Dahl and La Grace Volcano (2009).
10. For China, see Wang (2021); for Thailand, see (Sinnott 2004); for Hong Kong, see Lai (2020); for Taiwan, see Chao (2010).
11. See Wijewardena (2007). See also Blackwood (2010).
12. See, for a discussion on political homophobia, Serrano-Amaya (2018) and Kulick (2009).
13. See, for instance, Ellis (1913), Karsch-Haack (1911) and Robinson (1989).
14. See Wieringa (2009). See also Pallotta-Chiarolli (2020).
15. See Geller (2017).
16. Ruth Benedict, whose early insights into such 'patterns of culture' have influenced generations of feminist anthropologists, already maintained that people who do not fit into a particular social construct are accused of having 'abnormal traits' (1934).
17. See Bennett (2005), Blackburn (2004), Brenner (1998) and Suryakusuma (1996, 2011).
18. See Boellstorff (2005) for gay men and *waria*. See also Wijaya and Davies (2019).
19. See Aspinall and Berenschot (2019) for a discussion on the transactional character of the Indonesian electoral system.
20. See Smith, Son and Kim (2014), quoted in Badgett (2017).
21. See https://www.pewresearch.org/global/2020/06/25/global-divide-on-homosexual ity-persists/. Accessed 27 March 2022. In the 2020 version, Malaysia was not included.
22. See Pinandita (2020).
23. See Wieringa (2020b).
24. On civic space, see Janti (2022a). On social media, see *The Jakarta Post* (2022), 'Indonesia Preparing Tough New Curbs for Online Platforms', 24 March, https://www. thejakartapost.com/indonesia/2022/03/24/indonesia-preparing-tough-new-curbs-for-online-platforms.html.
25. See Sutrisno (2020).
26. Sexual deviation is defined as sadism, masochism, homosexuality and lesbian, and incest.
27. T. Pawestri and T. Mann (2022), https://indonesiaatmelbourne.unimelb.edu.au/indonesia-finally-has-a-law-to-protect-victims-of-sexual-violence-but-the-strug gle-is-not-over-yet/. Indonesia Finally has a Law to Protect Victims of Sexual Violence but the Struggle is not over yet. Posted May 19. Rigorous lobbying was involved, spearheaded by APIK's director of advocacy, Ratna Batara Munti.
28. Sexual harassment, sexual exploitation, forced contraception, forced abortion, rape, forced marriage, forced prostitution, sexual slavery, sexual torture. See Janti (2022b).
29. See Yosephine (2016b).

30. See Imam Hamdi (2022), 'Penjelasan KPU tentang Isu Transgender Transpuan dalam Pemilu'. 15 September. https://koran.tempo.co/read/berita-utama/476488/penjelasan-kpu-tentang-isu-transgender-transpuan-dalam-pemilu. Accessed 15 September 2022.
31. See Andayani (2021).
32. The Ardhanary Institute has documented both cases of sex change, accepted by the state (168 cases between 2008 and now) and court cases of identity fraud.
33. See also Butt (2010).
34. They are not the only anti-gender groups. Other groups include CGS Indonesia tanpa pacaran (Indonesia without dating), Hijrah dari Feminisme (Evacuation from Feminism), Aliansi Cerahkan Negeri (Alliance to Illuminate the Country), Hijab Alila, Indonesia Tanpa Feminis (Indonesia without Feminism) and Jakarta Tanpa Feminis.
35. See Dini (2020).
36. See https://thisisgender.com/direktur-centre-gender-studies-cgs-islam-tidak-bias-gender/, Direktur Centre Gender Studies CGS Islam Tidak Bias Gender. Accessed 21 September 2022.
37. Personal communication by Lies Marcoes, October 2021. She is the coordinator of the group Rumah KitaB, which carries out research on the 'covert ideologization' towards conservative fundamentalist values via religious study groups or media campaigns that espouse the ideas of radical Islamist groups like Jihad Islam but which do not directly advocate violence, and thus remain under the radar. Rumah KitaB is a pun playing with the words for house (rumah), kita (our) and kitab (holy) Book.
38. See Syakriah (2019).
39. Aqil (2021).
40. See 'Lihat Pasangan Gay; Bobby Nasution Tegaskan Kota Medan Anti-LGBT', 2 January 2023. https://news.detik.com/berita/d-6493598/lihat-pasangan-gay-bobby-nasution-tegaskan-kota-medan-anti-lgbt.
41. See Adil Raja Siregar (2022), 'Gubernur Riau Minta LGBT Bertobat Buntut Kasus HIV-AIDS Tinggi', 30 December. https://news.detik.com/berita/d-6489684/gubernur-riau-minta-lgbt-bertobat-buntut-kasus-hivaids-tinggi.
42. See Muin Ashrawi (2023), 'DPRD Makassar Usulkan Ranperda Tentang LGBT'. 6 January. https://sulsel.idntimes.com/news/sulsel/ashrawi-muin/dprd-makassar-usulkan-ranperda-tentang-lbgt?page=Times.
43. See also Waites (2020). As Pallotta-Chiarolli (2020) argues, we need an analysis of the whole spectrum of the multicultural, multi-faith, LGBTIQ community in all its intersections with other social structures.
44. See Agung Pramono (2022), 'Disebut Tolak Bissu di Hari Jadi Bone ke 692. Begini Respons Andi Sudirman'. 28 March. https://www.detik.com/sulsel/berita/d-6004638/disebut-tolak-bissu-di-hari-jadi-bone-ke-692-begini-respons-andi-sudirman.
45. See Izrahuddin (2013), quoting Bourchier (1998: 206).
46. See also Boellstorff (2005), Hegarty (2019a) and Rodriguez (2022).
47. Rodriguez and Suvianita (2020), 'How Indonesia's LGBT Community is Making a Difference amid COVID 19'. 26 June. https://theconversation.com/how-indonesias-lgbt-community-is-making-a-difference-amid-covid-19-140063.
48. State surveillance continues to increase. Private Israeli companies sold espionage and intelligence gathering software to some 100 countries, including Indonesia, as it was revealed by the Israeli newspaper *Haaretz* in October 2018. Using these

new technologies a database of LGBT rights activists was created (Shezaf and Jacobson 2018).

49. See, for instance, Moeis et al. (2020).
50. Viral, Video Mahasiswa Unhas Diusir karena Sebut Dirinya Non-Binary..... https://makassar.kompas.com/read/2022/08/21/203021578/viral-video-mahasiswa-unhas-diusir-karena-sebut-dirinya-non-binary.
51. See 'Apologizes for Discriminatory Behavior towards Non-Binary Student'. 22 August 2022. https://coconuts.co/jakarta/news/indonesian-university-apologizes-for-discriminatory-behavior-towards-non-binary-student/. Accessed 22 August 2022.
52. Particularly in the form of the so-called gingerbread model, in which the differences between anatomical sex, gender identity and gender expression are graphically explained. See also Wijaya (2019) and Agustine, Sutrismo and Candraningrum (2015).
53. See Wieringa (2016a) for a critique of the concept of queer as an umbrella term. But see Blackwood and Johnson (2012) for a defence of its applicability in Southeast Asia. Boellstorff (2007) and Wijaya (2020) apply the term widely for the Indonesian LGBT movement. See also Rodriguez (2019, 2022).
54. See Wieringa (2003).
55. See Aspinall and Berenschot (2019) for the nature of patronage politics in relation to social movements in post-Reformasi Indonesia.
56. See Badgett (2017).
57. See Power and Warburton (2020).
58. The 'Blasphemy Law' is incorporated in the Criminal Code.
59. See Sugiharti (2018), 'Watch Your Remarks in Virtual Space', *Jakarta Post*, 6 August.
60. See Power (2020).
61. See Dijk (1981).

References

Adam, Barry D., Jan Willem Duyvendak and Andre Krouwel. 1999. 'Gay and Lesbian Movements Beyond Borders: National Imprints of a Worldwide Movement'. In Barry D. Adam, Jan Willem Duyvendak and Andre Krouwel (eds), *The Global Emergence of Gay and Lesbian Politics: National Imprints of a Worldwide Movement*. Philadelphia: Temple University Press: 244–373.

Ad'han, Syamsurijal, and Muh. Mabrur. N.d. *Komunitas Bissu; Resistensi yang Enggan Membisu*. Jakarta: Mimeo.

Adinda. N.d. *Lesbian*. Djakarta: Senatra.

Agustine, RR Sri. 2001. 'Kekerasan dalam Rumah Tangga Terhadap Lesbian'. *Semai untuk Keadilan dan Demokrasi. Koalisi Perempuan Indonesia*. Jakarta: Koalisi Perempan Indonesia. 14th edn. September: 6–7.

Agustine, RR Sri. 2004. *Belajar dari Sejarah: 'Sentul' dan 'Kantil' Menelusuri Asal-Usul Istilah Identitas Dirinya Sendiri*. Jakarta: Mimeo: 1–7.

Agustine, RR Sri. 2008. 'Rahasia Sunyi: Gerakan lesbian di Indonesia'. *Jurnal Perempuan* 58: 59–72.

Agustine, RR Sri. 2021. 'Kotak Hitam Tersembunyi: Perkosaan Korrektif Terhadap Lesbian (Perempuan) Biseksual dan Transgender Laki-Laki'. *Jurnal Perempuan* 109: 51–63.

Agustine, RR Sri, Gadis Arivia and Dewi Candraningrum. 2015. *Modul Panduan Media Meliput LGBT*. Jakarta: Ardhanary Institute and Yayasan Jurnal Perempuan.

Agustine, RR Sri, Evi Lina Sutrisno and Dewi Candraningrum. 2015. 'Diri, Tubuh dan Relasi: Kajian atas Transgender FTM'. *Jurnal Perempuan* 20/4, issue 87: 48–74.

Agustine, RR Sri, and Ayu Regina Yolanda Sari. 2021. *Kekerasan Terhadap Lesbian, Biseksual, Dan Transgender Lelaki Di Jakarta, Makassar, Dan Pontianak*. Jakarta: Ardhanary Institute and TIFA.

Ahmed, Sara. 2006. *Queer Phenomenology; Orientation, Objects, Others*. Durham NC: Duke University Press.

AILA Indonesia. 2019. *Transformasi Menuju Fitrah: LGBT dalam Perspektif Keindonesiaan*. Bandung: AILA.

Aldous, Susan, and Pornchai Sereemongkonpol. 2008. *Ladyboys: The Secret World of Thailand's Third Gender*. Dunboyne: Maverick House.

Aldrich, R. 2002. *Colonialism and Homosexuality*. London: Routledge.

Al-Ghafari, Iman. 2013. 'Lesbian Existence in Arab Cultures: Historical and Sociological Perspectives'. In Saskia Wieringa and Horacio Sivori (eds), *The Sexual History of the Global South; Sexual Politics in Africa, Asia and Latin America*. London: Zed Books: 144–68.

Ali, Kecia. 2016. *Sexual Ethics and Islam: Feminist Reflections on Qur'an, Hadith and Jurisprudence*. London: Oneworld Publications.

Allen, Pam. 2007. 'Challenging Diversity? Indonesia's Anti-Pornography Bill'. *Asian Studies Review* 31(2): 101–15.

Amiruddin, Mariana. 2018. 'Tindak Pidana Zina, Kerentanan Perempuan dan Stigma Gerakan Perempuan'. *Jurnal Perempuan* 23(2): 83–101.

Andajani, Sari, Dinar Lubis and Sharyn Graham-Davies. 2015. 'Razia terhadap LGBT sebagai Agenda Moralitas Palsu: Kajian Pemberitaan Media di Indonesia'. *Jurnal Perempuan* 20/4, issue 87: 97–108.

Andaya, Leonard Y. 2000. 'The Bissu: Study of a Third Gender in Indonesia'. In Barbara Watson Andaya (ed.), *Other Pasts, Women, Gender and History in Early Modern Southeast Asia*. Manoa: University of Hawai'i Press: 27–47.

Andaya, Barbara Watson. 2006. *The Flaming Womb; Repositioning Women in Early Modern Southeast Asia*. Honolulu: University of Hawai'i Press.

Anderson, B. 1987. 'How Did the Generals Die?'. *Indonesia* 43: 109–34.

Anderson, Benedict R. O'G (ed.). 1990. 'Professional Dreams; Reflections on Two Javanese Classics'. In *Language and Power; Exploring Political Cultures in Indonesia*. Ithaca: Cornell University Press: 271–98.

Anderson, Benedict R. O'G. 1996. *Imagined Communities: Reflections on the Origin and Spread of Nationalism*. London: Verso.

Anderson, Benedict R. O'G. 2001. 'Dari Serat Tjentini sampai Gaya Nusantara'. In Dede Oetomo (ed.), *Memberi suara pada yang bisu*. Yogyakarta: Pustaka Marwa: XI–XXVII.

Anderson, Shelley. 1991. *Out in the World; International Lesbian Organizing*. Ithaca: Firebrand Books.

Ann, Martha, and Dorothy Myers Imel. 1993. *Goddesses in World Mythology: A Biographical Dictionary*. Oxford: Oxford University Press.

Anoegrajekti, Novi. 2003. 'Tandhak Ludruk: Ambiguitas dan Panggung Identitas'. *Srinthil* 5 Oktober: 103–14.

Anoegrajekti, Novi. 2007. 'Penari Gandrung: Kontrol Agama, Masyarakat dan Kekuatan Pasar'. *Jurnal Perempuan* 54: 51–73.

Anonymous. 1930s. 'Pendeta Bantji Bangsa Toradja'. In C. Hooykaas (ed.), *Modern Maleis Zakelijk Proza* (1947). Groningen-Batavia: Wolters: 12–16.

APTN (Asia Pacific Transgender Network). 2020. *There Was No Bencong in Our Ancestors; Bencong Is the Devil: Conversion Therapy Practices in Indonesia*. Bangkok: Mimeo.

APTN (Asia Pacific Transgender Network). 2021. *Conversion Therapy Practices in Indonesia*. https://www.aidsdatahub.org/sites/default/files/resource/conversion-ther apy-2020- indonesiacountry-snapshot.pdf. Accessed 18 February 2022.

Ardhanary Institute. 2016. *Konversi Terapi LGBT Dalam Praktik Ruqiyah Secara Keagamaan*. Jakarta: Ardhanary Institute Mimeo: 24.

Ariati, Ni Wayan Pasek. 2010. ' The Journey of a Goddess: Durga in India, Java and Bali'. Phd Thesis. Darwin: Charles Darwin University.

Ariyanto. 2008. Pemberantasan Komunitas Bissu p 31–34 *OUTZINE Newsletter Arus Pelangi*, Edisi XII/Juni. Jakarta: Arus Pelangi: 31–4.

Ariyanto and Rido Triawan. 2008. *Jadi, kau tak Merasa Bersalah? Studi Kasus Diskriminasi terhadap LGBTI*. Jakarta: Arus Pelangi.

Arus Pelangi. 2013. *Menguak Stigma, Kekerasan & Diskriminasi pada LGBT di Indonesia: Studi Kasus di Jakarta, Yogyakarta dan Makassar*. Jakarta: Arus Pelangi.

Arus Pelangi. 2019. *Catatan Kelam; 12 Tahun Persekusi LGBTI di Indonesia*. Jakarta: Arus Pelangi.

Ashley, Florence. 2019. 'Homophobia, Conversion Therapy, and Care Models for Trans Youth: Defending the Gender-Affirmative Approach'. *Journal of LGBT Youth*. September. https://www.tandfonline.com/doi/abs/10.1080/19361653.2019.1665610. Accessed 26 February 2022.

Aspinall, E., and M. Mietzner (eds). 2010. *Problems of Democratisation in Indonesia; Elections, Institutions and Society*. Singapore: ISEAS.

Aspinall, E., and Ward Berenschot. 2019. *Democracy for Sale. Elections, Clientelism and the State in Indonesia*. Ithaca: Cornell University Press.

Astrea and MamaCash. 2020. 'Vibrant yet Underresourced'. https://www.astraeafoundat ion.org/stories/vibrant-yet-under-resourced-our-lbq-report-is-finally-here/. Accessed 19 June 2022.

Atkinson, Jane Monnig. 1990. 'How Gender Makes a Difference in Wana Society'. In Shelly Errington and Jane Monnig Atkinson (eds), *Power and Difference in Island Southeast Asia*. Stanford: Stanford University Press: 59–93.

Atmojo, Kemala. 1986. *Kami Bukan Lelaki*. Jakarta: Pustaka Grafitipers.

Baal, J. van. 1984. 'The Dialectics of Sex in Marind-Anim Culture'. Gilbert G. Herdt (ed.), *Ritualized Homosexuality in Melanesia*. Berkeley: University of California Press: 128–68.

Badgett, Lee, Amira Hasenbush and Winston Ekaprasetia Luhur. 2017. *LGBT Exclusion in Indonesia and Its Economic Effects*. Los Angeles: UCLA School of Law, the Williams Institute.

Badil, R., and Rangkuti Nurhadi. 1992. *Rahasia di Kaki Borobudur: The Hidden Foot of Borobudur*. Jakarta: Katalis.

Balzer, Marjorie Mandelstam. 1996. 'Sacred Gender in Siberia; Shamans, Bear Festivals and Androgyny'. In Sabrina Petra Ramet (ed.), *Gender Reversals and Gender Cultures; Anthropological and Historical Perspectives*. London: Routledge: 164–83.

Barad, Karen. 2006. 'Posthumanist Performativity: Toward an Understanding of how Matter Comes to Matter'. In Deborah Orr, Linda López McAllister, Eileen Kahl and Kathleen Earle (eds), *Belief, Bodies and Being: Feminist Reflections on Embodiment*. Lanham, MD: Rowman & Littlefield: 11–37.

Barad, Karen. 2007. *Meeting the Universe Halfway: Quantum Physics and the Entanglement of Matter and Meaning*. Durham, NC: Duke University Press.

Baroni, Helen. 2002. *The Illustrated Encyclopedia of Zen Buddhism*. New York: Rosen Publishing Group.

Bauer, Edgar J. 2006. 'Magnus Hirschfeld: Panhumanism and the Sexual Cultures of Asia'. *Intersections: Gender, History and Culture in the Asian Context*, no. 14 (November). http://intersections.anu.edu.au/issue14/bauer.html.

Bayu, Gracia. 2001. 'Antara Ketakutan Sosial dan Pengakuan Diri'. In *Semai untuk Keadilan dan Demokrasi*. 14th edn. Jakarta: Koalisi Perempuan Indonesia: 3–4.

Benedict, Ruth. [1934] 1959. *Patterns of Culture*, with a New Preface by Margaret Mead. Boston: Houghton Mifflin.

Bennett, Linda Rae. 2005. *Women, Islam and Modernity; Single Women, Sexuality and Reproduction Health in Contemporary Indonesia*. New York: Routledge.

Bateson, Mary Catherine. 1984. *With a Daughter's Eye; a Memoir of Margaret Mead and Gregory Bateson*. New York: Morrow.

Bennett, Linda Rae, and Sharyn Graham Davies (eds). 2015. 'Introduction'. In *Sex and Sexualities in Contemporary Indonesia: Sexual Politics, Health, Diversity, and Representations*. London: Routledge: 1–27.

Beauvoir, Simone de. [1949] 1970. *The Second Sex*, 1st edn. New York: Bantam.

Beynon, John C. 2003 'Lady Mary Wortley Montagu's Sapphic Vision'. In Philip Holden and Richard J. Ruppel (eds), *Imperial Desire; Dissident Sexualities and Colonial Literature*. Minneapolis: University of Minneapolis Press: 21–44.

Bhabha, Homi. 1994. *The Location of Culture*. London: Routledge.

Bhaiya Abha, and Saskia Wieringa. 2007. *Manual on Sexual Rights & Sexual Empowerment*. Jakarta: Kartini Network; Jakarta and Delhi: Jagori.

Blackburn, Susan. 2004. *Women and the State in Modern Indonesia*. Cambridge: Cambridge University Press.

Blackwood, Evelyn. 1995. 'Falling in Love with an-Other Lesbian; Reflections on Identity in Fieldwork'. In Don Kulick and Margaret Willson (eds), *Taboo; Sex, Identity and Erotic Subjectivity in Anthropological Fieldwork*. London: Routledge: 51–76.

Blackwood, Evelyn. 2010. *Falling into the Lesbi World, Desire and Difference in Indonesia*. Honolulu: University of Hawai'i Press.

Blackwood, Evelyn. 2005. 'Gender Transgression in Colonial and Postcolonial Indonesia'. *Journal of Asian Studies* 64(4): 849–79.

Blackwood, Evelyn. 2007. 'Regulation of Sexuality in Indonesian Discourse: Normative Gender, Criminal Law and Shifting Strategies of Control'. *Culture, Health & Sexuality* 9(3): 293–307.

Blackwood, Evelyn, and Mark Johnson. 2012. 'Queer Asian Subjects: Transgressive Sexualities and Heteronormative Meanings'. *Asian Studies Review* 36(4): 441–51.

Blackwood, Evelyn, and Saskia E. Wieringa. 2007. 'Globalization, Sexuality and Silence: Women's Sexualities and Masculinities in an Asian Context'. In Saskia E. Wieringa, Evelyn Blackwood and Abha Bhaiya (eds), *Women's Sexualities and Masculinities in a Globalizing Asia*. New York: Palgrave: 1–23.

Bland, Lucy, and Laura Doan (eds). 1998. *Sexology in Culture; Labelling Bodies and Desires*. Cambridge: Polity Press.

Bleys, Rudi C. 1995. *The Geography of Perversion: Male-to-Male Sexual Behaviour Outside the West and the Ethnographic Imagination, 1750–1918*. New York: New York University Press.

Bloembergen, Marieke. 2011. Being Clean Is Being Strong: Policing Cleanliness and Gay Vices in the Netherlands Indies in the 1930s. In Kees van Dijk and Jean Gelman Taylor (eds), *Cleanliness and Culture*. Leiden: KITLV Press: 117–45.

Boellstorff, Tom. 1999. 'The Perfect Path: Gay Men, Marriage, Indonesia'. *GLQ* 5(4): 475–509. doi: 10.1215/10642684-5-4-475.

Boellstorff, Tom. 2004. 'The Emergence of Political Homophobia in Indonesia: Masculinity and National Belonging'. *Ethnos* 69(4): 465–86. doi: 10.1080/0014184042000302308.

Boellstorff, Tom. 2005. *The Gay Archipelago: Sexuality and Nation in Indonesia*. Princeton, NJ: Princeton University Press.

Boellstorff, Tom. 2007. *A Coincidence of Desires: Anthropology, Queer Studies, Indonesia*. Durham, NC: Duke University Press.

Boellstorff, Tom. 2004. Playing Back the Nation: *Waria*, Indonesian Transvestites'. *Cultural Anthropology* 19(2): 159–95.

Boellstorff, Tom. 2005. *The Gay Archipelago: Sexuality and Nation in Indonesia*. Princeton, NJ: Princeton University Press.

Boellstorff, Tom. 2007. 'Waria, National Transvestites'. In *A Coincidence of Desires: Anthropology, Queer Studies, Indonesia*. Durham, NC: Duke University Press: 78–113.

Boomgaard, P. 2012. 'Male-Male Sex, Bestiality, and Incest'. In R. A. G. Reyes and W. G. Clarence-Smith (eds), *Sexual Diversity in Asia, c. 600–1950*, 1st edn. London: Routledge.

Bosia, M., and M. L. Weiss. 2013. 'Political Homophobia in Comparative Perspective'. In M. L. Weiss and M. J. Bosia (eds), *Global Homophobia*. Urbana: University of Illinois Press: 1–29.

Boswell, John. 1995. *Same-Sex Unions in Premodern Europe*. New York: Vintage Books.

Bourchier, David. 2015. *Illiberal Democracy in Indonesia: The Ideology of the Family State.* London: Routledge.

Bourdieu, Pierre. 1990. *The Logic of Practice.* Stanford: Stanford University Press.

Braidotti, Rosi. 2011. *Nomadic Subjects: Embodiment and Sexual Difference in Contemporary Feminist Theory.* New York: Columbia University Press.

Brandes, J. L. A (ed.). 1920. *Pararaton (Ken Arok) of het Boek der Koningen van Tumapel en van Majapahit* 2e druk, Verhandelingen van de Bataviasche Genootschap No. 62 Batavia.

Brenner, Suzanne. 1998. *The Domestication of Desire: Women, Wealth, and Modernity in Java.* Princeton, NJ: Princeton University Press.

Brooten, Bernadette J. 1996. *Love between Women; Early Christian Responses to Female Homoeriticism.* Chicago: University of Chicago Press.

Bruinessen, Martin van. 2013. *Contemporary Developments in Indonesian Islam;Explaining the 'Conservative Turn'.* Singapore. ISEAS Publishing.

Budiarti, Hari. 2007. 'Taking and Returning Objects in a Colonial Context: Tracing the Collections Acquired during the Bone-Gowa Military Expeditions'. In Pieter J. ter Keurs (ed.), *Colonial Collections Revisited.* Leiden: CNWS Publications: 123–44.

Budiman, Amen. 1979. *Lelaki Perindu Lelaki: Sebuah Tinjauan Sejarah dan Psikologi Tentang Homoseks dan Masyarakat Homoseks di Indonesia.* Semarang: Tanjung Sari.

Budiman, Amen. 1982. *Wadam: Pengertian dan Masalahnya.* Semarang: Penerbit Tanjung Sari.

Budiman, Amen. 1992. 'Introduction'. In Sutjipto (ed.), *Jalan Hidupku: Autobiografi Seorang Gay Priyayi Jawa Awal Abad XX (My Life: An Autobiography of a Javanese Aristocratic Gay of the Early 20th Century).* Jakarta: Apresiasi Gay Jakarta: IX–XV.

Budiman, Arief, Barbara Hatley and Damien Kingsbury. 1999. *Reformasi, Crisis and Change in Indonesia.* Clayton: Monash Asian Institute.

Buehler, M. 2016. *The Politics of Shari'a Law: Islamist Activists and the State in Democratic Indonesia.* Cambridge: Cambridge University Press.

Butler, Judith. 1993. *Bodies That Matter: On the Discursive Limits of 'Sex'.* New York: Routledge.

Butt, Simon. 2010. 'Regional Autonomy and Legal Disorder: The Proliferation of Local Laws in Indonesia'. *Singapore Journal of Legal Studies.* July: 1–21.

Butt, Simon. 2019. 'The Constitutional Court and Minority Rights: Analysing the Recent Homosexual Sex and Indigenous Belief Cases'. In Greg Fealy and Ronit Ricci (eds), *Contentious Belonging: The Place of Minorities in Indonesia.* Singapore: ISEAS Indonesia Update Series: 55–74.

Capriati, W., and Y. S. Permana. 2008. 'Gerak Progresif Gerakan Gay Kontemporer di Yogyakarta'. *Jurnal Ilmu Sosial dan Ilmu Politik* 12(1): 59–77.

Carey, Peter, and Vincent Houben. 1987. 'Spirited Srikandhis and Sly Sumbadras: The Social, Political and Economic Role of Women at the Central Javanese Courts in the 18th and 19th Centuries'. In Elsbeth Locher-Scholten and Anke Niehof (eds), *Indonesian Women in Focus; Past and Present Notions.* Dordrecht: Foris: 12–42.

Carey, Peter. 2020. 'Towards the Great Divide: Race, Sexuality, Violence and Colonialism in the Dutch East Indies, from Daendels (1808–1811) to the Java War (1825–1830)'. In Farish A. Noor and Peter Carey (eds), *Racial Difference and the Colonial Wars of 19th Century Southeast Asia.* Amsterdam: Amsterdam University Press: 31–73.

Case, Sue-Ellen. 1993. 'Toward a Butch-Femme Aesthetic'. In Henry Abelove, Michèle Aina-Barale and David Halperin (eds), *The Lesbian and Gay Studies Reader.* New York: Routledge: 294–307.

Ceperiano, Arjohn M., Emmanuel C. Santos Jr, Danielle Celine P. Alonzo and Mira Alexis P. Ofreneo. 2016. 'Girl, Bi, Bakla, Tomboy: The Intersectionality of Sexuality, Gender and Class in Urban Poor Contexts'. *Philippines Journal of Psychology* 49(2): 5–34.

Chabot, H. T. 1950. *Kinship, Status and Gender in South Celebes*. Leiden: KITLV Press.

Chao, Antonia. 2010. 'Global Metaphors and Local Strategies in the Construction of Taiwan's Lesbian Identities'. *Culture, Health and Sexuality* 2(4): 377–90.

Cheney, Kristen. 2012. 'Locating Neocolonialism, "Tradition", and Human Rights in Uganda's "Gay Death Penalty"'. *African Studies Review* 55(2): 77–95.

Chiang, Howard, and Alvin K. Wong. 2017. 'Asia Is Burning: Queer Asia as Critique'. *Culture, Theory and Critique* 58(2): 121–6.

Chua, Lynette J. 2019. *The Politics of Love in Myanmar: LGBT Mobilization and Human Rights as a Way of Life*. Stanford. Stanford University Press.

Clancy-Smith, Julia, and Frances Gouda (eds). 1998. 'Introduction'. In *Domesticating the Empire; Race, Gender and Family Life in French and Dutch Colonialism*. Charlottesville: University Press of Virginia: 1–21.

Clarence-Smith, William G. 2012. 'Same-Sex Relations and Transgender Identities in Islamic Southeast Asia from the Fifteenth Century'. In Raquel A. G. Reyes and William G. Clarence-Smith (eds), *Sexual Diversity in Asia, c.600–1950*. London: Routledge: 67–86.

Connell. Raewyn. 2009. *Gender in World Perspective*. Cambridge: Polity Press.

Conner, Randy P., David Hatfield Sparks and Mariya Sparks. 1997. *Cassell's Encyclopedia of Queer Myth, Symbol and Spirit: Gay, Lesbian, Bisexual, and Transgender Lore*. London: Cassell.

Conway, Susan. 2006. *The Shan: Culture, Arts and Crafts*. Gistrup, Denmark: River Books.

Cordoba, Sebastian. 2020. 'Non-Binary Sexualities: the Language of Desire, Practice and Embodiment'. In Zowie Davy, Ana Cristina Santos, Chiara Bertone, Ryan Thoreson and Saskia E. Wieringa (eds), *The Sage Handbook of Global Sexualities*. London: Sage: 877–97.

Coté, Joost. 1995. *On Feminism and Nationalism. Kartini's Letters to Stella Zeehandelaar 1899–1903*. Clayton, NC: Monash University.

Creese, Helen. 2004. *Women of the Kakawin World. Marriage and Sexuality in the Indic Courts of Java and Bali*. Armonk, NY: Sharpe.

Creese, Helen. 2008. 'The Regulation of Marriage and Sexuality in Precolonial Balinese Law Codes'. In *Intersections: Gender and Sexuality in Asia and the Pacific*. Issue 16, March: 1–17.

Crouch, Harold. 2010. *Political Reform in Indonesia after Soeharto*. Singapore: ISEAS.

Dahl, Ulrika. 2010. 'Femme on Femme: Reflections on Collaborative Methods and Queer Femme-inist Ethnography'. Kath Browne, Catherine J. Nash (eds), *Queer Methods and Methodologies; Intersecting Queer Theories and Social Science Research*. London: Routledge: 143–68.

Dahl, Ulrika, and Del La Grace Volcano. 2009. *Femmes of Power; Exploding Queer Femininities*. London: Serpent's Tail.

Daniel. 2012. *HER Story; Perempuan Luar Biasa Berkisah tentang Hidupnya*. Surabaya: Universitas Surabaya and Dipayoni.

Daniélou, Alain. 1964. *Hindu Polytheism*. New York: Random House.

Daniélou, Alain. 1992. *Gods of Love and Ecstasy: The Traditions of Shiva and Dionysus*. Rochester, VT: Inner Traditions International.

Darmawan. 2018. 'Implementasi Fungsi Satuan Polisi Pamong Praja di Kabupaten Gresik'. *Airlangga Development Journal*. file:///C:/Users/Gebruiker/Downloads/adminadj,+3.+vol+2,+No+1,+2018-Darmawan.pdf.

Dave, N. N. 2011. 'Indian and Lesbian and What Came Next: Affect, Commensuration and Queer Emergences'. *American Ethnologist* 38(4): 650–65.

Davies, Sharyn Graham. 2010. *Gender Diversity in Indonesia*. London: Routledge.

Davies, Sharyn Graham. 2015. 'Sexual Surveillance in Indonesia'. Linda Rae Bennett and Sharyn Graham Davies (eds), *Sex and Sexualities in Contemporary Indonesia; Sexual Politics, Health, Diversity and Representations*. London: Routledge: 29–51.

Davies, Sharyn Graham. 2004. 'Hunters, Wedding Mothers and Androgynous Priests: Conceptualising Gender among Bugis in South Sulawesi', *Indonesia*. PhD Thesis. University of Western Australia, Perth.

Davies, Sharyn Graham. 2015. 'Surveilling Sexuality in Indonesia'. In Linda Rae Bennett and Sharyn Graham Davies (eds), *Sex and Sexualities in Contemporary Indonesia: Sexual Politics, Health, Diversity and Representations*. London: Routledge: 29–51.

Davies, Sharyn Graham. 2018. 'Gender and Sexual Plurality in Indonesia: Past and Present'. In Robert W. Hefner (ed.), *Routledge Handbook of Contemporary Indonesia*. London: Routledge: 322–34.

Davies, Sharyn Graham.2020. 'Sexual Citizenship Re-centred: Gender and Sexual Diversity in Indonesia'. In Zowie Davy, Ana Cristina Santos, Chiara Bertone, Ryan Thoreson and Saskia E. Wieringa (eds), *The Sage Handbook of Global Sexualities*. London: Sage: 688–705.

Davies, Sharyn Graham, and Linda Rae Bennett. 2014. 'Introduction: Mapping Sex and Sexualities in Contemporary Indonesia'. Linda Rae Bennett and Sharyn Graham Davies (eds), *Sex and Sexualities in Contemporary Indonesia: Sexual Politics, Health, Diversity and Representations*. London: Routledge: 1–27.

Davy, Zowie. 2020. 'Freedom Effects in Trans Erotica'. In Zowie Davy, Ana Cristina Santos, Chiara Bertone, Ryan Thoreson and Saskia E. Wieringa (eds), *The Sage Handbook of Global Sexualities*. London: Sage: 969–92.

D'Emilio, John. 1997. 'Capitalism and Gay Identity'. In Roger N. Lancaster and Micaela di Leonardo (eds), *The Gender/Sexuality Reader: Culture, History, Political Economy*. New York: Routledge: 169–78.

Deojha. 2006. *Lesbian Laki-Laki; Pengakuan Getir Kehidupan Seorang Butchie*. Yogyakarta: Pinus.

Dessens, Arianne D. 2008. 'Female Masculinities in Patients with a Disorder of Sex Development – Psychological Aspects of DSD'. Presentation at Symposium on Female Masculinities, 5–6 September 2008, University of Amsterdam.

Dessens, A. B., M. B. C. M. Cools, A. Richter-Unruh, L. H. J. Looijenga, J. A. Grootegoed and S. L. S. Drop. 2009. 'Genetic Defects of Female Sexual Differentiation'. In D. Pfaff, A. Arnold, A. Etgen, S. Fahrbach and R. Rubin (eds), *Hormones, Brain and Behaviour*, 2nd edn, vol. 5, chapter 113. Amsterdam: Elsevier: 3207–34.

Diamond, Lisa M.2008. *Sexual Fluidity; Understanding Women's Love and Desire*. Cambridge, MA: Harvard University Press.

Dibia, I. W. 2005. 'Silang Gender dalam Dramatari Arja di Bali'. In *Cross Gender*. Malang: Sava Media: 77–87.

Dijk, C. van. 1981. *Rebellion under the Banner of Islam: the Darul Islam in Indonesia*. Den Haag: Martinus Nijhoff.

Djajadiningrat-Nieuwenhuis, Madelon. 1987. 'Ibuism and Priyayization. Path to Power?'. In Elsbeth Locher-Scholten and Anke Niehof (eds), *Indonesian Women in Focus. Past and Present Notions*. Dordrecht: Foris Publications: 42–51.

Dunn, Philip. 2004. *The Perfumed Garden* (based on the original translation of Sir Richard Burton's text by Al-Nafzawi). London: Hamlyn.

Dreger, Alice Domurat. 1998. *Hermaphrodites and the Medical Invention of Sex.* Cambridge, MA: Harvard University Press.

Drucker, Donna J. 2014. *The Classification of Sex: Alfred Kinsey and the Organization of Knowledge.* Pittsburgh: University of Pittsburgh Press.

Dwyer, Leslie K. 2002. 'Spectacular Sexuality: Nationalism, Development and the Politics of Family Planning in Indonesia'. In Tamar Mayer (ed.), *Gender Ironies of Nationalism: Sexing the Nation.* London: Routledge: 25–62.

Dzulkarnain, Iskandar. 2006. *Perilaku Homoseksual di Pondok Pesantren.* Skripsi M.A., Yogyakarta: University of Gadjah Mada.

Ediati, Anastasia. 2014. 'Disorders of Sex Development in Indonesia'. Rotterdam: Erasmus University Rotterdam, PhD thesis. https://repub.eur.nl/pub/50331/140115.

Ellis, Havelock. 1913. *Studies in the Psychology of Sex*, 2 volumes. New York: Random House.

Ellis, Havelock, and John Addington Symonds. [1897] 1994. *Sexual Inversion.* Reprint. London: Wilson and Macmillan.

Endraswara, Suwardi. 2002. *Seksologi Jawa.* Jakarta: Wedatama Widya Sastra.

Eng, David. 2010. *The Feeling of Kinship.Queer Liberalism and the Racialization of Intimacy.* Durham, NC: Duke University Press.

Eng, David L., and Jasbir K. Puar. 2020. 'Introduction: Left of Queer'. In *Social Text* 4/145. Durham, NC: Duke University Press: 1–24.

Engebretsen, Elisabeth L. 2014. *Queer Women in Urban China: An Ethnography.* New York: Routledge.

Epprecht, M. 2004. *Hungochani: The History of a Dissident Sexuality in Southern Africa.* McGill: Queen's University Press.

Epprecht, Marc. 2008. *Heterosexual Africa? The History of an Idea from the Age of Exploration to the Age of AIDS.* Athens: Ohio University Press.

Errington, Shelly. 1990. 'Recasting Sex, Gender and Power: A Regional Theoretical Overview'. In Jane Monnig Atkinson and Shelly Errington (eds). *Power and Difference: Gender in Island Southeast Asia.* Stanford: Stanford University Press: 1–58.

Equal Rights Trust. n.d. *New Russian Law Conflicts with International and European Legal Obligations.* https://www.equalrightstrust.org/news/new-russian-law-conflicts-áintern ational-and-european-legal-obligations. Accessed 3 March 2022.

Fachrudin, Azis Anwar. 2016. *Homoseksualitas dan Fikih.* https://azisaf.wordpress. com/2016/02/18/homoseksualitas-dan-fikih/. Accessed 21 February 2012.

Faderman, L. 1980. *Surpassing the Love of Men: Romantic Friendship and Love between Women from the Renaissance to the Present.* London: Junction Books.

Fausto-Sterling, Anne. 2000. *Sexing the Body: Gender Politics and the Construction of Sexuality.* New York: Basic Books.

Fealy, Greg. 2019. '*Reformasi* and the Decline of Liberal Islam'. In Thushara Didley and Michele Ford (eds), *Activists in Transition: Progressive Politics in Democratic Indonesia.* Ithaca: Cornell University Press: 117–34.

Feinberg, Leslie. 1996. *Transgender Warriors; Making History from Joan of Arc to Dennis Rodman.* Boston: Beacon Press.

Feinberg, Leslie. 1992. 'Letter to a Fifties Femme from a Stone Butch'. In Joan Nestle (ed.), *The Persistent Desire: A Femme-Butch Reader.* Boston: Alyson Publications: 102–9.

Fenwick, S. 2018. 'Eat, Pray, Regulate: The Indonesian Ulama Council and the Management of Islamic Affairs'. *Journal of Law and Religion* 33(2): 271, https://doi.org/10.1017/jlr.2018.23.

Fernández, Daniel Ahmed. 2020. 'Queer Muslim Challenges and Resistances within the Context of Globalized Sexualities'. In Zowie Davy, Ana Cristina Santos, Chiara Bertone, Ryan Thoreson and Saskia E. Wieringa (eds), *The Sage Handbook of Global Sexualities*. London: Sage: 731–48.

Florida, Nancy. 1996. 'Sex Wars, Writing Gender Relations in Nineteenth-Century Java'. In Laurie J. Sears (ed.), *Fantasizing the Feminine in Indonesia*. Durham, NC: Duke University Press: 207–25.

Foley, Kathy. 2015. 'The "Ronggeng", the "Wayang", the "Wali", and Islam: Female or Transvestite Male Dancers-Singers-Performers and Evolving Islam in West Java'. *Asian Theatre Journal* 32(2): 356–86.

Forrester, Geoff, and R. J. May (eds). 1998. *The Fall of Soeharto*. Bathurst: Crawford.

Forum LGBTQI. 2013. *Laporan situasi HAM LGBT di Indonesia tahun 2012; Pengabaian Hak Asasi Berbasis Orientasi Seksual dan Identitas Gender: Kami tidak Diam*. Jakarta: Forum LGBTIQ Indonesia.

Foucault, Michel. 1978. *The History of Sexuality: An Introduction*, vol. 1. New York: Vintage.

Foucault, Michel. 1982. 'Power'. In James D. Faubion (ed.), *Essential Works of Foucault 1954–1984*, 1st edn, vol. 3. New York: New Press.

Foucault, Michel. 1980. *Power/Knowledge: Selected Interviews and Other Writings 1972–1977*. New York: Pantheon.

Foucault, Michel. 1985. *The Use of Pleasure: The History of Sexuality*, vol. 2. New York: Vintage Books.

Foucault, Michel. 1988a. *The Care of the Self: the History of Sexuality*, vol. 3. New York: Vintage Books.

Foucault, Michel. 1988b. 'Technologies of the Self'. In L. H. Martin, H. Gutman and P. H. Hutton (eds), *A Seminar with Michel Foucault*. Amherst: University of Massachusetts Press.

Foxwell, Chelsea. 2010. 'Merciful Mother Kannon and its Audiences'. *Art Bulletin* 92(4): 326–47.

Friedericy. H. J. [1947] 1965. *Bontorio, de Laatste Generaal*. Amsterdam: Contact.

Friedericy. H. J. 1958. *De Raadsman* Amsterdam: Querido.

Friedericy. H. J. 1961. *De Eerste Etappe*. Amsterdam: Querido.

Frühstück, Sabine. 2003. *Colonizing Sex: Sexology and Social Control in Modern Japan*. Berkeley: University of California Press.

Ga, Ester Mariani. 2008. 'Lesbian Dalam Penafsiran Agama'. *Jurnal Perempuan* 58: 21–47.

Gamalama, Dorce. 2005. *Aku Perempuan: Jalan Berliku Seorang Dorce Gamalama*. Depok: GagasMedia.

Garcia, Neil C. 1996. *Philippine Gay Culture: Binabae to Bakla, Silahis to MSM*. Hong Kong: Hong Kong University Press.

Gayatri, B. J. D. 1996. 'Indonesian Lesbians Writing Their Own Script: Issues of Feminism and Sexuality'. In M. Reinfelder (ed.), *Amazon to Zami: Towards a Global Lesbian Feminism*. New York: Cassell: 86–97.

Gayatri, B. J. D. 2005. 'Citra Seksualitas Perempuan Jawa (Representasi dari Candi, Mitologi dan Wayang)'. *Jurnal Perempuan* 41: 80–8.

Gayatri, B. J. D. 1993. 'Coming out but Remaining Hidden: A Portrait of Lesbians in Java'. Paper presented at ICAES 13, Mexico City.

Gayatri B. J. D. 2015. 'Selarung Gerakan Lesbian dalam Epidemi Kebencian: Awal Advokasi SOGIE di Nusantara'. *Jurnal Perempuan* 20(4), issue 87: 8–47.

Geertz, Clifford. 1960. *The Religion of Java*. Chicago: University of Chicago Press.

Geller, Pamela L. 2017. *The Bioarchaeology of Social-Sexual Lives: Queering Common Sense about Sex, Gender, and Sexuality*. New York: Springer.

Gerlach, R. 2018. *Political Recruitment and Representation in the Case of the First Female President of Indonesia – Megawati Sukarnoputri*. PhD Thesis. Vienna: University of Vienna.

Geertz, Clifford. 1976. *The Religion of Java*. Chicago: University of Chicago Press.

Giddens. Anthony. 1992. *The Transformation of Intimacy; Sexuality, Love and Eroticism in Modern Societies*. Stanford: Stanford University Press.

Giti. 1996. *Sakhiyani, Lesbian desire in Ancient and Modern India*. London: Cassell.

Goldberg, E. 2002. *Lord Who Is Half Woman: Ardhanarisvara in Indian and Feminist Perspective*. Albany: State University of New York Press.

Gopinath, Gayatri. 2018. *Unruly Visions: The Aesthetic Practices of Queer Diaspora*. Durham, NC: Duke University Press.

Gouda Frances. 1998. 'Good Mothers, Medeas and Jezebels: Feminine Imagery in Colonial and Anticolonial Rhetoric in the Dutch East Indies, 1900–1942'. In University of Julia Clancy-Smith and Frances Gouda (eds), *Domesticating the Empire; Race, Gender and Family Life in French and Dutch Colonialism*. Charlottesville: University Press of Virginia: 236–55.

Gouda, F. 1995. *Dutch Culture Overseas: Colonial Practice in the Netherlands Indies, 1900–1942*. Amsterdam: Amsterdam University Press.

Graham, Penelope. 1983. 'The Power of Transcendence: An Analysis of the Literature on Iban Shamanism'. Canberra ANU. Unpublished PhD Thesis.

Graham, Sharyn. 2004. 'It's Like One of Those Puzzles: Conceptualising Gender among Bugis'. *Journal of Gender Studies* 13(2): 107–16.

Graham, Sharyn. 2010. *Gender Diversity in Indonesia; Sexuality, Islam and Queer Selves*. London: Routledge.

Green, Jamison. 2004. *Becoming a Visible Man*. Nashville: Vanderbilt University Press.

Grewal, Inderpal, and Caren Kaplan. 1994. *Scattered Hegemonies: Postmodernity and Transnational Feminist Practices*. Minneapolis: University of Minnesota Press.

Groenendael van, V. M. C. 2008. *Jaranan: The Horse Dance and Trance in East Java*. Leiden: KITLV Press.

Gurning, Agnes Theodora. 2003. *Organisasi Lesbian dan Aktivitasnya sebagai Wujud Gerakan Sosial. Studi Kasus Organisasi Lesbian di Jakarta*. Depok: Fakultas Ilmu Sosial and Ilmu Politik Universitas Indonesia.

Habib, S. 2007. *Female Homosexuality in the Middle East: Histories and Representations*. New York: Routledge.

Habib, Samar. 2009. *Arabo-Islamic Texts on Female Homosexuality (850–1780 AD)*. New York: Teneo Press.

Hadiz, V. R. 2017. 'Indonesia's Year of Democratic Setbacks: Towards a New Phase of Deepening Illiberalism?'. *Bulletin of Indonesian Economic Studies* 53(3): 261–78.

Hakim, Abdul. 2014. *A Long Path of Bissu in South Sulawesi, Indonesia from Glory to Disappearance*. Halmahera: Mimeo.

Hakim, Abdul. N.d. *Islam and the Transformation of 'Sacred Gender'*. Jakarta: Mimeo.

Halberstam, Judith. 1998. *Female Masculinity*. Durham, NC: Duke University Press.

Halim, Kevin. 2019. *Penerimaan: Kumpulan Cerita Penerimaan Orang Tua Dengan Anak Trans Puan*. Jakarta: Gaya Warna Lentera Indonesia (GWL INA).

Halperin, David M. 1990. *One Hundred Years of of Homosexuality*. London: Routledge.

Hamdi, Ahmad Zainul. 2010. 'Membongkar yang Disembunyikan: Homoseksualitas dalam Islam'. *Jurnal Gandrung Jurnal Kajian Seksualitas Kritis* 1(1): 142–62.

Hamid, Usman. 2021. *Khutbah Idul Fitri Tahun 1442 H /2021 M. Wawasan Kebangsaan Dan Kewajiban Membela Keadilan.* Jakarta: Mimeo.

Hamka, Buya. 1981. *Tafsir Al-Azhar Juzu' XIX.* 2nd ed. Surabaya: Yayasan Latimojong.

Hardeland August. 1839–59. *Wörterbuch der Priestersprache der Ngaju-Dayak: (Bahasa Sangiang – Ngaju-Dayakisch--Bahasa Indonesia--Deutsch).* Berlin: De Gruyter Mouton.

Hatley, Barbara. 2008. *Javanese Performances on an Indonesian Stage: Celebrating Culture, Embracing Change.* Honolulu: University of Hawaii.

Hefner, Carl, J. 1994. *Ludruk Folk Theatre of East Java: Toward a Theory of Symbolic Action.* PhD thesis. Honolulu: University of Hawai'i,

Hefner, Robert W. 1987. 'The Politics of Popular Art: Tayuban Dance and Culture Change in East Java'. *Indonesia* 43: 75–94.

Hefner, Robert W. 2000. *Civil Islam: Muslims and Democratization in Indonesia.* Princeton: Princeton University Press.

Hefner, Robert. W. 2011. 'Where Have All the Abangan Gone? Religionization and the Decline of Non-Standard Islam in Contemporary Indonesia'. In M. Picard and R. Madinier (eds), *The Politics of Religion in Indonesia: Syncretism, Orthodoxy and Religious Contention in Java and Bali.* London: Routledge: 71–91.

Hegarty, Benjamin. 2019a. *Becoming Incomplete: The Transgender Body and National Modernity in New Order Indonesia (1967–1998).* PhD thesis. Canberra: Australian National University.

Hegarty, Benjamin. 2019b. 'The Perfect Woman: Transgender Femininity and National Modernity in New Order Indonesia, 1968–1978'. *Journal of the History of Sexuality* 28(1): 44–65.https://doi.org/10.7560/JHS28102.

Hekma, Gert. 1996. 'A Female Soul in a Male Body: Sexual Inversion as Gender Inversion in Nineteenth-Century Sexology'. In Gilbert H. Herdt (ed.), *Third Sex, Third Gender: Beyond Sexual Dimorphism in Culture and History.* New York: Zone Books.

Helminiak, Daniel. [1994] 2000. *What the Bible Really Says about Homosexuality.* San Francisco: Alamo Square Press.

Heraty, Toeti. 2006. *Calon Arang.Kisah Perempuan Korban Patriarki.* Yogyakarta: Yayasan Obor Indonesia.

Herlambang, W. 2013. *Kekerasan Budaya Pasca 1965: Bagaimana Orde Baru Melegitimasi Anti-komunisme melalui Sastra dan Film.* Yogyakarta: Galang Press.

Herlinatiens. 2003. *Garis Tepi Seorang Lesbian.* Yogyakarta: Galand Press.

Hidayana, Irwan M. 2013. 'Budaya Seksual dan Dominasi Laki-Laki dalam Perikehidupan Seksual Perempuan'. *Jurnal Perempuan* 18(2): 57–68.

Hidayana, Irwan, Diana T. Pakasi and Saskia Wieringa. 2012. *Desk Review; Sexual Diversity in Indonesia.* Amsterdam: Dance4Life and Rutgers WPF.

Hildebrandt, Timothy, and Lynette J. Chua.2017. 'Negotiating In/visibility: The Political Economy of Lesbian Activism and Rights Advocacy'. *Development and Change* 48(4): 639–62.

Hollibaugh, Amber. 2000. 'My Dangerous Desires; Falling in Love with Stone Butches: Passing Women and Girls (Who Are Guys) Who Catch My Eye'. In Amber L. Hollibaugh (ed.), *My Dangerous Desires. A Queer Girl Dreaming Her Way Home.* Durham, NC: Duke University Press: 253–71.

Honig, Emily. 1985. 'Burning Incense, Pledging Sisterhood: Communities of Women Workers in the Shanghai Cotton Mills, 1919–1949'. *Signs: Journal of Women in Culture and Society* 10(4): 700–14.

Horner, Jessica. 2019. 'Undoing the Damage: Working with LGBT Clients in Post-Conversion Therapy'. *Columbia Social Work Review* 8(1): 8–16. https://doi.org/10.7916/cswr.v8i1.1963.

Hooker, B. M. 2003. *Indonesian Islam: Social Change through Contemporary Fatawa*. Honolulu: University of Hawai'i Press.

Hosen, N. 2004. 'Behind the Scenes: Fatwas of the Majelis Ulama Indonesia (1975–1998)'. *Journal of Islamic Studies* 15(2): 147–79.

Howard, R. S. 1996. 'Falling into the Gay World: Manhood, Marriage, and Family in Indonesia'. PhD thesis. Graduate College of the University of the Illinois at Urbana-Champaign.

Hughes-Freeland, Felicia. 2008a. *Cross-Dressing Across Cultures: Genre and Gender in the Dances of* Didik Nini Thowok. Seri Makalah No. 108. Singapore: Asia Research Institute, National Univ. of Singapore.

Hughes-Freeland, Felicia. 2008b. 'Gender, Representation, Experience: The Case of Village Performers in Java'. *Dance Research: The Journal of the Society for Dance Research* 26(2): 140–67.

Human Rights Watch. 2016a. *These Political Games Ruin our Lives'. Indonesia's LGBT Community under Threat*. New York: Human Rights Watch. http://www.hrw.org/1-91.

Human Rights Watch. 2016b. 'Human Rights Watch Submission to the Universal Periodic Review of Indonesia'. September 2016. https://www.hrw.org/news/2017/04/28/human-rights-watch-submission-universal-periodic-review-indonesia.

Human Rights Watch. 2017. 'Indonesia: Gay Porn Arrests Threaten Privacy'. *Human Rights Watch*, 4 May. https://www.hrw.org/news/2017/05/04/indonesia-gay-porn-arrests-threatenprivacy.

Human Rights watch. 2018. *Scared in Public and now no Privacy; Human Rights and Public Health Impact of Indonesia's anti-LGBT Moral Panic*. New York: Human Rights Watch.

Husaini, Adian. 2015. *LGBT Di Indonesia: Perkembangan Dan Solusinya*. Jakarta: INSISTS.

Idrus, Nurul Ilmi. 2006. 'It's a Matter of One's Feelings: Gender, Desire and Identity among Female-Same-Sex Relationships in Globalised South Sulawesi'. *Antropologi Indonesia* 30(1): 7–20.

Indirastuti, Catharina Theresia. 2016. Calabai dan Negosiasi Cair Subjektivitas Gender: Posisi-Posisi Kompleks Waria Dalam Masyarakat Bugis di Kabupaten Pangkajene dan Kepulauan, Sulawesi Selatan. PhD Thesis. Jakarta: Universitas Indonesia.

IPT 1965. 2016. *Final Report of the International People's Tribunal on Crimes against Humanity in Indonesia*. Bandung: Ultimus.

Irigaray, Luce. 1977. *This Sex Which Is Not One*. Ithaca: Cornell University Press.

Iskandar, Dzulkarnain. 2006. 'Homosexual Behaviour in the Pesantren. [Perilaku Homoseksual di Pondok Pesantren]'. MA dissertation. Yogyakarta: Universitas Gajah Mada.

Ismoyo, Petty Jessy, and Amar Alfikar. 2022. *The Long and Winding Road: Weaving Narrative of Queer Muslims in Indonesia*. Denpasar: UNHI Press.

Isnaeni, Hendri F. 2015. 'Si Putih, Waria Penunjuk Jalan Jenderal Soedirman'. http://historia.id/persona/si-putih-waria-penunjuk-jalan-jenderal-soedirman. Accessed 9 June 2015.

Izharuddin, Alicia. 2013. 'Same-Sex Intimacies in Syariffudin's Mairil and the Queering of Authenticity'. *Inter-Asia Cultural Studies* 14(4): 538–50. doi: 10.1080/14649373.2013.831193.

Jackson, Peter. 2003. 'Performative Genders, Perverse Desires: A Bio-History of Thailand's Same-Sex and Transgender Cultures'. *Intersections: Gender, History and Culture in the Asian Context* no. 9 (August). http://intersections.anu.edu.au/issue9/jackson.html.

Jackson, Peter A, and Sullivan, Gerard (eds). 1991. *Lady Boys, Tomboys, Rent Boys: Male and Female Homosexualities in Contemporary Thailand*. New York: Haworth Press.

Jacobs, Julius. 1883. *Eenigen tijd onder de Baliërs. Eene Reisbeschrijving met Aanteekeningen betreffende Hygiëne, Land-en Volkenkunde van de Eilanden Bali en Lombok*. Batavia: Kolff.

Jacobs, Julius. 1894. *Het Familie- en Kampongleven op Groot-Atjeh. Eene Bijdrage tot de Ethonographie van Noord-Sumatra*. Leiden: Brill. Two Volumes.

Jaffrey, Sana. 2020. 'In the State's Stead? Vigilantism and Policing of Religious Offence in Indonesia'. In Thomas Power and Eve Warburton (eds), *Democracy in Indonesia; from Stagnation to Regression?* Singapore: ISEAS: 303–26.

Jakarta Capital Region Representative Council. 1972. *Peraturan Daerah Daerah Khusus Ibukota Jakarta Tentang Ketertiban Umum Dalam Wilayah Daerah Khusus Ibukota Jakarta No. 3 1972 [Regulation Concerning Public Order in the Jakarta Capital Region Number 3, 1972]*. Vol. 10/36/9–253.

Jakarta Capital Region Representative Council. 1968a. 'Korban2 Lesbianisme'. *Mingguan Djaja*, 30 November 1968.

Jakarta Municipal Government. 1968b. 'Bentjong (Bantji)'. *Mingguan Djaja*, 12 October 1968.

Jamal, A. 2001. 'The Story of Lut and the Quran's Perception of the Morality of Same-Sex Sexuality'. *Journal of Homosexuality* 4(1): 1–88.

Jauhola, Marjaana. 2010. *Building Back Better? Negotiating Normative Boundaries of Gender Mainstreaming and Post-Tsunami Reconstruction in Nanggroe Aceh Darussalam, Indonesia*. 22 January. https://www.cambridge.org/core/journals/rev iew-of-international-studies/article/abs/building-back-better-negotiating-normat ive-boundaries-of-gender-mainstreaming-and-posttsunami-reconstruction-in-nangg roe-aceh-darussalam-indonesia/A5F0ABE79A79A8F4923B28B70FB5E166.

Jeumpa, Bunga and Ulil. 2007. 'Quo Vadis, lesbians?'. *Inside Indonesia* 44, April–June. https://www.insideindonesia.org/editions/edition-6641/quo-vadis-lesbians. Accessed 2 July 2021.

Jokowi and Jusuf Kalla. 2014. *Jalan Perubahan untuk Indonesia yang Berdaulat, Mandiri dan Kepribadian; Visi, Misi dan Program Aksi* (Nawacita), Jakarta.

Jolly, Susan. 2002. 'Queering Development. Exploring the Links between Same-Sex Sexualities, Gender and Development'. *Gender and Development* 8(1): 78–88.

Johnson, Mark. 1997. *Beauty and Power: Transgendering and Cultural Transformation in the Southern Philippines*. Oxford: Berg.

Jordan-Young, Rebecca M. 2010. *Brainstorm: The Flaws in the Science of Sex Differences*. Cambridge, MA: Harvard University Press.

Jordan-Young, Rebecca M. 2012. 'Hormones, Context and "Brain Gender": A Review of Evidence from Congenital Adrenal Hyperplasia'. *Social Science& Medicine* 74: 1738–44.

Joseph, Suad. 2003. 'Family Law'. *Encyclopedia of Women in Islamic Cultures*; Leiden: Brill.

Juniarto, Achmad Zulfa. 2014. *Disorders of Sex Development in Indonesia: Natural Course and the Implications of a Stepwise Multidisciplinary Approach*. PhD Thesis. Rotterdam: Erasmus University.

Kadir, Hatib Abdul. 2007. *Tangan Kuasa dalam Kelamin; telaah Homoseks, Pekerja Seks dan Seks Bebas di Indonesia*. Yogyakarta: INSISTPress.

Käng, Dredge Byung'chu. 2012. 'Kathoey "In Trend": Emergent Genderscapes, National Anxieties and the Re-Signification of Male-Bodied Effeminacy in Thailand'. *Asian Studies Review* 36(4): 475–94.

Karsch-Haack, Ferdinand. 1911. *Das Gleichgeschlechtlige Leben der Naturvölker*. München: Reinhardt.

Kartomi, Margaret J. 1976. 'Performance, Music and Meaning of Reyog Ponorogo'. *Indonesia* 22: 85–130.

Katjasungkana, Nursyahbani. 2002. *Kasus-Kasus Hukum Kekerasan Terhadap Perempuan*. Yogyakarta: Galang.

Katjasungkana, Nursyahbani. 2012. 'Indonesia in the Grip of Fundamentalism: Legal Issues and Responses from the Women's Movement'. In Nursyahbani Katjasungkana and Saskia E. Wieringa (eds), *The Future of Asian Feminisms Confronting Fundamentalisms, Conflicts and Neo-Liberalism*. Newcastle upon Tyne: Cambridge Scholars Publishing: 319–47.

Katjasungkana, N., and S. E. Wieringa. 2003. 'Sexual Politics and Reproductive Rights in Indonesia', *Development* 46(2): 63–7.

Katjasungkana, Nursyahbani. 2013. 'The Indonesian Family as a Contested Site of Women's Rights: Implementation of the Domestic Violence Act'. In Maznah Mohamad and Saskia E. Wieringa (eds), *Family Ambiguity and Domestic Violence in Asia: Concept, Law and Process*. Sussex: Academic Press: 169–92.

Katjasungkana, Nursyahbani, and Saskia E. Wieringa. 2016. *Creeping Criminalisation of Women's and LGBTI Rights*. New York OutRight.

Keeler, Ward. 1990. 'Speaking of Gender in Java'. In Jane Monnig Atkinson and Shelly Errington (eds), *Power and Difference: Gender in Island Southeast Asia*. Redwood City, CA: Stanford University Press: 127–52.

Kendall. 1999. 'Women in Lesotho and the (Western) Construction of Homophobia'. In Evelyn Blackwood and Saskia E. Wieringa (eds), *Female Desires*. New York: Columbia University Press: 157–81.

Kendall, Lauren. 1985. *Shamans, Housewives and Other Restless Spirits: Women in Korean Ritual Life*. Honolulu: University of Hawaii Press.

Kennedy, Elisabeth Lapovsky, and Madeline D. Davis. 1993. *Boots of Leather, Slippers of Gold. The History of a Lesbian Community*. New York: Routledge.

Kerkhof, Gosse.1992. 'Het Indische Zedenschandaal. Een Koloniaal Incident'. In Raymond Feddema (ed.), *Wat Beweegt de Bamboo? Geschiedenissen in Zuidoost Azië*. Amsterdam: Het Spinhuis: 92–118.

Kersten, C. 2015. *Islam in Indonesia: The Contest for Society, Ideas and Values*. London: Hurst & Company.

Khanis, Suvianita. 2013. 'Human Rights and the LGBTI Movement in Indonesia'. *Journal of Women's Studies* 19(1): 127–38.

Kholifah, Dwi Rubiyanti. 2012. 'Contesting Discourses on Sexuality in Pesantren: Santriwati Negotiating their Sexual Life'. In Nursyahbani Katjasungkana and Saskia E. Wieringa (eds), *The Future of Asian Feminisms. Confronting Fundamentalisms, Conflicts and Neo-Liberalism*. Newcastle upon Tyne: Cambridge Scholars: 396–417.

Kinney, Ann, with Marijke Klokke en Lydia Kieven. 2003. *Worshiping Siva and Buddha: The Temple Art of East Java*. Honolulu: University of Hawai'i Press.

Koeswinarno. 1996. *Waria dan Penyakit Menular Seksual: Kasus Dua Kota di Jawa* [*Waria and Sexually Transmitted Disease: The Cases of Two Cities in Java*]. Yogyakarta. Pusat Penelitian Kependudukan, Gajah Mada University.

Koeswinarno. 1999. 'Sex, Language and Identity; A Study about "Being Waria" in the Yogyakarta World of Waria'. *Jurnal Antropologi* 2(3): 83–111.

Koeswinarno. 2004. *Hidup sebagai Waria*. Yogyakarta: LKiS.

Komisi Penyiaran Indonesia [Indonesian Broadcasting Commission]. 2008. 'Permintaan Penghentian Tayangan Kebanci-Bancian Di Televisi' [Request to Stop Showing Gender Transgression on Television]. 30 August. http://www.kpi.go.id/index.php/sia ran-pers-1/2505-permintaan-penghentiantayangan-kebanci-bancian-di-televisi.

Komisi Penyiaran Indonesia. 2016. 'KPI Larang Promosi LGBT Di TV Dan Radio' [KPI Bans the Promotion of LGBT on TV and Radio]. 12 February. http:// www.kpi.go.id/index.php/lihatterkini/38-dalam-negeri/33218-kpi-larang-prom osi-lgbt-di-tv-dan-radio.

Komnas HAM. 2016. *Upaya Negara Menjamin Hak-Hak Kelompok Minoritas di Indonesia; Sebuah Laporan Awal*. Jakarta: Komisi Nasional Hak Asasi Manuria Republik Indonesia.

Komnas Perempuan. 2010. *Atas Nama Otonomi Daerah: Pelembagaan Diskriminasi dalam Tatanan Negara Bangsa Indonesia*. Jakarta: Komnas Perempuan.

Komnas Perempuan 2013. *Korban Berjuang, Publik Bertindak: Mendobrak Stagnasi Sistem Hokum; Catatan KTP Tahun 2012*. Jakarta: Komnas Perempuan

Komnas Perempuan. 2014a. *Hasil Eksaminasi Publik terhadap Putusan Mahkamah Agung no. 16 P/HUM/2006 dan no. 26 P/HUM/2007 tentang Permohonan Judicial Review atas Perda Kota Tangerang dan Kebupatem Bantul tentang Pelarangan Prostitusi*. Jakarta: Komnas Perempuan.

Komnas Perempuan. 2014b. *Kegentingan Kekerasan Seksual: Lemahnya Upaya Penanganan Negara; Catatan Kekerasan Terhadap Perempuan Tahun 2013*. Jakarta: Komnas Perempuan 2014.

Komnas Perempuan. 2019. *Korban Bersuara, Data Bersuara: Sahkan RUU Penghapusan Kekerasan Seksual sebagai Wujud Komitmen Negara – Catatan Kekerasan terhadap Perempuan 2018*. Jakarta: Komnas Perempuan.

Koolhof, Sirtjo. 2017. 'La Galigo: Karya Sastra Agung dari Tana Uqiq'. In Rétna Kencana Colliq Pujié Arung Pancana Toa, La Galigo menurut Naskah NBG 188. Three parts, trans. Muhammad Salin. Jakarta: Yayasan Obor Indonesia, Yayasan la Galigo and KITLV: 1–51.

Kosem, Samak. 2017. 'Pondan under the Pondok: Reflexive Ethnography of "Queer Muslim" and Childhood Memories in the Religious School', *Thammasat Journal of History* 4(1) (January–June): 161–206.

Niekerk Kooten, Anja van, and Sacha Wijmer. 1985. *Verkeerde Vriendschap*. Amsterdam: Feministische Uitgeverij Sara.

KPI (Koalisi Perempuan Indonesia). 2002. *Women's Rights, Sexual Health and HIV/AIDS. A Training Manual*. Jakarta: KPI.

Krafft-Ebing, R. von. 1886. *Psychopatia Sexualis. Eine Klinisch-Forensische Studie*. Stuttgart: Verlag von Ferdinand Enke.

Kristeva, Julia. 1982. *Powers of Horror: An Essay on Abjection*. New York: Columbia University Press.

Kroef, Justus M. van der. 1954. 'Transvestitism and the Religious Hermaphrodite in Indonesia'. *University of Manila Journal of East Asiatic Studies* 3(3): 257–65.

Krom, N. J. 1926. *Hindoe-Javaansche Geschiedenis*. Den Haag: Nijhof.

Kruyt, J. A. 1877. *Atjeh en de Atjehers, twee Jaren Blokkade op Sumatra's Noord-Oost Kust*. Leisden: Kolff.

Kulick, Don. 2009. 'Can There Be an Anthropology of Homophobia? In David Murray (ed.), *Homophobias: Lust and Loathing Across Time and Space*. Durham, NC: Duke University Press.

Kumar, Ann. 1980. 'Javanese Court Society and Politics in the Late Eighteenth Century: The Record of a Lady Soldier, Part I: The Religious, Social and Economic Life of the Court'. *Indonesia* 29: 1–46.

Kumar, Ann. 2000. 'Imagining Women in Javanese Religion: Goddesses, Ascetes, Queens, Consorts, Wives'. In Barbara Watson Andaya (ed.), *Other Pasts: Women, Gender and History in Early Modern Southeast Asia*. Honolulu: University of Hawai'i: 87–104.

Kusumaningrum, Ade. 2008. 'Lesbian dan Mainstream Media; Sebuah Pengalaman Pribadi Menghadapi Media Massa Sebagai Narasumber Lesbian'. *Jurnal Perempuan* 58: 109–22.

Lai, Franciska Yuenki. 2020. *Maid to Queer; Asian Labour Migration and Female Same-Sex Desires*. Hong Kong: Hong Kong University Press.

Laksmini, Ayu Rai. 2008. 'Lesbian: Sebuah Penerimaan Diri'. *Jurnal Perempuan* 58: 97–107.

Larasati, Rachmi Diyah. 2013. *The Dance that Makes You Vanish: Cultural Reconstruction in Post Genocide Indonesia*. Minneapolis: University of Minnesota Press.

Lathief, H. 2004. *Bissu: Pergulatan dan Peranannya di Masyarakat Bugis*. Depok: Desantara for Latar Nusa.

Laqueur, Thomas. 1990. *Making Sex; Bodies and Gender from the Greeks to Freud*. Cambridge, MA: Harvard University Press.

Lee H., C. G. Streed, H. Yi, S. Choo and S. S. Kim. 2021. 'Sexual Orientation Change Efforts, Depressive Symptoms, and Suicidality among Lesbian, Gay, and Bisexual Adults: A Cross-Sectional Study in South Korea'. *LGBT Health* 8(6): 427–32. doi: 10.1089/lgbt.2020.0501.

Lee, Po-Han. 2016. 'LGBT Rights versus Asian Values: De/reconstructing the Universality of Human Rights'. *International Journal of Human Rights* 20(7): 978–92.

Leemans, Mitchke. 1995. 'Sihaq en Sekse; Lesbische Seksualiteit in Middeleeuws Arabische Literatuur'. MA thesis. Utrecht: Utrecht University.

Lemke, Thomas. 2001. 'The Birth of Bio-politics: Michel Foucault's Lecture at the Collège de France on Neo-Liberal Governmentality'. *Economy and Society* 30(2): 190–207.

Lewin, Ellen, and William L. Leap. 1996. *Out in the Field. Reflections of Gay and Lesbian Anthropologists*. Urbana: University of Illinois Press.

Lindsey, Tim. 2019. 'Minorities and Discrimination in Indonesia: The Legal Framework'. Greg Fealy and Ronit Ricci (eds), *Contentious Belonging: The Place of Minorities in Indonesia*. Singapore: ISEAS Indonesia Update Series: 36–55.

Ling, Tan Tjiauw. 1968. 'Beberapa Segi Daripada Laporan Preminier Research Bantji'. *Djiwa* 1(2): 45–54. (research project at UI).

Lewi, Olivia. 2012. 'Bissu, Pendeta Agama Bugis Kuno Yang Kian Terpinggirkan' [Bissu, the Priests of Ancient Bugis Religion are increasingly Marginalized]. *National Geographic Indonesia*, 10 July. http://nationalgeographic.co.id/berita/ 2012/07/bissu-pendeta-agama-bugis-kuno-yang-kianterpinggirkan. Accessed 30 June 2014.

Listiorini, D. 2020. 'Online Hate Speech'. *Inside Indonesia* 26 January. https://www.insidein donesia.org/online-hate-speech. Accessed 18 June 2018.

Listiorini, D., and S. G. Davies. 2017. 'Online Dating Apps Blocked'. *Inside Indonesia*. http://www.insideindonesia.org/online-dating-apps-blocked.

Loulan, JoAnn. 1990. *The Lesbian Erotic Dance, Butch, Femme, Androgyny and Other Rhythms*. San Francisco: Spinsters Book.

Lyon, J. M. B. de. 1941. 'Over de Waroks en Gemblak van Ponorogo'. *Koloniaal Tijdschrift* 31: 740–60.

Mackie, Vera. 2017. 'Rethinking Sexual Citizenship: Asia-Pacific Perspectives'. *Sexualities* 20(1–2): 143–58.

Mahkamah Konstitusi Republik Indonesia (Indonesian Constitutional Court). 2016a. *Risalah Sidang perkara Nomor 46/PUU-XIV/2016*. 1 August. Jakarta: Mahkamah Konstitusi Republik Indonesia.

Mahkamah Konstitusi Republik Indonesia (Indonesian Constitutional Court). 2016b. *Risalah Sidang Perkara Nomor 46/PUU-XIV/2016*. 28 November. Jakarta: Mahkamah Konstitusi Republik Indonesia.

Maimunah. 2008a. Indonesian Queer: Non-Normative Sexualities in Indonesian Film, 2003–2006. Skripsi M.A. Sydney: University of Sydney.

Maimunah. 2008b. 'Indonesia's Q!Film Festival. Indonesia's Q! Film Festival: Young Indonesians Are Using an Alternative Film Festival to Promote Awareness of Sexual Diversity'. *Inside Indonesia* 93. www.insideindonesia.org/indonesia-s-q-film-festival-2.

Mak, Geertje. 1997. *Mannelijke Vrouwen; over Grenzen van Sekse in de Negentiende Eeuw*. Amsterdam: Boom.

Manalastas, Eric Julian, T. T. Ojanen, B. A. Torre, R. Ratanasheforn, B. C. C. Hong, V. Kumaresan and V. Veeramuthu. 2017. 'Homonegativity in Southeast Asia: Attitudes towards Lesbians and Gay Men in Indonesia, Malaysia, the Philippines, Singapore, Thailand and Vietnam. *Asia-Pacific Social Science Review* 17(1): 25–33.

Mangunwijaya, Y.B. 1988. *Roro Mendut. Novel Sejarah*. Jakarta: Gramedia.

Mariana, Anna. 2011. 'Politik Seksual atas Tubuh Perempuan: Sejarah Perbudakan Seksual pada Masa Fasisme Jepang dan Neo-fasisme Orde Baru di Indonesia, sebuah Perbandingan'. MA thesis. Yogyakarta: Universitas Gajah Mada.

Marshall, Paul. 2018. 'The Ambiguities of Religious Freedom in Indonesia'. *Review of Faith & International Affairs* 16(1): 85–96.

Matthes, B. F. 1872. 'Over de Bissoe's of Heidensche Priesters en Priesteressen der Boeginezen' [About the Bissu or Heathen Priests and Priestesses of the Buginese] *Verhandelingen der Koninklijke Akademie van Wetenschappen, Afdeling Letterkunde* 17: 1–50.

Mazdafiah, Siti, and Wulan Widaningrum (eds). 2012. *Herstory; Perempuan Luar Biasa Berkisah tentang Hidupnya*. Surabaya: Dipayoni and Universitas Surabaya.

Mead, Margaret. 1972. *Blackberry Winter: My Earlier Years*. New York: Simon & Schuster.

McClintock, Anne. 1995. *Imperial Leather; Race, Gender and Sexuality in the Colonial Contest*. New York: Routledge.

McGregor, K. 2007. *History in Uniform: Military Ideology and the Construction of Indonesia's Past*. Singapore: National University of Singapore Press.

McGregor, Katharine, Ana Dragojlovic and Hannah Loney (eds). 2020. *Gender, Violence and Power in Indonesia*. London: Routledge.

McIntosh, Mary. 1968. 'The Homosexual Role'. *Social Problems* 12: 182–92.

McIntosh, Mary. [1967] 1981. 'The Homosexual Role'. Reprinted in Kenneth Plummer (ed.), *The Making of the Modern Homosexual*. London: Hutchinson: 53–75.

McQueen, Paddy. 2020. 'Sexuality, Identity and the Politics of Recognition'. In Zowie Davy, Ana Cristina Santos, Chiara Bertone, Ryan Thoreson and Saskia E. Wieringa (eds), *The Sage Handbook of Global Sexualities*. London: Sage: 621–44.

Melvin, Jess. 2018. *The Army and the Indonesian Genocide: Mechanics of Mass Murder*. London: Routledge.

Mepschen, Paul, JanWillem Duyvendak and Evelien Tonkens. 2010. 'Sexual Politics, Orientalism and Multicultural Citizenship in the Netherlands'. *Sociology* 44: 962–80.

Mernissi, Fatima. 1983. *Sex, Idéologie, Islam*. Paris: Tierce.

Mernissi, Fatima. 1985. *Beyond the Veil: Male-Female Dynamics in Modern Muslim Society*. London: Saki.

Meyboom-Italiaander, Jos. 1924. *Javaansche Sagen, Mythen en Legenden*. Zutphen: Thieme: 16–48.

Mignolo, Walter, and Catherine E. Walsh. 2018. *On Decoloniality: Concepts, Analytics and Praxis*. Durham, NC: Duke University Press.

Mietzner, Marcus and Burhanuddin Muhtadi. 2019. 'The Mobilisations of Intolerance and its Trajectories: Indonesian Muslims' Views of Religious Minorities and Ethnic Chinese'. Greg Fealy and Ronit Ricci (eds), *Contentious Belonging: The Place of Minorities in Indonesia*. Singapore: ISEAS Indonesia Update Series: 155–75.

Mira, W. 1994. *Relung-relung Gelap Hati Sisi*. Jakarta: Gramedia.

Moeis, Isnarmi, Junaidi Indrawad, Nurman S. and Zaky Farid Luthfi. 2020. 'Content Analysis of the Pancasila Education Curriculum in Preventing LGBT Behavior'. Global Conferences Series:Social Sciences, Education and Humanities (GCSSSEH), vol. 5, *Progress in Social Science, Humanities and Education Research Symposium*. 136–9. doi: https://doi.org/10.32698/GCS-PSSHERS360.

Mogrovejo, Norma. 1999. 'Sexual Peeference, the Ugly Duckling of Feminist Demands: The Lesbian Movement in Mexico'. In Evelyn Blackwood and Saskia E. Wieringa (eds), *Female Desires: Same-Sex Relations and Transgender Practices across Cultures*. New York: Columbia University Press: 71–89.

Mookerjee, Ajit. 1988. *Kali: The Feminine Force*. London: Thames and Hudson.

Moore, Henriette A. 1994. *A Passion for Difference: Essays in Anthropology and Gender* Bloomington: Indiana University Press.

Morgan, Ruth, and Saskia Wieringa. 2005. *Tommy Boys, Lesbian Men and Ancestral Wives*. Johannesburg: Jacana Publishers.

Mosse, George L. 1985. *Nationalism and Sexuality; Middle Class Morality and Sexual Norms in Modern Europe*. London: University of Wisconsin Press.

Muhyidin, Depe. 2013. 'Mairil dari Imam Syafii Hingga Robert K. Merton Fikrah'. *Rahima Edition* 41 (Online magazine), as published in www.rahima.or.id/index.php?opt ion=com_content&view=article&id=1042:mairil-dari-imam-syafii-hingga-robert-k-merton-fikrah-swara-rahimaedisi41&catid=38:fikrah&itemid=271.

MUI (Majelis Ulemah Indonesia' [Indonesian Council of Islamic Scholars]). 1980. *Operasi Perubahan/Penyempurnaan Kelamin* [Operation to Change or Perfect the Genitals], Fatwa 6 (1 June).

Mukhotib, M. D. (ed.) 2002. *Seksualitas: Menggugat Konstruksi Islam*. Yogyakarta Yayasan Kesejahteraan Fatayat (YKF).

Mulia, Siti Musdah. 2004. *Counter Legal Draft. The Compilation of Indonesian Islamic law*, Jakarta: Ministry for Religious Affairs of the Republic of Indonesia.

Mulia, Siti Musdah. 2008. 'Allah Hanya Melihat Taqwa, Bukan Orientasi Seksual Manusia, Wawancara Dewi Setyarini'. *Jurnal Perempuan* 58: 122–35.

Mulia, Siti Musdah. 2010a. 'Islam dan Homoseksualitas: Membaca Ulang Pemahaman Islam'. *Jurnal Gandrung* 1(1): 9–31.

Mulia, Siti Musdah. 2010b. *Islam dan Hak Asasi Manusia: Konsep dan Implementasi*. Yogyakarta: Naufan Pustaka.

Mulia, Siti Musdah. 2012. 'Contesting Fundamentalism: Humanizing Women'. In Saskia E. Wieringa and Nursyahbani Katjasungkana (eds), *The Future of Asian Feminisms;*

Confronting Fundamentalisms, Conflicts and Neo-Liberalism. Newcastle upon Tyne: Cambridge Scholars Publishing: 283–99.

Murray, A. J. 1991. *No Money No Honey: A Study of Street Traders and Prostitutes in Jakarta*. Singapore: Oxford University Press.

Murray, A. J. 1999. 'Let Them Take Ecstasy: Class and Jakarta Lesbians'. In E. Blackwood and S. Wieringa (eds), *Female Desires: Same-Sex Relations and Transgender Practices across Cultures*. New York: Columbia University Press: 139–57.

Murray, Stephen O. 1998. 'Diversity and Identity. The Challenge of African Homosexualities'. In Murray, *Boy-Wives and Female Husbands; Studies of African Homosexualities*. New York: St Martin's Press.

Murray, Stephen O., and W. Roscoe. 1997. *Islamic Homosexualities; Culture, History and Literature*. New York: New York University Press.

Murtagh, Ben. 2013. *Gender and Sexualities in Indonesian Cinema: Constructing Gay, Lesbi and Waria Identities on Screen*. Hoboken: Routledge.

Mustaqfiroh, Rahayu. 2014. 'Constructing Sexuality in Panopticon Pesantren'. In Bianca J. Smith and Mark Woodward (eds), *Gender and Power in Indonesian Islam; Leaders, Feminists, Sufis and Pesantren Selves*. London: Routledge: 175–86.

Muthmaniah, Yulianti. 2015. 'Hak-Hak Asasi Manusia LGBT dalam Kebijakan dalam Negeri Indonesia'. *Jurnal Perempuan* 20(4): 142–75.

Nahas, Omar. 2001. *Islam en Homoseksualiteit*. Amsterdam en Utrecht: Bulaaq/Yousuf.

Najih, Mokhammad. 2018. 'Indonesian Penal Policy; Toward Criminal Law Reform Based on Pancasila'. *Journal of Indonesian Legal Studies* 3(2): 149–74.

Nestle, Joan. 1984. 'The Fem Question'. In Carole Vance (ed.), *Pleasure and Danger Exploring Female Sexuality*. Boston: Routledge and K. Paul: 232–41.

Nestle, Joan (ed.). 1992. *The Persistent Desire; a Femme-Butch Reader*. Boston: Alyson Publications.

Nestle, Joan. 1998. *A Fragile Union*. San Francisco: Cleis Press.

Newfield, Emily, Stacey Hart, Suzanne Dibble and Lori Kohler. 2006. 'Female-to-Male-Transgender Quality of Life'. *Quality of Life Research* 15: 1447–8.

Newton, Esther. 1972. *Mother Camp: Female Impersonators in America*. Englewood Cliffs: Prentice Hall.

Newton, Esther. 1993. *Cherry Grove, Fire Island. Sixty Years in America's First Gay and Lesbian Town*. Boston: Beacon Press.

Newton, Esther. 2000. *Margaret Mead Made Me Gay; Personal Essay, Public Ideas*. Durham, NC: Duke University Press.

Niehof, Anke, and Firman Lubis. 2003. *Two Is Enough: Family Planning in Indonesia Under the New Order 1968-1998*. Leiden: KITLV Press.

Nihom, M. 1986. 'The Identification of the Original Site of a Cult Statue on East Java: The Jaka Dolog'. *Journal of the American Oriental Society* 106(3): 485–99, 501.

Noerdin, Edriana, Lisabona Rahman, Ratna Laelasari Y. and Sita Aripurnami. 2005. *Representasi Perempuan dalam Kebijakan Publik di Era Otonomi Daerah* [The Representation of Women in Public Policy in the Era of Regional Automony]. Jakarta: Women Research Institute.

Nurish, Amanah. 2010. 'Women's Same-Sex Relations in Indonesian Pesantren'. *Gender, Technology and Development* 14(2): 267–77.

Nyanzi, Stella. 2013. 'Dismantling Reified African Culture through Localised Homosexualities in Uganda'. *Culture, Health & Sexuality: An International Journal for Research, Intervention and Care* 15(8): 952–67. doi: 10.1080/13691058.2013.798684.

Oetomo, D. 1991. 'Homoseksualitas di Indonesia'. *Prisma* 7: 84–96.

Oetomo, D. 1996. 'Gender and Sexual Orientation in Indonesia'. In L. J.Sears (ed.),
    Fantasizing the Feminine in Indonesia. Durham, NC: Duke University Press. https://
    doi.org/10.1215/9780822396710-012.

Oetomo, D. 2000. 'Masculinity in Indonesia'. In Richard Guy Parker, Regina Maria
    Barbosa and Peter Aggleton (eds), *Framing the Sexual Subject: The Politics of Gender,
    Sexuality, and Power*. Berkeley: University of California Press: 46–59.

Oetomo, D. 2001a. *Memberi Suara pada yang Bisu*. Yogyakarta: Galang Press.

Oetomo, D. 2001b. 'Ludruk Theater; Survival in Transformation'. *Latitudes*,
    September: 17–22.

Oetomo, D. 2007. 'Gay Identities'. *Inside Indonesia*. 30 September. https://www.insidein
    donesia.org/gay-identities. Accessed 23 August 2017.

Offord, B. 2011. 'Singapore, Indonesia and Malaysia: Arrested Development!' In M.
    Tremblay, D. Paternotte and C. Johnson (eds), *The Lesbian and Gay Movement and the
    State; Comparative Insights into a Transformed Relationship*. London: Ashgate: 135–52.

O'Flaherty, M. 2015. 'The Yogyakarta Principles at Ten'. *Nordic Journal of Human Rights*
    33(4): 280–98.

O'Flaherty, M., and J. Fisher 2008. 'Sexual Orientation, Gender Identity and International
    Human Rights Law: Contextualising the Yogyakarta Principles'. *Human Rights Law
    Review* 8(2): 207–48.

O'Flaherty, Wendy Doniger. 1980. *Women, Androgynes and Other Mythical Beasts*.
    Chicago: University of Chicago Press.

O 'Connor, Karen, and Alexandra B. James. 2010. *Gender and Women's Leadership; a
    Reference Handbook*. London: Sage.

Okado, Kaori. 2011. 'When Women are Kings: Cross-Gendered Expression in an All-
    Female Central Javanese Court Dance-Drama and its Public Reception'. *UrbanScope*
    2: 19–30.

Ong, Hok Ham. 1972. 'The Wayang Topeng of Malang'. *Indonesia* 14: 111–24.

Ong, Hok Ham. 1991. 'Kekuasaan dan Seksualitas: Lintasan Sejarah Pra dan Masa
    Colonial'. *Prisma* 7: 15–23.

Onstenk, Annemiek. 1983. *Van Brede Schouders tot Hoge Hakken; Veranderde
    Beeldvorming over Lesbische Vrouwen in de Periode 1939–1965*. Amsterdam: SUA.

Pallotta-Chiarolli, Maria. 2020. 'Pre-Colonial Actualities, Post-Colonial Amnesia and
    Neo-Colonial Assemblage'. In Zowie Davy, Ana Cristina Santos, Chiara Bertone, Ryan
    Thoreson and Saskia E. Wieringa (eds), *The Sage Handbook of Global Sexualities*.
    London: Sage: 57–82.

Pande, Alka. 2004. *Ardhanarishvara the Androgyne: Probing the Gender Within*. New
    Delhi: Rupa.

Paramaditha, Intan. 2018. 'Q! Film Festival as Cultural Activism: Strategic Cinephilia and
    the Expansion of a Queer Counterpublic'. *Visual Anthropology* 31(1–2): 74–92.

Parker, Andre, Mary Russo, Doris Sommer and Patricia Yaeger. 1992. *Nationalisms and
    Sexualities*. New York: Routledge.

Pauka, Kirstin. 1998. 'The Daughters Take Over? Female Performers in Randai Theatre'.
    Drama Review 42(1): 113–21. doi: 10.1162/105420498760308706.

Pausacker, Helen. 1991. 'Srikandhi and Sumbadra: Stereotype Role Models or Complex
    Personalities?'. In Chandra Lokesh (ed.), *The Art and Culture of South-East Asia*.
    London: Sheba Feminist Publishers: 271–97.

Pausacker, Helen. 2015. 'Indonesian Beauty Queens'. In Linda Rae Bennett and Sharyn
    Graham Davies (eds), *Sex and Sexualities in Contemporary Indonesia: Sexual Politics,
    Health, Diversity, and Representations*. London. Routledge: 273–92.

Pausacker, Helen. 2021. 'Homosexuality and the Law in Indonesia'. In Tim Lindsey and Helen Pausacker (eds), *Crime and Punishment in Indonesia*. Abingdon. Routledge: 430–63.

Pawestri, Tunggal. 2016. More Hard Times for Indonesian LGBT People. http://www.the jakartapost.com/academia/2016/08/22/more-hard-times-for-indonesian-lgbt-people. html. Accessed 22 August 2016.

Peacock, James L. 1967. 'Javanese Clown and Transvestite Songs: Some Relations between "Primitive Classification" and "Communicative Events"'. In June Helm (ed.), *Essays on the Verbal and Visual Arts: Proceedings of the 1966 Spring Meeting*. Seattle: American Ethnological Society.

Peacock, J. 1987. *Rites of Modernization: Symbolic Aspects of Indonesia Proletarian Drama*. Chicago: University of Chicago Press.

Pelangi, Arus. 2013. *Menguak Stigma, Kekerasan dan Diskriminasi Pada LGBT di Indonesia: Studi Kasus di Jakarta, Yogyakarta dan Makassar*. Jakarta: Arus Pelangi.

Peletz, Michael G. 2009. *Gender Pluralism: Southeast Asia since Early Modern Times*. New York: Routledge.

Pelras, C. 1996. *The Bugis*. Oxford: Blackwell Publishers.

Perelaer, M. T. H. 1870. *Ethnografische Beschrijving der Dajaks*. Zaltbommel: Noman

Petchesky, Rosalind Pollack. 2001. 'Sexual Rights; Inventing a Concept. Mapping an International Practice'. In Mark Blasius (ed.), *Sexual Identities; Queer Politics*. Princeton, NJ: Princeton University Press: 118–41.

Petkovic, Josko. 1998. 'Waiting for Karila: Bending Time, Theory and Gender in Java and Bali. *Intersections*. http://www.sshe.murdoch.edu.au/hum/as/intersections/current2/ Josko.html.

Phelim, Kine. 2017. 'Indonesian Religion Minister's Contradictory LGBT "Embrace"'. https://www.hrw.org/news/2017/12/19/indonesian-religion-ministers-contradict ory-lgbt-embrace.

Pigeaud, Th. G. Th. 1963. *Javaanse Volksvertoningen*. Batavia: Volkslectuur.

Pigeaud, Th. G.Th. 1963. *Java in the Fourteenth Century; Study in Cultural History the Nagara – Kertagama by Rakawi Prapanca of Majapahit 1365 A.D.* KITLV Translation Series 4, 5 volumes. The Hague: Nijhoff.

Platt, Maria, Sharyn Graham Davies and Linda Rae Bennett. 2018. 'Contestations of Gender, Sexuality and Morality in Contemporary Indonesia'. *Asian Studies Review* 42(1): 1–15. doi: 10.1080/10357823.2017.1409698.

Plummer, K. 2003. *Intimate Citizenship; Private Discussions and Public Dialogues*. Seattle: University of Washington Press.

Povinelli, Elizabeth A., and George Chauncey. 1999. 'Thinking Sexuality Transnationally'. *GSQ: A Journal of Lesbian and Gay Studies* 5(4): 439–50.

Power, Thomas P. 2020. 'Assailing Accountability: Law Enforcement Politicisation, Partisan Coercion and Eexecutive Aggrandisement under the Jokowi Administration'. In Thomas P. Power and Eve Warburton (eds), *Democracy in Indonesia; from Stagnation to Regression*? Singapore: ISEAS: 277–303.

Power, Thomas P. and Eve Warburton. 2020. *Democracy in Indonesia; from Stagnation to Regression*? Singapore: ISEAS.

Praag, S. van. n.d. *Sexualiteit en Huwelijk bij de Volkeren der Aarde*. Amsterdam: De Gulden Ster.

Pramodhawardani, Jaleswari. 2003. Konstruksi Kaum Lesbian atas Realitas Homoseksual: Analisis Isi Feminis terhadap Situs Web Swara Srikandi. Jakarta: Univesrsitas Indonesia.

Prawirakusumah, R. Prie, and Ramadhan K. H. 1988. *Menguak Duniaku: Kisah Sejati Kelainan Seksual.* Jakarta: Pustaka Utama Grafiti.

Puar, Jasbir. 2007. *Terrorist Assemblages; Homonationalism in Queer Times.* Durham, NC: Duke University Press.

Pucci, Adriana. 1992. *Bhima Swarga. The Balinese Journey of the Soul.* Boston: Bulfinch.

Rafael, Vicente L. 2019. 'The Sovereign Trickster'. *Journal of Asian Studies* 78(1): 141–66. https://doi.org/10.1017/S0021911818002656.

Raffles,Thomas. 1817. *History of Java.* London: Murray.

Rapoport, Eva. 2018. 'Jathilan Horse Dance: Spirit Possession Beliefs and Practices in the Present-Day Java'. *Indonesian Journal of Southeast Asian Studies* 2(1). https://doi. org/10.22146/ikat.v2i1.37389. Accessed 20 September 2020.

Ras, J. J. 1976. *De Schending van Soebadra; Javaans Schimmenspel.* Amsterdam: Meulenhof.

Rassers, Willem Huibert. 1922. *De Pandji-Roman.* Leiden: Uniersiteit van Leiden.

Ratri, M. 2002. *Lines; Kumpulan Cerita Perempuan di Garis Pinggir.* Jakarta: Millennium.

Ratri, M. 2008. 'Lesbian dan Hak-Hak Sipil'. *Jurnal Perempuan* 58: 47–59.

Reddy, Vasu. 2002. 'Perverts and Sodomites; Homophobia as Hate Speech in Africa'. *Southern African Linguistics and Applied Language Studies* 20(3): 163–75.

Reinfelder, Monika (ed.) 1996. *Amazon to Zami: Towards a Global Lesbian Feminism.* London: Cassell.

Rétna Kencana Colliq Pujié Arung Pancana Toa. 2017. *La Galigo menurut Naskah NBG 188.* Three parts, trans. Muhammad Salin. Jakarta: Yayasan Obor Indonesia, Yayasan la Galigo and KITLV.

Rich, Adrienne. 1980. 'Compulsory Heterosexuality and Lesbian Existence'. *Signs Journal of Women in Culture and Society* 5(4): 631–60.

Richardson, Diane. 2000a. 'Constructing Sexual Citizenship. Theorizing Sexual Rights'. *Critical Social Policy* 20(1): 105–35.

Richardson, Diane. 2000b. *Rethinking Sexuality.* London: Sage.

Rinaldo, Rachel. 2019. 'The Women's Movement and Indonesia's Transition to Democracy'. In Thushara Didley and Michele Ford (eds), *Activists in Transition: Progressive Politics in Democratic Indonesia.* Ithaca: Cornell University Press: 135–52.

Robinson, Geoffrey. 2018. *The Killing Season: A History of the Indonesian Massacres, 1965– 1966.* Princeton, NJ: Princeton University Press.

Robinson, Kathryn. 2009. *Gender, Islam and Democracy in Indonesia.* Abingdon: Routledge.

Robinson, Kathryn. 2015. 'Masculinity, Sexuality and Islam'. In Linda Rae Bennett and Sharyn Graham Davies (eds), *Sex and Sexuality in Contemporary Indonesia.* London: Routledge: 51–68.

Robinson, Paul. [1976] 1989. *The Modernization of Sex; Havelock Ellis, Alfred Kinsey, William Masters and Virginian Johnson.* Ithaca: Cornell University Press.

Roces, Mina. 2022. *Gender in Southeast Asia.* Cambridge: Cambridge University Press.

Rodriguez, Diego Garcia. 2018. 'Reclaiming Indonesian Citizenship'. *Inside Indonesia* 134: October–December. https://www.insideindonesia.org/reclaiming-indonesian-citi zenship?.

Rodriguez, Diego Garcia. 2019. 'Queer Religious Geographies? Qu(e)erying Indonesian Muslim Selves'. *Gender, Place & Culture* 27(9): 1326–47. doi: 10.1080/0966369X.2019.1693343.

Rodriguez, Diego Garcia. 2022. 'Who Are the Allies of Queer Muslims? Situating Pro-Queer Religious Activism in Indonesia'. *Indonesian and the Malay World* 50(146): 96– 117. doi : 10.1080/13639811.2002.2015183.

Romli, Mohamad Guntur. 2008. 'Lesbian dalam Seksualitas Islam'. *Jurnal Perempuan* 58: 74–95.

Roosa, John. 2006. *Pretext for Mass Murder: The September 30th Movement & Suharto's Coup d'Etat in Indonesia*. Madison: University of Wisconsin Press.

Roosa, John. 2020. *Buried Histories: The Anticommunist Massacres of 1965–1966 in Indonesia*. Madison: University of Wisconsin Press.

Rosenbloom, Rachel (ed.). 1996. *Unspoken Rules; Sexual Orientation and Women's Human Rights*. London: Cassell.

Rosjidi, Ajip. 1983. *Chandra Kirana* Retold. Jakarta: Pustaka Jaya.

Rubin, Gayle. 1975. 'The Traffic in Women. Notes on the Political Economy of Sex'. In Rayna Rapp Reiter (ed.), *Towards and Anthropology of Women*. New York: Monthly Review Press: 157–211.

Rubin, Gayle. 1984. 'Thinking Sex. Notes for a Radical Theory of the Politics of Sexuality'. In Carole Vance (ed.), *Pleasure and Danger*. New York: Routledge and Kegan, Paul. 274–345.

RutgersWPF, Aliansi Satu Visi and Dance4Life. N.d. *Mainstreaming Sexual and Gender Diversity in SRHR and HIV Programming in Indonesia; Final Report on a Thematic Learning Programme (TLP)*. Jakarta: Rutgers WPF Indonesia.

Ryan, Caitlin, Russell B. Toomey, Rafael M. Diaz and Stephen T. Russell. 2018. 'Parent-Initiated Sexual Orientation Change Efforts with LGBT Adolescents: Implications for Young Adult Mental Health and Adjustment'. *Journal of Homosexuality*. Published online 7 November. doi: 10.1080/00918369.2018.1538407.

Sa'dan, Masthuriah. 2015. 'LGBT, Agama dan HAM: Kajian Pemikiran Khaled M. Abou el-Fadl'. *Jurnal Perempuan* 87: 176–94.

Safitri, Dian Maya. 2013. 'The Politics of Piety in the Pnodok Pesantren Khusus Waria Al-Fattah Senin-Kamis Yogyakarta: Negotiating the Islamic Religious Embodiment'. In Jajat Burhanudin and Kees van Dijk (eds), *Islam in Indonesia Contrasting Images and Interpretations*. Amsterdam: ICAS: 91–109.

Sabaroedin, Syarifah. 2001. 'Apa Arti Homoseksualitas yang Dipaksakan. Semai untuk Keadilan dan Demokrasi'. *Koalisi Perempuan Indonesia* edisi XIV (September): 5.

Sabaroedin, Syarifah. 2006. *Kebertubuhan Perempuan dalam Pornografi*. Jakarta: Yayasan Kota Kita.

Sa'dan, Masthuriah. 2015. 'LGBT, Agama dan HAM: Kajian Pemikiran Khaled M. Abou el-Fadl'. *Jurnal Perempuan* 87: 176–94.

Saifuddin, Zuhri. 2006. The Dalaq of the Pesantren [Dalaq di Pesantren]. MA thesis. Yogyakarta: Universitas Gajah Mada.

Saleh, L., and N. Sood. 2020. *Vibrant Yet Under-Resourced: The State of Lesbian, Bisexual, and Queer Movements*. New York: Astraea Lesbian Foundation for Justice and MamaCash.

Samudera, Hera. 2016. *Tomboi vs Lesbi*.Yogyakarta: Pohon Cahaya.

Santos, Ana Cristina, Saskia E. Wieringa, Ryan Thoreson, Chiara Bertone and Zowie Davy. 2020. 'Editors' Introduction'. In Zowie Davy, Ana Cristina Santos, Chiara Bertone, Ryan Thoreson and Saskia E. Wieringa (eds), *The Sage Handbook of Global Sexualities*. London: Sage: 1–31.

Santoso, Soewito. 2006. *The Centhini Story: The Javanese Journey of Life*. Singapore: Marshall Cavendish Editions.

Sauer, Arn, and Aranka Podhora. 2013. 'Sexual Orientation, Gender Identity and Human Rights Impact Assessment'. *Impact Assessment and Project Appraisal (IAPA) Journal* 31(2): 135–45.

Sawitri, Cok. 2001. 'The Girls Play House'. *Latitudes*. September: 40–4.

Sharlet, Jeff. 2009. *The Family: The Secret Fundamentalism at the Heart of American Power.* New York: HarperCollins.

Schiller, Anne. 1991. 'On "the Watersnake Which Is also a Hornbill". Male and Female in Ngaju Dayak Mortuary Symbology'. In Vinson H. Sutlive (ed.), *Female and Male in Borneo: Contributions and Challenges to Gender Studies.* Borneo Research Council Monograph Series. Williamsburg, VA: Borneo Research Council Department of Anthropology College of William and Mary in Virginia: 414–35.

Schuyf, Judith. 1994. *Een Stilzwijgende Samenzwering; Lesbische Vrouwen in Nederland, 1920–1970.* Amsterdam: IISG.

Scott, Peter Dale. 1985. 'The United States and the Overthrow of Sukarno, 1967–1967'. *Pacific Affairs* 58(2): 239–64.

Sedgwick, Eve Kosofsky. 1990. *Epistemology of the Closet.* Berkeley: University of California Press.

Sempol, Diego. 2013. 'Violence and the Emergence of Gay and Lesbian Activism in Argentina, 1983–90'. In Saskia Wieringa and Horacio Sivori (eds), *The Sexual History of the Global South: Sexual Politics in Africa, Asia and Latin America.* London: Zed Books: 99–120.

Serrano-Amaya, José Fernando. 2018. *Homophobic Violence in Armed Conflict and Political Transition.* Cham: Palgrave-MacMillan.

Setiawan, Ikwan. 2016. *Transformation of Ludruk Performances: From Political Involvement and State Hegemony to Creative Survival Strategy.* Matatimoer Institute. 22 March. https://matatimoer.or.id/2016/03/22/transformation-of-ludruk-performan ces-from-political-involvement-and-state-hegemony-to-creative-survival-strategy/. Accessed 18 September 2020.

Setiawan, Ken M. P., and Dirk Tomsa. 2022. *Politics in Contemporary Indonesia: Institutional Change, Policy Challenges and Democratic Decline.* London: Routledge.

Setiawati, Sri. 2017. 'Jaringan Sosial Organisasi Lesbian, Bisexual Dan Transgender: Studi Kasus Organisasi Ardhanary Institute Di Jakarta'. *Jurnal Antropologi: Isu-Isu Sosial Budaya* 18(2): 153–71.

Shannahan, D. S. 2010. 'Some Questions from a Muslim Faith Perspective'. *Sexualities* 13(6): 67–84.

Shefaz, Hagar, and Jonathan Jacobson. 2018. 'Revealed: Israel's Cyber-Spy Industry Helps World Dictators Hunt Dissidents and Gays'. *Haaretz*, 20 October. https://www.haaretz. com/israel-news/.premium.MAGAZINE-israel-s-cyber-industry-helps-world-dictat ors-hunt-dissidents-and-gays.html.

Shukla, Surabhi. 2018. '*Navtej Singh Johar and Ors. v Union of India* Writ Petition Criminal Code (No) 76/2016'. *Law and Sexuality*. https://lawandsexuality. com/2018/09/10/navtej-singh-johar-and-ors-v-union-of-india-writ-petition-crimi nal-no-76-2016/.

Simpson, Bradley R. 2008. *Economists with Guns: Authoritarian Development and U.S.-Indonesian Relations, 1960–1968.* Stanford: Stanford University Press.

Sinnott, Megan. 2004. *Toms and Dees: Transgender Identity and Female Same-Sex Relationships in Thailand.* Honolulu: University of Hawai'i Press.

Sinyo. 2014. *Anakku Bertanya tentang LGBT.* Bandung: Quanta.

Siradj, Said Aqiel. 2009. 'LGBT dalam Pandangan Islam'. *Tantri, Warta Istri, Putri dan Santri* 2(2): 10–16.

Situmorang, Bernadeth Sinta, and Ratna Batara Munti. 2007. 'Bukan Cinta Biasa: Kisah Perempuan yang Mencintai Perempuan dan Perjalanan Menentukan Identitas Diri'. In Dalam Endah Sulistiyowati (ed.), *Hegemoni Hetero-normativitas: Membongkar Seksualitas Perempuan yang Terbungkam*. Yogyakarta: LKiS: 85–178.

Smith, Barbara. 1993. 'Homophobisa – Why Bring It Up?'. In Henry Abelove, Michèle Aina-Barale and David Halperin (eds), *The Lesbian and Gay Studies Reader*. New York: Routledge: 99–103.

Snouck Hurgronje, Christiaan.1906. *The Acehnese*. Leiden: Brill.

Soelarto, B., and S'Ilmi. 1976. *Kesenian Rakyat Gandrung dari Banyuwangi*. Jakarta: Departemen Pendidikan dan Kebudayaan.

Soneji, Davesh. 2012. *Unfinished Gestures: Devadasis, Memory and Modernity in South Asia*. Chicago: University of Chicago Press.

Stepan, N. L. 1991. *The Hour of Eugenics: Race, Gender and Nation in Latin America*. Ithaca: Cornell University Press.

Stoler, Ann Laura. 1989. 'Making Empire Respectable: The Politics of Race and Sexual Morality in 20th-Century Colonial Cultures'. *American Ethnologist* 16(4): 634–60.

Stoler, Ann Laura. 1995. *Race and the Education of Desire. Foucault's History of Sexuality and the Colonial Order of Things*. Durham: NC: Duke University Press

Stoler, Ann Laura. 2002. *Carnal Knowledge and Imperial Power; Race and the Intimate in Colonial Rule*. Berkeley: University of California Press.

Suara Ibu, Peduli. 1999. *Catatan Perjalanan Suara Ibu Peduli*. Jakarta: Yayasan Perempuan Indonesia.

Sugianto, L. 2015. *Eksistensi Calalai dalam Budaya Sulawesi Selatan*. Jakarta: Ardhanary Institute.

Sukanjata. 1956. *Komplot Homosex*. Djakarta: Analisa.

Sumbogo, Priyono B. 2004. 'Gay Indonesia. Forum Utama; Legalisasi Perkawinan Homo'. *Forum Keadilan* No. 45, April 18: p. 11.

Sunardi, Christine. 2009. 'Pushing at the Boundaries of the Body: Cultural Politics and Cros-Gender Dance in East Java'. *Bijdragen tot de Taal-land- en Volkenkunde* 165(4): 459–92.

Sunarti, Euis. 2021. *Jangan Sampai Menyesal; Lindungi Keluarga dan Generasi Penerus Bangsa dari Gerakan Kebebasan Orientasi dan Perilaku Seksual Penyimpang*. Bandung: IPB Press.

Suliyati, Titiek. 2018. 'Bissu, Keistimewaan Gender dalam Tradisi Bugis'. *Endogami Jurnal Ilmiah Kajian Antropologi* 2(1): 52–61.

Supiastutik and Kusumayanti, D. D. 2008. 'Tren Lesbian dalam Novel Perempuan Penulis Pasca-Saman: Kajian Sastra Feminis'. *Sosiohumaniora* 1(1): 88–99.

Surabhi, Shukla. 2020. 'Transgender Persons in the Indian Courtroom'. Zowie Davy, Ryan Thoreson, Chiara Bertone Christine and Saskia E. Wieringa (eds), *The Sage Handbook of Global Sexualities*. Los Angeles: Sage: 705–29.

Suroso, Suar. 2013. *Akar dan Dalang; Pembantaian Manusia tak Berdosa dan Penggulingan Bung Karno*. Bandung: Ultimus.

Suryakusuma, Julia. 2011. *State Ibuism: The Social Construction of Womanhood in New Order Indonesia*. Depok: Komunitas Bambu.

Suryakusuma, Julia. 1996. 'The State and Sexuality in New Order Indonesia'. In Laurie J. Sears (ed.), *Fantasizing the Feminine in Indonesia*. Durham, NC: Duke University Press: 92–119.

Sutjipto. 1992. *Jalan Hidupku: Autobiografi Seorang Gay Priyayi Jawa Awal Abad XX* [My Life: an Autobiography of a Javanese Aristocratic Gay of the Early 20th Century]. Jakarta: Apresiasi Gay Jakarta.

Sutlive, Vinson H. 1992. 'The Iban Manang in the Sibu District of the Third Division of Sarawak: An Alternate Route to Normality'. In Stephen O. Murray (ed.), *Oceanic Homosexualities*. Garland Gay and Lesbians Series No. 7. New York: Garland Publishing: 273–84.

Sutlive, Vinson H., and George N. Appell. 1991. 'Introduction'. In Sutlive, Vinson H (ed.), *Female and Male in Borneo: Contributions and Challenges to Gender Studies*. Borneo Research Council Monograph Series. Williamsburg, VA: Borneo research Council Department of Anthropology College of William and Mary in Virginia: XI–XLVI.

Suvianita, Khanis. 2013. *Laporan Situasi HAM LGBTI di Indonesia Tahun 2012; Pengabaian Hak Asasi Berbasis Orientasi Seksual dan Identitas Gender: Kami Tidak Diam*. Jakarta: Forum LGBTIQ Indonesia and Gaya Nusantara.

Syarifuddin. 2005. *Mairil: Sepenggal Kisah Biru di Pesantren*. Yogyakarta: Idea.

Syarifah, S. 2001. 'Apa Arti Heteroseksualitas Yang Dipaksakan?'. In *Semai untuk Keadilan dan Demokrasi*. 14th edn. Jakarta: Koalisi Perempuan Indonesia. September: 5.

Tang, Shawna. 2017. *Postcolonial Lesbian Identities in Singapore. Re-Thinking Global Sexualities*. London: Routledge.

Teresia, Kadek Genia. 2019. *Kelompok Minoritas Seksual Dalam Terpaan Pelanggaran HAM*. Jakarta: Lembaga Bantuan Hukum Masyarakat.

Thadani, Giti. 2008. *Sambhog; Pleasure Constellations of the Feminine*. New Delhi: Mimeo.

Thadani, Giti. 1996. *Sakhiyani: Lesbian Desire in Ancient and Modern India*. London: Cassell.

Thajib, Ferdiansyah. 2018. 'The Making and Breaking of Indonesian Muslim Queer Safe Spaces'. *Borderlands* 17(1): 1–24.

Thamaona, Ijhal. 2003. 'Abbiasang ri Ulleng Langi [Closing the Path to Heaven and Earth]. *Srinthil* (October): 32–9.

Tietmeyer, Elisabeth. 1985. *Frauen Heiraten Frauen. Studien zur Gynaegamie in Afrika*. Hohenschäftlarn: Klaus Renner Verlag.

Tidey, Sylvia. 2019. 'AIDS as an "Entry Point" for LGBT Rights Discourse'. *Inside Indonesia* 138: October–December. https://www.insideindonesia.org/ aids-as-an-entry-point-for-lgbt-rights-discourse.

Tiwon, Sylvia, 1996, 'Models and Maniacs: Articulating the Female in Indonesia'. In Laurie J. Sears (ed.), *Fantasizing the Feminine in Indonesia*. Durham, NC: Duke University Press: 47–71.

Toer, Pramoedya Ananta. 1999. *Arok Dedes*. Jakarta: Hasta Mitra.

Tohari, Ahmad. 1982. *Ronggeng Dukuh Paruk*. Jakarta: Gramedia.

Toomistu. Terje. 2019. *Embodied Lives, Imagined Reaches: Gendered Subjectivity and Aspirations for Belonging among Waria in Indonesia*. PhD thesis. ÜLikooli: University of Tartu.

Topley, Marjorie. 1975. 'Marriage Resistance in Rural Kwangtung', In Margery Wolf and Roxane Witke (eds), *Women in Chinese Society*. Stanford: Stanford University Press.

U (anonymous). 2001. 'Lesbian Adalah Pilihan Hidukpu'. In *Semai untuk Keadilan dan Demokrasi*. 14th edn. Jakarta: Koalisi Perempuan Indonesia. September: 8–10.

UN General Assembly. 2008. *Joint Statement on Human Rights, Sexual Orientation and Gender Identity*, 22 December. www.sxpolitics.org/wp-content/uploads/2009/03/ un-document-on-sexual-orientation.pdf. Accessed 20 March 2019.

UNDP and APTN. 2017. *Legal Gender Recognition: A Multi-Country Legal and Policy Review in Asia*. Bangkok: UNDP.

UNDP/USAID. 2014 *Being LGBT in Asia; Indonesia Country Report. A Participatory Review and Analysis of the Legal and Social Environment for Lesbian, Gay, Bisexual and Transgender Persons and Civil Society*. Bangkok: UNDP.

Vance, Carole S. 1999. 'Anthropology Rediscovers Sexuality: A Theoretical Comment'. In Richard Parker and Peter Aggleton (eds), *Culture, Society and Sexuality; a Reader*. London: Routledge: 41–59.

Vanita, Ruth, and Saleem Kidwai (eds). 2000. *Same-Sex Love in India; Readings from Literature and History*. New Delhi: Macmillan.

Vargas, V., and Saskia Wieringa. 1998. 'The Triangle of Empowerment: Processes and Actors in the Making of Public Policy for Women'. In Geertje Lycklama a Nijeholt,Vargas, Virginia and Saskia Wieringa (eds), *Women's Movements and Public Policy in Europe, Latin America and the Caribbean*. New York: Garland.

Vicinus, Martha. 1992. 'They Wonder to Which Sex I Belong. The Historical Roots of the Modern Lesbian Identity'. *Signs* 8(3): 467–99.

Vickers, Adrian. 2012. *Bali: A Paradise Created*. Clarendon, VT: Tuttle.

Wachirianto, Iwan. 1991. *Gembalakan dalam Perspectif Sosiologis* [Gemblak, A Sociological Perspective]. Surabaya: Fisip Universitas Airlangga.

Wadud, Amina. 1992. *Qur'an and Women. Rereading the Sacred Text from a Woman's Perspective*. Wisconsin: University of Michigan.

Wadud, Amina. 2006. Inside the Gender Jihad: Women's Reform in Islam. Oxford: Oneworld.

Waidzunas, T. 2015. *The Straight Line: How the Fringe Science of Ex-Gay Therapy Reoriented Sexuality*. Minneapolis: University of Minnesota Press.

Waites, Matthew. 2020. 'Global Sexualities: Towards a Reconciliation between Decolonial Analysis and Human Rights'. In Zowie Davy, Ana Cristina Santos, Chiara Bertone, Ryan Thoreson and Saskia E. Wieringa (eds), *The Sage Handbook of Global Sexualities*. London: Sage: 33–57.

Wang, Yiran. 2021. 'Passionate Aesthetics': T-P Gender Practices and Discourses, and the Hierarchies within Lesbian (lala) Communities in Contemporary Mainland China'. *Journal of Gender Studies* 30(5): 561–72. doi: 10.1080/09589236.2021.1929094.

Webster, Tracy Wright. 2004. Beyond the 'Closet': The Voices of Lesbian Women in Yogyakarta. MA thesis. Yogyakarta: Centre for Women's Studies IAIN (Institut Agama Islam Negeri) Sunan Kalijaga. .

Webster, Tracy.Wright. 2006. 'Strategic Communities: The Notion of Keluarga in Indonesia and among Female Same-Sex Attraction in Yogyakarta'. Paper presented at the 16th Biennial Conference of the Asian Studies Association of Australia in Wollongong, 26 June–29 June 2006.

Wee, Vivienne. 2012. 'The Politicization of Women's Bodies in Indonesia: Sexual Scripts as Charters for Action'. In Anissa Hélie and Homa Hoodfar (eds), *Sexuality in Muslim Contexts Restrictions and Resistance*. London: Zed Books.

Weeks, Jeffrey. [1986] 2010. *Sexuality*, 3rd edn. London: Routledge.

Wekker, Gloria. 1994. *Ik ben een Gouden Munt, ik ga door Vele Handen, maar Verlies mijn Waarde niet: Subjectiviteit en Seksualiteit van Creoolse Volksklasse Vrouwen in Paramaribo*. Amsterdam: Vita.

Wekker, Gloria. 2006. *The Politics of Passion: Women's Sexual Culture in the Afro-Surinamese Diaspora*. New York: Columbia University Press.

Welch, David (ed.). 2014. *Nazi Propaganda; Power and Limitations*. London: Croom Helm.

Wichelen, Sonja van. 2010. *Religion, Politics and Gender in Indonesia; Disputing the Muslim Body.* Oxon: Routledge.

Wieringa, Saskia E. 1987. *Uw Toegenegen Dora D., Reisbrieven.* Amsterdam: Furie.

Wieringa, Saskia E. 1992. 'Essentialism versus Constructivism: an Essential Conflict?' Lecture given at University of West Indies, February 7.

Wieringa, Saskia E. 1989. 'An Anthropological Critique of Constructionism: Berdaches and Butches.: Dennis Altman at alii'. *Homosexuality, Which Homosexuality?* London: GMP.

Wieringa, Saskia E. 1993.'Two Indonesian Women's Organizations: Gerwani and the PKK'. *Bulletin of Concerned Asian Scholars* 25(2): 17–31.

Wieringa, Saskia E. 1995. 'The Perfumed Nightmare: Indonesian Women's Organizations after 1950'. In B. Hering (ed.), *Pramoedya Ananta Toer 70 Tahun, Essays to honour Pramoedya Ananta Toer's 70th Year.* Stein: Yayasan Kabar Seberang: 257–83.

Wieringa, Saskia E. 1999. 'Desiring Bodies or Defiant Cultures: Butch-Femme Lesbians in Jakarta and Lima'. In E. Blackwood and S. Wieringa (eds), *Female Desires: Same-Sex Relations and Transgender Practices across Cultures.* New York: Columbia University Press.

Wieringa, Saskia E. 2000. 'Communism and Women's Same-Sex Practices in Post-Suharto Indonesia'. *Journal of Culture, Health & Sexuality* 2(4): 441–57.

Wieringa, Saskia E. 2002. *Sexual Politics in Indonesia.* London: Palgrave/McMillan.

Wieringa, Saskia E. 2003. 'The Birth of the New Order State in Indonesia: Sexual Politics and Nationalism'. *Journal of Women's History* 15(1): 70–92.

Wieringa, Saskia E. 2005. 'Woman Marriages and Other Same Sex Practices; Historical Reflections on African Women's Same Sex Relations'. In Ruth Morgan and Saskia Wieringa (eds), *Tommy Boys, Lesbian Men and Ancestral Wives.* Johannesburg: Jacana Publishers: 281–309.

Wieringa, Saskia E. 2007a. ' "If There is no Feeling…" The Dilemma between Silence and Coming Out in a Working Class Butch/Fem Community in Jakarta'. In Mark B. Padilla, Jennifer S. Hirsch, Miguel Muñoz-Laboy, Robert E. Sember and Richard G. Parker (eds), *Love and Globalisation; Transformations of Intimacy in the Contemporary World.* Nashville: Vanderbilt University Press: 70–93.

Wieringa, Saskia E. 2007b. *Het Krokodillengat.* Roman. Utrecht: La-Vita. (Published as The Crocodile Hole in English, Jakarta: Jurnal Perempuan 2015).

Wieringa, Saskia E. 2007c. 'Silence, Sin and the System Women's Same Sex Practices in Japan'. In Saskia E. Wieringa, Evelyn Blackwood and Abha Bhaiya (eds), *Women's Same Sex Experiences in a Globalizing As*ia. London: Palgrave McMillan: 23–47.

Wieringa, Saskia E. 2007d. 'The Admonishment of Vegetarian Great Aunt'. Inaugural address at the University of Amsterdam.

Wieringa, Saskia E. 2008. 'From Sacred Gender to Social Stigma: Changing Cultural Perceptions of Intersex Persons'. Paper presented at Intersex Conference, Diponegoro University, Semarang, 7–19 October: 17.

Wieringa, Saskia E. 2009. 'Postcolonial Amnesia: Sexual Moral Panics, Memory and Imperial Power'. In Gilbert Herdt (ed.), *Moral Panics, Sex Panics; Fear and the Fight over Sexual Rights.* New York: New York University Press: 205–34.

Wieringa, Saskia E. 2010. 'Gender Variance in Asia: Discursive Contestations and Legal Implications'. *Journal of Gender, Technology and Development* 14(2): 143. https://doi.org/10.1177/097185241001400202.

Wieringa, Saskia E. (ed.). 2011. *Women-Loving-Women in Africa and Asia.*Trans/sign project, Report of Research Findings. Amsterdam: Riek Stienstra Fund, Kartini Asia Network, Hivos and MamaCash, Amsterdam.

Wieringa, Saskia E. 2012a. 'Gender Variance in Southeast Asia: Discursive Contestations and Legal Implications'. Nursyahbani Katjasungkana and Saskia E. Wieringa (eds), *The Future of Asian Feminisms;Cconfronting Fundamentalisms, Conflicts and Neo-Liberalism*. Newcastle upon Thyme: Cambridge Scholars Publishing: 447–76.

Wieringa, Saskia E. 2012b. 'Passionate Aesthetics and Symbolic Subversion; Heteronormativity in India and Indonesia'. *Asian Studies Review* 36(4): 515–30.

Wieringa, Saskia E. 2012c. 'Dildos: Passionate Aesthetics and the Plasticity of Desires'. In Lenore Manderson (ed.), *Technologies of Sexuality, Identity and Sexual Health*. London: Routledge: 165–85.

Wieringa, Saskia E. 2015a. 'Gender Harmony and the Happy Family: Islam, Gender and Sexuality in Post-Reformasi Indonesia'. *Journal of South East Asian Research* 23(1): 5–27.

Wieringa, Saskia E. 2015b. 'Discursive Contestations Concerning Intersex in Indonesia: Stigma, Rights and Identities'. In Linda Rae Bennett and Sharyn Graham Davies (eds), *Sex and Sexualities in Contemporary Indonesia: Sexual Politics, Health, Diversity and Representations*. London: Routledge: 169–83.

Wieringa, Saskia E. 2015c. 'Sexualities, Asia and the Pacific'. In Patricia Whelehan and Anne Bolin (eds), *The International Encyclopedia of Human Sexuality*. Malden, MA: Wiley-Blackwell: 5.

Wieringa, Saskia E. 2016a. *Heteronormativity, Passionate Aesthetics and symbolic subversion in Asia*. Eastbourne: Sussex Academic Publishers.

Wieringa, Saskia E. 2016b. 'The Crocodile Hole in Ubud: How a Feminist Lunch Evades a Book Ban'. *Tijdschrift voor Genderstudies* 19(1): 107–13.

Wieringa, Saskia E. 2018. 'When a History Seminar Becomes Toxic: A Reading of the Attack on LBH Jakarta in September 2017'. *Archipel, Etudes interdisciplinaires sur le monde insulindien* 95: 195–211.

Wieringa, Saskia E. 2019a. 'Criminalisation of Homosexuality in Indonesia: The Role of the Constitution and Civil Society'. *Australian Journal of Asian Law* 20(1): 1–19.

Wieringa, Saskia E. 2019b. 'Is the Recent Wave of Homophobia Unexpected?' In Greg Fealy and Ronit Ricci (eds), *Contentious Belonging: The Place of Minorities in Indonesia*. Singapore: ISEAS Indonesia Update Series: 113–33.

Wieringa, Saskia E. 2019c. *Rule of Law in Indonesia from the Eyes of Poor Women and Vulnerable Groups: Legal Empowerment and the APIK Gender Justice Index (AGJI)*. Jakarta: APIK.

Wieringa, Saskia E. 2020a. 'Heteronormativity and Passionate Aesthetics'. In Zowie Davy, Ana Cristina Santos, Chiara Bertone, Ryan Thoreson and Saskia E. Wieringa (eds), *The Sage Handbook of Global Sexualities*. London: Sage: 291–313.

Wieringa, Saskia E. 2020b 'The Impact of Indonesia's 2019 Presidential Campaign on the Human Rights Movement: Narrow Solidarity versus Affinity'. *Open Journal of Political Science (OJPS)* 10(4). https://m.scirp.org/papers/103504.

Wieringa, Saskia E. 2021. 'Gay Couple Caned in Aceh, Indonesia'. *People's Charter for Southeast Asia*. 7 February. https://forsea.co/gay-couple-caned-in-aceh-indonesia/.

Wieringa, Saskia E. 2022a. 'Dorce Gamalama's Burial and Indonesia's Transgender Traditions'. *Inside Indonesia*, 2 August. https://www.insideindonesia.org/dorce-gamalama-s-burial-and-indonesia-s-transgender-traditions.

Wieringa, Saskia E. 2022b. 'Nationalism and Two Sexual Moral Panics in Indonesia'. In Claudia Derichs, Sumrin Kalia, Lina Knorr, and Andrea Fleschenberg (eds), *Local Responses to Global Challenges. A Transregional Studies Reader*. Singapore: World Scientific Publishing.

Wieringa, Saskia E. with Evelyn Blackwood. 1999. 'Sapphic Shadows: Challenging the Silence in the Study of Sexuality'. In S. Wieringa and E. Blackwood (eds), *Culture, Identity and Sexuality; Women's Same-sex Relations Crossculturally*. New York: Columbia University Press: 39–67.

Wieringa, Saskia E., with Evelyn Blackwood. 2009a. *Hasrat Perempuan; Relasi Seksual sesama Perempuan dan Praktek Perempuan Transgender di Indonesia*. Jakarta: Ardhanary Institute.

Wieringa, Saskia E., Evelyn Blackwood and Abha Bhaiya (eds). 2007. *Women's Sexualities and Masculinities in a Globalizing Asia*. New York: PalgraveMcMillan.

Wieringa, Saskia E., and Horacio Sivori. 2013. 'Sexual Politics in the Global South: Framing the Discourse'. In Saskia Wieringa and Horacio Sivori (eds), *The Sexual History of the Global South; Sexual Politics in Africa, Asia and Latin America*. London: Zed Books.

Wieringa, Saskia E., with Jess Melvin and Annie Pohlman. 2019. *The International People's Tribunal for 1965 and the Indonesian Genocide*. New York: Routledge.

Wieringa, Saskia E., and Nursyahbani Katjasungkana. 2012. *The Future of Asian Feminisms; Confronting Fundamentalisms, Conflicts and Neo-Liberalism*. Newcastle upon Tyne: Cambridge Scholars Publishing.

Wieringa, Saskia E., with Nursyahbani Katjasungkana. 2018. *Propaganda and the Genocide in Indonesia; Imagined Evil*. New York: Routledge.

Wijaya, Hendri Yulius. 2019. 'Localizing Queer Identities; Queer Activism and National Belonging in Indonesia'. In Greg Fealy and Ronit Ricci (eds), *Contentious Belonging: The Place of Minorities in Indonesia*. Singapore: ISEAS Indonesia Update Series: 133–55.

Wijaya, Hendri Yulius. 2020. *Intimate Assemblages; the Politics of Queer Identities and Sexualities in Indonesia*. Singapore: Palgrave Macmillan.

Wijaya, Hendri Yulius, and Sharyn Graham Davies. 2019. 'The Unfulfilled Promise of Democracy: Lesbian and Gay Activism and Indonesia'. In Thushara Dibley, Michele Ford and Yatun L. M. Sastramidjaja (eds), *Activists in Transition: Progressive Politics in Democratic Indonesia*. Ithaca: Southeast Asia Program Publications, an imprint of Cornell University Press: 153–70.

Wijewardena, Shermal. 2007. ' "But No One Has Explained to Me Who I Am Now...": "Trans" Self-Perceptions in Sri Lanka'. In Saskia E. Wieringa, Evelyn Blackwood and Abha Bhaiya (eds), *Women's Sexualities and Masculinities in a Globalizing Asia*. New York: Palgrave Macmillan: 101–19.

Wilken, G. A. 1912. Het Shamanisme bij de Volken van den Indische Archipel. In de Verspreide Geschriften van and Dr G. A. Wilken (eds), *Geschriften over Animisme en daarmede verband houdende Geloofsuitingen*, vol. 3. Semarang: Van Dorp: 232–397.

Winter, J. W. 1902. 'Beknopte Beschrijving van het Hof Soerakarta in 1824'. *Bijdragen tot de taal-Land-en Volkenkunde* 54: 15–172.

Wilson, Ara. 2004. *The Intimate Economies of Bangkok: Tomboys, Tycoons, and Avon Ladies in the Global City*. Berkeley: University of California Press.

Wilson, Ian Douglas. 2008. ' "As Long as It's Halal": Islamic Preman in Jakarta'. In Greg Fealy and Sally White (eds), *Expressing Islam: Religious Life and Politics in Indonesia*. Singapore: ISEAS: 192–211.

Wilson, Ian Douglas. 1999. 'Reog Ponorogo. Spirituality, Sexuality and Power in a Javanese Performance Traditions'. *Intersections: Gender and Sexuality in Asia and the Pacific* Issue 2, 2. May.

Wittig, Monique. 1992. *The Straight Mind and Other Essays*. New York: Harvester/ Wheatsheaf.

Yash. 2003. *Transseksualisme. Sebuah Studi Kasus Perkembangan Transeksual Perempuan ke Laki-Laki*. Semarang: Penerbit Aini.

The, Yik Koon. 2002. *The Mak Nyahs: Malaysian Males to Female Transsexuals*. Singapore: Eastern Universities Press.

The Yogyakarta Principles Comic. 2010. Jakarta: Institut Pelangi Perempuan.

Yolandasari, Ayu Regina. 2015. 'Penyebab atau Penyembuh? Kekerasan Seksual terhadap Lesbian, Biseksual, dan Transgender Female-to-Male di Indonesia'. *Jurnal Perempuan* 20(4) issue 87: 86–96.

Yulia, Dian. 2012. 'Konperensi ILGA dalam Ingatan Saya'. In Daniel and others (eds), *HER Story; Perempuan Luar Biasa Berkisah tentang Hidupnya*. Surabaya: Universitas Surabaya and Dipayoni.

Zakiah, Naila Rizqi, and Armadina Az Zahra. 2017. *LGBT=Nuklir? Indonesia Darurat Fobia*. Jakarta: LBH Masyarakat.

Zakiah, Naila Rizqi. 2018. *Bahaya Akut Persekusi LGBT*. Jakarta: LBH Masyarakat.

Zimmerman, Bonnie. 2000. 'Asian Lesbian Network'. In *Lesbian Histories and Cultures*. London: Routledge: 75–6.

Zuhrah, Ni'matuz. 2021. *Penyimpangan Seksual (LGBT) Perspektif Hadis Nabi Saw*. Phd thesis. Makassar: Universitas Islam Negeri Alauddin.

Films mentioned in the text

Akulah Vivian. 1977. M. Endraatmadja.

Arisan [the Gathering], part 1 2003. Nia Dinata.

Arisan [the Gathering], part 2 2011. Nia Dinata.

Calalai – In-betweenness. 2015. Febriyanti, K.

Children of Srikandhi. 2012. Children of Srikandhi Collective.

Kucumbu Tubuh Indahku [Memories of My Body]. 2018. Garin Nugroho.

Madame X. 2010. Lucky Kuswandi.

The Sun, the Moon and the Hurricane. 2014. Andri Cung.

Wariazone. 2011. Terje Toomistu and KIWA.

TV programmes watched

Channel 7, Peristiwa, 4 March 2003.

Jiwa sang Penari, TV documentary, broadcast Metro TV, 8 January 2020.

Newspaper articles

Adjie, Moch, and Fiqih Prawira. 2020. 'TNI Slammed for Anti-LGBT Campaign after Jailing Soldier'. *Jakarta Post*, 19 October. https://www.thejakartapost.com/paper/2020/10/18/tni-slammed-for-anti-lgbt-campaign-after-jailing-soldier.html.

Afiie, Marguerite Afra. 2016. 'Tumblr to Be Blocked in Indonesia due to Pornography, LGBT Content: Govt'. Jakartapost.com, 18 February. http://www.thejakartapost.

com/news/2016/02/18/tumblr-be-blocked-indonesia-due-pornography-lgbt-cont
ent-govt.html.

Afif. 2016. 'Kelompok LGBT Dilarang Keras Jadi Pekerja Salon di Bireuen Aceh'.
Merdeka.com, 19 March. https://www.merdeka.com/peristiwa/kelompok-lgbt-dilar
ang-keras-jadi-pekerja-salon-di-bireuen-aceh.html.

Adyatama, Egi. 2020. 'TNI Vows Firm Actions against Soldiers Linked to LGBT'. Tempo
15 October. https://en.tempo.co/read/1396403/tni-vows-firm-actions-against-soldi
ers-linked-to-lgbt.

Allard, T., and A. B. Da Costa. 2017. ' "Red Scare" Puts Pressure on Indonesian President'.
Reuters, 28 September.

Amahl S. Azwar. 2021. ' "Conversion therapy" Website Haunts Indonesian LGBT Activists'.
Jakarta Post, 17 February. https://www.thejakartapost.com/life/2021/02/17/convers
ion-therapy-website-haunts-indonesian- lgbtactivists.html.

Amindoni, Ayomi. 2019. 'Qanun Jinayat di Aceh Dianggap 'Diskriminatif: 'Kalau Rakyat
Kecil Membuat Kesalahan, Langsung Dibawa Jalur Hukum'. BBC News Indonesia, 17
December. https://www.bbc.com/indonesia/indonesia-5081881.

Andrianto, Aris. 2014. 'Tragedi 1965 dan Kebencian LGBT Meminggirkan Lengger
Lanang'. Tempo.co, 16 November. https://investigasi.tempo.co/291/tragedi-1965-dan-
kebencian-lgbt-meminggirkan-lengger-lanang. Accessed 17 June 2020.

Armando, Ade. 2015. 'Ade Armando, Allah tidak Mengharamkan LGBT'. Republika,
6 July. www.m.republika.co.id/berita/nasional/umum/15/07/06/nqyqw2-ade-arma
ndo-allah-tidak-mengharamkan-lgbt. Accessed 6 July 2015.

Aqil, A. Muh. Ibnu. 2021. 'KPK to Lose Investigators who Reportedly Failed Test'. *Jakarta
Post*, 4 May. https://www.thejakartapost.com/news/2021/05/04/kpk-to-lose-investigat
ors-who-reportedly-failed-test.html.

Bayuni, Endy. 2018. 'Commentary: New Penal Code: How Are We Worse Than the
Dutch?' 13 February. www.thejakartapost.com/academia/2018/02/13/commentary-ne
w-penal-code-how-are-we-worse-than-the-dutch.html.

Budiman, Arief. 1969. ' "Wanita-Adam" – Sebuah Persoalan'. *Kompas*, 16 January: 1.

Cahya, Gemma Holliani. 2020. 'Sinaga Case: What Indonesia Can Learn from the
Manchester Police'. *Jakarta Post*, 10 January. https://www.thejakartapost.com/
news/2020/01/10/sinaga-case-what-indonesia-can-learn-from-the-manchester-pol
ice.html.

Charolin, Pebrianti. 2022. 'detikjatim, "Menguak Hubungan Gemblak-Warok di Reog,
Seperti Apa Sebenarnya?" ' *detikjatim*, 13 April. https://www.detik.com/jatim/bud
aya/d-6030946/menguak-hubungan-gemblak-warok-di-reog-seperti-apa-sebenarnya.

Coconuts Jakarta. 2016. 'Anti-LGBT Academics Petition Constitutional Court to
Criminalize Homosexual Acts'. 2 August. http://jakarta.coconuts.co/2016/08/02/
anti-lgbt-academics-petition-Constitutional-court-criminalize-homosexual-acts.

Coconuts Jakarta. 2017. 'Indonesian University Refuses to Accept LGBT Students, Citing
Protection of the "Rights" '. Coconuts, 3 May. https://coconuts.co/jakarta/lifestyle/ind
onesian-university-refuses-accept-lgbt-students-citing-protection-rights/.

Coconuts Jakarta. 2018a. '87.6% of Indonesians See LGBT as a Threat, but Slim Majority
Say They Deserve Right to Life and Protection: Survey. Coconuts, 25 January.

Coconuts Jakarta. 2018b. 'Indonesian Talk Show Sanctioned for Discussion of
'Transgender Issues' by Broadcasting Commission. Coconuts, 10 April. https://cocon
uts.co/jakarta/lifestyle/indonesian-talk-show-sanctioned-discussion-transgender-iss
ues-broadcasting-commission.

Coconuts Jakarta. 2018c. 'Indonesian City Says It'll Work with Exorcists That Expel Female Genies from Men to "Cure" LGBT Behavior'. Coconuts, 21 November. https:// coconuts.co/jakarta/news/indonesian-city-says-itll-work-exorcists-remove-female-gen ies-men-cure-lgbt-behavior/?fbclid=IwAR1bNxsxpdfrNXOqaeWBu1-eYf-xw1tJDkNo _rT5EANXTzFTPb3mjnlFvFs.

Di Ilio, Nicole. 2019. 'Inside the World's Only Islamic School for Transgender Students'. www.vice.com › Home › LGBTQ, 6 August.

Dini, Mala. 2020. 'GiGa Indonesia Gelar Dialog Nasional Soal Ketahanan Keluarga'. Depok News, 1 July. https://www.depoknews.id/giga-indonesia-gelar-dialog-nasio nal-soal-ketahanan-keluarga/July 1.

Dipa, Arya. 2018. 'Gay Couple Arrested in Bandung as Anti-LGBT Wave Grips W. Java'. *Jakarta Post*, 20 October. http://www.thejakartapost.com/news/2018/10/20/gay-cou ple-arrested-in-bandung-as-anti-lgbt-wave-grips-w-java.html.

Erdianto, Kristian. 2016. 'Aktivis HAM: Surat Edaran KPI Diskriminasi LGBT'. *Kompas*, 29 February. http://nasional.kompas.com/read/2016/02/29/11492801/Aktivis.HAM. Surat.Edaran.KPI.Diskriminasi.LGBT.

Evan, Fania. 2020. 'Indonesians Are Turning to Exorcisms to "Cure" Members of the LGBTQ Community. 17 February. https://www.vice.com/en/article/n7j3y7/indonesia-exorcism-lgbtq-conversion-therapy.

Fachriansyah, Rizki. 2018. 'Facebook Page for Gay Students Stirs Controversy in Garut'. *Jakarta Post*, 10 October. http://www.thejakartapost.com/news/2018/10/10/faceb ook-page-for-gay-students-stirs-controversy-in-garut.html.

Fikri, Chairul. 2022. 'Trans Woman Dorce Gamalama Buried as Man'. Jakarta Globe, 16 February. https://jakartaglobe.id/lifestyle/trans-woman-dorce-gamalama-bur ied-as-man. See also Wieringa (2022).

Gatra, Edisi No. 46, Tahun IX, 4 Oktober 2003.

Gaya Lestari, Edisi 3, Oktober & Desember 1993.

Gaya Lestari, Edisi 4 February 1994.

Gaya Lestari, Edisi 5 April 1994.

Gaya Lestari, Edisi 6 Juni 1994.

Gunawan, Apriadi. 2019. 'Court Rejects Student Journalists' Lawsuit against Being Sacked Over LGBT Story'. *Jakarta Post*, 16 November. https://www.thejakartapost. com/news/2019/11/15/court-rejects-student-journalists-lawsuit-against-being-sac ked-over-lgbt-story.html.

Hajramurni, Andi. 2017. 'Police Ban Transgender Cultural Event in South Sulawesi'. *Jakarta Post*, 20 January. https://www.thejakartapost.com/news/2017/01/20/pol ice-ban-transgender-cultural-event-in-south-sulawesi.html.

Halim, Haeril. 2020. 'Aceh Unveils New Female Flogging Squad'. *Jakarta Post*, 28 January. https://newgelora.thejakartapost.com/news/2020/01/28/aceh-unveils-new-female-flogging-squad.html.

Harahap, Lia. 2021. https://www.merdeka.com/peristiwa/kpppa-apresiasi-kominfo-blo kir-video-soal-lgbt.html. KPPPA Apresiasi Kominfo Blokir Video Soal LGBT. 15 September.

Hari, Agustinus. 2020. 'North Sulawesi Church Hosts Discussion on LGBT Support'. *Jakarta Post*, 7 February. https://www.thejakartapost.com/news/2020/02/07/north-sulawesi-church-hosts-discussion-on-lgbt-support.html.

HarianHalu.com. 2016. 'Wagub: Usir LGBT dari Sumbar'. 19 February. https://www.haria nhaluan.com/news/detail/48754/wagub-usir-lgbt-dari-sumbar.

Harsono, Andreas. 2018. 'Indonesian Police Harass Transgender Women'. Human Rights Watch, 8 November. https://www.hrw.org/news/2018/11/08/indonesian-police-har ass-transgender-women.

Harsono, Andreas. 2019. 'Quasi Ban Imposed on Award-Winning Indonesian Film'. *Jakarta Post*, 12 May. https://www.thejakartapost.com/academia/2019/05/12/ban-kucu mbu-tubuh-indahku-garin-nugroho.html.

Haynes, Suyin. 2018. 'Indonesia's Crackdown on LGBT Rights Is Fueling an HIV Epidemic, Rights Group Warns'. *Time*, 2 July. http://time.com/5324621/indonesia-lgbt-crackdown-hiv-human-rights-watch/.

Hermawan, Ary. 2016. 'Why AILA Is a Bigger Threat to Freedom Than FPI'. *Jakarta Post* 30 August. https://www.thejakartapost.com/news/2016/08/30/comment ary-why-aila-is-a-bigger-threat-to-freedom-than-the-fpi.html.

Hermawan, Ary. 2018. 'Commentary: #2019GantiPresiden Shows All That Is Wrong with Our Democracy'. *Jakarta Post*, 5 September. http://www.thejakartapost.com/acade mia/2018/09/05/commentary-2019gantipresiden-shows-all-that-is-wrong-with-our-democracy.htm.

Hidayana, Irwan Martua. 2018. 'On Gender Diversity in Indonesia'. *The Conversation*, 12 September. https://theconversation.com/on-gender-diversity-in-indonesia-101087.

Hidayatullah. 2014. 'Gaya Hidup yang Diedukasi Doktrin Feminisme Jadi Pendorong Lahirnya Perilaku LGBT'. 3 February. https://www.hidayatullah.com/berita/wawanc ara/read/2014/02/03/15911/nilai-dan-gaya-hidup-yang-diedukasi-doktrin-femini sme-jadi-pendorong-lahirnya-perilaku-lgbt.html.

Ibrahim, Raka. 2022. 'Familial Taboo: Stories of Children Who Cut Off Contact with Their Parents'. *The Jakarta Post*, 3 February. https://www.thejakartapost.com/cult ure/2022/02/03/familial-taboo-stories-of-children-who-cut-off-contact-with-their-parents.html.

Ishaq, Taufiq. 2018. 'Meski Dibatalkan, AILA Curiga Kontes Mister dan Miss Gaya Dewata Tetap Berjalan', Kiblat.net, 11 October. https://www.kiblat.net/2018/10/11/meski-dibatalkan-aila-curiga-kontes-mister-dan-miss-gaya-dewata-tetapberjalan/.

Ishomuddin, Muhammad. 2019. 'Reog Dance Proves Homosexuality Is an Ancient Tradition in Indonesia'. https://www.vice.com/en/article/vb9m8b/the-reog-dance-proves-homosexuality-is-an-ancient-tradition-in-indonesia. 24 April. Accessed 19 August 2021.

Irsyad, Aldila. 2018. 'Blaming Women, Minorities for Natural Disasters'. *Jakarta Post*, 24 October. http://www.thejakartapost.com/academia/2018/10/24/blaming-women-min orities-for-natural-disasters.html.

The Jakarta Post. 2015. 'Police Urged to Release Women Accused of Being Lesbians'. 4 October. www.thejakartapost.com/news/2015/10/04/police-urged-release-women-accused-being-lesbians.

The Jakarta Post. 2016a. 'Aceh Clamps Down on LGBT People, Threatens Caning'. 15 March. www.thejakartapost.com/news/2016/03/15/aceh-clamps-down-lgbt-people-threatens-caning.html. 15 March.

The Jakarta Post. 2016b 'Indonesian Clerics Declare LGBT Groups Haram'. 17 February. www.thejakartapost.com/news/2016/02/17/indonesian-clerics-declare-lgbt-gro ups-haram.html.

The Jakarta Post. 2016c. 'Kalla Requests UNDP to Not Fund LGBT Groups'. 15 February. https://www.thejakartapost.com/news/2016/02/15/kalla-requests-undp-not-fund-lgbt-groups.html.

The Jakarta Post. 2016d. 'LGBT Not Welcome at University: Minister'. 25 January. www.the jakartapost.com/news/2016/01/25/lgbt-not-welcome-at-university-minister.

The Jakarta Post. 2016e. 'Luhut Agrees LGBTs Need Rights Protected but Says They Are Diseased'. 16 February. https://www.thejakartapost.com/news/2016/02/16/luhut-agrees-lgbts-need-rights-protected-says-they-are-diseased.html.

The Jakarta Post. 2016f. 'Poor Knowledge Leads to Prolonged Discrimination against LGBT People'. 14 March. www.thejakartapost.com/news/2016/03/14/poor-knowledge-leads-prolonged-discrimination-against-lgbt-people.html.

The Jakarta Post. 2018. 'Anti-LGBT Team Established in Depok'. 19 February. https://www.thejakartapost.com/news/2018/02/19/anti-lgbt-team-established-in-depok.html

The Jakarta Post. 2019a. 'House Agrees to Include Controversial Morality Articles in Criminal Code'. 30 June. www.thejakartapost.com/news/2019/06/30/house-agrees-to-include-controversial-morality-articles-in-criminal-codebill.html.

The Jakarta Post. 2019b. 'We Just Want the Normal Ones: AGO Justifies Refusal to Recruit LGBT People as Civil Servants'. 23 November. https://www.thejakartapost.com/.news/2019/11/23/we-just-want-the-normal-ones-ago-justifies-refusal-to-recruit-lgbt-people-as-civil-servants.html.

The Jakarta Post. 2019. 'Instagram Grants Indonesia's Request, Shuts Down Account Featuring Gay Muslim Comic Strips'. 13 February. https://www.thejakartapost.com/news/2019/02/13/instagram-grants-indonesias-request-shuts-down-account-featuring-gay-muslim-comic.html.

The Jakarta Post. 2020. 'Court-Martial of Gay Soldier Form of Discrimination, Activists Say'. 18 March. https://www.thejakartapost.com/news/2020/03/18/court-martial-of-gay-soldier-form-of-discrimination-activists-say.

Janti, Nur. 2022a. 'Activists Face Danger Amidst Shrinking Civic Space'. *The Jakarta Post*, 22 March. https://www.thejakartapost.com/indonesia/2022/03/21/activists-face-danger-amid-shrinking-civic-space.html.

Janti, Nur. 2022b. 'House to Deliberate Sexual Violence Bill Next Session Puan'. *The Jakarta Post*, 19 February. https://www.thejakartapost.com/paper/2022/02/24/house-to-deliberate-sexual-violence-bill-next-session-puan.html.

Kampai, Jeka. 2018. 'Warga Payakumbuh Sumbar Deklarasi Perangi LGBT'. *DetikNews*, 5 November. https://news.detik.com/berita/4287946/warga-payakumbuh-sumbar-deklarasi-perangi-lgbt.

Karmini, Niniek. 2016. 'Indonesia Warns Messaging Apps to Drop Same-Sex Emoticons'. *Jakarta Post*. 12 February. http://www.thejakartapost.com/news/2016/02/12/indonesia-warns-messaging-apps-drop-same-sex-emoticons.html.

Khalik, Abdul. 2008. 'Islam "Recognized Homosexuality"'. *The Jakarta Post*, 28 March. http://www.thejakartapost.com/news/2008/03/27/islam-recognized-homosexuality.

Khumaini, A. 2014a. '*Fenomena Mairil: Menyingkap Tirai Bisu Pesantren*'. https://www.qureta.com/post/fenomena-mairil-menyingkap-tirai-bisu-pesantren.

Khumaini, A. 2014b. 'Di Ponorogo ada Gemblak, di Pesantren ada Mairil'. Merdeka.com, 11 May. https://www.merdeka.com/peristiwa/di-ponorogo-ada-gemblak-di-pesantren-ada-mairil.html. Accessed 24 July 2022.

Kine, P. 2015. 'Dispatches: Challenging Indonesia's Intolerant Muslim Clerics'. Human Rights Watch, 17 March. https://www.hrw.org/news/2015/03/17/dispatches-challenging-indonesias-intolerant-muslim-clerics. Accessed 26 May 2022.

Kompas. 1968. 'Di Djakarta Terdapat 15,000 Bantji', 5 August.

Kompas. 1969. 'Razzia Wadam', 17 January 1969.

Kompas. 1973. 'Para Wadam Ibukota Memprotes Polisi', 28 February 1973.

Kompas. 1977. 'Bang Ali Dan Wadam, Kompas', 27 June 1977.

Kurniawan, Budi. 2003. 'Cinta Tabu Sesama Bunga; Lesbian Blak-Blakan'. *Medium Tinjauan Berita Dwi Mingguan.* Year 1, No. 8 June 4–17: 86–94.

Kustiani, Rini. 2019. 'Arus Pelangi: 1850 Korban Persekusi dari 2006, Diperburuk KUHP'. Tempo, 24 September. https://nasional.tempo.co/read/1251533/arus-pelangi-1-850-kor ban-persekusi-dari-2006-diperburuk-rkuhp.

Lashmar, Paul, Nicholas Gilby and James Oliver. 2022. 'UKs Propaganda Leaflets Inspired 1960s Massacre of Indonesian Communists'. *The Guardian*, 23 January. https://www. theguardian.com/world/2022/jan/23/uks-propaganda-leaflets-inspired-1960s-massa cre-of-indonesian-communists.

Maharani, Shinta. 2015. 'Tragedi 1965 dan Kebencian LGBT Meminggirkan Lengger Lanang'. Tempo Investigasi 17 November. https://investigasi.tempo.co/291/ tragedi-1965-dan-kebencian-lgbt-meminggirkan-lengger-lanang.

Marbun Julfikli. 2014. 'MUI: Penyimpangan Seksual Bertentangan dengan HAM'. Republika, 5 May. https://nasional.republika.co.id/berita/nasional/hukum/n53lmy/ mui-penyimpangan-seksual-bertentangan-dengan-ham.

Marching, Soe Tjen. 2020. 'Reynhard Sinaga and Our Responsibilities'. *Jakarta Post*, 9 January. https://www.thejakartapost.com/academia/2020/01/09/reynhard-sin aga-and-our-responsibilities.html.

Muryanto, Bambang. 2016. 'Hard-liners Visit Yogyakarta Transgender Islamic School'. *The Jakarta Post*, 20 February. http://www.thejakartapost.com/news/2016/02/20/hard-lin ers-visit-yogyakarta-transgender-islamic-school.html.

Muryanto, Bambang. 2020. 'Women's Wing of Nahdlatul Ulama Offers Hand to Transgender Boarding School in Yogyakarta'. *Jakarta Post*, 27 January. https://www.the jakartapost.com/news/2020/01/27/womens-wing-of-nahdlatul-ulama-offers-hand-to-transgender-boarding-school-in-yogyakarta.html.

Muslimah, Salmah. 2016. 'PKS: Virus LGBT Harus Dienyahkan dari Negara RI yang Relijius'. Detiknews, 10 February. http://news.detik.com/berita/3138822/ pks-virus-lgbt-harus-dienyahkan-dari-negara-ri-yang-relijius.

Nathan, G. 2016. 'ESQ: Dari Segala Sisi, LGBT Bisa Merusak'. http://nasional.republika. co.id/berita/nasional/umum/16/02/21/o2vr3r330-esq-dari-segala-sisi-lgbt-bisa-meru sak Ahad, 21 Februari 2016.

Okezone. 2016. 'KSAL Ingatkan Prajurit Waspadai Kelompok Pendukung LGBT'. 17 February. http://news.okezone.com/read/2016/02/17/337/1314448/ksal-ingatkan-praju rit-waspadai-kelompok-pendukung-lgbt.

OUTZINE Newsletter Arus Pelangi Edisi XII/Juni. 2020. Jakarta: Arus Pelangi.

Pangestika, Dyaning, and Ghina Ghaliya. 2019. 'They Have "Rights to Get Decent Job": Gerindra Defends LGBT Jobseekers through Twitter'. *Jakarta Post*, 29 November. https://www.thejakartapost.com/news/2019/11/29/they-have-rights-to-get-decent-job-gerindra-defends-lgbt-jobseekers-through-twitter.html.

Pawestri, Tunggal. 2016. 'More Hard Times for Indonesian LGBT People'. *Jakarta Post*, 22 August. http://www.thejakartapost.com/academia/2016/08/22/more-hard-times-for-indonesian-lgbt-people.html.

Pawestri, Tunggal, and T. Mann. 2022. https://indonesiaatmelbourne.unimelb.edu.au/ indonesia-finally-has-a-law-to-protect-victims-of-sexual-violence-but-the-strug gle-is-not-over-yet/. Posted 19 May.

Pinandita, Apriza. 2020. 'More Indonesians Tolerant of Homosexuality, though Vast Majority Still Say No: Pew Survey'. *Jakarta Post*, 26 June. https://www.thejakartapost. com/news/2020/06/26/more-indonesians-tolerant-of-homosexuality-though-vast-majority-still-say-no-pew-survey.html.

Rappler.com. 2016. 'NU Muda Beda Pendapat dengan PBNU Soal LGBT'. 8 February. http://www.rappler.com/indonesia/121532-nu-muda-beda-pendapat-den gan-pbnu-soal-lgbt.

Republika.co.id. 2016a. 'LGBT Ancaman Serius', 24 January. www.republika.co.id/berita/ koran/halaman-1/16/01/24/o1gi281lgbt-ancaman-serius?fb_comment_id=1259288317 421000_1265791670103998#f1654dafd2bd974.

Republika.co.id. 2016b. 'Ini Pandangan MUI Soal LGBT', 17 February. http://khazanah. republika.co.id/berita/duniaislam/islam-nusantara/16/02/17/o2ok3u384-ini-pandan gan-mui-soal-lgbt.

Republika.co.id. 2016c. 'RUU LGBT Penting untuk Melindungi Rakyat Indonesia'. 10 March. www.republika.co.id/berita/nasional/umum/16/03/10/o3sw24361-ruu-lgbt-penting-untuk-melindungi-rakyatindonesia.

Republika.co.id. 2016d. 'Menteri Khofifah Klarifikasi Soal Ingin Merebus LGBT'. 14 March. http://nasional.republika.co.id/berita/nasional/umum/16/03/14/o4074v328-menteri-khofifah-klarifikasi-soal-inginmerebus-lgbt.

Republika. 2016. 'LGBT Ancaman Serius'. 24 January. https://www.republika.co.id/berita/ koran/halaman -1/16/01/24/olgi281-lgbt-ancaman-serius.

Retaduari, Elza Astari. 2016. 'Rekomendasi Mukernas, PKB Tolak Perkawinan Sejenis'. http://news.detik.com/berita/3136482/rekomendasi-mukernas-pkb-tolak-perkawi nan-sejenis. 6 February.

Rezkisari, I. 2016. 'Menteri Khofifah Klarifikasi Soal Ingin Merebus LGBT'. Republika, 14 March. https://news.republika.co.id/berita/o4074v328/menteri-khofifah-klarifik asi-soal-ingin-merebus-lgbt. Accessed 14 March 2016.

Riau Daily. 2016. 'Kata Wakil Ketua MPR: LGBT Langgar Sila Pertama', RiauDaily. com, 23 February. http://riaudaily.com/news/detail/16249/2016/02/23/-kata-waki l-ketua-mpr:-lgbt-langgar-sila-pertama.

Rodriguez, D. G., and Suvianita K. (2020), 'How Indonesia's LGBT Community is Making a Difference amid COVID 19'. 26 June. https://theconversation.com/how-indones ias-lgbt-community-is-making-a-difference-amid-covid-19-140063. Accessed 26 June 2020.

Rostanti, Qommarria. 2016. 'KPI Sudah Sejak Lama Larang Tayangan Kebanci-bancian'. Republika, 19 February. http://www.republika.co.id/berita/nasional/umum/16/02/19/ o2sh4d354-kpi-sudah-sejak-lama-larang-tayangan-kebancibancian.

Rosawita. 1993. 'Asian Lesbian Network (ALN) Jaringan Kerja Sama Lesban Asia'. *Gaya Nusantara* no. 19.

Salim, T., and I. Parlina. 2016. 'NU, PKB Take Tough Stance against LGBT Community'. *Jakarta Post*, 6 February. http://www.thejakartapost.com/news/2016/02/06/ nu-pkb-take-tough-stance-against-lgbt-community.html.

Sidiq, Fachrul. 2018. 'Waria' Told to Leave Their Home in Jakarta Amid Anti-LGBT Campaign'. *Jakarta Post*, 18 November. http://www.thejakartapost.com/ news/2018/11/18/waria-told-to-leave-their-home-in-jakarta-amid-anti-lgbt-campa ign.html.

Simone, Daniel De. 2020. 'Reynhard Sinaga: How the Manchester Rapist Found His Victims'. BBC News, 6 January. https://www.bbc.com/news/uk-50688975.

Sugiharti, S. 2018. 'Watch Your Remarks in Virtual Space', *Jakarta Post*, 6 August.

Suryakusuma, Julia. 2016. 'State Hysteria Leading Nation with Homophobia'. *Jakarta Post*, 24 February. https://www.thejakartapost.com/news/2016/02/24/view-point-state-hyste ria-leading-nation-with-homophobia.html.

Syakriah, Ardila. 2020. 'No Link between Crimes; Sexual Orientation Post Rreynhard Anti-LGBT Sentiment Condemned'. *Jakarta Post*, 17 January. https://www.thejakartap ost.com/news/2020/01/17/no-link-between-crimes-sexual-orientation-post-reynh ard-anti-lgbt-sentiment-condemned.html.

Sheany. 2020. 'Despite Death Threats, Queer Singer Kai Mata Still Wants to Fight for LGBT Visibility in Indonesia'. Coconuts, 30 June. https://coconuts.co/bali/features/ despite-death-threats-queer-singer-kai-mata-still-wants-to-fight-for-lgbt-visibility-in-indonesia/.

Shezaf, Hagar, and Jonathan Jacobson. 2018. 'Revealed: Israel's Cyber-Spy Industry Helps World Dictators Hunt Dissidents and Gays'. *Haaretz*, 20 October. https://www.haar etz.com/israel-news/.premium.MAGAZINE-israel-s-cyber-spy-industry-aids-dictat ors-hunt-dissidents-and-gays-1.6573027.

Singgih, V. P. 2016. 'Hanura Calls for Law against LGBT People', *Jakarta Post*, 21 March.

Sinuko, Damar. 2015. 'Universitas Diponegoro Tolak Diskusi Soal Gay'. CNN Indonesia, 13 November. www.cnnindonesia.com/nasional/20151113140504-20-91469/universi tas-diponegoro-tolak-diskusi-soal-gay.

Sundaryani, Ferdina S. 2016. 'Commission Wants TV, Radio Free of LGBT'. *Jakarta Post*, 14 February.

Sutrisno, Budi. 2020. 'Bedroom Bill: Proposed "Family Resilience" Law Would Require LGBT People to Report for "Rehabilitation"'. *Jakarta Post*, 19 February. https:// www.thejakartapost.com/news/2020/02/19/bedroom-bill-proposed-family-resilie nce-law-would-require-lgbt-people-to-report-for-rehabilitation.html?

Syakriah, Ardila. 2019. 'It's "Deviation" and "Mental Disability": Some Indonesian Institutions Put Ban on LGBT Applicants'. *Jakarta Post*, 18 November. https://www.the jakartapost.com/news/2019/11/18/its-deviation-and-mental-disability-some-state-insti tutions-put-ban-on-lgbt-applicants.html.

Syakriah, Ardila. 2020. 'Depok Mayor Calls for More Anti-LGBT Raids in Wake of Reynhard Sinaga Case'. *Jakarta Post*, 11 January. https://www.thejakartapost.com/ news/2020/01/11/depok-mayor-calls-for-more-anti-lgbt-raids-in-wake-of-reynhard-sinaga-case.html.

Tan, Poedjiati. 2020. 'Razia LGBT Walikota Depok Merupakan Tindakan Pelecehan dan Diskriminatif terhadap LGBT'. Konde, 15 January. https://www.konde.co/2020/01/ razia-lgbt-walikota-depok-tindakan.html. Accessed 15 February 2021.

Tehusijarana, Karina M. 2019. 'Conservative Muslims Reject Antirape Bill over "Pro-adultery, LGBT" Concerns'. *Jakarta Post*, 2 February. www.thejakartapost.com/ news/2019/02/01/conservative-muslims-reject-antirape-bill-over-pro-adultery-lgbt-concerns.html.

Tehusijarana, Karina M., and Ghina Ghaliya. 2020. 'Anti-Sexual Deviance Propaganda Bill Mysteriously on Priority List'. *Jakarta Post*, 17 January. https://www.thejakartapost. com/news/2020/01/17/anti-sexual-deviance-propaganda-bill-mysteriously-on-prior ity-list.html.

Tempo. 1981a. 'The Love Story of Aty and Nona'. 23 May, 26–7.

Tempo. 1981b. 'The Story of Jossie and Bonnie'. 30 May, 51–3.

Tempo.co. 2016a. 'Minister: LGBT Movement More Dangerous Than Nuclear Warfare'. 23 February. http://en.tempo.co/read/news/2016/02/23/055747534/Minister-LGBT-Movement-More-Dangerous-than-NuclearWarfare.

Tempo.co. 2016b. 'Din Syamsuddin: LGBT Jangan Dimusuhi'. 5 March. https://m.tempo. co/read/news/2016/03/05/173750992/din-syamsuddin-lgbt-jangan-dimusuhi.

Thamrin, Mahandi Yoanata. 2019. 'Ketoprak Jawa pernah dibunuh dua kali?'. https://nationalgeographic.grid.id/read/131715339/ketoprak-jawa-pernah-dibu nuh-dua-kali?page=all.

Topsfield, Jewel. 2017. 'Suspicion that LGBT Rights Are "Western Agenda" Fuels Indonesian Crackdown'. *Sydney Morning Herald*, 21 October. https://www.smh.com. au/world//suspicion-that-lgbt-rights-are-western-agenda-fuels-indonesiancrackdown-20171020-gz5fao.html.

Tribun Lampung. 2015. 'Rektor Unila: Mahasiswa dan Dosen Terlibat LGBT Akan Dipecat!'. 3 December. https://lampungtribunnews.com.

Tuasikal, Rio. 2016. 'Ruqyah LGBT, Arus Pelangi: Itu Seperti Harapan Kosong'. KBR, 15 March. http://kbr.id/berita/032016/ruqyah_lgbt__arus_pelangi__itu_seperti_harapan _kosong/79404.html.

Ulung, Kurniawan A. 2022. 'Harrowing Times: The Challenges Facing Yogyakarta's Trans Women's Crisis Center'. *Jakarta Post*, 20 February. https://www.thejakartapost.com/ paper/2022/02/20/harrowing-times-the-challenges-facing-yogyakartas-trans-wom ens-crisis-center.html.

Varagur, Krithika. 2016. 'How Saudi Arabia's Religious Project Transformed Indonesia'. *The Guardian*, 16 April. https://www.theguardian.com/news/2020/apr/16/how-saudi-arabia-religious-project-transformed-indonesia-islam.

Westcott, Ben. 2018. 'Fear and Horror among Indonesia's LGBT Community as Gay Sex Ban Looms'. CNN World, 26 February. https://edition.cnn.com/2018/02/25/asia/ indonesia-lgbt-criminal-code-intl/index.html.

Wibisono, Gunawan. 2016. 'Catatan Komisi VIII DPR ke Kemenag Soal LGBT'. 17 February. http://news.okezone.com/read/2016/02/17/337/1314872/catatan-kom isi-viii-dpr-ke-kemenag-soal-lgbt.

Wijanarko, Bagus. 2016. 'Menristek Sebut LGBT Tak Dibolehkan Masuk Kampus'. CNN Indonesia, 23 January. www.cnnindonesia.com/nasional/20160123211552-20-106213/ menristek-sebut-lgbt-tak-bolehkan-masuk-kampus.

Wijaya, Callistasia Anggun. 2016. 'Don't Expel LGBT People from Society: Minister'. *Jakarta Post*, 4 March. www.thejakartapost.com/news/2016/03/04/don-t-expel-lgbt-people-society-minister.html.

Yosephine L. 2016a. 'Indonesian Psychiatrists Label LGBT as Mental Disorders'. *Jakarta Post*, 24 February. http://www.thejakartapost.com/news/2016/02/24/indonesian-psychi atrists- label-lgbt-as- mental-disorders.

Yosephine, L. 2016b. 'Komnas HAM Slams Vilification of LGBT by Officials'. *Jakarta Post*, 5 February.

Yosephine, L. 2016c. 'Sexual Violence Doesn't Discriminate: Activists'. *Jakarta Post*. 19 May. https://www.thejakartapost.com/news/2016/05/19/sexual-violence-doesnt-discr iminate-activists.html.

Yosephine, L. 2016d. 'World Psychiatric Association Opposes "Reparative Therapy" for LGBT People'. *Jakarta Post*, 24 March. http://www.thejakartapost.com/ news/2016/03/24/world-psychiatric-association-opposes-reparative-therapy-lgbt-peo ple.html.

Yulius, Hendri. 2016. 'Narcissus dan LGBT Masuk Kampus'. Tempo, 27 January. Http:// Koran.Tempo.Co/Konten/2016/01/27/392344/Narcissus-Dan-LGBT-Masuk-Kampusr.

Yuniar, Resty Woro. 2021. 'Exorcism and Corrective Rape Inside Indonesia Controversial: LGBT Indonesia'. *South China Morning Post*, 25 April. https://www.

scmp.com/week-asia/people/article/3130861/exorcisms-and-corrective-rape-inside-indonesia-controversial-lgbt-Indonesia.

Yuono. 1994. 'Gaya Nusantara. Homologi; Dilema Gay Beragama'. *Gaya Nusantara* No. 33, September.

Zaman. 1983a. 'Sehari dengan Joice Erna: Jangan Tanya Masa Lalu'. 18 June: 19–23.

Zaman. 1983b. 'Menikmati Dosa'. 25 June: 11–14.

Laws

Indonesia. 1945. Undang-Undang Dasar Negara Republik Indonesia Tahun 1945 (UUD NRI Tahun 1945) amandemen keempat.

Indonesia. 1974. Undang-Undang tentang Perkawinan, UU No. 1 Tahun 1974, LN 1, TLN 3019.

Indonesia. 1999. Undang-Undang tentang Hak Asasi Manusia, UU No. 39 Tahun 1999, LN 165, TLN 3886.

Indonesia. 1999. Undang-Undang tentang Pers, UU No. 40 Tahun 1999, LN 166, TLN 3887.

Indonesia. 2003. Undang-Undang tentang Ketenagakerjaan, UU No. 13 Tahun 2003, LN 39, TLN 4279.

Indonesia. 2005. Undang-Undang tentang Pengesahan International Covenant on Economic, Social and Cultural Rights, UU No. 11 Tahun 2005, LN 118, TLN 4557.

Indonesia. 2006. Undang-Undang tentang Administrasi Kependudukan, UU No. 23 Tahun 2006, LN 124, TLN 4674.

Indonesia. 2007. Peraturan Pemerintah tentang Pelaksanaan Pengangkatan Anak, PP No. 54 Tahun 2007, LN 123, TLN 4768.

Indonesia. 2007. Peraturan Pemerintah tentang Pelaksanaan Undang-undang Nomor 23 Tahun 2007 tentang Administrasi Kependudukan, PP No. 37 Tahun 2007, LN 80, TLN 4736.

Indonesia. 2008. Undang-Undang tentang Pornografi, UU No. 44 Tahun 2008, LN 181, TLN 4928.

Law No. 18/2014 on mental health guidelines categorizes homosexuals and bisexuals as 'people with psychiatric problems' whilst transgender people are said to have 'mental disorders' – the distinction being that psychiatric conditions, if not treated, will put people 'at risk of developing a mental disorder'.

Index

www.ingramcontent.com/pod-product-compliance
Lightning Source LLC
Chambersburg PA
CBHW071840270326
41929CB00013B/2058